REVELATION UNVEILED

OTHER BOOKS BY TIM LAHAYE . . .

Non-Fiction

The Act of Marriage (with Beverly LaHaye)
Anger Is a Choice
How to Win Over Depression

Fiction

Left Behind Series
  Left Behind
  Tribulation Force
  Nicolae
  Soul Harvest
  Apollyon
  Assassins

REVELATION UNVEILED

A revised and updated edition of
Revelation Illustrated and Made Plain

TIM LAHAYE

ZondervanPublishingHouse
Grand Rapids, Michigan

A Division of HarperCollins*Publishers*

Revelation Unveiled
Copyright © 1999 by Tim LaHaye

A revised and updated edition of *Revelation Illustrated and Made Plain*

Requests for information should be addressed to:

Zondervan Publishing House
Grand Rapids, Michigan 49530

Library of Congress Cataloging-in-Publication Data

LaHaye, Tim F.
    Revelation unveiled / Tim LaHaye
       p.   m
    Includes bibliographic references.
    ISBN: 0-310-23005-5 (pbk.)
    1. Bible. N.T. Revelation—Commentaries.   I. Title.
BS2825.3.L332   1999
228'.077—dc21
                                          99-18860
                                             CIP

Published in association with Alive Communications, Inc., 1465 Kelly Johnson Blvd. #320, Colorado Springs, CO 80920

Printed in the United States of America

00 01 /❖ DC/ 22 21 20 19 18 17 16 15 14 13 12

This book is gratefully dedicated to my mother,
MARGARET LaHAYE,
former Child Evangelism Director, Lansing, Michigan.

Her consistent Christian life and earnest prayers helped
guide me during my rebellious years and ultimately led me
into the ministry. It was her keen interest in Bible prophecy
that sparked my own. I could wish for every young man
such a dedicated Christian mother.

CONTENTS

Preface   9
Preliminary Considerations   15

Part 1—Christ and the Church Age

Introduction (Rev. 1:1–8)   25
1. The Christ of the Churches (Rev. 1:9–20)   33
2. The Church of Ephesus (Rev. 2:1–7)   43
3. The Church of Smyrna (Rev. 2:8–11)   51
4. The Church of Pergamum (Rev. 2:12–17)   57
5. The Church of Thyatira (Rev. 2:18–29)   65
6. The Church of Sardis (Rev. 3:1–6)   72
7. The Church of Philadelphia (Rev. 3:7–13)   78
8. The Church of Laodicea (Rev. 3:14–22)   84
9. Christ's Description of Himself (Rev. 1–3)   92

Part 2—Christ and the Tribulation

10. Rapture Before Tribulation (Rev. 4:1–2)   99
11. The Throne of God (Rev. 4–5)   113
12. The Seven-Sealed Scroll (Rev. 5)   124
13. The Tribulation Period (Dan. 9:24–27)   132
14. The Seal Judgments (Rev. 6)   141
15. The 144,000 Servants of God (Rev. 7)   148
16. The Seven Trumpet Judgments (Rev. 8–9)   163
17. The Mighty Angel and the Little Scroll (Rev. 10)   178
18. Two Super Witnesses (Rev. 11:1–14)   182
19. The Seventh Trumpet Judgment (Rev. 11:15–19)   192
20. Satan Versus Israel (Rev. 12)   196
21. The Antichrist (Rev. 13)   207
22. The Beast Out of the Sea (Rev. 13:1–10)   214
23. The False Prophet (Rev. 13:11–18)   222
24. Another 144,000 Servants (Rev. 14)   228
25. Another Glimpse of Heaven (Rev. 15)   243

26. The Seven Bowl Judgments (Rev. 16)   250
27. Religious Babylon Destroyed (Rev. 17)   260
28. Commercial Babylon Destroyed (Rev. 18)   278

Part 3—Christ and the Future

29. The Heavenly Hallelujah Chorus (Rev. 19:1–6)   289
30. The Marriage Supper of the Lamb (Rev. 19:7–10)   293
31. The Glorious Appearing of Jesus Christ (Rev. 19:11–16)   299
32. The Battle of the Great Day of God Almighty
    (Rev. 19:17–21)   308
33. Satan Bound in the Abyss (Rev. 20:1–3; 19:20)   317
34. The First Resurrection (Rev. 20:4–6)   325
35. The Millennium and Church History (Rev. 20:1–6)   330
36. The Coming Kingdom of Christ (Rev. 20:1–10)   339
37. The Great White Throne (Rev. 20:11–15)   349
38. The New Heaven and New Earth (Rev. 21)   355
39. The New Jerusalem (Rev. 21:9–27)   360
40. Heaven on Earth (Rev. 22)   367
Notes   375
Bibliography   377

PREFACE

The book of Revelation is easily the most fascinating book in the Bible, for it gives a detailed description of the future. Everyone is interested in what is going to happen to them and their loved ones after death, what will happen to the people of the earth, and what the future holds for this planet. Revelation not only answers all these questions but also gives them in great detail. This book not only answers questions unknowable from any other source but as the first line informs us, it is "the revelation of Jesus Christ."

The fascination for this book that details more future events than any other is as old as the book itself. And that fascination is not limited to "extremists" or the under-educated or those easily persuaded; it was held by the man considered by many scientists as "the most brilliant man who ever lived," Sir Isaac Newton. Not only was he the discoverer of the law of gravity and scores of other scientifically important findings, but he also loved the book of Revelation. I have in my possession a copy of his seventeenth-century commentary on the entire book. Obviously he loved the Christ it reveals and treasured the insights it provides on future life after death.

It should not be surprising that even in the twenty-first century the book has not lost its charm. In fact, if the incredible interest in our fiction series *Left Behind* (written with Jerry Jenkins), which has remained at the top of the best-seller list every month since it appeared four years ago, is any indication, the fascination for this subject is increasing. For that entire series is based on the future events found in the book of Revelation. Modern men and women want answers to the future and Revelation provides them. Thousands of readers of the *Left Behind* series have written or e-mailed us to say our prophetic novels have inspired them to read the book of Revelation for the first time (some several times) and found it thrilling. That should not be surprising, particularly in light of the fact that it is the only source we have for definitive answers for those events of the future that intrigue us all. Besides, we may be living on the threshold of the fulfillment of those future events.

In addition, the book of Revelation is the only book in the New Testament that presents Jesus Christ as He really is today. The gospels introduce Him as the "man of sorrows, and familiar with suffering" during his incarnation. Revelation presents Him in His true glory and majesty after His resurrection and ascension into heaven, never again to be reviled, rebuked, and spat upon. No wonder John entitled it "The Revelation of Jesus Christ."

The study of this book will warm your heart as you perceive the true Christ and His ministry to the churches for the past two thousand years. You will thrill to see myriads of angels bowing before Him and singing His praises. You will also view His dynamic triumph over Satan and all the forces of evil.

The book of Revelation makes it clear that Christ and Christians are the ultimate winners in the game of life. In fact, a study of this book is essential for a comprehensive view of the rest of Scripture. It finalizes God's wonderful purposes for His favorite creatures—the human race.

A proper understanding of this book will help the Bible student know what God has in store for this world before it comes to pass, so he may prepare himself and not be taken unaware. It will also afford him a confident faith with which to confront the political, social, and religious chaos that is imminent. Only a biblical illiterate is unable to see that these are the last days.

No book in the Bible has been more discredited than Revelation except for its counterpart in the Old Testament, the book of Daniel. Because Revelation deals predominantly with prophecy and the future, and because it exposes Satan as a deceptive fraud, the archenemy of humankind has tried his hardest to discredit the book. The last thing he wants is for people to become aware of Christ's majesty, Satan's treachery, and the Christian's final triumph when this old world system ultimately fails.

I have found that the proper understanding of Revelation motivates Christians to consistent dedication and service. It lifts their spirits and gives them a hope in the future that no other book in the world provides. Most of all, the study of this book will give you a vital love for Jesus Christ and the souls of lost people about you, for it not only reveals the Lord and His wonderful plan to redeem His Church but also discloses the awful plight of this world and of those who reject Him.

Writing the original version of *Revelation Illustrated and Made Plain* was the fulfillment of a twenty-five-year dream. I had studied the book diligently for years, taught it at least ten times, and saw the electrifying effect it had on two congregations I pastored. Somehow I knew that if someone wrote a down-to-earth easy-to-understand commentary on the book, together with the charts and diagrams my congregations found so helpful in the presentations, it would help many others to understand this great book. Very honestly, I hoped it would sell at least 50,000 copies, which for a commentary on any single book in the Bible is very good. I am pleased to say that almost six times that number are already in print. Hundreds of pastors and Bible teachers have written and indicated they have used it in preparation for their teaching.

Now twenty-five years later there is an even greater need for this book, particularly among the millions who are reading the *Left Behind* novels and becoming acquainted with the field of Bible prophecy for the first time. This new updated edition is even clearer than the first. It includes several new charts and graphics and a number of new insertions that will make the exciting truths of this book even clearer. In addition, the publishers are allowing the purchaser of this book to copy its charts to use with an overhead projector, thus enabling teachers of Revelation to better present the truth and time events of the book. It is my prayer that this new edition will stir the heart of every reader and inspire him or her to greater service and preparation for the rapidly approaching day when we will see Him who said, "Behold, I am coming soon!"

—Tim LaHaye
1999

Scenes in Heaven

Opening of the
seven-sealed scroll
(4:1–5:15)

Scenes on the Earth

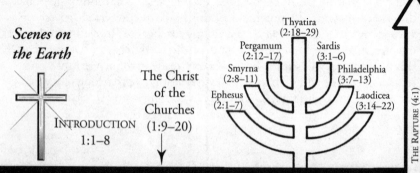

Thyatira
(2:18–29)

Pergamum
(2:12–17)

Sardis
(3:1–6)

Smyrna
(2:8–11)

Philadelphia
(3:7–13)

Ephesus
(2:1–7)

Laodicea
(3:14–22)

The Christ
of the
Churches
(1:9–20)

INTRODUCTION
1:1–8

THE RAPTURE (4:1)

Christ and the Church Age
(2:1–3:22)

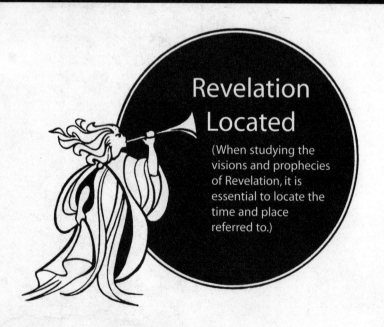

Revelation
Located

(When studying the
visions and prophecies
of Revelation, it is
essential to locate the
time and place
referred to.)

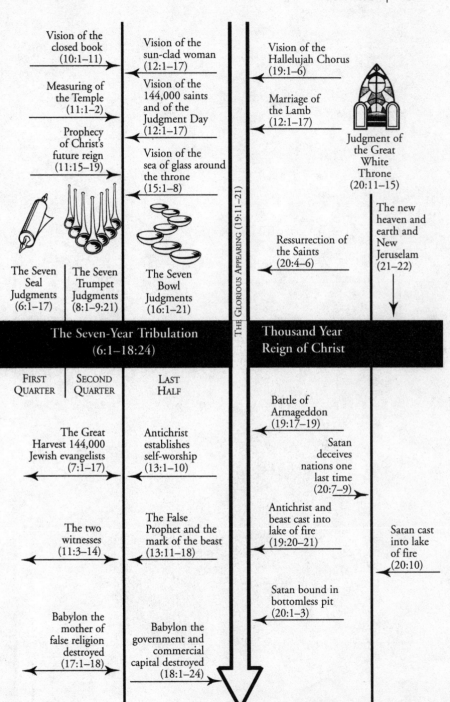

Vision of the closed book (10:1–11)

Vision of the sun-clad woman (12:1–17)

Vision of the Hallelujah Chorus (19:1–6)

Measuring of the Temple (11:1–2)

Vision of the 144,000 saints and of the Judgment Day (12:1–17)

Marriage of the Lamb (12:1–17)

Judgment of the Great White Throne (20:11–15)

Prophecy of Christ's future reign (11:15–19)

Vision of the sea of glass around the throne (15:1–8)

The new heaven and earth and New Jeruselam (21–22)

Ressurection of the Saints (20:4–6)

| The Seven Seal Judgments (6:1–17) | The Seven Trumpet Judgments (8:1–9:21) | The Seven Bowl Judgments (16:1–21) |

THE GLORIOUS APPEARING (19:11–21)

The Seven-Year Tribulation (6:1–18:24) | **Thousand Year Reign of Christ**

| FIRST QUARTER | SECOND QUARTER | LAST HALF |

The Great Harvest 144,000 Jewish evangelists (7:1–17)

Antichrist establishes self-worship (13:1–10)

Battle of Armageddon (19:17–19)

Satan deceives nations one last time (20:7–9)

The two witnesses (11:3–14)

The False Prophet and the mark of the beast (13:11–18)

Antichrist and beast cast into lake of fire (19:20–21)

Satan cast into lake of fire (20:10)

Satan bound in bottomless pit (20:1–3)

Babylon the mother of false religion destroyed (17:1–18)

Babylon the government and commercial capital destroyed (18:1–24)

PRELIMINARY CONSIDERATIONS

Almost one hundred years ago the author of the *Scofield Reference Bible* said in his notes on Revelation, "Doubtless, much which is designedly obscure to us will be clear to those for whom it was written as *the time approaches*." Most prophecy scholars believe that time is at hand, and many things are clearer today than they were in Dr. Scofield's day. It is my hope that these notes, charts, and pictures gathered from writers new and old, plus the leading of the Holy Spirit, will further clarify these things for "those for whom they were written"—which could well be this generation. One thing is certain, our generation has more reason to believe Christ could rapture His church in our lifetime than any generation in the almost two thousand years of church history, and as we will see, the Rapture triggers a host of prophetic events that are forecast in this book.

THE VALUE OF STUDYING REVELATION

To many, the book of Revelation is a closed book. More than one Bible teacher has taken a class from Matthew through the book of Jude, only to return to the book of Matthew rather than face the unusual teachings of the book of Revelation. It cannot be denied that it has confused many people. Nor can we deny that this book has been of immeasurable blessing to others. The following are some valuable reasons for studying this great book:

1. A special blessing is promised to those who read this book (1:3). There is blessing in reading any portion of God's Word, but this is the only book that promises special blessing for those who read and hear its words. Keep in mind too that the book closes with a restatement of this blessing for those who, in addition to reading and hearing the Word, also "keep it" (22:7).

2. It reveals God's wonderful Plan for the future. A keen interest in future events is a universal desire of the human race, particularly in days like ours when world conditions are so uncertain. Many people anxiously ask, "What does the future hold for me?" The student of the book of Revelation need not be taken unaware as

these events unfold, for it is possible through the study of this book to know that future plan.

3. This book gives clearer detail concerning Bible prophecy than any other book in the Bible. For example, John describes the glorious appearing of Jesus Christ (Rev. 19); the governmental operation of the man of sin, the terrible events of the Tribulation Period, the ultimate end of Satan, the future glorification of the Church, the future position of the saints, and the city Christ is preparing for His Church. Without Revelation we would have only scant information regarding these future events.

4. This book completes the circle of Bible truths. As the Word of God, the Scriptures predictably reveal superb planning and organization. We see that clearly in the book of Revelation, for it completes the great truths begun in Genesis and in other passages of the Bible. Here are some examples:

Genesis shows humanity's beginning in a beautiful paradise.
Revelation shows the wonderful paradise to come.

Genesis shows how human beings lost a chance to eat of the tree of life (Gen. 3:22–24).
Revelation shows that humankind will yet eat of that tree (Rev. 22:2).

Genesis tells of humanity's first rebellion against God (Gen. 3–4).
Revelation promises an end to humanity's rebellion against God.

Genesis records the first murderer, drunkard, and rebel.
Revelation promises a city where "nothing impure will ever enter it, nor will anyone who does what is shameful or deceitful, but only those whose names are written in the Lamb's book of life" (Rev. 21:27).

Genesis reveals the tragic sorrow that resulted from sin (Gen. 3–4).
Revelation promises, "[God] will wipe every tear from their eyes" (Rev. 21:4).

Genesis records the first death (Gen. 4:8).
Revelation promises that "there will be no more death" (Rev. 21:4).

Genesis shows the beginning of the curse (Gen. 3:15–18).
Revelation shows the curse lifted (Rev. 22:3).

Genesis introduces the devil for the first time as the tempter of the human race (Gen. 3:1–18).
Revelation shows the final doom of Satan (Rev. 20:10).

Genesis promises that Satan's head will be bruised (Gen. 3:15).
Revelation shows Satan bruised and defeated (Rev. 19:20).

Genesis shows Satan's first attempt at discrediting the Word of God when he asked Eve, "Did God really say?" and his first attempt at denying the Word of God, "You will not surely die" (Gen. 3:1–5). Sad to say, the thousands of years since then finds human beings still believing Satan and not God. Today the Bible is not believed by the majority of people but rather is subjected to the criticism of skeptics in education, the entertainment industry, science, and even the liberal ministry. This skepticism has tragically resulted in the doom of many unsuspecting souls.

Revelation promises a curse on all such infidels who detract from God's holy Word, "And if anyone takes words away from this book of prophecy, God will take away from him his share in the tree of life and in the holy city, which are described in this book" (Rev. 22:19).

SPECIAL SUGGESTIONS FOR STUDYING THIS BOOK

1. Follow the golden rule of interpretation: When the plain sense of Scripture makes common sense, seek no other sense; therefore, take every word at its primary, ordinary, usual, literal meaning unless the facts of the immediate text, studied in the light of related passages and axiomatic and fundamental truths, clearly indicate otherwise. This rule, suggested by the late Dr. David L. Cooper, provides basic guidelines for properly interpreting the many signs and symbols in the book.

2. Locate the scene of activity. Hopeless confusion will be generated in the study of Revelation unless one keeps firmly in mind whether the scene under discussion takes place in heaven or on earth. The action should also be followed closely, for sometimes a scene in heaven results in activity on the earth. For example, chapters 4 and 5 are scenes in heaven, chapter 6 a scene on earth. The preceding chart, besides showing the chronology of Revelation, shows the scene of activity for each event.

3. With the exception of chapters 12 and 17, most of Revelation unfolds chronologically. It is easier to understand this book if one expects it to fall into chronological sequence except for these two chapters. This is particularly important in the events of the Tribulation. The student of the book of Revelation should memorize immediately the fact that the seal judgments of chapter 6 comprise the first quarter of the Tribulation and the trumpet judgments of chapters 8 and 9 comprise the second quarter of the Tribulation. The bowl judgments of chapter 16 comprise the last half, or three-and-a-half years of the Tribulation. Everything else has to be studied in the context of the period with which it coincides. The following chart shows the chronological sequence of the Seven-Year Tribulation that covers most of the book.

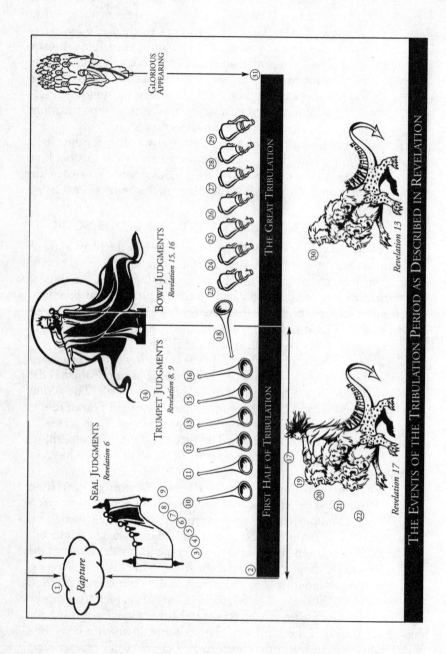

THE EVENTS OF THE TRIBULATION PERIOD AS DESCRIBED IN REVELATION

FOUR INTERPRETATIONS

The interpretation one gives the book of Revelation will obviously determine its message. There are four basic interpretations that are worthy of note.

Futurist Interpretation

The futurist view, which seems to me to be the most satisfactory, accepts the book of Revelation as prophecy that primarily is yet to be fulfilled, particularly from chapter 4 on. This was the interpretation of the early church during its most evangelistic history, from the apostles until the fourth century. Today it is the accepted position by most premillennial Bible teachers.

A safe rule to follow in the study of the book of Revelation is to accept the book as literal unless the facts are obviously to the contrary.

Historical Interpretation

The historical view suggests that John was describing the major events that would take place during the history of the Church. It therefore suggests that we can see these events as we look back at history. This, of course, calls for the juggling of historical events to fit the prophecy. This is historically unsound and tends to distort the plain or literal meaning.

Spiritualizing Interpretation

There are those who believe everything in the book should be taken figuratively or metaphorically, that John was talking about a spiritual conflict and not a physical experience. This view is held by most amillennialists and postmillennialists. Until the turn of the century, postmillennialism gained many followers with the idea that the world was getting better and better and we were about to usher in the kingdom. The perpetual degeneracy of the human race during the twentieth century, two world wars, and over 160 million deaths to communist dictators have rendered this a most untenable position.

Preterist Interpretation

The preterist view holds that John wrote the book prior to the destruction of the temple in A.D. 70 and was referring to events of his own day. This requires mental gymnastics that are unnecessary if one would apply the Golden Rule of Interpretation. The Roman emperors Nero or Domitian could scarcely fulfill the requirements of this book for the Antichrist, much less the desecration of the temple for forty-two months or for the worldwide cataclysms that are yet future.

AN OUTLINE OF THE BOOK OF REVELATION

Since the book of Revelation is the "Revelation of Jesus Christ," it should not seem strange that an outline of the book should revolve around the person, work, and future plans of Jesus Christ.

I. CHRIST AND THE CHURCH AGE (CHS. 1–3)
   A. Introduction (1:1–8)
   B. The Christ of the churches (1:9–20)
   C. Christ's message to His churches (chs. 2–3)
      1. The church of Ephesus (2:1–7)
      2. The church of Smyrna (2:8–11)
      3. The church of Pergamum (2:12–17)
      4. The church of Thyatira (2:18–29)
      5. The church of Sardis (3:1–6)
      6. The church of Philadelphia (3:7–13)
      7. The church of Laodicea (3:14–22)

II. CHRIST AND THE TRIBULATION (CHS. 4–18)
   A. John caught up to heaven (ch. 4)
   B. Christ receives glory in heaven (ch. 5)
   C. The seven seals—the first quarter of the Tribulation (ch. 6)
      1. Revival under the 144,000 Jewish witnesses (ch. 7)
      2. The preaching of the two witnesses (11:1–14)
   D. The trumpet judgments—the second quarter of the Tribulation (chs. 8–9)
      1. Israel persecuted by Satan (ch. 12)
      2. The beast (Antichrist) and the False Prophet (ch. 13)
      3. Ecclesiastical Babylon destroyed by the kings of the earth (ch. 17)
   E. Heavenly visions
      1. Vision of the little scroll (ch. 10)
      2. Vision of the glorious appearing of Christ (11:15–19)
      3. Satan cast down to the earth (12:7–12)
      4. Vision of the martyrs secure with Christ; doom pronounced on the beast worshipers (ch. 14)
      5. Vision of the coming bowl judgments (ch. 17)
   F. The seven bowls—last half of the Great Tribulation (chs. 15–16)
      1. The commercial city of Babylon destroyed by God (ch. 18)

III. CHRIST AND THE FUTURE (CHS. 19–22)
   A. Christ's marriage to His Church (19:1–10)
   B. Christ's glorious appearing (19:11–21)

C. Christ's millennial kingdom (20:1–11)
   1. Satan bound a thousand years (20:1–3)
   2. Resurrection of believers (20:4–6)
   3. Satan loosed to test man's will (20:7–9)
   4. Satan doomed (20:10)
D. Christ's judgment of unbelievers (20:11–15)
E. Christ's creation of new things (21:1–22:7)
   1. New heaven and earth (21:1–2)
   2. New conditions for men (21:3–8)
   3. New Jerusalem (21:9–27)
   4. The new paradise (22:1–7)
F. Christ's last message (22:8–21)

KEY VERSE OF REVELATION

Revelation 1:19 is the key verse that unlocks the door to the entire outline of the book. It is further evidence of the threefold division of this great Revelation. John was told expressly by Christ to write—

1. "what you have seen
2. what is now . . .
3. what will take place later"

From this, it seems evident that the book is made up primarily of future events. It includes some things that existed in John's day (chs. 2–3), all based on the things he saw. From this, we see that the futurist interpretation of the book of Revelation is the valid one.

PART ONE

Christ and the Church Age

The Seven Churches of Revelation

	EPHESUS The Apostolic Church Rev. 2:1–7	SMYRNA The Persecuted Church Rev. 2:8–11	PERGAMUM The Indulged Church Rev. 2:12–17	THYATIRA The Pagan Church Rev. 2:18–29	SARDIS The Dead Church Rev. 3:1–6	PHILADELPHIA The Church Christ Loved Rev. 3:7–13	LAODICEA The Lukewarm Church Rev. 3:14–22
	A.D. 30–100	A.D. 100–312	A.D. 312–606	A.D. 606–Tribulation	A.D. 1520–Tribulation Protestant Reformation	A.D. 1750–Rapture	A.D. 1900–Tribulation
COMMENDATION I know your...	Good works, labor, patience. Hated Nicolaitians.	Works, tribulation, poverty.	Works. Held fast my name. Has not denied my faith.	Good works, love, service, faith, patience.	Works. A name that you live.	Works. Missions. Little strength. Kept my word. Not denied my name.	Not one word!
CONDEMNATION I counsel you...	You have left your first love.	Not one word!	You have false teachers of Balaam and the Nicolaitans.	You allow Jezebel to teach idolatry and compromise.	You are dead. Works not complete.	Not one word!	You are lukewarm, wretched, miserable, poor, blind and naked.
COUNSEL I counsel you...	Remember from where you are fallen and repent.	Fear not. Be faithful.	Repent.	Hold fast what you have until I come.	Watch. Strengthen the things that remain. Remember, hold fast and repent.	Hold fast what you have.	Buy gold tried by fire and white raiment. Anoint your eyes. Be zealous and repent.
CHALLENGE To him that overcomes...	Will give to eat of the tree of life	Will not be hurt by the second death.	Will give hidden manna and a white stone.	Will give millennial leadership and the Morning Star.	Will be clothed in white raiment. I will not blot his name out of the book of life.	Will make him a pillar and write upon him the name of God and My new name.	Will grant to sit with me on my throne.

RAPTURE OF THE CHURCH

INTRODUCTION

Revelation 1:1–8

The revelation of Jesus Christ, which God gave him to show his servants what must soon take place. He made it known by sending his angel to his servant John, who testifies to everything he saw—that is, the word of God and the testimony of Jesus Christ. Blessed is the one who reads the words of this prophecy, and blessed are those who hear it and take to heart what is written in it, because the time is near.

John,

to the seven churches in the province of Asia:

Grace and peace to you from him who is, and who was, and who is to come, and from the seven spirits before his throne, and from Jesus Christ, who is the faithful witness, the firstborn from the dead, and the ruler of the kings of the earth.

To him who loves us and has freed us from our sins by his blood, and has made us to be a kingdom and priests to serve his God and Father—to him be glory and power for ever and ever! Amen.

Look, he is coming with the clouds,
  and every eye will see him,
even those who pierced him;
  and all the peoples of the earth will mourn because of him.
    So shall it be! Amen.

"I am the Alpha and the Omega," says the Lord God, "who is, and who was, and who is to come, the Almighty."   (Rev. 1:1–8)

THE SUBJECT OF REVELATION

"The revelation of Jesus Christ. . . ." The word "revelation" is a translation of the Greek word *apokalypsis*, which means "an unveiling." It is not a new word in the New Testament, for it occurs eighteen times (Luke 2:32; Gal. 1:12; 2 Thess. 1:7; 1 Pet. 1:7; etc.). The word means "to show or expose to view," as the unveiling of a painting is a "revelation." This book, then, is the unveiling of Jesus Christ. But not just Jesus Christ, for John has already presented Him very clearly as the divine Son of God in the Gospel that bears his name. Further on in the verse we find that this is the revelation of Jesus Christ "to show his servants what must soon take place." Again we see that the emphasis of the book is on future events.

"He made it known by sending his angel." The KJV word for "made known" is "signify." This word has been abused by many godly scholars in their study of this book. Some suggest that it means "sign-ify," that is, to write in signs. True, there are some symbols in the book and God calls them symbols, for example, Revelation 12:1, 3, and 15:1. However, it is wrong to classify the entire book as a book of signs and symbols, suggesting that they cannot be taken literally. On the contrary, the figurative language of Revelation is figurative of fact. There is far more in the book of Revelation that should be accepted literally than should be spiritualized.

THE SCRIBE AND DATE OF REVELATION

"... his servant, John." Among those who take the Bible literally there has never been any serious question about either the author of the book or the date when it was written. The Apostle John was the most venerated Christian leader throughout Asia Minor, particularly around Ephesus, where he had been the pastor for much of the last half of the first century. He outlived all the other apostles, in fulfillment of Jesus' prophecy in John 21:20–24. The Gospel that bore his name (written about A.D. 85) was an instant success among late first-century Christians so that a book by him about ten years later, given almost totally to prophecy and graphically different, was nonetheless accepted and used in the churches for over three hundred years.

All the external evidence points to the writing of Revelation by John when he was banished to the Isle of Patmos during the reign of Roman emperor Domitian (A.D. 91–96) for, as he said, "the word of God and the testimony of Jesus Christ." Evidence has been found that Patmos and surrounding islands were indeed used to incarcerate prisoners or the so-called "enemies of the state" at that period of history. That would make the writing of Revelation in and around the traditionally accepted date of A.D. 95, near the very end of John's life. Since he was the last of the apostles, it makes this unique revelation of Jesus Christ and the wonderful prophetic plan God has for humankind a fitting closure for the entire library of the sixty-six books of God's revelation to humankind.

The only objections offered to the authenticity of the book did not come until late in the second and third century by the Eastern Church centered in Alexandria. This was the headwaters of the Greek-inspired allegorical method of interpretation (through Philo and other Greek philosophers) that so influenced the Eastern Church. This method of interpreting Scripture was advanced by the brilliant Origen (branded a heretic by the early church), and ultimately brought into the church of Rome in the fifth century by Augustine, who also came from Alexandria. There is probably no heresy so harmful in the history of the church as the over-spiritualizing or allegorizing of Scripture. Even today the principal excuse by those who ignore the 28 percent of Scripture that is prophetic is that it must be taken "allegorically or symbolically." In truth, prophecy cannot be understood when taken that way. As we have seen, it should be understood literally unless the facts of the immediate context clearly indicate otherwise.

During the past century many post- or amillennialists (those who either think the church will convert the world prompting Christ's return, or that there will be no specific Millennium), suggest that Christ is now on earth in control. Or they have tried to assert that the book of Revelation was written during the reign of Nero, about A.D. 64. They claim that the prophecies of the Apocalypse were fulfilled by the fall of Jerusalem in A.D. 70. Such an idea is fraught with all kinds of distortions of history; it contradicts the known statements of Irenaeus and other early church fathers that it was written by John during the reign of Domitian and even ignores internal scriptural evidence to the contrary. For example, Christ's message to the first-century church of Ephesus was they "had forsaken their first love." If Revelation were written in A.D. 64 or 65, as they claim, that would mean the early church became cold in their zeal for Christ just thirty years after His ascension, while Peter and Paul were still alive! History confirms that was the very period of enormous evangelistic zeal when the gospel was preached "to every creature under heaven" (Col. 1:23). Such an idea is preposterous!

Another bit of internal evidence that John wrote Revelation late in the first century is found in our Lord's message to the church of Laodicea. He said the church was "increased with goods, rich and needs nothing." That was impossible in A.D. 64–66. The entire city had been destroyed by an earthquake in A.D. 62 and would not have had time to rebuild by then. Thirty or more years later, in A.D. 95, yes, but no city in those days could rebuild to its original level or prominence in just three or four years after such a devastating earthquake.

The preterist view—that Revelation was written prior to the destruction of Jerusalem in A.D. 70—cannot be supported either externally (historically) or internally (scripturally). The truth is the preterists advocate this theory because they need it to support their allegorizing or spiritualization system for interpreting prophecy. They would have us believe the whole book was fulfilled prior to the destruction of Jerusalem in 70 A.D. Their main thrust is to try to nullify the effectiveness of Revelation 20 that six times gives the length of the future millennial kingdom of Christ as "one thousand years." They can only do that by trying to prove that the book of Revelation was written prior to the destruction of Jerusalem in A.D. 70. This enables them to claim that the prophecies of the book have already been fulfilled and that there is no one-thousand-year kingdom era yet to come. The traditional date of A.D. 95, which as we have seen was the official view of the Western Church and all churches through the centuries that took the Bible literally, utterly destroys their view for it automatically shows the prophecies of Revelation to be yet future (including the 1000-year earthly reign of Christ).

It is difficult to understand why anyone would question the A.D. 95 date for the writing of Revelation when it was so readily accepted by the early church. No other date was offered for almost four centuries, and even then it was not taken seriously. Irenaeus, a disciple of Polycarp (who was a disciple of the Apostle John) wrote *Against Heresies* around A.D. 180. He is accepted by all scholars as a reliable authority on the first 150 years of Christianity. He wrote that John received the book of Revelation on the Isle of Patmos "toward the end of Domitian's reign."[1] And it is a known fact of history that Domitian was murdered in the year A.D. 96. Moreover, he was famous for banishing people to Patmos and other Greek islands. Irenaeus' statement was accepted as accurate by such early church fathers as Clement, Victorinus, Tertullian, Jerome, Eusebius, and others. The fact that he was only one generation removed from the Apostle John has traditionally carried great weight with historians.

It is interesting to note that all the second and third century compilations of the New Testament included the book of Revelation. Historian H. Grattan Guinness writes, "That the Apocalypse was the subject of extensive and constant study by the early church is evident from the significant fact that practically the entire book is reproducible from the Christian writers of the first three centuries."[2]

For most students of Revelation, it is easier to accept the clear statement of highly regarded Irenaeus, supported by several of the other early church fathers that supported his view of the A.D. 95 date of the writing of the book, than the early date suggestion of those who lived eighteen hundred years removed from the events. These preterists, as they are called, prefer the A.D. 64 date, not because there is sufficient scriptural or historical evidence to confirm it but because they need it. They know that if Revelation was indeed written when early church tradition confirms it was—A.D. 95—then the book is about the future. As we will see, that view best fits the normal reading of the book. Except for the seven church ages, some of which are still in progress, all the other events in the book are yet to come. The book is primarily about "what will take place later" (Rev. 1:19).

THE SPIRITUAL BLESSING OF REVELATION

We have already seen that a blessing is offered to those who read, hear, and keep the words of this book. The word "blessing" in Scripture is similar in meaning to the word "happy." As you know, happiness is not found in the things of this world but comes from God. The book of Revelation is a source of happiness to anyone who will read it, hear it in the depths of his heart, and obey its instructions. If ever a generation needed to study this book it is ours. As mentioned, we are probably living at the time when these things will begin to come to pass.

THE SOURCE OF REVELATION

It is important that we keep in focus the true source of the book of Revelation. It did not originate with John but came to him through a four-fold sequence of transmission: *God—Christ—angel—John: to the Church.* The true source of the book of Revelation is God. That is probably the reason that the Greek writing of the text is somewhat different from John's Gospel. He was more of an amanuensis in this book than in his Gospel.

THE TRINITY

"... who is, and who was, and who is to come." This is a reference to the Holy Trinity or the triune God. Whenever the word God appears in Scripture, the context should be examined closely to determine whether it is referring to God the Father, God the Son, or God the Holy Spirit. It is erroneous to assume that the title God always refers to God the Father. Many times it refers to the triune God. The expression "who is, and who was, and who is to come" is an encompassing expression that connotes the eternity of God. It is significant to note that this great book has its origin in the Trinity. The triune nature of God is again revealed in 1:8.

THE SALUTATION OF REVELATION

"Grace and peace to you." *Grace* is the Greek method of greeting; *peace* is the Hebrew form of greeting. Both of these generate from God, not human beings. Grace and peace are not the prerogatives of people. One's relationship to God determines one's possession of grace and peace.

This verse shows that the Trinity shares in the dispensing of grace and peace: God the Father—"from him who is, and who was, and who is to come"; God the Spirit—"and from the seven spirits before his throne"; and God the Son—"and from Jesus Christ." ("The seven spirits" is a reference to the sevenfold work of the Spirit as revealed in Isaiah 11:2, where He is called "the Spirit of the Lord ... the Spirit of wisdom and of understanding, the Spirit of counsel and of power, the Spirit of knowledge and of the fear of the Lord." The number *seven* denotes perfection or completeness; the expression "seven spirits" does not mean seven Holy Spirits but the seven ministries of the Holy Spirit.)

THE SAVIOR OF REVELATION

Right here in the introduction we have the first of many descriptions in this book of Jesus Christ in the glory and majesty befitting His person and nature. In our Lord's first coming, He was "despised and rejected by men, a man of sorrows, and familiar with suffering" (Isa. 53:3). In His next coming, He will be adored and worshiped, for He will come "with power and great glory" (Luke 21:27). The book of Revelation presents the Lord Jesus more magnificently than any other book in the Bible. For a true picture of the whole nature of Jesus Christ, one must understand Him as He is revealed in this book. Verses 5, 6, and 7 describe the past, present, and future work of Jesus Christ, the Lord.

"... the faithful witness." The Lord Jesus Christ is the faithful witness. All that we need to know about God is revealed through Him. As He said to Philip, "Anyone who has seen me has seen the Father" (John 14:9). Though there are other witnesses of the person of Christ, such as God the Father (who spoke from heaven), John the Baptist, Jesus' miracles, and the Scriptures (5:31–39), His witness is sufficient. For this reason He could say of Himself, "I am ... the truth" (14:6).

"... the firstborn from the dead." This phrase means that Christ is "the firstfruits" of those who are raised from the dead (1 Cor. 15:23). Christ is not the first being raised from the dead, for Elisha and Elijah raised the dead, and Christ Himself raised three people from the dead. However, these people all died natural deaths later; they were not raised "imperishable" (15:42). Christ is the first one ever to have been resurrected in His glorified body, an event that also guarantees our ultimate resurrection.

"... the ruler of the kings of the earth." Jesus Christ is in control of this world, though He is permitting human beings certain latitude; nevertheless, His control of the world rulers of this day is evident in the fact that He ultimately permits them to be put down. It seems that He permits world rulers certain latitudes which have kept one person from ever controlling this world since the time of Christ. For example, Napoleon met his Waterloo, Kaiser Wilhelm met his, and Adolph Hitler met his, just as the communist tyrants of our twentieth century have met theirs. The ultimate meaning, of course, is in reference to that day when He will reign physically as King of kings and Lord of lords on this earth.

The Present Work of Christ

He "who loves us" denotes continual action. Not only did He give Himself for us, but today He continues to love us with an everlasting love.

"... and freed [KJV, washed] us from our sins by his blood." All those who have received Jesus Christ by faith have been cleansed by His blood. This is not a universal experience but a unique washing by Christ of those who personally call on Him. The Bible tells us, "The blood of Jesus, [God's] Son, purifies us from all sin" (1 John 1:7). But this is based on the condition that we confess our sin. Let me pause here to ask: Have you confessed your sin? Have you called personally on the name of the Lord

Jesus Christ? Unless you have, you are still in your sins. But the blood of Jesus Christ will be applied to those sins in cleansing power if you will but ask the Savior for His cleansing and turn your life over to Him.

Dr, John Walvoord, the dean of all living prophecy scholars, likes to tell the story that when he was fifteen years old, he realized for the first time that he had never had the personal experience of being born again by faith in Jesus Christ. He had been raised in a Christian home, was baptized, and was a member of the church, yet had never personally received Christ. He had even pledged his life for the gospel ministry but had never personally been saved. Under the preaching of a visiting evangelist he realized for the first time that no one becomes a Christian by good works. That night he said he accepted the grace of Christ by faith when he personally called on the name of the Lord for forgiveness and salvation. That is the only way anyone becomes a Christian—by personally calling on the name of the Lord.

". . . and has made us to be a kingdom and priests to serve his God and Father." Amazing as it may seem, once we become Christians by faith, Christ makes us kings and priests. We may not look like kings today, but there is a day coming when, because we are the children of God by faith, we will rule and reign with Him—that is, if we have been born into His spiritual kingdom, having been translated from the power of darkness into the kingdom of the Son of His love in whom we have redemption, the forgiveness of our sins (Col. 1:13–14).

Our present condition does not accurately convey our future realization, but it is as certain as the eternal God. In the meantime, however, we are to do our work faithfully as priests unto God, which means that we are to intercede on behalf of those who need Christ and cannot pray for themselves. One of the great needs of the Church of Jesus Christ today is to be actively engaged in the work of intercessory prayer.

The Future Work of Christ

> Look, he is coming with the clouds,
>   and every eye will see him,
> even those who pierced him;
>   and all the peoples of the earth will mourn because of him.
>   So shall it be! Amen.   (Rev. 1:7)

Christ is coming again. Yes, Jesus is coming again! This is a certified, guaranteed promise. The angelic messengers in Acts 1:11 said, "This same Jesus, who has been taken from you into heaven, will come back in the same way you have seen him go into heaven." This can only mean that He will come visibly to the earth. This is a reference to His coming at the end of the Tribulation Period to set up His millennial kingdom.

"Look, he is coming with the clouds." He ascended in a cloud (Acts 1:9) and will return in a cloud. Jesus Himself said that He would come in a cloud (Matt. 24:30).

". . . and every eye will see him." This does not mean only those who are on the earth at that time. It means *every eye*. Jesus Himself said to Caiaphas, the high priest, "But I say to all of you: In the future you will see the Son of Man sitting at the right hand of the Mighty One and coming on the clouds of heaven" (Matt. 26:64). Caiaphas is now dead and, unless he repented with those on the day of Pentecost, is in Hades. Thus we see that even those in Hades will see Him along with those "who pierced him," meaning that all those who lent their assent to the crucifixion of Jesus will face Him again, for He is coming visibly in power and great glory. It could not be said more majestically than the manner in which the Lord Jesus Himself stated it in Matthew 24:30–31:

> At that time the sign of the Son of Man will appear in the sky, and all the nations of the earth will mourn. They will see the Son of Man coming on the clouds of the sky, with power and great glory. And he will send his angels with a loud trumpet call, and they will gather his elect from the four winds, from one end of the heavens to the other.

It is no wonder that God predicts that "all the peoples of the earth will mourn because of him." The peoples of the earth mourn because they are earthly; that is, they have rejected the Christ and are eternally lost. If the book of Revelation teaches us nothing else, it teaches that Jesus Christ is coming again to judge this world, and the basis of judgment will be whether or not people have received Him as Savior and Lord.

ONE

The Christ of the Churches

Revelation 1:9–20

> I, John, your brother and companion in the suffering and kingdom and patient endurance that are ours in Jesus, was on the island of Patmos because of the word of God and the testimony of Jesus. On the Lord's Day I was in the Spirit, and I heard behind me a loud voice like a trumpet, which said: "Write on a scroll what you see and send it to the seven churches: to Ephesus, Smyrna, Pergamum, Thyatira, Sardis, Philadelphia and Laodicea." (Rev. 1:9–11)

THE APOSTLE JOHN

The early church was not given to ecclesiasticism! This deadly teaching that has created a division between "clergy" and "laity" has done much harm to the Church of Christ through the centuries. The Apostle John was the oldest living apostle of our Lord at the time of this writing. He was probably esteemed as the most revered saint of his day. Instead of attracting attention to this, he immediately identified himself with the people by stating, "I, John, your brother and companion in . . . suffering." This "suffering" (KJV, "tribulation") is different from the Great Tribulation, which John speaks of later as a future event (chs. 4–18). He was going through suffering as a member of the early church that was persecuted so unmercifully by the emperors of Rome, who had already claimed the lives of Peter and Paul and probably most of the other apostles.

He further identified himself as their companion "in the . . . kingdom and patient endurance that are ours in Jesus." The "kingdom" here is obviously the spiritual kingdom that Jesus set up on the day of Pentecost, which is in operation today and can be entered into only by being born again (John 3:3). The "patient endurance" of this kingdom is seen in our faithfully enduring until he comes at the end of this age.

Imprisoned at Patmos

The Isle of Patmos, located in the Mediterranean Sea just off the mainland of Asia from the city of Miletus, is a tiny island to which John had probably been banished by the Roman government "because of the

word of God and the testimony of Jesus." It is noteworthy that even at
the venerable age of approximately ninety, John refused to compromise
his faithful preaching concerning the resurrected, glorified Christ. One
cannot resist the temptation of quoting the dying words of another
Christian saint, Polycarp, who was burned at the stake, refusing to recant
his faith in Jesus Christ and who, just as the torch was applied to the
wood stacked at his feet, said, "Eighty and six years have I served Him,
and He never did me any wrong. How could I blaspheme my King and
my Savior now?" The history of the Christian Church is replete with
countless thousands who chose death rather than faithlessness to the
Word of God and the testimony of Jesus Christ. Who can say that the
church age will not end the same way it began? In fact, the 60 million
Christians in the house or underground churches of China believe it
already is.

In the Spirit on the Lord's Day

Some consider John's reference to the Lord's Day to be the first time
the expression "the Lord's Day" was applied to the first day of the week,
when the Christians gathered together to worship. It is true that they
were freed from the law as a testimony to Israel and that, to express their
belief in the resurrection, they did not meet on the Sabbath but on Sunday. Many modern-day Christians do not realize that our Sunday is not
a Sabbath day, since to the Christian every day is a holy day. Nowhere in
the New Testament are we commanded to observe the Sabbath. In fact,
all the other nine Old Testament commandments are repeated in the
New Testament—only the one regarding observing the Sabbath is omitted. Most Bible scholars believe the reason is that it was not intended for
the church. The Bible teaches that we are not to esteem one day above
another. We should keep in mind Romans 14 and Colossians 2, which
suggest that we go to the Lord's house on what we call "the Lord's Day"
as a testimony that we believe Jesus Christ rose bodily from the dead on
the first day of the week.

Meaning of "the Lord's Day"

John's use of "the Lord's Day" in this connection with being "in the
Spirit," however, probably does not refer to being in the Spirit on the
first day of the week. Rather, it is a reference to the fact that by the power
of the Holy Spirit John was lifted in prophetic vision beyond the church
age to "the day of the Lord." This specifically refers not only to the glorious appearing of Christ to the earth, but also incorporates the many
events of the Tribulation Period, including the Rapture of the Church
and the seven years of Tribulation and culminating with the glorious
appearing of Christ and the establishment of His millennial kingdom.

THE SEVEN CHURCHES

The seven churches of Asia selected by Christ in verse 11 are worthy of close scrutiny. We will treat them individually when we come to chapters 2 and 3, for there is a world of meaning contained in these messages. Opinion is divided as to the extent to which the teachings gained in the study of these messages to the churches can be taken. It is generally agreed, however, that these messages can have four applications.

1. The Seven Churches of John's Day

Obviously, these were literal churches with which John was familiar, for much of his ministry had been conducted throughout that area of Asia. The question that naturally comes to mind is: Why of the hundreds of churches located in cities all over the world by this time (about sixty-three years after the day of Pentecost) were these seven churches selected? It is suggested that they also represent the seven basic divisions of church history.

2. The Seven Basic Divisions of Church History

A study of history reveals that the Church has gone through seven basic periods or stages. Some prophecy scholars show how they parallel the same types of our Lord's parables of the kingdom in Matthew 13, which depict the church during these past almost two thousand years. These will be dealt with in detail in subsequent chapters; however, here I would like to quote prophecy professor Gary Cohen.

> The theory that the seven churches of Revelation 2–3 are prophetical, that they represent seven consecutive periods in ecclesiastical history, seems to have first been suggested by some of the words of the martyr Victorinus, Bishop of Pettau (died c. A.D. 303). This belief as held today does not deny that at the same time the seven churches are also historical and representative. It asserts that the prophetical element is in addition to these other elements and wholly compatible with them. Thus it beholds the seven congregations (1) as historically existent at the time of John's writing in A.D. 95–96, (2) as representing the entire church through the seven types of local churches which shall exist throughout the dispensation, and (3) as prefiguring seven aspects of the professing church which would successfully rise into prominence before Christ's second coming.
>
> The seven periods are generally given approximately as follows:
>
> 1. Ephesus—Apostolic church (A.D. 30–100)
> 2. Smyrna—Persecuted church (A.D. 100–313)
> 3. Pergamos—State church (A.D. 313–590)
> 4. Thyatira—Papal church (A.D. 590–1517)
> 5. Sardis—Reformed church (A.D. 1517–1790)
> 6. Philadelphia—Missionary church (A.D. 1730–1900)
> 7. Laodicea—Apostate church (A.D. 1900–)[3]

Although this time-honored belief that Christ's message to the seven churches includes a prophecy of the seven stages of church history has never been unanimous, it is held by most premillennialists. Even Phillip Schaff, the writer of the classic eight-volume set *History of the Christian Church*, accepts that position.

3. The Seven Types of Churches That Exist Today

Although most of these phases of church history are now concluded, nevertheless their influence still carries over from stage to stage, and some trends are still in existence even in our own day.

4. The Seven Characteristics That Can Exist in Any Church or Christian

This suggestion is merely the practical application of the message to these churches on a personal and individual basis. As we come to them, we can readily see that these seven churches comprise seven methods of attack by Satan on the Church or individual Christians within the Church, demanding that we take unto ourselves the whole armor of God (Eph. 6:10–18) and "resist the devil" (James 4:7; cf. 1 Pet. 5:9).

THE SEVEN LAMPSTANDS

"I saw seven golden lampstands" (1:12). We can be most dogmatic on the meaning of the seven lampstands here because they are interpreted for us in 1:20, where the Lord Jesus Himself told John that "the seven lampstands are the seven churches." These seven churches were uniquely elected by Christ for the purposes we already designated. A lampstand is a fitting symbol for the church. While in this world, Jesus Christ was the light of the world; but He told His disciples, "You are the light of the world" (Matt. 5:14).

Though we give light, we do not originate light; just as a lampstand does not originate light, but gets its light from the oil or electricity generating through it, so the child of God is a means of light. Christ is the light, but He uses the churches and the children of God in the churches as lampstands to convey this light. We can either yield ourselves unstintingly to Christ and, by letting Him shine through us, be used to illuminate the darkness that has engulfed humanity, or we can commit the sins of several of the churches of Asia and dim that light. Christ has ordained the Church to be His torchbearer in this generation. The only limitation placed on the brilliance of the light is the yieldedness of the lampstand, the Church!

THE VISION OF THE CHRIST OF THE CHURCHES

I turned around to see the voice that was speaking to me. And when I turned I saw seven golden lampstands, and among the lampstands was someone "like a son of man," dressed in a robe reaching down to his feet and with a golden sash around his chest. His head and hair were white like wool, as white as snow, and his eyes were like blazing fire. His feet were like bronze glowing in a furnace, and his voice was like the sound of rushing waters. In his right hand he held seven stars, and out of his mouth came a sharp double-edged sword. His face was like the sun shining in all its brilliance.

When I saw him, I fell at his feet as though dead. Then he placed his right hand on me and said: "Do not be afraid. I am the First and the Last. I am the Living One; I was dead, and behold I am alive for ever and ever! And I hold the keys of death and Hades.

"Write, therefore, what you have seen, what is now and what will take place later. The mystery of the seven stars that you saw in my right hand and of the seven golden lampstands is this: The seven stars are the angels of the seven churches, and the seven lampstands are the seven churches." (Rev. 1:12–20)

This vision of Christ is graphically descriptive, not only of Christ in His glory, but of His relationship to the churches of His day and churches of all ages.

The Ten Characteristics of Christ Envisioned by John

As John turned to see who it was that was speaking to him, he saw seven golden lampstands and a person in their midst. He lists ten details of that person that are most descriptive. Notice that only the stars and the lampstands are interpreted for us. Nothing about the person of Christ is interpreted. One might ask, Why is this true? It is because the Holy Spirit has interpreted these details on other occasions in Holy Writ. As we contemplate this fact, we recognize the basic principle of Bible study that we should compare Scripture with Scripture. We will take each of these characteristics of John's vision and note their meaning from Scripture.

1. "... someone 'like a son of man'" indicates that this person was not a grotesque creature of the supernatural world; rather, He was human in His appearance. "Son of Man" is one of the most frequent titles Jesus applied to Himself. It is used of the Messiah in all four Gospels as well as in Daniel 7:13.

2. "... dressed in a robe reaching down to his feet." This was typical of the long robes of the high priests as they ministered in the Holy Place in the Temple. Hebrews tells us Jesus is our great high priest pertaining to all things in our relationship with God.

3. "... with a golden sash around his chest" refers to a symbol of strength and authority common in the ancient world. The average working man wore a short tunic of loose-fitting clothes. Only those in authority wore a girdle. Remember, Jesus said of Himself, "All authority in heaven and on earth has been given to me" (Matt. 28:18).

4. "His head and hair were white like wool, as white as snow," conveys the thought of antiquity and reminds us of the vision of Daniel 7:9–13, where Christ is called the "Ancient of Days." The whiteness here, of course, also speaks of the righteousness of God, who is from everlasting to everlasting.

5. "... his eyes were like blazing fire." The Greek construction is literally, "his eyes shot fire," indicating that Christ was indignant over something; as we progress with the vision, we find that He was indignant over the indifference, in some cases, of the apostate churches. Whenever the Church of Jesus Christ is not what it should be, we can be sure it arouses the indignation of Christ.

6. "... his feet were like bronze glowing in a furnace." The bronze speaks to us of judgment. It reminds us of the brazen altar of the tabernacle, where sin was judged.

7. "... his voice was like the sound of rushing waters." This simile can best be illustrated by Niagara Falls. When you come to the edge of the great falls, all other sounds are eliminated from your hearing as you are engulfed by the deafening roar of the turbulent waters. This figure seems to indicate the attitude of the Son of God as He comes on the Day of the Lord in judgment. Far too many cannot hear His voice today, but they will hear it then. The call of worldliness, materialism, science, education, psychology, and all other voices calling to the souls of human beings seem to take precedence over the voice of Jesus Christ today. In that day all other voices will be stilled by the deafening, overpowering voice of the Son of God, to whom all people will give heed, for they will be entering into their hour of judgment. However, the church or Christian that so desires can hear His voice today if he or she will but listen.

8. "In his right hand he held seven stars." The Lord Himself interpreted to John the meaning of the seven stars. In verse 20 "the seven stars are the angels of the seven churches." The meaning of the Greek word translated "angels" is literally "messengers."

Many godly Bible scholars believe the word "angels" here refers, not to supernatural angelic beings, but to the messengers divinely appointed by God to lead local congregations. For example, the spiritual leader or pastor at the church of Ephesus was addressed in 2:1: "To the angel of the church in Ephesus write." Once I heard Dr. J. Vernon McGee, the radio Bible teacher, say regarding this, "I like to think that it refers to the local pastors. It is good to hear a pastor being called an angel; sometimes we are called other things."

Another view is that the messenger is an actual angel, a supernaturally created being especially assigned to that church. This could mean that churches all have a guardian angel, just as Christ indicated that little children have a guardian angel (Matt. 18:10). The main objection to this suggestion is that some of the angels obviously failed in keeping their churches pure. However, in answer to that, even angels, though supernatural, are not divine. Nor can they supersede the human will, because this is a liberty given by God. If Christ has subjected Himself to the position of being on the outside of the door of the church, knocking for entrance (Rev. 3:20), we can scarcely imagine the angels doing more. If a church has failed in its mission, it is not because its angel has been irresponsible, but because the church has rejected the Holy Spirit's leading.

Of the two views suggested, I lean to the thought that the meaning here is "angel." With all the enemies armed against the church, both natural and supernatural, I like to think that we have a specially assigned angel working for us. Certainly we need one!

9. ". . . out of his mouth came a sharp double-edged sword." Ephesians 6 refers to the Word of God as "the sword of the Spirit." Hebrews 4:12 tells us that the Word of God is "sharper than any double-edged sword." Evidently the spoken word of Christ will go forth as a sharp sword against which there will be no defense in the day of judgment. Thus we can see that there will really be no battle with the Antichrist, for he will be indefensible against the presence of Christ at His coming (Rev. 19–20).

10. "His face was like the sun shining in all its brilliance." This speaks of the divine nature of Christ and reminds us of the event that took place on the Mount of Transfiguration, where Christ "was transfigured before them. His face shone like the sun, and his clothes became as white as the light" (Matt. 17:2). For just a moment during His earthly ministry, Peter, James, and John saw Jesus in His divine glory, just as John saw Him here in this vision. Let there be no doubt about it: This is Jesus the Christ, the divine Son of God. Amen!

John's Reaction to His Vision of Christ

Although we are the sons of God, "co-heirs with Christ" (Rom. 8:17), let it be clearly understood that we will never be divine or "deities." Christ is so exalted beyond us that even in our glorified state we will willingly worship at his feet. This John who prostrated himself at the feet of the resurrected Christ is the same John who was familiar enough with the Lord Jesus to lay his head on His breast in the upper room. Now we find John falling at His feet "as though dead," knocked cold by His glory. Anyone truly in touch with the Spirit of God instinctively bows in adoration to Jesus Christ. Any spirit that motivates one in defiance of Christ is not the Holy Spirit.

FOUR REASONS WHY CHRISTIANS SHOULD NOT FEAR

Cold, naked fear is gripping the hearts of human beings everywhere today because of chaotic world conditions. For the first time in human history the proliferation of nuclear bombs makes it possible for terrorists or rogue nations to destroy cities or whole nations. Those without Christ have every right to fear! This never should be the case for the child of God! "For God did not give us a spirit of timidity, but a spirit of power, of love and of self-discipline" (2 Tim. 1:7).

As Jesus laid His right hand on John and said to him, "Do not be afraid," He was enunciating in the form of His essential deity what He had announced to the disciples on many occasions while in His incarnate state. He often used the terms "do not be afraid," "peace be with you," and "do not let your heart be troubled." These messages not only admonished the disciples of Jesus' day but reflect the attitude that should characterize His disciples in every age, for He said, in giving the Great Commission, "And surely I am with you always" (Matt. 28:20). The greatest cure for one's natural fear is the personal presence of Jesus Christ. Notice Jesus' four reasons why we need not fear:

1. "I am the First and the Last" speaks of Christ's eternity. He is before all things; and after all things are through, He will still be in control.

2. "I am the Living One; I was dead" speaks of Christ's sacrificial death for our sins and His resurrection. This phrase attests to the fact that we worship a risen, living Christ.

3. "I am alive for ever and ever!" The Scripture tells us that Christ "died for sins once for all" (1 Pet. 3:18). He will not die again. He will not change His state. He will always be! Oh, that people might realize the decision of accepting or rejecting Jesus as an eternal decision; just as He is able to save "for ever and ever," so He is able to damn forever those who reject Him.

4. "And I hold the keys of death and Hades." This is a detail that John did not record in his description, but Jesus stated that in His hand He held "the keys of death and Hades." These keys were evidently purchased with His own blood, for according to Hebrews 2:14–15, "by his death he might destroy him who holds the power of death—that is, the devil—and free those who all their lives were held in slavery by their fear of death."

The Christian need not fear death or Hades. The unseen abode of the unbelieving dead currently is Hades, often called "hell." After the Great White Throne Judgment of Revelation 20, death and Hades will be "thrown into the lake of fire. The lake of fire is the second death" (20:14). Those outside of Jesus Christ have every reason to fear that event! The child of God, however, should never fear death, Hades, or the lake of fire. Why? Because Christ our Savior has the keys of death and Hades, and a key is a symbol of release.

Years ago I was taken to see a prisoner by the special representative of the warden's office in the reformatory at St. Cloud, Minnesota. While there, I noted that new inmates obviously feared the institution and the long-anticipated confinement; however, I did not fear the institution. Why? Because the representative of the warden's office held the keys to the institution for me, even though I passed through sixteen heavy steel doors all securely locked. In a similar manner, those who know Jesus Christ need never fear Hades and death, for He holds the key that unlocks the door to this dreaded place.

The big question is, *Do you know Him? Is He your Savior?* Though Jesus Christ died for the sins of the whole world, He has not saved all the people of the world, for He has chosen to leave it up to each person's will whether he or she will accept or reject Him. When the Philippian jailer asked the Apostle Paul, "What must I do to be saved?" he received the emphatic reply, "Believe in the Lord Jesus, and you will be saved" (Acts 16: 31). That is, trust in the Lord Jesus Christ. Have you trusted in Him? If not, I urge you to commit your soul, by faith, to Him today by asking Him to come into your heart, cleanse your sin, and save your soul.

TWO

The Church of Ephesus

Revelation 2:1–7

The church of Jesus Christ was founded on the testimony of His personal deity (Matt. 16:18). He said of it, "The gates of Hades will not overcome it." He could speak prophetically of the future destiny of the Church because He intended to see to it personally that the Church He established would be protected. Nowhere is this seen more clearly than in John's heavenly vision, which we have already examined, portraying Christ walking among the lampstands (the churches), shining forth the light they received from Him to a lost world floundering in darkness.

Chapters 2 and 3 of Revelation give the message of Christ to the seven churches of Asia and go beyond them to the churches which will come later. Christ's divine commendation, condemnation, counsel, and challenge are just as vital today as in the day they were written.

THE APOSTOLIC CHURCH, A.D. 30–100

Commendation: "I know your deeds, your hard work and your perseverance. I know that you cannot tolerate wicked men, that you have tested those who claim to be apostles but are not, and have found them false. You have persevered and have endured hardships for my name, and have not grown weary. . . . You hate the practices of the Nicolaitans, which I also hate."

Condemnation: "You have forsaken your first love."

Counsel: "Remember the height from which you have fallen! Repent and do the things you did at first."

Challenge: "To him who overcomes, I will give the right to eat from the tree of life, which is in the paradise of God."

Ephesus is considered by Bible scholars to have been one of the finest and largest churches of New Testament times. It was begun by the Apostle Paul at the end of his second missionary journey (Acts 18:19–20). Located in a wicked city given over to the worship of the goddess Artemis, the church exhibited a spiritual vitality that carried over from Paul's habit of preaching "publicly and from house to house," ministering to them "with great humility and with tears" (20:19–20). For a good description of the founding of this church, read Acts 18–20. One cannot help being impressed with the deep spirituality of the Ephesian elders who came to Miletus to see Paul before he went to Jerusalem (20:17–38).

The Ephesian or Apostolic Period

Of the seven churches mentioned in Revelation 2 and 3, this is the only one where reference is made to the apostles. This would bear out the thought that the message of Christ to the church at Ephesus was directed not only to one local church, but to the church of the first century, usually called "the early church" or "the apostolic church." This covered the period of time from the day of Pentecost (about A.D. 30) to A.D. 100.

The name Ephesus means "desired one." This was the most desirable of all the churches or church ages. It was characterized by fervent evangelism. One of the main reasons for this was the large percentage of Jewish converts that made up the church. The Church of Jesus Christ owes much to the Jews, through whom we have the Bible and our Savior, Jesus Christ. The success of the early church was due largely to a preponderance of Jewish leadership and their contagious belief that Jesus could come in their lifetime.

The Early Church Preached the Gospel Around the World

There is strong scriptural indication that the early church preached the gospel around the world. Romans 10:18 tells us, "But I ask: Did they not hear? Of course they did: Their voice has gone out into all the earth, their words to the ends of the world." Romans 16:26 relates that the gospel is "made known through the prophetic writings by the command of the eternal God, so that all nations might believe and obey him." In Colossians 1:6, speaking of the gospel, the Holy Spirit asserts through the Apostle Paul that it "has come to you. All over the world this gospel is bearing fruit and growing. . . ." In 1:23 we find, ". . . if you continue in your faith, established and firm, not moved from the hope held out in the gospel. This is the gospel that you heard and that has been proclaimed to every creature under heaven, and of which I, Paul, have become a servant."

Putting these four passages of Scripture together, we find that before the Scripture canon had been completed, the early church accomplished more widespread preaching of the gospel through the ministry of the Jewish Christians than has ever been done since the Church has become predominantly led by Gentiles. In fact, even with our modern means of communication and jet travel today, we are unable to equal their evangelistic success. It is interesting to note that apostasy and indifference were characteristics of the Church of Jesus Christ under the administration of Gentiles, whereas evangelism was a characteristic of Jewish leadership. This is highlighted by the prophetic truth, found in Revelation 7, that the only other time the Gospel will be proclaimed around the world will again be under Jewish leadership when the 144,000 Jewish Christian witnesses will go forth, preaching the gospel to reach "a great multitude that no one could count" (7:9).

CHRIST'S COMMENDATION

A Working Church

The speaker in this vision in 2:1–7, of course, is Christ, described by John as walking in the midst of the seven golden lampstands. This indicates that Christ and His power have always been available to the Church. He is thus fulfilling His words to the apostles in Matthew 28:20, "teaching them to obey everything I have commanded you. And surely I am with you always, to the very end of the age."

"I know your deeds, your hard work and your perseverance." Christ commended this early church for its faithful works of Christian service. Service for Jesus Christ is work. It is a joyous labor of love for the child of God who is "abiding in Christ," but it is nonetheless a labor. Christ knows and records all faithful service. He said in Matthew 10:42, "And if anyone gives even a cup of cold water to one of these little ones because he is my disciple, I tell you the truth, he will certainly not lose his reward."

No act of service is too small to escape the Savior's notice. Dr. M. R. DeHaan, the great prophetic Bible teacher, once stated, "To come to Christ costs nothing, to follow Christ costs something, but to serve Christ cost everything." Jesus said, "Whoever finds his life will lose it, and whoever loses his life for my sake will find it" (Matt. 10:39).

Every Christian should have a thorough understanding of Ephesians 2:8–10. We are all familiar with the principle of salvation by grace through faith as stated in verses 8–9, but few understand that after this transaction we go on "to do good works, which God prepared in advance for us to do."

A Separated Church

"I know that you cannot tolerate wicked men." The word for "church" in the Greek is *ecclesia*, literally meaning "called-out ones." A true church is a church *in* the world but not *of* the world. One of the things that characterized the early church, but not some of the other churches, was the refusal to fraternize with loose Christians. The early church heeded the injunctions of the Holy Spirit to "watch out for those who cause divisions and put obstacles in your way that are contrary to the teaching you have learned. Keep away from them" (Rom. 16:17). Church discipline is almost unheard of today. The early church practiced it, and the truly separated church that is filled with the Spirit today will still practice it.

Some years ago, while visiting the church of the Tzeltal Indians of southern Mexico, I saw what it meant for a group of believers to observe church discipline, having only the Bible to instruct them. One man was standing outside, watching while the services were being conducted. We were informed that this was because he had been going with an unsaved woman in the village, which compromised his Christian witness and was considered an offense by that church. They would not permit him to sit inside through the services until he repented. We were also informed that others of that church were not permitted to take communion or give their tithes and offerings if they were not in fellowship with the Lord. What a stir it would create in the modern church if such practices were conducted faithfully; but who can say they should not be?

A Pure Church

"I know ... you have tested those who claim to be apostles but are not, and have found them false." Satan sowed weeds in the Lord's wheat field immediately after the day of Pentecost. Some of these weeds disguised themselves as apostles and went about deceiving some of the early churches in their innocence, for they had no written copy of the Scriptures. Of course, God is faithful, and those churches that truly looked to Him and tried the spirits, "to see if they are of God," were not deceived. The church at Ephesus was one of these and would not be taken in by false apostles.

The current Church of Jesus Christ needs to heed this message, for there are many false apostles going about disguised as servants of Jesus Christ but who are really enemies of the cross, seeking their own personal gain. The ecclesiastical sickness of "ecumania" (a one-world church regardless of one's faith), which has caught the fancy of many church leaders, has a deadening effect on the true Church wherever it is found. We can expect this trend to continue with increasing ferocity until the Lord comes. We have every right today to test people to see if they are of God. If their teachings are not consistent with and faithful to the Word of God, they should be rejected. Because of the devil's use of semantics, we have to examine what people mean by the words they employ, as well as the words themselves.

An Enduring Church

"You have persevered and have endured hardships for my name, and have not grown weary." The structure of these words clearly indicates that the church at Ephesus was a consistent church, enduring through its entire history in faithful propagation of the gospel message, not being fainthearted, but courageously presenting the gospel of Christ. The entire commendation is a tribute to the faithfulness of this godly church.

An Autonomous Church

"You hate the practices of the Nicolaitans, which I also hate." The word "Nicolaitans" comes from two Greek words: *niko,* meaning "to conquer, overthrow," and *laos,* meaning "the people, laity." It seems that in the early days of the church the followers of Nicolai held two serious heretical views: They practiced sensuality by completely separating one's spiritual and physical nature, thus giving themselves license to sin. And they tried to establish an ecclesiastical order. This latter heresy is known as "Nicolaitanism." Evidently an effort was made to set up bishops, archbishops, cardinals, and popes. This is an unscriptural idea, which causes the local church to become enslaved by one man or a small group of men whose spiritual life can determine the spiritual success of the church. This is a most dangerous principle indeed, since every human being is dependent on an abiding relationship with Jesus Christ to maintain spiritual vitality. "Holy men" may cease "abiding" after taking office, to the great detriment of the church. Another evil of this practice is that it causes the local church to look to human beings for the solution to their problems rather than to the Holy Spirit. The Lord Jesus said that He would send the Holy Spirit, who "will guide you into all truth" (John 16:13).

Nicolaitanism, which is synonymous with modern day ecclesiasticism, is a concept about which Jesus Christ said, "I also hate." Would to God that the Church of Jesus Christ could learn the valuable lesson that it is not by ecclesiasticism or organization or promotion or administration, but "by my Spirit, says the Lord." The greatest single curse in modern Christendom is ecclesiasticism. When human beings get control of the spiritual training of other people and are in a position to dominate the church, their theological position will eventually dominate that church.

The history of the Church of Jesus Christ is a continuous cycle of autonomous churches amalgamating into great conventions or denominations of ecclesiastical hierarchies that eventually become apostate. This in turn causes a breaking away on the part of the minority group that seeks to be faithful to the Scripture and to be autonomous, depending only on the Holy Spirit. Evidently the church at Ephesus and the early apostolic church were successful in withstanding the work of the Nicolaitans, which was accepted later by the church of Pergamum (Rev. 2:15).

CHRIST'S CONDEMNATION

"Yet I hold this against you: You have forsaken your first love." There was only one condemnation against this early church—but a serious one indeed. Although basically faithful, it had unconsciously succumbed to the natural tendency of letting even the most wonderful experience become commonplace. The generation of the apostles had passed from the scene, except for the Apostle John, and their children had taken their places by the time this message was given. Although the Ephesians loved the Lord, they had lost the spontaneous sparkle of their love for Him. This has been illustrated many times in human experience by marriages that fall onto dangerous ground when the husband and wife begin taking each other for granted. Honeymoon love erodes and becomes just routine married life. As devastating as this is in marriage, it is many times worse in the relationship of an individual or a church with Christ.

The thrilling flush of new-found conversion and experience with Jesus Christ must be guarded by submission to the Holy Spirit all during one's Christian experience. Most Christians' lives consist of a "first love experience," which develops into a routine walk of having "forsaken your first love." During this latter period they take for granted "the marvelous grace of God" and the thrilling "new creation in Christ Jesus." Many later come to heed the words in this message and return to a day-by-day intimate fellowship with and love for the Lord Jesus Christ. This is essential in experiencing the abundant Christian life.

THE COUNSEL OF CHRIST

The Christ of the churches counsels the church of Ephesus to do three things:

- "Remember the height from which you have fallen." Christ sternly admonishes the believers at Ephesus to recall their faithfulness of earlier years and to take inventory of their spiritual life. This is also a need of the twentieth-century church.
- "Repent." They are to turn back from their coldness and indifference to a vital relationship with Christ.
- "Do the things you did at first." This completes Christ's counsel and stands as a test of their love. The Lord Jesus said, "By their fruit you will recognize them" (Matt. 7:16); so it is today that by a church's or an individual's "works" He will know them. Those that truly love Jesus Christ with all their heart obey Him. The Savior Himself said, "If you love me, you will obey what I command" (John 14:15). The children of God who excuse their indulgence and lack of consecration only prove by their conduct that they do not love the Lord Jesus Christ with all their heart, with all their soul, and with all their mind. Christians who are unwilling to yield all their talents and capabilities to Jesus Christ have a love problem; that is, they do not sufficiently love Christ. It is safe to conclude that if our love for Christ Jesus is what it should be, no task is too great, no sacrifice too much for Him.

THE CHALLENGE OF CHRIST

The challenge of Christ to the church of Ephesus falls into two main divisions: "Hear what the Spirit says" and "to him who conquers. ..."

Hear What the Spirit Says

"He who has an ear, let him hear what the Spirit says to the churches." This was an expression of the Lord Jesus Christ that appears in many of His parables (e.g., Matt. 13:9). The statement implies three kinds of individuals:

1. Those without ears. This, of course, could not refer to physical ears, for everyone is equipped with them. He is obviously referring to those who are not attuned to the Holy Spirit by the new birth—that is, those who have not been born again and thus are not anointed with the Holy Spirit. Consequently, they cannot hear the voice of God when He speaks.

2. Those who are dull of hearing. Not all born-again Christians are willing to hear the Spirit of God when He speaks. The Holy Spirit upbraided the Hebrew Christians for being "slow to learn" (Heb. 5:11). This is in reference to those Christians who are in rebellion against the Spirit of God and His mastery of their lives—a most dangerous condition in which to live.

3. Those spiritually minded Christians who are willing to hear what the Spirit says to the churches. The test of this hearer is seen in his conduct, for the Scripture teaches that we should be "doers of the word and not hearers only" (James 1:22, KJV).

Eternal Life for Overcomers

"To him who overcomes, I will give the right to eat from the tree of life, which is in the paradise of God." The Tree of Life, of which those who overcome are given the opportunity to eat, is unquestionably the tree from which Adam and Eve were forbidden to eat after their sin. A symbol of eternal life, it is pictured as having a prominent place in the paradise of God that awaits those who put their trust in Him (Rev. 22:2).

The tree of eternal life will be eaten only by "overcomers." Who is an overcomer? First John 5:4–5 gives us the answer. "For everyone born of God overcomes the world. This is the victory that has overcome the world, even our faith. Who is it that overcomes the world? Only he who believes that Jesus is the Son of God."

Overcoming the world is the experience that takes place in the life of the individual who puts his or her faith in Jesus Christ. There is no other way by which a man or woman can become an overcomer.

A PRACTICAL OBSERVATION

The people of the Ephesian age church can almost be excused for forsaking their first love, for they did not have a Bible to read everyday to keep their spiritual life alive. Bibles were scarce, having to be laboriously copied by hand. First-century churches were fortunate to have one copy that could be read each Lord's Day; only by memorizing the Word heard at church could most Christians feed their spiritual life on God's Word between Sundays. We modern Christians have no such excuse—the average Christian has access to three to ten Bibles at any one time. I have found the best way for believers to retain their first love is to "let the word of Christ dwell in you richly" (Col. 3:16), by reading, studying and memorizing it on a daily basis.

THREE

The Church of Smyrna

Revelation 2:8–11

The church in Smyrna was a much-persecuted church in a wealthy city that had little time for Christians. The city itself, founded about three centuries before Christ, was a well-planned accomplishment of Alexander the Great. The commercial center of Asia Minor, it was on the direct trade route from India and Persia to Rome. The large variety of coins found by archaeologists in the city clearly indicates that it was a wealthy city. The Jewish segment of the population seems to have been most irreligious and neglectful of spiritual things. Few specific details are known of the history of the Smyrna church other than what is given here in the book of Revelation. It can be safely deduced, however, that it was a most faithful church in the face of persecution. From this account, the known characteristics of the conditions in the church at Smyrna indicate that the judgment seat of Christ will reveal this church to be one of the most outstanding local bodies of believers in all of church history.

THE PERSECUTED CHURCH, A.D. 100-312

Commendation: "I know your afflictions and your poverty—yet you are rich!"

Condemnation: Not one word!

Counsel: "Do not be afraid of what you are about to suffer.... Be faithful, even to the point of death."

Challenge: "He who overcomes will not be hurt at all by the second death."

The Smyrna period of church history is probably the greatest time of persecution the Church of Christ has ever known. Satan unleashed a violent attack on the church in an effort to obliterate it, for it became evident to him that the apostolic church, because of its faithful preaching of the gospel, had become a serious threat to his worldwide godless empire. That he was unsuccessful in this attempt is easily seen in a study of church history, for God overruled and Satan learned a valuable lesson. The more he persecuted the church during this period, the more the church overcame the one condemning characteristic of the apostolic age, that of having left its first love. Not one word of condemnation was hurled by Christ at this church. From this Satan learned a great secret: Persecution will not stamp out the Church of Christ! Consequently, the age ended with the easing of persecution; then Satan used what turned out to be one of his most effective weapons to weaken the Church, that of indulgence or endorsement.

Some Persecutions of This Age

As predicted by the Lord Himself in verse 10, "You will suffer persecution for ten days." This church age saw eight of the ten periods of persecution under Roman emperors.

Nero	A.D. 54–68	Paul beheaded and Peter crucified
Domitian	A.D. 81–96	John exiled
Trajan	A.D. 98–117	Ignatius burned at the stake
Marcus Aurelius	A.D. 161–180	Justin Martyr killed
Severus	A.D. 193–211	
Maximinius	A.D. 235–238	
Decius	A.D. 249-251	
Valerian	A.D. 253–260	
Aurelian	A.D. 270–275	
Diocletian	A.D. 284-305[4]	

Diocletian is considered the worst emperor in Rome's history and the greatest antagonist of the Christian faith. He led a violent attempt to destroy the Bible from the face of the earth. Under his leadership many Roman cities had public burnings of the sacred Scriptures.

During the second and third centuries this persecution age saw hundreds of Christians brought into the amphitheater of Rome to be fed to hungry lions while thousands of spectators cheered. Many were crucified; others were covered with animal skins and tortured to death by wild dogs. They were covered with tar and set on fire to serve as torches. They were boiled in oil and burned at the stake, as was Polycarp in the city of Smyrna itself in A.D. 156. One church historian has estimated that during this period, five million Christians were martyred for the testimony of Jesus Christ.

A Thriving Church

Evidence of the supernatural nature of the Church can be seen in the fact that the Church reached its greatest numbers in proportion to world population during this period of persecution. In addition to the establishment of churches in many parts of the world, this church age distinguished itself by its production of many hand-copied manuscripts of the sacred Scriptures and the translation of Scripture into many languages.

Early in this period, the Bible was translated into Syriac, in what is known as the Peshito manuscripts, which became the official Scriptures of the Eastern churches and from which translations were made into Arabic, Persian, and Armenian. In the second century the Bible was translated into Latin in what is called the Old Latin Version. This became the Bible of the Western churches for more than a thousand years and has been translated into many different languages.

The more the Scriptures were disseminated and used by the people, even in the face of persecution, the more the Church advanced in numbers until it was such a dominant factor in the Roman Empire that Christianity was established as the state church by Emperor Constantine in A.D. 312. However, the cessation of persecution turned out to be a master stroke of Satan and a great tragedy to the Church. This will be borne out in Christ's next message to the church of Pergamum, which was assimilated by paganism, lost its fire, and received serious condemnation from our Lord.

THE MESSAGE OF CHRIST TO SMYRNA

"These are the words of him who is the First and the Last, who died and came to life again." It is interesting to note that Christ introduces each message to the churches by reaching back to the vision of Himself in chapter 1 and picking out one of the characteristics of His nature. To Ephesus He referred to Himself as the one who "holds the seven stars in his right hand and walks among the seven golden lampstands" (2:1), emphasizing that He faithfully provides for the churches. To Smyrna He emphasizes His eternal nature—"the First and the Last"; His death for their sins—"I was dead"; and His resurrection—"and behold I am alive for ever and ever" (1:18).

Again we see the unique characteristic of Christianity in that we do not worship a dead man, as do the Muslims, the Buddhists, or the Confucianists, but a Christ who is alive. Because of this, He is able to work on behalf of his children in any age.

THE COMMENDATION OF CHRIST

The message to the church of Smyrna is the shortest of all Christ's messages. However, one of the greatest commendations to this church is the fact that He does not condemn it. Christ's commendation highlights three characteristics of the church: tribulation, poverty, and affliction.

A Persecuted Church

"I know ... your afflictions." This was a severely persecuted church. Since the word "works" of verse 9 (cf. KJV) does not appear in the best manuscripts, the emphasis is placed here not on the faithful works of the church, which no doubt were many, but on the fact that they had undergone much persecution.

A Poor Church

"I know ... your poverty—yet you are rich!" The believers in Smyrna were poor and yet rich. In addition to the physical persecution, it would seem that the church there went through a severe period of financial persecution. Smyrna was not only a trade city but also a city of guilds that closely regulated the craftsmen of the day much as unions do today. Because of the intense hatred for Christians, when a man took a stand for Jesus Christ, his shop was boycotted or his employment was severed or some other means was used to limit his economic opportunity. Those Christians who were rich in this world's goods went bankrupt. Consequently, the church enjoyed few monetary assets. This was true not only of the church of Smyrna, but also of the second and third century churches.

Someone has said that the churches of the first three centuries were marked by material poverty and spiritual power, whereas the churches of our day are marked by material wealth and spiritual weakness. Sad to say, this seems to be true. Today Christians are cursed with material things that are not conducive to their spiritual development. Christians living under economic impoverishment should praise God that during such a time He will prove Himself faithful and, if they let Him, will bring them much spiritual blessing.

"... yet you are rich!" This highlights a divine principle that, regardless of one's economic state, knowing Jesus Christ brings wealth in this life and in the life to come! Many who are as poor as the proverbial "church mouse" are rich in this life in the things that money cannot buy: joy, peace, happiness, contentment, and eternal accomplishment.

This unseen wealth available to the child of God is seen in the statement of the Apostle Paul in 2 Corinthians 6:10, "... sorrowful, yet always rejoicing; poor, yet making many rich; having nothing, and yet possessing everything."

The Apostle Paul had not one thing in this world materially, but he was able to impart riches and said of himself, "yet possessing everything." Only the Christian is truly rich in those things that are important. Oh, that God's people in this twentieth and twenty-first centuries could realize the principle our Savior is here setting forth to the church of Smyrna. Riches can never be provided by this world! Our oneness with Jesus Christ determines the realization of our wealth in this world. The closer we are to Jesus Christ today, the richer we are. The further we are from Him, notwithstanding the balance of our bank account, the poorer we are. Christian, on this basis, how much are you worth?

An Afflicted Church

"I know the slander of those who say they are Jews and are not, but are a synagogue of Satan." The believers in Smyrna were an afflicted church, afflicted by false teachers who had claimed to be Jews but really were not. The New Testament definition of a Jew is one who is circumcised in "the heart, by the Spirit, not by the written code" (Rom. 2:29). It is never sufficient to obey the teachings of the Word legalistically. Submission of the heart to God, not adherence to a prescribed set of rules, is His desire for us.

The Synagogue of Satan

Satan has his own religious faith. He also has his churches, called "synagogues of Satan." Any church that preaches a gospel other than the gospel of Jesus Christ is a synagogue of Satan, regardless of what it is called. Many so-called "Christian" churches today are like the Jews at Smyrna—they are not Christians at all and are condemned by the Savior Himself because they preach a message other than the one laid down in the Word of God. In reality, they are the synagogue of Satan, not the Church of Jesus Christ.

Two Basic Heresies

The two basic heresies that emanate from the synagogue of Satan in the name of Christianity were apparent before the end of the second century. In fact, they existed at the time Christ gave His message to the churches of Ephesus and Smyrna. These heresies are a false doctrine of Christ and a mixing of law and grace. The latter was the work of the Judaizers, condemned by the Savior in verse 10.

Practically every false religious system and cult coming out of Christianity can be traced to one of these two heresies. Either people are confused about the personal deity of our blessed Lord, suggesting that though He was a good man, He was not the virgin-born Son of God who lived a sinless life, died a sacrificial death, rose bodily from the grave, ascended physically into heaven, and promised to return physically to this earth some day. Or they add to salvation "by grace through faith," saying that in addition to believing on Jesus, we should also keep the Sabbath, observe certain rites and ceremonies, eat or not eat certain kinds of food, etc. The church of the first three centuries in large measure successfully withstood these two insidious teachings that are deceiving many people today in one cult or another.

THE COUNSEL OF CHRIST

The Christ of the churches counsels the church of Smyrna and the Smyrna age of the Church to two things:—"Do not be afraid," and "Be faithful, even to the point of death."

"Do not be afraid of what you are about to suffer." The Lord Jesus predicted the suffering that would come to this church, telling them that "the devil will put some of you in prison to test you, and you will suffer persecution for ten days." These ten days are considered by many Bible teachers to be the ten periods of persecution referred to previously. Some Bible teachers suggest it refers to the last ten years of the age, A.D. 303–312, during which the Church suffered intense persecution under Diocletian.

The counsel of our Lord to this dear church was the same advice He gives the believers of every age when they fall into tribulation: "Fear not." Those who have Jesus Christ have enough, regardless of the intensity of the persecution! When grace is needed, grace is supplied; when courage is needed, courage is supplied; for we have the divine promise that our God is able to "meet all your needs according to his glorious riches in Christ Jesus" (Phil. 4:19).

"Be faithful, even to the point of death, and I will give you the crown of life." Further riches are involved in this promise of our Lord. We will "reign with Him for a thousand years" (Rev. 20:6) in direct proportion to our faithfulness in Christian service. The Lord Jesus said, "Store up for yourselves treasures in heaven" (Matt. 6:20). Only Christians are permitted to "store up" for eternity. A popular saying states, "You can't take it with you!" That is not entirely true for the Christian, because through the economy of God Christians can send their riches ahead of them by storing up "treasures in heaven." In this connection, it would be good to study the judgment of the believer's work as described in 1 Corinthians 3:9–20 and our Lord's parable of the ten minas in Luke 19:11–27.

THE CHALLENGE OF CHRIST

Again, the challenge of Christ comes to those who have spiritual ears to "hear what the Spirit says to the churches," and it is a challenge to overcome. As we have already seen, this is dependent on one's personal faith in Jesus Christ.

"He who overcomes will not be hurt at all by the second death." We have already seen in the vision of the Christ of the churches in Revelation 1:18 that Christ holds in His hand the keys of hell and death. God's children have Christ's personal promise that they will never be hurt by the second death, described in Revelation 20 as the time when Hades (the present abode of the unbelieving dead) and death are cast into the lake of fire. "The lake of fire is the second death" (20:14).

One must understand what the Bible means by death. It is the Bible's term for the complete ruin of a person's life so they can never fulfill God's plan for their life, which is eternal. Death occurs when a person is forever separated from God instead of united with Him, as was His intention. The second death is that state when people who have died in unbelief are resurrected and cast alive into an eternal state of separation from God in the place called "the lake of fire" (Rev. 20:15). This second death need never cause the child of God to fear, for it will have no power over them.

FOUR

The Church of Pergamum

Revelation 2:12–17

Pergamum was the capital city of Asia until the close of the first century. It was a city given over to the worship of many Greek idols. Local Roman rulership, unable to cope with the multitude of religious differences in the city, demanded the cooperation of all groups. Two of the most prominent religious systems of the city were the worship of Bacchus (the god of revelry) and the worship of Asclepius (the god of healing).

Verse 13 twice refers to the city as the place "where Satan has his throne" or "where Satan lives." A detailed commentary on this condition can scarcely be given with accuracy, for we do not have access to the historical details. However, we can say that the following conjecture to a large degree is representative of the truth. Satan has a kingdom; Babylon has from earliest times been considered the capital of this kingdom. Idolatry gained its start in Babylon through Nimrod and his mother, inspired by Satan. As long as Babylon was a dominant world power, it made an excellent headquarters for Satan's attack on the human race. However, when Babylon's glory began to decline and it was left desolate, Satan looked for another location. He selected Pergamum because of its strong idolatrous religions. Missionaries have been in areas so pagan in their religions that it seemed as though the very atmosphere was charged with the presence of Satan. No doubt these were the conditions under which the little church of Pergamum was faithfully preaching the gospel of Jesus Christ.

THE INDULGED CHURCH, A.D. 312–606

Commendation: "I know where you live—where Satan has his throne. Yet you remain true to my name. You did not renounce your faith in me, even in the days of Antipas, my faithful witness, who was put to death in your city—where Satan lives."

Condemnation: "Nevertheless, I have a few things against you: You have people there who hold to the teaching of Balaam, who taught Balak to entice the Israelites to sin by eating food sacrificed to idols and by committing sexual immorality.

Likewise you also have those who hold to the teaching of the Nicolaitans."

Counsel: "Repent therefore! Otherwise, I will soon come to you and will fight against them with the sword of my mouth."

Challenge: "To him who overcomes, I will give some of the hidden manna. I will also give him a white stone with a new name written on it, known only to him who receives it."

The Indulged Church Age

Satan learned from his attack on the church of Smyrna that persecution only causes the Church to flourish and continue in a perpetual state of revival. After Diocletian's unsuccessful attack on the Church, Constantine succeeded him as emperor of Rome. Constantine's ascendancy to the throne was not without controversy, and it had far-reaching effects on the Christian Church of the fourth, fifth, and sixth centuries.

Roman history tells us that Constantine contended for the throne with Maxentius after the death of Galerius. Both Roman history and church tradition indicate that Constantine, already attracted by Christianity, allegedly saw a vision of a fiery cross in the sky and heard a voice saying, "In this sign conquer."

Constantine believed this vision was a message from God that if he would embrace the Christian religion, he would be able to conquer his enemies. He accepted the Christian faith and declared himself to be its defender and protector. There are some who accept this as a bona fide conversion on the part of Constantine; however, a careful examination of his life indicates that either he had a poor concept of Christianity or he had never been truly born again by the Spirit of God. One commendable thing he did was to order Eusebius, bishop of Rome, to supervise the production of fifty copies of the Holy Scriptures to be used by the churches. Some of these manuscripts comprise our oldest existing copies of God's Word.

When Constantine became emperor of Rome, he became the virtual emperor of the Western world. As the self-styled "protector of the Christian faith," he issued an edict of toleration for Christianity and showered many favors on the Christian Church. The government provided money for the operation of the church, and many of the pagan temples were taken over by Christians. To please the emperor, these leaders adopted customs that were parallel to pagan practices. One compromise invariably leads to another, and what seemed at the start to be a great blessing ended up a great curse. During the succeeding three centuries of this period, many anti-Christian practices of pagan origin were adopted, which robbed the church of its fire and its evangelistic fervor.

Pagan Practices Introduced Into the Church

The influence of paganism on the Church increased over the years step by step. The Church began to shroud itself in "mystery" and ritualism that had a strong resemblance to Babylonian mysticism. The Chaldean tau, which was the elevation of a large "T" on the end of a pole, was changed to the sign of a cross. The rosary of pagan origin was introduced. Celibacy of priests and nuns, which has no scriptural verification but finds a counterpart in the vestal virgins of paganism, was conceived. The following is a partial list of unscriptural changes introduced during this age. Gradually these changes became more prominent than the original teachings of Christianity.

A.D. 300—Prayers for the dead
A.D. 300—Making sign of the cross
A.D. 375—Worship of saints and angels
A.D. 394—Mass first instituted
A.D. 431—Worship of Mary begun
A.D. 500—Priests began dressing differently than laypeople
A.D. 526—Extreme unction
A.D. 593—Doctrine of purgatory introduced
A.D. 600—Worship services conducted in Latin
A.D. 600—Prayers directed to Mary[5]

From A.D. 312 on, the Church became more Roman and less Christian in its practices. The Roman Catholic Church of today is hard put to trace its ancestry beyond A.D. 312. Until that time the Church was an independent collection of local churches, working together whenever possible but not dominated by central authority. The name Pergamum literally means "marriage" or "elevation." As the Church became married to governmental authority and elevated to a place of acceptance, it declined in spiritual blessing and power.

Postmillennialism Introduced

The blessed doctrine of the imminent return of Christ, espoused by the Church of the first three centuries, producing an evangelistic, consecrated, fervent Church, began to change when Christianity was made the state religion. As the Church became rich and powerful, it was suggested that the world was getting better and better, that Christ's kingdom was already ushered in, and that He would come at the *end* of the thousand-year reign. This demanded a reinterpretation of the status of Israel, which was accomplished by suggesting that Israel had been "cast off forever" and the promises of Israel now applied to the Church. Not until fourteen hundred years later was the coming of Jesus Christ reemphasized, and with it came a return to evangelistic fervor. Whenever a local church or denomination has maintained a strong emphasis on the second coming of our blessed Lord, it has been an evangelistic, missionary-sending station. Where this doctrine has been neglected, the church has become cold, indifferent, and worldly.

The Nature of Christ Revealed to Pergamum

"These are the words of him who has the sharp, double-edged sword." We have previously seen that Christ selected one of the aspects of His nature as revealed to John in his vision and presented it to each individual church. To Pergamum He revealed the "sharp, double-edged sword," which, without question, refers to the Word of God. The cure for the problems of the local church at Pergamum, of the Pergamum age of the Church, or of any church is the Word of God. Christ used that Word to sanctify His Church (John 17:17), to clean it (15:3), to bring it joy (15:11), and to bring it peace (16:33). Had the church of Pergamum and the Pergamum age heeded the Word of God, the evils of the Dark Ages could well have been avoided.

CHRIST'S COMMENDATION TO PERGAMUM

The commendation of our Lord to Pergamum, as recorded in verse 13, falls into three basic categories.

1. "I know where you live—where Satan has his throne." We have already seen the evil nature of this city where Satan made his headquarters, which later was moved to Rome. From there Satan directed the affairs of his worldwide kingdom, perverting the souls of human beings. Through the Roman emperors, as we have already seen, Satan had learned during the first three centuries that attacking Christians would never conquer them; thus, he changed his approach during the Pergamum period to one of indulgence and "elevation."

2. "Yet you remain true to my name." Criticism cannot be hurled against the doctrine of this church or Church age, for they were doctrinally pure. But they sinned by taking in the ceremonies of paganism, which later were supported by artificial doctrines of an unscriptural nature that went on to pollute the true doctrines of the Church. The truth of the matter is that many outstanding leaders were produced during this Pergamum age. It was during this time that the Arian controversy was fought at the Council of Nicea in A.D. 325. Arius and his followers denied the personal deity of our Savior.

Actually, their concept of Christ was much like that of modern-day Jehovah's Witnesses: Christ was the greatest of all created beings, but not one with the Father. At this council, presided over by Constantine himself, this question inspired heated debates. It must have seemed strange indeed for a governmental leader to preside over a Christian assembly while at the same time bearing the title of previous emperors, namely, high priest of the heathen religions. Dr. H. A. Ironside, in his book *Lectures on the Book of Revelation,* tells this story. During the council, feelings ran so high that Constantine had to intervene on several occasions. At one point, the brilliant Arius seemed almost to have stopped all opposition

> when a hermit from the deserts of Africa sprang to his feet, clad chiefly in tiger's skin. This latter he tore from his back, disclosing great scars (the result of having been thrown into the arena among the wild beasts). With his back dreadfully disfigured by animal claws exposed to their view, he dramatically cried, "These are the brand marks of the Lord Jesus Christ, and I cannot hear this blasphemy." Then he proceeded to give so stirring an address, setting forth clearly the truth as to Christ's eternal deity, that the majority of the council realized in a moment that it was indeed the voice of the Holy Spirit.

> Dr. Ironside continues,

> Whether this story be actually true or not, I cannot say; but it well sets forth the spirit pervading many who participated in the council, most of whom had passed through the terrible persecution of Diocletian. The final outcome of the Council of Nicea was that Jesus Christ was declared to be "very God of very God," "perfection of perfection," and "God and man in one person."[6]

Because this church held fast to Christ's name, the organized church did not teach anything but the personal deity of Jesus Christ for over a thousand years. Not until rationalism came in and produced nineteenth and twentieth century modernism could the Church be found guilty of a false doctrine regarding our Lord. The devil did succeed in subverting this teaching by making it merely a dogmatic doctrine rather than a vital relationship with a person. However, most so-called Christian churches today at least pay lip service to the deity of Christ.

3. "You did not renounce your faith in me." Much of this has already been covered, related to the doctrinal purity of this church and Church age. The Antipas referred to in verse 13 is unknown by Bible scholars. It is suggested that he was a local Christian in the city of Pergamum who had, like many during the first century, sealed the testimony of his faith with his own blood.

CONDEMNATION

The condemnation of Christ given to the church of Pergamum reveals that, although their theological doctrine was correct, their practical doctrines were radically evil. These false doctrines fell into two main categories.

> Nevertheless, I have a few things against you: You have people there who hold to the teaching of Balaam, who taught Balak to entice the Israelites to sin by eating food sacrificed to idols and by committing sexual immorality.
> (Rev. 2:14)

1. The Doctrine of Balaam

To properly evaluate this doctrine, one should be familiar with Numbers 22–31. In short, Balaam tried for filthy lucre's sake to prophesy a curse against Israel. Balak, the king of Moab, was afraid of the children of Israel as they were coming through his land. He hired Balaam to use his gift of prophecy against Israel, and Balaam sought every means at his disposal to do so. However, he encountered a major problem: God was with Israel! Every time Balaam opened his mouth to curse them, out came a blessing. Finally, in desperation, he gave Balak the suggestion of enticing the Israelites to making an unholy alliance with the Moabites through intermarriage with them; thus we find fulfilled what is referred to in Revelation 2:14: ". . . Balaam, who taught Balak to entice the Israelites to sin by eating food sacrificed to idols and by committing sexual immorality." At Balaam's suggestion, the Israelites intermarried with the Moabites, contrary to the will of God. Thus the people were polluted socially and spiritually. The only way to deal with paganism and false doctrines is to condemn them and root them out. Paul's advice to the Colossian church in Colossians 2:6–8 is most appropriate in such cases.

This was typical of the church of Pergamum in that, although the believers there were faithful to Christ's name and held the faith regarding theological doctrine, they did not remain separated from the world, but amalgamated with paganism. As we have already seen, paganism soon predominated, as it always does!

The only time Christians have the unlimited power of the Holy Spirit at their disposal is when they are obedient to the will of God. When they disobey God and make alliances with the world, they are entering into a powerless state that will enmesh and ruin them. An illustration of this homogenized state that crept into the Church, here called the doctrine of Balaam, is seen in a coin that today resides in the British Museum in London, stamped during the days of Constantine. On one side are Christian emblems, on the other side emblems of heathen gods. Some early tradition suggests that when large heathen basilicas were given to the Christian Church for meeting places to satisfy the emperor, the pagan names were chiseled off idols and the names of Christian saints were inscribed; they were then used as statues. Whether or not this is true, the church that traces its origin back to Rome today bears evidence that somewhere in its history the idolatry of paganism crept in.

2. The Doctrine of the Nicolaitans

"Likewise you also have those who hold to the teaching of the Nicolaitans." The doctrine of the Nicolaitans has already been examined under the church of Ephesus, though the Ephesian church and the Apostolic Age rejected this heresy. It was, however, accepted by the church of Pergamum and the indulged or Pergamum Age. Nicolaitanism is the doctrine of a strong ecclesiastical hierarchy ruling over the laity; this has never been conducive to a strong spiritual condition in the Church. Laypeople were given no voice in Church affairs, but were required to obey blindly the decrees of the clergy. The clergy then gradually seemed to gravitate to an impractical ivory-tower type of existence that separated them more and more from the people. Whenever clergy lose contact with people, they cease to be effective tools in the hand of God.

In this modern age, the work of Church administration and Christian promotion often demand so much of a pastor's time and effort that he does not devote the proper amount of time to meeting the unsaved face-to-face. Although a faithful minister should "search the Scriptures" so he can "preach the Word of God," his work must always be flavored by Paul's admonition to Timothy to "do the work of an evangelist" (2 Tim. 4:2, 5). This spirit of evangelism is most effective when the minister has been faithfully dealing personally with those who are unsaved. Some of the greatest Bible sermons ever preached have been occasioned by the inspiration of the Holy Spirit given to a man of God as he dealt with an unsaved soul.

The Lord Jesus gave His opinion about hierarchical systems of Church government when He referred to the doctrine of the Nicolaitans as that "which I also hate" (Rev. 2:6). This teaching has ruined more churches and denominations than any other.

COUNSEL

The counsel of Christ to the church of Pergamum is a simple statement of a basic principle of God that, reduced to the barest minimum, states: Repent or be judged by the Word of God. This principle, which has never been changed, applies to both individuals and churches. Unless we are willing to repent of our sins or our violations of the stated Word of God and return in obedience to the Word, we will be judged by the Word, "the double-edged sword." Be sure of this—if there is a principle in the Word of God to which you have refused to submit yourself in this life, you will face that principle when you stand before the Lord Jesus at His coming. It is better to heed the Word of God in 1 Corinthians 11:31,

"But if we judged ourselves, we would not come under judgment," thus guaranteeing that we will hear the Master's "well done, good and faithful servant!" (Matt. 25:21) instead of His condemnation.

CHRIST'S CHALLENGE TO THE CHURCH OF PERGAMUM

Our Lord's challenge to the church of Pergamum is directed to overcomers (1 John 5:4) and is divided into two beautiful symbols loaded with meaning—"hidden manna" and "a white stone."

The Hidden Manna

The hidden manna is a symbol that is readily understood by the Bible student. Manna was the heavenly food sent by God to the children of Israel in the desert. It typifies the spiritual food provided by God in His Word. It should be clearly understood that this is an individual feeding, not a Church function. Just as the Israelites had to go individually and gather the manna in the desert, so the child of God in the Pergamum Church Age or in any Church age is dependent on God for his or her individual spiritual supply. No matter what life's dilemma, if God's children will only look to Him, their needs will be supplied: "And my God will meet all your needs according to his glorious riches in Christ Jesus" (Phil. 4:19).

The White Stone

The symbolic meaning of the white stone is not as easy to determine as the hidden manna. Bible commentators are not agreed on this subject, though there is a basic tone of agreement—that of assurance. White in the Bible refers to the righteousness of God. In this connection I like to think of an ancient custom as being the key that unlocks the meaning of this stone. It seems that in ancient times a white stone meant acquittal. For example, if a man had been tried by a court, the jurors published their vote on his case by laying down a white stone, signifying that they were acquitting him of the crime. This would certainly be in accord with many other passages of Scripture that indicate that Christ has given an acquittal to the child of God who has called on Him for forgiveness and salvation. Such a one is, according to Romans 5:1, "justified through faith." The big difference, of course, is that we are guilty. Nevertheless, because Christ died guiltless, we receive the white stone of acquittal with a name for Christ on it that is yet unknown to us. The white stone, then, stands as a beautiful symbol of the eternal acquittal we gain through faith in the Lord Jesus Christ.

FIVE

The Church of Thyatira

Revelation 2:18–29

The city of Thyatira was probably founded by Alexander the Great some three hundred years before Christ. It was a wealthy city in Macedonia, noted in the ancient world for its outstanding color dyes. It has been suggested that the city was evangelized by the Ephesian church or perhaps by Paul's first convert in Philippi, Lydia (Acts 16:14). The main characteristic of this church seemed to be its "works" toward people rather than doctrinal belief. In fact, as we will see, it was indicted for permitting a false teacher to spread her soul-damning heresy.

THE PAGAN CHURCH, A.D. 606 to the Tribulation (The Dark Ages)

Commendation: "I know your deeds, your love and faith, your service and perseverance, and that you are now doing more than you did at first."

Condemnation: "You tolerate that woman Jezebel, who calls herself a prophetess. By her teaching she misleads my servants into sexual immorality and the eating of food sacrificed to idols."

Counsel: "Only hold on to what you have until I come."

Challenge: "To him who overcomes and does my will to the end, I will give authority over the nations—'He will rule them with an iron scepter; he will dash them to pieces like pottery'—just as I have received authority from my Father. I will also give him the morning star."

The Church of the Dark Ages

The Church Age of Thyatira produced what is known in history as the Dark Ages. "Dark" indicates that the program of merging paganism with Christianity, begun under the church of Pergamum, increasingly emphasized paganism, which is darkness. The light that Jesus Christ entrusted to His Church all but flickered out during the Dark Ages and was not rekindled until the days of the Reformation.

Continuing the history of the Church where we left off in the church of Pergamum, we note the following changes and doctrines that have their source in paganism added to the Church during this period.

A.D. 607—Boniface III made first Pope
A.D. 709—Kissing the Pope's foot
A.D. 786—Worshiping of images and relics
A.D. 850—Use of "holy water" begun
A.D. 995—Canonization of dead saints
A.D. 998—Fasting on Fridays and during Lent
A.D. 1079—Celibacy of the priesthood
A.D. 1090—Prayer beads
A.D. 1184—The Inquisition
A.D. 1190—Sale of indulgences
A.D. 1215—Transubstantiation
A.D. 1220—Adoration of the wafer (Host)
A.D. 1229—Bible forbidden to laypeople
A.D. 1414—Cup forbidden to people at Communion
A.D. 1439—Doctrine of purgatory decreed
A.D. 1439—Doctrine of seven sacraments affirmed
A.D. 1508—The *Ave Maria* approved
A.D. 1534—Jesuit order founded
A.D. 1545—Tradition granted equal authority with Bible
A.D. 1546—Apocryphal books put into Bible
A.D. 1854—Immaculate conception of Mary
A.D. 1864—*Syllabus of Errors* proclaimed
A.D. 1870—Infallibility of the Pope declared
A.D. 1930—Public schools condemned
A.D. 1950—Assumption of the Virgin Mary
A.D. 1965—Mary proclaimed Mother of the Church[7]

Since the above changes and additions have been made, as substantiated by history, it seems ironic that the Church of Rome today likes to boast that "Rome is always the same." The tragedy is that, in spite of the drastic changes cited above, many believe this assertion.

"Continual Sacrifice"—Rome's Greatest Heresy

"Thyatira" comes from two words meaning "sacrifice" and "continual"; this introduces the central heresy that has produced other false doctrines. That is, the Church of Rome denies the finished work of Christ but believes in a continuing sacrifice that produces such things as sacraments and praying for the dead, burning candles, and so forth. All of these were borrowed from mystery Babylon, the mother of all pagan customs and idolatry, none of which is taught in the New Testament. During this period, between A.D. 607 to today, the Universal (Catholic) Church headquartered in Rome gradually became more Babylonian than Christian.

Heresy falls into one of two basic categories: a false concept of the personal deity of Christ or mixing works with faith. The Church of Rome can scarcely be accused of teaching a false concept of the personal deity of Christ; however, their emphasis on the "continual sacrifice" and rejection of our Lord's finished work breeds a concept that causes people to try to earn their own salvation by works, penance, indulgences, and many other satanically conceived ideas labeled by our Lord in Revelation 2:24 as "Satan's so-called deep secrets."

One of the dangerous trends during the twentieth century in the Church of Rome is the elevation of Mary to a status just short of deity. News media reports indicate that millions have petitioned the Pope to declare her a member of the Trinity, though the official line is that it is not going to happen—yet. Already she is referred to as "the mother of God" or "the queen of Heaven" and in some instances appears to be the dispenser of salvation, which contradicts many Scriptures. Notice Jesus' own words in John 14:6, "I am the way and the truth and the life. No one comes to the Father except through me." To even suggest that anyone, even Mary the human mother of Jesus, participates in dispensing the gift of eternal life is not only heresy, it is blasphemous. As the Apostle Peter, when speaking exclusively of Jesus as the official dispenser of salvation said, "there is no other name under heaven given to men by which we must be saved" (Acts 4:12). Scripturally speaking, there is only one person under Heaven who dispenses salvation to humankind and it isn't Mary.

Rome's Similarity to Paganism

A few years ago my wife and I had the privilege of flying to Mexico City where, together with another family in our church, we toured the largest Roman cathedral on the North American continent, the Shrine of Guadeloupe. I was deeply impressed with the unscriptural conduct of the service and how similar their service was to pagan rituals I had seen previously. For example:

Penance. Many were crawling on their hands and knees over hundreds of yards of concrete (in many instances causing gashes and blood on their knees and legs) in an effort to punish themselves, whereas the Scripture teaches, "For it is by grace you have been saved, through faith—and this not from yourselves, it is the gift of God—not by works, so that no one can boast" (Eph. 2:8–9).

Darkness. The room was so dark that photographs could not be taken and everything was kept in a gloomy state; the Scriptures teach, "But whoever lives by the truth comes into the light" (John 3:21).

Mystery. The mysterious nature of the service could be seen in the fact that individuals could not understand the Latin being spoken during the mass, and no message was given in a language they recognized. Parents came to the glass-encased form representing a dead saint, thinking that by rubbing the casket and placing an offering in the slot provided they could then rub blessing on the forehead of their infant children or other loved ones. In contrast, the Lord Jesus talked about those who hear the Word and *understand it* (Matt. 13:23).

Idolatry. Prominently located on every wall were idols representative of Christ, the apostles, or other saints. I counted seventeen such idols. Though idolatry is typical of pagan worship, it is forbidden in the Bible. "You shall not make for yourself an idol in the form of anything in heaven above or on the earth beneath or in the waters below" (Ex. 20:4).

Chanting. During the service much chanting was performed by the priests. Individuals who had come to worship prayed by saying the same word repetitiously, whether they knew its meaning or not. By contrast our Lord has warned: "When you pray, do not keep on babbling like pagans, for they think they will be heard because of their many words" (Matt. 6:7).

Mary the Central Figure. A large picture of Mary framed in gold occupies the most prominent place in the cathedral, while the idol representing Christ is off to the left and not nearly so prominent. To the contrary, the Bible teaches "that in everything he [Christ] might have the supremacy" (Col. 1:18).

Crucifix. A crucifix, well known in Roman forms of worship, was all that could be seen of our blessed Lord, whereas the Scriptures speak not of "continual sacrifice" but, in the words of Christ Himself speaking of the sacrifice, "It is finished"; the angel on the day of resurrection said, "He is not here; he has risen, just as he said" (Matt. 28:6). Oh, that these people might recognize the principle conveyed in the words of our Lord: "I am the Living One; I was dead, and behold I am alive for ever and ever! And I hold the keys of death and Hades" (Rev. 1:18).

One of the obvious differences between Catholics and Protestants is the cross they use to symbolize their faith. The Catholic cross usually depicts Christ on the cross, commemorating his continual sacrifice for our sins. The Protestant cross is empty, depicting that Christ died for our sins, was buried, and rose again the third day (cf. 1 Cor. 15:3–4).

Christ's Character Revealed

"These are the words of the Son of God, whose eyes are like blazing fire and whose feet are like burnished bronze." Our Lord's selection of the title "Son of God" for Himself is most instructive when compared to 1:13, where He selects the title "like a son of man." These titles are synonymous or interchangeable. This should be borne in mind in this day when false teachers are prone to advocate the human nature of Christ at the exclusion of His divine nature. Also, it is instructive to those in the Church of Rome who are prone to think of Him as the "Son of Mary."

"Eyes . . . like blazing fire" and "feet . . . like burnished bronze" denote that Christ is looking with piercing judgment on the Church because she has permitted false teaching to creep into her midst and "mislead my servants."

CHRIST'S COMMENDATION

Our Lord's commendation to the church of Thyatira comes in the form of six words (Rev. 2:19). He commends them for their (1) "deeds"—indicating that many through Rome's long history have been faithfully serving Jesus Christ as a result of receiving Him; (2) "love"—a love for humankind characterized this church, for in ancient times hospitals and sanitariums were almost exclusively the work of the church through its nuns and priests; (3) "faith"—although it is not given the prominence of works and love, it nevertheless is a characteristic of that age and church, with the main exception noted in the paragraph above; (4) "service" means ministry; (5) "perseverance" means endurance and speaks of the long time period of this church; (6) "now doing more than you did at first"—the good works of the Church of Rome (except for such periods as the Inquisition, when many were wantonly murdered) are commendable.

It should also be borne in mind that, although the vast majority of members have been held in ignorance and darkness, many have been faithful to the Lord Jesus Christ. Some outstanding products of that period are John Wycliffe, John Hus, Savonarola, and many others who earned the martyr's crown because they refused to give up their adherence to the Word of God and Christ Jesus the Lord. In fact, one of the bleakest marks on the history of the Church of Rome is that it burned at the stake men like Wycliffe and Hus, whose only sin was trying to translate the Bible into the mother tongue of the common people. Historically no jailer has ever kept a prisoner in total confinement the way the Church of Rome kept the Bible from God's people for over a millennium! No wonder this age as been referred to as "The Dark Ages." The Bible is the "light of the world"—it is the church's commission to let that light shine.

CHRIST'S CONDEMNATION

"Nevertheless, I have this against you: You tolerate that woman Jezebel, who calls herself a prophetess. By her teaching she misleads my servants into sexual immorality and the eating of food sacrificed to idols." Our Lord's condemnation on the church of Thyatira took two forms: (1) He condemned her for permitting a false teacher to enslave or to lead astray His servants, and (2) He condemned her for not repenting when she had opportunity.

Jezebel, the False Prophetess

The Lord Jesus reaches back into the Old Testament for the name of a woman who brought Baalism into Israel and perverted the nation, using her as a point of comparison for those who brought paganism and its devilish teachings into the church. (Whenever a woman is used symbolically to convey a religious teaching, she always represents a false religion.) Our Lord's parable in Matthew 13:33–35 concerning the woman who took leaven (a symbol of evil) and hid it in three measures of meal "until it worked all through the dough" is a prophetic glimpse of what took place during the false teaching of this period.

The teaching of the false prophetess, Jezebel, took two forms: (1) "By her teaching she misleads my servants into sexual immorality," which is a symbol of the idolatry brought in during this period, and (2) "and the eating of food sacrificed to idols," a symbol of the union of the church with the world. During this time Rome sought to bring the kingdom of the world under the domination of the Pope in Rome. Though contrary to the teachings of our Lord, who said, "My kingdom is not of this world" (John 18:36), Church leaders seriously attempted to make their kingdom of this world.

Opportunity to Repent

"I have given her time to repent of her immorality, but she is unwilling." Plenty of opportunity was given to this church to repent; almost a thousand years was granted, yet "she is unwilling."

Christ's Future Judgment of This Church

"So I will cast her on a bed of suffering, and I will make those who commit adultery with her suffer intensely, unless they repent of her ways." Our Lord here predicts that this church and those that are persuaded to follow her false teachings will go into the Great Tribulation, when she will, according to Revelation 17, be the Church of the Tribulation. This warning should speak to every Bible-believing Christian in the world about having any entangling affiliation with the ecumenical movement. Pope John XXIII popularized through his ecumenical Council the concept that "all of them will be one." Protestant unbelievers and heretics are advancing this program on every hand. God's faithful followers should be careful to measure everything according to the stated Word of God and, if need be, to stand alone.

One other thing Pope John XXIII did was issue an encyclical that encouraged Catholic followers to read the Confraternity Edition of the Scriptures. In so doing he opened the door to millions of Catholics to read God's Word for the first time, many of whom have received Christ personally. According to a Gallup Poll as many as thirteen million Catholics in this country claim to be born again. Only God knows how many are truly born again worldwide. We can hope there are multiplied millions.

"I will strike her children dead. Then all the churches will know that I am he who searches hearts and minds, and I will repay each of you according to your deeds." "Death," according to Greek scholar Vincent, is literally a reference to the "second death," when all unbelievers regardless of religious affiliation will be cast into the lake of fire (Rev. 20:15).

"I will repay each of you according to your deeds" is an obvious reference to the equitable judgment of the Great White Throne, when all will stand before Christ (see Rev. 20:11–15). Unfortunately, as we will see when we examine that text, all who appear at that judgment are lost because they did not personally receive Jesus.

CHRIST'S COUNSEL

Our Lord's counsel to the church at Thyatira was apparently directed to the faithful individuals within that church who rejected the false doctrines. "Only hold on to what you have until I come" refers to the fact that many during the Tribulation will refuse to knuckle under to the false religious system, called "the prostitute" in Revelation 17.

CHRIST'S CHALLENGE

"To him who overcomes and does my will to the end, I will give authority over the nations." There are two aspects of the challenge of our Lord to the individual overcomer of this period: (1) He will give such a one a position of leadership and authority during the millennial age if he or she is faithful in this age; (2) "I will also give him the morning star." This beautiful title is clearly understood in the light of our Lord's word in Revelation 22:16, where He explains that He is the "the bright Morning Star." This promise is clearly the promise of Christ to come and "abide" if you "overcome." Who is an overcomer? First John 5:1–4 clarifies that it is "everyone who believes that Jesus is the Christ!"

SIX

The Church of Sardis

Revelation 3:1–6

There is nothing worse than a dead church! It is like a man dying of thirst on the desert who sees a well off in the distance, only to find upon arrival that it is dry. Many thirsty souls stumble through the desert of this world and then finally see what they think is hope in the form of a church, only to find upon entering that it is completely dead. Such is the picture this text gives us of the church of Sardis and the age she represents—the Reformation.

Sardis, the capital city of Lydia, was prominent in Asia Minor. Noted for its carpet industry, it was a wealthy city that was finally destroyed by an earthquake. The local church there seems to have had an acceptable name in certain areas but was really dead. This is tragic in view of the fact that life is a characteristic of the born-again Christian. Jesus said, "I have come that they may have life, and have it to the full" (John 10:10).

There were, however, a few faithful believers "in Sardis who have not soiled their clothes."

THE DEAD CHURCH, A.D. 1520 to the Tribulation

Commendation: "I know your deeds; you have a reputation of being alive . . ."

Condemnation: ". . . but you are dead. . . . I have not found your deeds complete in the sight of my God."

Counsel: "Wake up! Strengthen what remains and is about to die. . . . Remember, therefore, what you have received and heard; obey it, and repent. But if you do not wake up, I will come like a thief, and you will not know at what time I will come to you."

Challenge: "He who overcomes will, like them, be dressed in white. I will never blot out his name from the book of life, but will acknowledge his name before my Father and his angels."

The Dead Church Age

Sardis means "escaping ones" or those who "come out." This name, together with our Lord's condemnation of this church, provides a perfect description of the Reformation churches. The Protestant Reformation developed as the result of the continued emphasis by the Church of Rome on pagan doctrines (see chapter 5) rather than adherence to scriptural principles. The basic emphasis of the Reformation churches originally was Martin Luther's watchword, taken from Scripture, "But the righteous will live by faith" (Rom. 1:17). They had recoiled from trying to make salvation the result of works and sparked a resurgence of interest in studying the Scriptures.

The tragedy of the Reformation churches that earned for them the condemnation by the Lord of being "dead" was twofold.

1. They became state churches. Luther, for example, sought the approval of the political leaders, and eventually the Lutheran Church became the state church of Germany, as did others throughout Europe. The danger of this is that the church then includes the entire population, thus eliminating the need for personal acceptance of Jesus Christ and an emphasis on the individual's relationship to God. Another danger is the tendency to please the government rather than God.

2. The Reformation churches did not sufficiently change many customs and teachings of the Church of Rome. Infant baptism was continued, in spite of the fact that there is no scriptural verification for it. Sprinkling was also continued, and ritualism, including some elements of the sacraments, was perpetuated. Ritual and formality, characteristic of pagan forms of worship, are not conducive to genuine worship, for they appeal to the sensuous human nature. The Bible teaches that God must be worshiped in *spirit* and in *truth*. Ritual that comes from paganism cannot be of the Holy Spirit and does not convey truth. The main purpose of a church is the propagation of the gospel of Jesus Christ. This should be done in song and word. If people leave a church with the mysterious feeling of "worship" but have not been brought face-to-face with Jesus Christ in a personal way, they have been worshiping in a dead church.

Christ's Nature Revealed to Sardis

The aspect of Christ's nature revealed to Sardis is most instructive. Reaching back into the complete vision of His nature imparted to John in Revelation 1, He selected two characteristics of Himself: "seven spirits" and "seven stars."

"These are the words of him who holds the seven spirits of God and the seven stars." The seven spirits refer to the Holy Spirit, who Jesus said is truth. The stars are the angels of the churches. This church had more than adequate opportunity to know the truth and to obey the Lord *if* they had heeded His warning. The natural explanation of their deficiency appears to be that they preferred to trust the State in a time of economic need instead of God. Had Luther and other Reformers depended solely on the Holy Spirit instead of governmental authorities and leaders, who can say but that the Reformation would not have been a far greater spiritual experience for millions more?

CHRIST'S COMMENDATION

The church of Sardis receives the shortest commendation from our Lord of any of the churches. In fact, some Bible scholars do not include any commendation for this church, but list the commendation as a condemnation because of the way it ends.

"I know your deeds." This may well refers to the early stages of the Reformation when Martin Luther and others chose to defy Roman authority, even at the risk of their own lives, to obey the Bible's teaching on salvation by faith.

"You have a reputation" probably refers to the fact that the Reformation church had a reputation as a church faithful to Christ, particularly in the earlier days of the movement.

"Of being alive" indicates that there was some life in the church. Certainly those who placed their faith in Jesus Christ "lived." It should be noted, however, that the act of placing one's trust in Jesus Christ and receiving His salvation does not guarantee consistent obedience to the Holy Spirit. Steadfast obedience is a result of a day-by-day submission to the will of God.

CHRIST'S CONDEMNATION

"But you are dead." This has already been covered in the introduction to this chapter, indicating that the ritual and ceremony of the Reformation Church often crowded out the true life underneath so that it was impotent and ineffective in the hand of God. This is defined in verse 2 by our Lord's statement, "for I have not found your deeds complete in the sight of my God." Although the Reformation leaders began well, they did not proceed to complete the works of reforming the church, but stopped far short of scriptural standards.

CHRIST'S COUNSEL

Our Lord counsels the church of Sardis to do five things that, if they obey, will make them acceptable to Him.

1. "Wake up!" is an expression that points up a serious deficiency in the teaching of the Reformation leaders. The word our Lord uses here is used in other passages of Scripture to indicate the attitude of life that should characterize His children in view of His promised return. The most serious deficiency in the Reformation teachings was that they lacked instruction in Bible prophecy and separation. Prophetically instructed

Christians are more apt to be separated, consecrated Christians than those unaware of the promises of our Lord's second coming.

2. "Strengthen what remains." This evidently refers to the need for strengthening the good doctrinal teachings of the early days of the Reformation, which were limited to salvation by faith, the total depravity of the human race, and the authority of the Word of God.

3. "Remember, therefore, what you have received and heard" indicates the need to return to the days of blessing as a result of searching the Scriptures and to depend on God rather than on the state church and ritual.

4. "Obey it" communicates a warning to adhere tenaciously to the doctrines clearly taught in the Scriptures they presently had. It was bad enough that they did not press far enough in the development of scriptural truth then, but it is even worse that the church of Sardis represents some of the denominations swept along in the advancing tide of neo-orthodoxy today, giving up or compromising the orthodox position that characterized the Reformers.

5. "... and repent." Repentance involves not only an act of turning to God, but a submissive heart. The Reformation churches needed to turn back to Christ, seeking His will and His Spirit's teaching, rather than to accept their own preconceived ideas about the interpretation of truth. Had they been willing to repent, doubtless the Holy Spirit would have guided them "into all truth."

Christ's Warning to Sardis

"But if you do not wake up, I will come like a thief, and you will not know at what time I will come to you." Because the Reformation churches have not heeded our Lord's warning, it is obvious that they are going to be taken unawares when our Lord comes. One of the many evidences of this prophetic ignorance on the part of Reformation churches is that they are leaders in the World Council of Churches' ecumenical program, which purposes to unite all Protestants, all Catholics, and eventually all religions. For shortly after the true Church has been raptured to be with Christ, the global church will unite all religious groups as one large religious organization. If they just understand the prophetic Word of God, they will realize that they are aiding and abetting the Antichrist's program, for that combined church will be his church during the first three-and-a-half years of the Tribulation.

Some Faithful Saints in Sardis

"Yet you have a few people in Sardis who have not soiled their clothes. They will walk with me, dressed in white, for they are worthy." As in all church ages, the Reformation had individuals who were faithful to their

Lord. They saw through the pageantry of ornate religious sacraments and ritual and came to the personal acceptance of Christ as Savior and Lord. Because of this faith in Him and obedience to His Word, they "have not soiled their clothes," that is, have not compromised with the attitude and conduct of the world, and rather chose to live a separated and godly life.

The Lord has promised that all who are faithful to Him during persecution will "walk with me, dressed in white, for they are worthy." The story is told that years ago, when our country established relief camps to help Armenian refugees, one young girl came and waited outside the tent for medical assistance. Her dark eyes betrayed a tremendous pain that racked her body. Someone asked her, "Have you been hurt?" To which she answered, "I am bearing the cross. I bear in my body the cross of Jesus Christ. Now I know how He suffered." The relief workers did not understand, but the nurse who assisted her in the medical tent, when she slipped off her dress, saw a cross branded on her shoulder with hot irons. The wound was swollen and burning with infection. The girl explained, "Every day they would say to me, 'Mohammed or Christ?' When I said 'Christ' on the last day, they branded my shoulder with this cross. Now as long as I live I will bear this cross, and someday when I see Jesus I will be glad."

Many of us who have never tasted the sting of persecution for the cause of Jesus Christ will stand aside and be thrilled at the Judgment Seat of Christ when those who have endured are rewarded.

Christ's Challenge to Sardis

Our Lord's challenge to this church, as to all the others, is directed to the individual. "He who overcomes," as we have already seen, is a direct reference to those who have been born again by faith in Christ (1 John 5:1–4). "He who overcomes will, like them, be dressed in white" refers to the righteousness of Christ with which we are clothed when we are born again (2 Cor. 5:21).

"I will never blot out his name from the book of life, but will acknowledge his name before my Father and his angels." This indicates the security with which a believer is held against the day of judgment described in Revelation 20:11–15. The Book of Life is the book that contains the names of all living individuals. It is possible to have one's name blotted out of that book for three reasons: (1) for sinning against God (Ex. 32:33); (2) for not being an overcomer, which is synonymous with being born again or putting one's trust in Christ Jesus (1 John 5:1–4); and (3) for taking away from the words of the prophecy of Revelation 22:19. In short, then, anyone who has sinned against God has his or her name blotted out of the Book of Life upon death.

Our Lord concludes, "He who has an ear, let him hear what the Spirit says to the churches." Whether or not you have heard is determined by whether you have heeded His warning to be born again. The way to guarantee that your name will never be blotted out of the Book of Life is to get on your knees and ask God right now to cleanse your sin and save you.

SEVEN

The Church of Philadelphia

Revelation 3:7–13

Having found the study of the three preceding somewhat depressing, we find it refreshing to consider the church of Philadelphia. This sixth church is a throwback to the first and second churches, Ephesus and Smyrna, of the first three centuries. Your heart will be stirred as you study this passage, and you will find yourself desiring to be identified with this kind of church.

The church of Philadelphia was located in a center of Greek civilization. Founded only 189 years before Christ, the city had a surprising influence on that area of the ancient world. This church must have been vital, for Philadelphia remained an independent Christian city until the close of the fourteenth century, when it was conquered by the Turks.

THE CHURCH CHRIST LOVED, A.D. 1750 to the Rapture

Commendation: "I know your deeds. See, I have placed before you an open door that no one can shut. I know that you have little strength, yet you have kept my word and have not denied my name."

Condemnation: Not one word!

Counsel: "I am coming soon. Hold on to what you have, so that no one will take your crown."

Challenge: "Him who overcomes I will make a pillar in the temple of my God. Never again will he leave it. I will write on him the name of my God and the name of the city of my God, the new Jerusalem, which is coming down out of heaven from my God; and I will also write on him my new name. He who has an ear, let him hear what the Spirit says to the churches."

The Philadelphia Age of Church History

The name Philadelphia literally means "brotherly love." Our Lord selected that church to describe the kind of church age that was initiated around the year 1750 and will continue to the Tribulation. Just as Sardis came out of Thyatira, so the Philadelphia age came out of Sardis. The

Reformation church, as we saw in the preceding chapter, became dead and cold as a state church. Philadelphia, however, was marked by vitality of life. In this church age, God worked in a thrilling manner that produced revivals in Europe and the British Isles, spreading even to America. These revivals in turn produced what is known today as the modern missionary movement.

It was this moving of the Spirit of God on the part of His people that caused an English shoe cobbler to become so burdened for the lost of India that in 1793 he became the first foreign missionary. William Carey was followed by other young people whom the Spirit of God touched, and thus the present-day "Faith Missionary Movement" was begun. As our Lord said, "I have placed before you an open door." This open door found such men as Adoniram Judson, David Livingstone, Jonathan Goforth, and literally thousands of other people, going out to Africa, China, Japan, Korea, India, South America, and the islands of the sea.

The Two Reasons for the Missionary Movement

One factor that led to the great missionary movement was the printing of the Bible in the language of the people and the natural tendency of the ordinary individual to take the Bible literally. Thus, when a young man like William Carey read our Lord's command, "Go into all the world and preach the good news to all creation," he was inclined to obey it.

The second factor that contributed to this missionary movement was the increased interest in the study of the doctrine of the second coming of our Lord. Around 1800 the doctrine of the premillennial return of Christ, which had been all but dead since the end of the third century, was revived. This teaching, as was pointed out in the previous chapter, contributed to a consecrated and separated church and increased her zeal for evangelism and missionary sacrifice to fulfill the Great Commission. In preparation for her Lord's return, she was willing to do whatever He commanded.

Christ's Nature Revealed

Four aspects of Christ's character are revealed to Philadelphia in verse 7, two of which are not found in His vision to John in chapter 1.

1. "Holy." Our Lord reminds this church of His holiness. It is good to be reminded at this point that He also said, "Be holy, because I am holy" (1 Pet. 1:16). This aspect of His nature may have been singled out to signify the practice of the church of Philadelphia in being separated from the world unto holiness.

2. "True." In several passages our Lord is referred to as Truth (John 14:6). Dr. J. Vernon McGee offers this interesting suggestion: "True means genuine with an added note of perfection and completeness.

Moses did not give the 'true bread.' Christ is the 'true bread'" (John 6:32–35). From this we see that Christ is not only truth, but the ultimate truth. No truth will be given to this world other than the truth revealed in Jesus Christ. This aspect of His nature may well have alluded to the movement toward doctrinal separation that characterized the age of Philadelphia.

3. "... who holds the key of David" is an obvious reference to the authority of Christ. It forecasts His eventual rulership of the world but still relates to Revelation 1:5: Although He gives latitude to the kings of the world, He nevertheless controls the extent to which they can govern.

4. "What he opens no one can shut, and what he shuts no one can open." The Lord Jesus gave His disciples the commission to "go into all the world and preach the good news," on the basis of what He had already said in Matthew 28:18, "All authority in heaven and on earth has been given to me." The doors of opportunity for preaching the gospel are controlled by the Lord Jesus Christ. Neither Moammer Gadhafi nor Saddam Hussein nor any world dictator can close the door to the preaching of the Gospel unless Christ so wills it. This is not only true of the missionary movement of the Philadelphia church age, but also of the individual.

The late Dr. Henrietta C. Mears was a great leader of young people. She often used Revelation 3:7 in challenging young people called of God to obey His word without fear or reservation. God is not limited in His ability to open doors. This is a message much needed by the Lord's servants today. There is a tendency to compromise in order to gain opportunities, whereas in truth it is our responsibility to do right and God's responsibility to open the doors of opportunity.

CHRIST'S COMMENDATION

Our Lord commended the church of Philadelphia for four things, which in turn invoked a promise from Him.

1. "I know your deeds. See, I have placed before you an open door that no one can shut." This evidently refers to the doors of opportunity open to them for the proclamation of the gospel, one of the chief characteristics of faithful service throughout this Church age. First Corinthians 16:9 indicates that the Apostle Paul considered an open door an opportunity for Christian service.

2. "You have little strength." This refers to the minority status of the believers in Philadelphia. Except for some churches in America, the Philadelphia Church Age is characterized by small congregations, which, according to human standards, are weak. This, of course, is real strength; for as the Holy Spirit tells us through Paul, "When I am weak, then am I strong."

3. "Yet you have kept my word." This church not only believed the Word of God, but obeyed it. The Reformation churches, past and present, believe the Word of God but are not characterized by obedience to it. The church of Philadelphia, a fitting contrast to this pattern, is characterized by obedience to His Word.

4. ". . . and have not denied my name." Satan always tries to counter an effective work of God. It is interesting to notice that the greatest increase in false Christs and false religions in the world's history began during this same period of time. One characteristic of this Church age is that it refuses to deny the name of the Lord, thereby offering a challenge that needs to be presented to every faithful Christian as he or she approaches the end of the age.

CHRIST'S PROMISE TO A COMMENDABLE CHURCH

This rather unique promise of Christ, resulting from the commendable attitude of this church, falls into two basic divisions: vindication and preservation.

1. Vindication: "I will make those who are of the synagogue of Satan, who claim to be Jews though they are not, but are liars—I will make them come and fall down at your feet and acknowledge that I have loved you." Christ promised that all the false religionists (religious impostors and false teachers) who claimed to be Jews, but were not, would some-day be subdued before them. These heretics will realize that, in perse-cuting the faithful Church of Christ, they have turned their backs on Him.

2. Preservation: "Since you have kept my command to endure patiently, I will also keep you from the hour of trial that is going to come upon the whole world to test those who live on the earth." The world has never known a universal period of tribulation. This passage is an obvi-ous reference to the Tribulation Period of seven years that will be cov-ered extensively in our study of Revelation 6 through 18. This promise, however, is to the church of Philadelphia: She will be raptured before that Tribulation begins.

It seems difficult to understand why some false teachers suggest that the Church must go through the Tribulation in view of this clear-cut statement of our Lord to "keep you" (in this case us) out of "the hour of trial"—which must be understood in the light of Jesus' description of that period in Matthew 24:21 as the time when "there will be great dis-tress, unequaled from the beginning of the world until now—and never to be equaled again." Obviously that period has never historically hap-pened—yet. Many believe, as we will see, that such a time of tribulation will not commence until the Antichrist signs a covenant with Israel for seven years. The Rapture of the Church, which will be covered when we get to Revelation 4, will precede that covenant signing. This explains why many think the next thing on the prophetic agenda is the Rapture of the Church.

CHRIST'S COUNSEL

"I am coming soon. Hold on to what you have, so that no one will take your crown." Our Lord's counsel to the church of Philadelphia is based on the promise of His second coming. It is interesting to note that the challenge is made on the basis that the church of Philadelphia will be in existence at His coming. It is clear from history that this church age, now almost three hundred years old, is one of the shorter periods of church history. Christ's counsel to them is to hold fast to what they have already been doing and to continue faithfully until the end. The church of Philadelphia is characterized by a spirit of revival that promotes evangelism and a missionary-minded church.

Dr. Adrian Rogers has suggested three basic essentials for building a spiritual church: evangelism, missions, and Bible teaching. His great ministry is as pastor of the 25,000-member Bellevue Baptist Church in Memphis, Tennessee, where he preaches to over seven thousand people twice each Sunday morning. When I visited that church a few months ago, I was impressed how it must have been like the church of the open-door of Philadelphia, open to the lost in their generation. Every week many receive Christ through the total ministry of that church.

One thing that makes Bellevue stand apart is that, like its Philadelphia counterpart, it shares their great emphasis on the second coming of Christ. At a time when many pastors were muted in seminary to the effective teaching on Christ's return, Dr. Rogers provides a refreshingly prophetic pulpit voice often heralding the Second Coming, not only in his church but also in his national TV ministry. Nothing ignites the fire of evangelism in the heart of a congregation like dynamic preaching on the promised return of Jesus.

The churches that are following this formula today are enjoying unprecedented growth. In fact, we are currently witnessing the development of large Philadelphia-type churches in almost every major American city. These churches have life and vitality, mute evidence of the power of the Spirit upon them.

This is in sharp contrast to the Sardis or Laodicean churches, which are having a hard time maintaining the status quo—and many are losing more members than they take in. Their problem is that they have not "kept his word" and they have "denied his name."

The emptiness of our Western civilization because of its atheistic humanistic philosophy has given the Philadelphia churches their greatest opportunity in their almost three-hundred-year history to harvest human souls. For the first time in centuries the human race is not only philosophically empty but also aware of that emptiness. Faithful churches with a Bible-teaching, evangelistic, missionary-minded ministry are leading many out of their philosophical desert into the abundant life Christ came to offer all humankind. If we would but seize the opportunity to trumpet the soon coming of Christ from our pulpits and in personal witnessing, we can capitalize on the twenty-first-century emptiness of heart.

That people are interested in future events and the return of Christ is demonstrated by the continuing popularity of our *Left Behind* series of prophetic novels. The incredible thing is the number of unsaved people who are reading them, many of whom are receiving Christ by faith. Now that these books have moved into secular bookstores everywhere, there is no telling how many will come to Christ in what may be as one of the last, if not the final great harvest of souls before the Rapture.

CHRIST'S CHALLENGE

The challenge of our Lord to overcomers (those that are born again) is threefold:

1. "Him who overcomes I will make a pillar in the temple of my God. Never again will he leave it." A pillar speaks of stability. Christians have stability in this life only in Christ. They are often buffeted and rejected for their faith; however, in the life to come they will not be outsiders, but will be on the "in" with relation to Christ.

2. "I will write on him the name of my God and the name of the city of my God, the new Jerusalem, which is coming down out of heaven from my God." The writing of the name of God is indicative of the fact that true believers are identified with Christ by the seal of the name of God, which entitles them to have entrance into the city of God. Christ promises to prepare a new Jerusalem that will come down to the new earth, as described in Revelation 21:9–22:6.

3. "... and I will also write on him my new name." Believers of the church of Philadelphia will have not only the name of God, which entitles them to entrance into the city of God, but also the name of Christ, which according to Revelation 22:3–4 entitles them to be "his servants. . . . They will see his face." One of the blessed promises in the Word of God to His children is that one day we will see the One who is the object of our affection, the Lord Jesus Christ, whom we have worshiped in spirit and in truth through the Word of God. That is, we will see Him face-to-face. This is an exclusive experience for all those who are overcomers. Those who are just hearers of the Word of God are not justified before God, but those who have received the Lord Jesus and accordingly are prepared to meet Him at His coming are justified before God.

EIGHT

The Church of Laodicea

Revelation 3:14–22

The last of the seven churches is the most disappointing. In fact, it is disgusting! Our Lord compares it to the nauseating experience of drinking anything lukewarm. In this sense it is a graphic prophecy of the modern-day apostate church.

Laodicea was a wealthy inland city about forty miles from Ephesus. Steeped in Greek culture and learning, it was a thriving center of commerce·and industry. The local church must have been wealthy, as evidenced by the fact that among present-day ruins are three churches dating back to the early days of Christianity. In spite of her wealth, nothing is known of the ministry of this church in preaching the gospel throughout the region around it as was characteristic of the church of Ephesus.

THE APOSTATE CHURCH OR THE PEOPLE'S CHURCH,
A.D. 1900 to the Tribulation

Commendation: Not one word!

Condemnation: "So, because you are lukewarm—neither hot nor cold—I am about to spit you out of my mouth. You say, 'I am rich; I have acquired wealth and do not need a thing.' But you do not realize that you are wretched, pitiful, poor, blind and naked."

Counsel: "I counsel you to buy from me gold refined in the fire, so you can become rich; and white clothes to wear, so you can cover your shameful nakedness; and salve to put on your eyes, so you can see."

Challenge: "To him who overcomes, I will give the right to sit with me on my throne."

The Laodicean Church Age

It should be kept in mind that the first three church ages differ from that last four in that each of the former stopped at the beginning of the next church. Ephesus was replaced by Smyrna, Smyrna by Pergamum, and Pergamum by Thyatira. A look at the chart at the beginning of Part

1 will show that we have Thyatira, Sardis, and Philadelphia with us at the present time. Thus Laodicea adds to this church age by arising from the three that preceded it.

The Laodicean church age began around 1900 and is increasing in intensity at a breathtaking pace. Laodicea could well be called the apostate ecumenical church that is gathering momentum at this very hour. The characteristics of the Laodicean church age can best be seen by a detailed examination of Christ's condemnation upon her.

Christ's Description of Himself to Laodicea

Only one of the three titles our Lord used to describe His nature to Laodicea is found in John's vision of chapter 1. It is the first.

1. "Amen" is a Hebrew word that means "true" and carries with it the meaning of finality. In this sense, Christ is the final truth. That is, all God's revelations to humankind about Himself are found in the person of Jesus Christ. If you want to know about God, all you have to do is study the life of Jesus Christ. Dr. Merrill C. Tenney has beautifully stated it: "Christ is the seal of God's revealed truth, the finality of all that the Father has spoken. Beyond Him, God has nothing more to say to man."

2. "... the faithful and true witness." The Lord Jesus is Truth and the faithful witness of Truth. Because He knows the end from the beginning, His Word can be accepted as absolute authority for two reasons: He is God, and "God gives the Spirit without limit" (John 3:34).

3. "... the ruler of God's creation." The word "ruler" here is more frequently translated "beginning" (KJV) or even "first cause." When considered in the light of the Word and parallel passages (Col. 1:15), this phrase is perhaps best translated "the beginner of the creation of God." It is obvious that all things are created through Christ's power when we consider John 1:3, "Through him all things were made; without him nothing was made that has been made," and Colossians 1:16–17, "For by him all things were created: things in heaven and on earth, visible and invisible, whether thrones or powers or rulers or authorities; all things were created by him and for him. He is before all things, and in him all things hold together."

Taken in reverse order, the three titles here selected by our Lord present Him as the beginner of creation, the faithful witness of everything that emanates from God, and the final authority (as He certainly will be at His second coming).

CHRIST'S COMMENDATION OF LAODICEA

The church of Laodicea has the distinction of being the only one whose conduct was so reprehensible that even the Christ of Glory, who knew all about her, could not find one thing on which to commend her. This is a tragic indictment, indeed, on so-called Christianity in the twentieth and approaching twenty-first century.

CHRIST'S CONDEMNATION OF LAODICEA

Our Lord's condemnation of Laodicea is twofold:

1. They are sickeningly lukewarm. "I know your deeds, that you are neither cold nor hot. I wish you were either one or the other!" Our Lord makes clear that He is fully aware of the neutral condition of the church in the last days. It is not "hot," meaning "zealous of good works," nor is it "cold," meaning "lifeless." Instead, it is "lukewarm" or indifferent. What a description of the modern-day church! All kinds of organizations, programs, committees, activities—but no power.

The Holy Spirit warned through Paul in 2 Timothy 3:5 that in the last days many will be characterized as "having a form of godliness but denying its power. Have nothing to do with them." The lukewarm church, which claims to represent Jesus Christ, never sees the transformation of a soul from darkness to life, but instead deceives many because they do not have the power of the gospel of Christ. These churches are usually more interested in social action than gospel action, more interested in reformation than transformation, more interested in planning than praying. Consequently, they are sickening to the Lord.

"So, because you are lukewarm—neither hot nor cold—I am about to spit you out of my mouth." The Lord Jesus Christ does not claim this church for Himself even though its members make broad their claim on Him.

2. They are deceived about themselves. "You say, 'I am rich; I have acquired wealth and do not need a thing.' But you do not realize that you are wretched, pitiful, poor, blind and naked." All deception is evil, but the most devastating deception is self-deception. The Laodicean church and the age she represents are deceived about themselves. This fact can easily be seen by a simple comparison of Laodicea's description of herself and the Lord's description of her.

Laodicea's Description of Herself

Laodicea says of herself, "I am rich; I have acquired wealth and do not need a thing." Material abundance is not conducive to spiritual vitality. The Laodicean church of today is "rich." Her churches are the finest. She has fabulous architecture, million-dollar buildings, fund-raising organizations, and a large (though unconsecrated) church membership. In saying, "I have acquired wealth and do not need a thing," she does not realize her poverty-stricken spiritual state. For Jesus said, "Apart from me you can do nothing."

Human beings can organize. They can build. They can promote. They can preach. They can teach. But only the Spirit of God can convict human souls. Only the Spirit of God can transform the lives of people. Only the Spirit of God can glorify Jesus Christ, who said of the Holy Spirit, "He will bring glory to me" (John 16:14). This offers a good test of any work claiming to be performed in the name of Jesus Christ: If it glorifies humanity, it is not the work of the Spirit!

The unique test of the Spirit is: Does it glorify Jesus Christ? This church age does not! For instead of preaching the gospel in Jesus' name to reach a maximum number of souls in these last days, they spend their time in doctrinal denial of the "faith that was once for all entrusted to the saints." As one mainline church (as they're often called) pastor told me recently, "I don't want to condemn anyone by telling them Christ is the only way of salvation, that would condemn their belief as wrong." Instead of grappling with and teaching the truth of the Bible, they spend their time in social causes. The Laodicean church today would be at the forefront of the gay rights and feminist movements and be leaders in the ordination of women and the feminizing of the deity. The message of our Lord is clear to such a church: "Have nothing to do with them."

The plight of the Laodicean church when she stands before Jesus Christ in the Judgment will be the same as that of the group of religionists described by our Lord Himself in Matthew 7:22–23: "Many will say to me on that day, 'Lord, Lord, did we not prophesy in your name, and in your name drive out demons and perform many miracles?' Then I will tell them plainly, 'I never knew you. Away from me, you evildoers!'"

Christ's Description of Laodicea

The true state of the Laodicean church can be seen by noting in detail what Christ saw in this church. To Him she was—

1. "Wretched, pitiful." Even though she gave herself lessons on positive thinking and read books on how to have peace, inwardly her people were an unhappy, wretched lot, for riches never satisfy the hungry human heart.

2. "Poor." Even though rich in material things, the Laodicean church members were poor because they did not know Christ. This is in accord with our Lord's statement in Mark 8:36, "For what good is it for a man to gain the whole world, yet forfeit his soul?"

3. "Blind." Although the Laodicean church members thought they knew and understood through their sophisticated education and appropriation of "wisdom," they did not understand the ways of God. This blindness is illustrated in twentieth-century Christendom's invasion of civil rights. The pulpits of churches are being used today as sounding boards for racial agitation, which depicts the blindness of these churches because they are striving to solve human racial problems externally or by means of education. That is impossible! Human nature must be changed internally, and only Jesus Christ can do that! The more people try to solve

these social problems without Christ, the more confused the problem will become.

4. "Naked." This twentieth-century Laodicean church is clothed with religion. She wraps her religious robes about her, burns her candles, waves her symbols, offers her chants, and reads her creeds; but Jesus Christ sees her as "naked," for she is not clothed by faith with the garments of righteousness. Oh, that this church age could realize that the name of Christ she uses, but does not believe in as the divine Son of God, has been excluded from her midst and that without Him she is nothing.

CHRIST'S COUNSEL TO LAODICEA

Our Lord counsels the church of Laodicea to do four things, all of which are part of the salvation experience, indicating that this church is not a born-again church.

1. "I counsel you to buy from me gold refined in the fire, so you can become rich." Eternal riches are not appropriated by material possessions. Instead, they have been appropriated by the blood of Jesus Christ and are available by faith. First Peter 1:7 indicates that "these have come so that your faith" may be more precious than gold. It is interesting to note that the Laodicean church, labeled "poor," is asked to buy something. How is this to be understood?

In the book of the prophet Isaiah (55:1), we read God's invitation to human beings to come and buy what they need "without money and without cost." Salvation is not purchased through human efforts. It has been purchased for us by the death of Christ on Calvary's cross. Therefore, the poorest of the poor can pay the price, which is to humble oneself, calling on the name of the Lord and believing in him.

2. "I counsel you to buy from me . . . white clothes to wear." This denotes the righteousness required to come into God's presence (referred to in 3:5). He knew their nakedness and their need for the "white clothes" that represent righteousness. In Isaiah 61:10 we read of God's provision of "garments of salvation" and the "robe of righteousness" as a bride or groom might wear. Righteousness is imputed to human beings when they call on the name of the Lord and are saved.

3. "I counsel you to buy from me . . . salve to put on your eyes, so you can see." This is an indication of a human being's need of spiritual illumination. No matter how brilliant people are in the flesh, unless they are indwelt by the Spirit of Jesus Christ, they will never understand the ways of God. Only the Holy Spirit, whom Jesus said would be our teacher, can cause human beings to understand the ways of God. "The man without the Spirit does not accept the things that come from the Spirit of God, for they are foolishness to him, and he cannot understand them, because they are spiritually discerned" (1 Cor. 2:14).

4. "So be earnest, and repent." This lukewarm, indifferent, material-istic church is challenged by our Lord, on the basis of His love for them even in that lost state, to repent of their sins and turn to Him.

CHRIST'S COUNSEL TO INDIVIDUALS

Christ's message to Laodicea contains a most interesting counsel that is specifically directed the individuals of this church age. Although the church has excluded Him, those who are willing to receive Him are given a special invitation that is also applicable to individuals of all church ages: "Here I am! I stand at the door and knock. If anyone hears my voice and opens the door, I will come in and eat with him, and he with me."

This verse of Scripture has been beautifully described by one saint of God as "the simplest explanation of the plan of salvation encompassed in so brief a statement within the lids of God's Word." The door referred to here is obviously the door to one's heart, that is, the center of one's being. The Bible says, "Above all else, guard your heart, for it is the wellspring of life" (Prov. 4:23). Consequently, we find Christ knocking at the door of this emotional center called the heart, asking entrance. He does not force His way, but patiently knocks: "If anyone hears my voice and opens the door, I will come in. . . ."

For almost two thousand years our Lord has faithfully, patiently, and wonderfully knocked on the doors of human hearts. How does He knock? In many ways, four of which I would like to share with you.

1. Through His Word. The Lord Jesus said, "I tell you the truth, who-ever hears my word and believes him who sent me has eternal life and will not be condemned; he has crossed over from death to life" (John 5:24). We must hear our blessed Lord's Word to be saved. Many have felt the gentle knock of the Savior at the door of their hearts as they read some portion of the Word of God. Sometimes this knocking evidences itself by violent reaction and rejection, but that does not minimize the fact that Christ has knocked.

2. Through His people. Another method our Lord uses to knock at the door of human hearts is through His children. The Scripture says, "And how can they hear without someone preaching to them?" (Rom. 10:14). We usually think of the great preachers of the Church as men like D. L. Moody, Billy Graham, Adrian Rogers, Charles Stanley, and many others. But if the truth were known—and it will be when we stand before the Judgment Seat of Christ—Jesus knocks through the ordinary, everyday, often obscure people.

The late Dr. Lee Scarborough, the great preacher from Texas, told of the conversion of a well-to-do businessman who came forward at the close of a service. The pastor asked who it was whom God used to speak to him about Christ. He had heard the preaching of D. L. Moody, Truett, and many other outstanding ministers, but he replied:

> None of those great preachers moved me. About eight years ago God saved my wife. I have watched her now these eight years as she has been faithful to Jesus Christ in poverty and in riches. Night after night I've watched her kneel beside our bed to pray. I've watched her as she went faithfully to prayer meeting and church services, putting Jesus Christ first in every area of her life. Last night as we retired, when she kneeled to pray, I began to think of the difference between her life and mine. As I lay there, I thought of my life as a little molehill of nothing and her life as a great mountain for God and righteousness. I got up out of bed and for the first time in eight years asked her to pray for my soul. Last night, by my bedside, I was lead to Jesus Christ—not by D. L. Moody or George Truett, but by my wife.

Yes, there is no question about it. Jesus knocks on the door of human hearts through His people.

3. Through His Holy Spirit. The Lord Jesus made it clear in John 14:8 that He sent the Holy Spirit to convict the heart of humankind of "sin and righteousness and judgment." Many who thought they had escaped the preacher and the Word of God have been awakened in the middle of the night to toss restlessly on their bed at the conviction of God's Spirit, which is the gentle knocking of Jesus at the door of one's heart.

4. Through providence. Usually I don't use the word "providence," for it is often misused as a rather impersonal reference to God. I am using it in this sense to mean God's gentle alignment of the affairs of a person's life that continually point him or her to the need of inviting Jesus into one's heart. Many who have felt the hot breath of death on them recognize that they were saved by the providence of God. They may not have recognized that this was the gentle knock of Jesus at their heart's door, but it was just the same.

Years ago, in a small town in Texas, a German merchant and his entire family came forward at the close of a service to receive Christ as Savior and Lord. When the pastor asked him to tell his experience, this is what he said:

> Yesterday I closed my store early and went for a ride with my family. We were crossing the railroad tracks when a train struck the back of our car. We went home and got out, all frightened. There was just one member of our family, little Mary, a member of your church, who was not frightened. We talked about it and Mary said, "Daddy, if we had been one second later in crossing that track all the family would have been in hell now but me." As soon as Mary said that, I called the family to prayer and asked Mary to lead us to heaven.

Perhaps you have heard the Lord Jesus knock at your heart's door in all of these ways: through His Word, His people, His Holy Spirit, His providence. The key question is: Have you opened the door and accepted His promise? "If anyone hears my voice and opens the door, I will come in and eat with him, and he with me." This indicates fellowship with Jesus. You are incomplete until you have fellowship with God through His Son Jesus Christ (1 John 1:3), which is only possible by inviting Him into your heart.

CHRIST'S CHALLENGE TO LAODICEA

The challenge of Christ to Laodicea, like His six other challenges, is to "overcome" or to become "born-again believers." The challenge is simply a promise to share His throne as He shares the Father's throne. This is a promise that we will rule and reign with Christ in His coming kingdom. The ultimate victory of the Christian, not seen in this life but in the life to come, is a challenge to faithfulness.

"He who has an ear, let him hear what the Spirit says to the churches." Have you heard what our Lord has said to the churches? The message of Christ to Laodicea indicates that as this age draws to a close, apostasy, deadness, and indifference will increase. It is no wonder our Lord asked of this age, "However, when the Son of Man comes, will he find faith on the earth?" (Luke 18:8). We should not expect to see revival as in the days of Moody, Finney, and others, but apostasy on the part of the Laodicean church. And who can deny that the ecumenical movings of this day clearly fulfill this prediction?

However, it would be just like our Heavenly Father, that great "shepherd of the sheep," to convict millions of people of their sins and offer them forgiveness in Jesus' name, just prior to the Rapture of the Church at the end of the Church Age. That is why I like to be ready at all times for those individuals who may be ready to receive the Savior before He returns for His church.

As we have come to the close of the messages of Christ to the seven churches, it is the burden of my heart that individuals will heed the Savior's invitation to open the door of their hearts. The picture of Christ knocking at the door is not only the picture of what He has been doing these past two thousand years but the picture of all He is going to do in this age to bring people to Him. If we refuse to voluntarily open the door of our heart, we reject Jesus Christ!

NINE

Christ's Description of Himself

Revelation 1–3

The book of Revelation is the only document in the Bible that contains Jesus Christ's personal description of Himself. It is of particular importance to us because it describes Him as He is today, not as He was during His thirty-three years of self-limitation on earth, when He came to suffer and die for our sins.

It will be exceedingly profitable for us to examine these statements. When placed together as a unit, they give a clear picture of the divine nature of our Lord. Let there be no doubt about it—Jesus Christ is God! For He said of Himself:

1:8: "I am the Alpha and the Omega."

1:17: "I am the First and the Last." This speaks of Christ's eternity.

1:18: "I am the Living One; I was dead...." This indicates His life on earth and His crucifixion.

1:18: "I am alive for ever and ever!" This speaks of His resurrection and eternity.

1:18: "And I hold the keys of death and Hades." Christ controls who goes to hell and the future of all believers.

2:1: "These are the words of him who holds the seven stars in his right hand." Christ controls the messengers of the churches.

2:1: "... and walks among the seven golden lampstands." Christ walks among the churches, easily accessible to them if they desire.

2:8: "These are the words of him who is the First and the Last, who died and came to life again." Here Christ combines a reference to His eternal nature with the fact of His death and resurrection.

2:12: "These are the words of him who has the sharp, double-edged sword." Christ presents the Word of God as His offensive weapon.

2:18: "... the Son of God." This asserts Christ's relationship to God as His divine Son.

2:18: "... whose eyes are like blazing fire." This is an obvious reference to His searching gaze on the work of His Church.

2:18: "... whose feet are like burnished bronze." Bronze, or brass, speaks of judgment. The Lord Jesus Christ will one day judge all people.

3:1: "These are the words of him who holds the seven spirits of God and the seven stars." The Holy Spirit will guide the "star" messengers of the churches. The Church has never been without guidance, if she would look for it.

3:7: "These are the words of him who is holy." His nature is holy.

3:7: ". . . and true." His testimony is right and can be relied upon.

3:7: ". . . who holds the key of David." Authority to rule over Gods' people is His.

3:7: "What he opens no one can shut, and what he shuts no one can open." Christ controls our opportunities to serve Him.

3:14: "These are the words of the Amen." He has final authority.

3:14: ". . . the faithful and true witness." He is *the* revelation of God.

3:14: ". . . the ruler [or beginner] of God's creation." Christ is the author and source of all God's creation.

3:20: "Here I am! I stand at the door and knock. If anyone hears my voice and opens the door, I will come in and eat with him, and he with me." The Lord of glory pictures Himself standing without, knocking at the door of a person's heart. He does not force His entrance, but leaves it to the individual to invite Him to come in.

Mr. Holman Hunt has painted a beautiful picture of Christ knocking at the heart's door. It is said that one day he unveiled this picture to a friend and asked, "What do you think of it?"

"It is a beautiful picture, but I think you have forgotten something," said the friend. "There is no latch on the door."

Mr. Hunt replied, "Ah, my friend, you have missed the point of the picture. The man at the door is the Lord Jesus Christ. The door is the entrance to the human heart and the latch is on the inside. Unless the one on the inside opens the door, Jesus will never come in.

A DESCRIPTION OF SALVATION BY CHRIST HIMSELF

Next to the person of Christ, the most important subject in the Bible is the doctrine of salvation. Since our Lord gave a descriptive phrase of salvation to each of the seven churches, we can combine them to produce the most complete picture of eternal life to be found in the Bible.

Each of Christ's definitions of salvation is given to "him who overcomes" or who has been born again (John 3:3, 7; 1 John 5:4–5).

2:7: "To him who overcomes, I will give the right to eat from the tree of life, which is in the paradise of God." Believers will live forever in God's paradise. This is suggestive of an eternal existence comparable to the Garden of Eden: no death, no sin, no heartache, nothing but the blessings of God.

2:11: "He who overcomes will not be hurt at all by the second death." Believers will not be "thrown into the lake of fire" (Rev. 20:15) but are saved from eternal death, which means eternal separation from God.

2:17: "To him who overcomes, I will give . . . a white stone with a new name written on it, known only to him who receives it." The stone indicates acquittal from our sins, and our new name, just as Christ renamed Peter and Paul after their conversions, points to the new life we have in Him.

2:26–27: "To him who overcomes and does my will to the end, I will give authority over the nations—'He will rule them with an iron scepter; he will dash them to pieces like pottery'—just as I have received authority from my Father." This indicates that believers will rule and reign with Christ in the Millennium.

2:28: "I will also give him the morning star." This is Christ's promise to come into the believer's heart and dwell with him or her.

3:5: "He who overcomes will, like them, be dressed in white." The believer's sinful nature is covered by the righteousness of Christ.

3:5: "I will never blot out his name from the book of life." Only those whose names are *not* written in the Book of Life are "thrown into the lake of fire." Believers need never fear hell, for Christ will see that our names remain in His Book of Life.

3:5: ". . . but [I] will acknowledge his name before my Father and his angels." Sinful human beings have no right to go to heaven in the presence of the Father and His angels; but Jesus will confess our names, thus giving us the right to be there.

3:12: "Him who overcomes I will make a pillar in the temple of my God. Never again will he leave it." Believers will have access to the Holy Place of God.

3:12: "I will write on him the name of my God and the name of the city of my God, the new Jerusalem, which is coming down out of heaven from my God." Believers will be eternally identified with Christ and thus have access to the Holy City, which is to come down from heaven.

3:12: "I will also write on him my new name." Believers will be eternally identified with Christ.

3:21: "To him who overcomes, I will give the right to sit with me on my throne." Believers will have a share in the ruling of Christ's coming kingdom.

Our first full-time church was in a beautiful suburb of Minneapolis, where we served six delightful years. After forty-two years we were invited back for the centennial celebration of that church. It was a wonderful reunion. Many of the people told me they had accepted Christ when I preached on the seven churches, particularly on the day I put a picture of Holman Hunt's masterful painting of Christ knocking at the heart's door in the church bulletin. What seemed so meaningful for several was that Hunt did not include a door latch, indicating that the only way the door that represented their hearts could be opened was from the inside.

That matchless invitation is not limited to the Laodicean church; it applies to individuals in every one of the churches throughout all these past two thousand years of church history. I sincerely hope you have opened that inside latch and invited the Savior into your heart.

> Here I am! I stand at the door and knock. If anyone hears my voice and opens the door, I will come in and eat with him, and he with me. (Rev. 3:20)

PART TWO

Christ and the Tribulation

TEN

Rapture Before Tribulation

Revelation 4:1–2

> After this I looked, and there before me was a door standing open in heaven. And the voice I had first heard speaking to me like a trumpet said, "Come up here, and I will show you what must take place after this." At once I was in the Spirit, and there before me was a throne in heaven with someone sitting on it. (Rev. 4:1–2)

It was no coincidence that the first thing to happen after John has described the seven churches (which we have seen represent not only a message to each individual church but also to the seven periods of church history) is his being taken up into heaven. Inasmuch as John was the last remaining apostle and a member of the universal Church, his elevation to heaven is a picture of the Rapture of the Church just before the Tribulation begins. It is also noteworthy that the invitation comes from Christ himself, who is the One who "first spoke" to John "like a trumpet" (1:10). Note how similar to this event is the promise of our Lord to His disciples near the end of His life about taking them to His Father's house (John 14:2–3):

> In my Father's house are many rooms; if it were not so, I would have told you. I am going there to prepare a place for you. And if I go and prepare a place for you, I will come back and take you to be with me that you also may be where I am.

Everyone knows God is in heaven, and Jesus ascended to heaven where He sits today at the right hand of God. Paul tells us that when he himself died, he (his spirit and soul) would "depart and be with Christ" (Phil. 1:23). He also said, "For though I am absent from you in body, I am present with you in spirit" (Col. 2:5). Obviously, then, when a Christian dies, his soul and spirit goes to be with Christ in the Father's house, that is, in heaven. His or her body, of course, remains in the grave until the resurrection, which for the Christian is at the end of the Church Age just before the Tribulation. That is why we locate the Rapture at this spot in the flow of events in the book of Revelation. There are at least four reasons for locating it here.

1. The location of this event is right for the Rapture. Chapters 4–5 present a vision in heaven, and chapter 6 introduces the Tribulation period. John, one of the first true members of the Church of Jesus Christ, is a fitting symbol of the Church being taken out of the world just before the Tribulation begins, as our Lord promised: "Since you have kept my command to endure patiently, I will also keep you from the hour of trial that is going to come upon the whole world to test those who live on the earth" (Rev. 3:10).

2. The absence of any mention of the Church in the rest of Revelation indicates that it is not on the earth during the Tribulation. There are sixteen references to the Church in Revelation 1–3, whereas chapters 6–18, which cover the Tribulation, do not mention the Church once. The natural conclusion drawn from this is that the Church that was so prominent during its two thousand-year history (as predicted in chapters 2–3) is not mentioned in chapters 4–18 because those chapters describe the Tribulation, which the Church does not endure.

3. The extensive use of Old Testament language and symbols in chapters 4–18 is an indication of Israel, not the Church. This is understandable since the Church Age is the time of the Gentiles, whereas the Tribulation is the time of Jacob's trouble or the seventieth week of Daniel, determined by God for His dealings with Israel. Some of these Old Testament symbols are the tabernacle, the ark of the covenant, the altar, elders, censers, cherubim, seals, trumpets, and plagues.

4. There is much similarity between the events of Revelation 4:1–2 and other scriptural teaching on the Rapture, such as 1 Thessalonians 4:13–18.

None of the above four reasons is sufficient in itself to insist that Revelation 4:1–2 refers to the Rapture of the Church. When, however, all of them are considered together, we are inclined to believe that this inference can rightly be made.

The Rapture of the Church is not explicitly taught in Revelation 4 but definitely appears here chronologically at the end of the Church Age and before the Tribulation. We will turn to other passages of Scripture that specifically deal with the Rapture so that we may be clearly informed of what the Bible teaches on the subject.

The first thing to occur in this vision of the future (after Jesus' own revelation of the Church Age described in chaps. 2–3) is the calling of John up to the Father's house in heaven; this fact has to be instructive. John obviously represents the Church, and because the door opening in heaven and the personal invitation of Christ Himself to "come up here" certainly parallels other prophetic passages (e.g., 1 Thess. 4:16–18), these factors all detail the Rapture of the Church.

Most prophecy scholars are reluctant to say that Revelation 4:1–2 are a direct teaching of the Rapture because it does not specifically say so or give us any additional details about that event. However, since John is the seer and is writing about future events even in his day, what better way to allude to the Rapture at this specific time—particularly since it is located right after the description of the Church Age and just prior to the revelation of the Antichrist (which we will describe beginning with chapter 6) and the beginning of the Tribulation?

The Apostle Paul was the special writer God chose to reveal to the Church the wonderful details of the Rapture, when all Christians, both the dead and the living, will be "caught up" (or raptured) to heaven to be with Christ (1 Thess. 4:16–17). Jesus mentioned it only once, in John 14:2–3 (see above). He spoke of his second coming many times, but in every other instance he had the climactic event Paul calls the "glorious appearing" in mind. That is usually the event most people think of when they speak of the many promises (318 total) in the New Testament regarding the second coming of Christ. We will examine that visible phase of His coming in detail when we get to Revelation 19. Care must be taken when examining Second Coming passages to determine whether they refer to the Rapture or the Glorious Appearing.

The following chart, used by permission from my friend, Dr. Thomas Ice, the executive director of the PreTrib Research Center, locates some of the main references to the two different phases of the Second Coming. You will note that most of those that describe the Rapture come from the writing of the Apostle Paul. This chart reveals that when all the promises of the Second Coming are pieced together, the Bible teaches one coming of Christ in two installments. The first is His coming in the air to rapture His Church prior to the Tribulation, and the second describes the Glorious Appearing, when He comes to the earth for everyone else at the end of the Tribulation period, just before He establishes His thousand-year kingdom—all subjects that we will study in this book.

RAPTURE—WHAT DOES IT MEAN?

Studying the second coming of Christ and future events as they are revealed to us in the prophetic books of the Bible is a perfectly legitimate subject. Not only because His coming is mentioned 318 times, but because it also occupied so much of the Apostle Paul's teaching ministry. The first book written in the New Testament was 1 Thessalonians, addressed to a small Greek church in the city of Thessalonica. Paul was there only three weeks before he was driven out of town by irate Jews. While he was with them, he had taught that Christ would come and rapture Christians out of this world to go with Him to His Father's house. After he left, however, some of their members had died. Consequently,

PHASES OF THE SECOND COMING

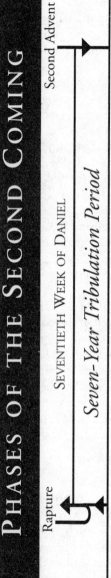

	SEVENTIETH WEEK OF DANIEL	Second Advent
Rapture	Seven-Year Tribulation Period	
RAPTURE PASSAGES	**SECOND COMING PASSAGES**	
John 14:1–3	Daniel 2:44–45	Acts 1:9–11
Romans 8:19	Daniel 7:9–14	Acts 3:19–21
1 Corinthians 1:7–8	Daniel 12:1–3	1 Thessalonians 3:13
1 Corinthians 15:51–53	Zechariah 12:10	2 Thessalonians 1:6–10
1 Corinthians 16:22	Zechariah 14:1–15	2 Thessalonians 2:8
Philippians 3:20–21	Matthew 13:41	1 Peter 4:12–13
Philippians 4:5	Matthew 24:15–31	2 Peter 3:1–14
Colossians 3:4	Matthew 26:64	Jude 14–15
1 Thessalonians 1:10	Mark 13:14–27	Revelation 1:7
1 Thessalonians 2:19	Mark 14:62	Revelation 19:11–20:6
1 Thessalonians 4:13–18	Luke 21:25–28	Revelation 22:7, 12, 20
1 Thessalonians 5:9		
1 Thessalonians 5:23		
2 Thessalonians 2:1		
1 Timothy 6:14		
2 Timothy 4:1		
2 Timothy 4:8		
Titus 2:13		
Hebrews 9:28		
James 5:7–9		
1 Peter 1:7, 13		
1 Peter 5:4		
1 John 2:28–3:2		
Jude 21		
Revelation 2:25		
Revelation 3:10		

these young Christians were perplexed about the status of their dead Christian members, so they wrote him a letter requesting an explanation. First Thessalonians is Paul's answer. In it he gives the most detailed description of the Rapture of the Church found in all of Scripture. Note 1 Thessalonians 4:13–18 carefully.

> Brothers, we do not want you to be ignorant about those who fall asleep, or to grieve like the rest of men, who have no hope. We believe that Jesus died and rose again and so we believe that God will bring with Jesus those who have fallen asleep in him. According to the Lord's own word, we tell you that we who are still alive, who are left till the coming of the Lord, will certainly not precede those who have fallen asleep. For the Lord himself will come down from heaven, with a loud command, with the voice of the archangel and with the trumpet call of God, and the dead in Christ will rise first. After that, we who are still alive and are left will be caught up together with them in the clouds to meet the Lord in the air. And so we will be with the Lord forever. Therefore encourage each other with these words.

To appreciate the contrast between this event and the Glorious Appearing at the end of the Tribulation, we should read our Lord's own description of that event in Matthew 24:27–31.

> For as lightning that comes from the east is visible even in the west, so will be the coming of the Son of Man. Wherever there is a carcass, there the vultures will gather. Immediately after the distress of those days
>
> > the sun will be darkened,
> >   and the moon will not give its light;
> > the stars will fall from the sky,
> >   and the heavenly bodies will be shaken.
>
> At that time the sign of the Son of Man will appear in the sky, and all the nations of the earth will mourn. They will see the Son of Man coming on the clouds of the sky, with power and great glory. And he will send his angels with a loud trumpet call, and they will gather his elect from the four winds, from one end of the heavens to the other.

Do not be surprised if you cannot correlate these two installments of our Lord's second coming. They are totally different. And when we include additional Rapture events like those described in 1 Corinthians 15:51–55 and add Glorious Appearing descriptions like the one we will study in Revelation 19:11–16, we can only conclude they are *not* describing the same event. In fact, I have discovered fifteen differences between the Rapture before the Tribulation and the Glorious Appearing after it. Please examine the accompanying chart carefully to get the impact.

15 Contrasting Events of the Second Coming

Rapture / Blessed Hope

1. Christ comes in air for His own
2. Rapture / translation of all Christians
3. Christians taken to the Father's House
4. No judgment on earth at Rapture
5. Church taken to Heaven at Rapture
6. Rapture imminent / could happen any moment
7. No signs for Rapture
8. For believers only
9. Time of joy
10. Before the Day of Wrath (Tribulation)
11. No mention of Satan
12. The Judgment Seat of Christ
13. Marriage of Lamb
14. Only His own see Him
15. Tribulation begins

Glorious Appearing

1. Christ comes with His own to earth
2. No one translated
3. Resurrected saints do not see Father's House
4. Christ judges inhabitants of earth
5. Christ sets up His kingdom on earth
6. Glorious appearing cannot occur for at least 7 years
7. Many signs for Christ's physical coming
8. Affects all humanity
9. Time of mourning
10. Immediately after Tribulation (Matthew 24)
11. Satan bound in Abyss for 1000 years
12. No time or place for Judgment Seat
13. His bride descends with Him
14. Every eye will see Him
15. 1000-year kingdom of Christ begins

Many important observations could be made about the fifteen contrasting events that describe the two phases of our Lord's coming. One is that it is impossible for them to be describing the same event! Only when you place these biblical descriptions beside each other is it possible to see that. This in one reason why many have never seen the distinction and think the Second Coming is a singular event rather than the coming of Christ in the air to take His Church to His Father's house as He promised, and seven years later His coming in power and great glory to the earth as He promised.

There is only one "Second Coming," but it occurs in two phases. The first phase is only for His church, that is, all living and dead believers since the church was founded in A.D. 33. The second phase is for all those living on the earth at the end of the Tribulation. That the Glorious Appearing will take place at the end of the Tribulation just before the Millennium cannot be questioned for Jesus predicted that His Glorious Appearing would come "immediately after the distress of those days" (Matt. 24:29).

THE GLORIOUS APPEARING CANNOT COME TODAY!

It may shock many of my readers to learn that the Second Coming of Christ to set up His Kingdom cannot come now or any time soon! In fact, the Glorious Appearing of Christ cannot come for at least seven years! Yet the early church for three hundred years lived almost every day in the light of His return, which is why they were so successful in reaching their world for Christ. Even today millions of Christians expect Christ to return at any moment, as the many Rapture passages listed above teach. He will not disappoint us! He will come—and His coming could be at any moment—but that coming is for His Church only, which is made up of all true believers everywhere who have received Him personally by faith. But to expect His return in power and majesty to take control of this earth and set up His Kingdom for at least seven years is to expect the impossible.

The differing passages relating to Christ's coming are harmonized when we see that some are exclusive for His Church and others include the entire world. I am convinced these two phases of Christ's return are what the Apostle Paul had in mind when he wrote to Titus, "looking for that blessed hope, and the glorious appearing . . ." (KJV). The "blessed hope" is the confident way we put our deceased Christian loved ones to rest in anticipation of that day just before the Tribulation when we will be gathered together with them to meet the Lord in the clouds and then be taken to His Father's house. The "glorious appearing" obviously refers to His coming to the earth in "power and great glory." To those who take the Bible literally, this interpretation passes the test of "making common sense" out of the Scripture.

THE RAPTURE COULD COME AT ANY MOMENT

Many of the texts cited above for the Rapture of the Church teach an imminent coming of Christ. That means He could come at any moment. Take, for example, one of the first teachings on the Rapture in 1 Thessalonians 1:9–10:

> . . . for they themselves report what kind of reception you gave us. They tell how you turned to God from idols to serve the living and true God, and to wait for his Son from heaven, whom he raised from the dead—Jesus, who rescues us from the coming wrath.

These Thessalonian Christians were not sitting around waiting for the Rapture, they were "serv[ing] the living and true God" in an attitude of expectancy "to wait for his Son." That is as it should be, for it could take place at any moment, or it could be a generation or more away. Philippians 3:20 is another example, a proper understanding of 2 Thessalonians 2:1–8 is another, and there are many others. But, it must be stressed again, the Rapture is scheduled prior to the Glorious Appearing. Almost all premillennialists (those who believe Christ will come back personally to set up His Kingdom, as we will see demonstrated in chapters 19–20), agree that there is a Rapture scheduled before the Glorious Appearing. The source of disagreement is how much time before the Glorious Appearing does the Rapture occur. The following chart locates the three main views according to their defenders.

The reader should keep in mind that these are all Christians, they all have scriptural reasons for their views, and they should all be regarded as fellow believers. Actually, they are only three to seven or more years apart. The time difference is significant, however, since it determines whether we are to look first for the Antichrist and Tribulation or first for the Rapture. Some of the mid- and post-tribulation believers are even now coming out with books instructing Christians to prepare for life in the Tribulation. I find that interesting in view of the fact that not one verse can be found in the New Testament instructing Christians on how to live during that seven-year period. The obvious reason is that Christians will not be living on earth at that time; they will be in heaven.

Those Tribulation "saints" we will study about in future chapters of Revelation are individuals who do not receive Christ until *after* the church has been raptured. It does seem strange that since so much prophetic content by both the Old Testament prophets and the New Testament apostles describes the seven-year Tribulation (more than any other prophetic subject except the Second Coming itself) that not even one

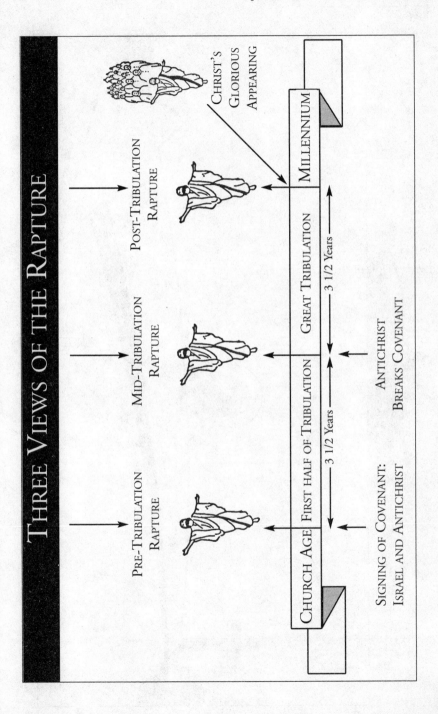

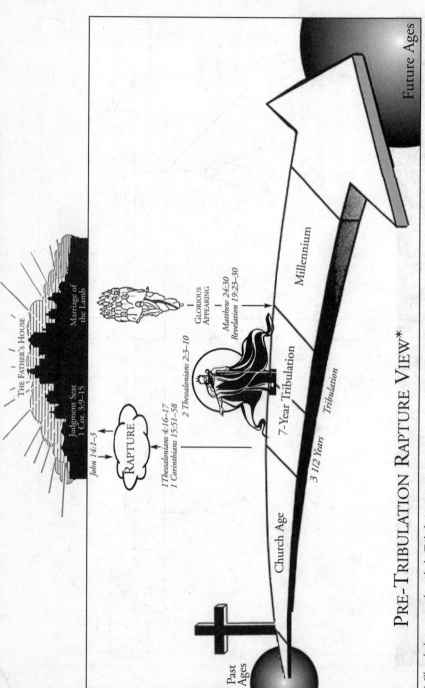

The Father's House

Judgment Seat
1 Cor. 3:9–15

Marriage of
the Lamb

John 14:1–3

RAPTURE

1 Thessalonians 4:16–17
1 Corinthians 15:51–58

2 Thessalonians 2:3–10

GLORIOUS
APPEARING

Matthew 24:30
Revelation 19:23–30

Past Ages

Church Age

7-Year Tribulation

3 1/2 Years   Tribulation

Millennium

Future Ages

PRE-TRIBULATION RAPTURE VIEW*

* Church does not go through the Tribulation

verse can be found instructing Christians on how to live during that period. This can only mean that the Church will not go through the Tribulation, as pictured by John, a member of the body of Christ, who was taken up by a vision into heaven before the vision of the events of the Tribulation period were revealed.

EXPECTING A PRE-TRIBULATION RAPTURE NOT NEW

For several years a popular argument against the pre-Tribulation theory of the "blessed hope" phase of Christ's return is that it was invented by John Darby in the last century (1828) and was never seen or mentioned by the early Christian fathers for almost nineteen centuries of church history. That argument is simply not true! In fact, one post-Tribulation writer advertised an offer of five hundred dollars to anyone who could prove a pre-Tribulation Rapture was seen before John Darby began to popularize it in Great Britain, the United States, and Canada in the 1840s. Subsequently, he had to pay that five-hundred-dollar challenge when someone discovered that the Reverend Morgan Edwards saw it back in 1742. Since then that minister has admitted his error and withdrawn his offer.

Reverend Morgan Edwards was a Baptist pastor in Philadelphia who included a discussion on the pre-Tribulation return of Christ for His Church in his book *Millennium, Last Days Novelties*, written in 1788. Although he saw only a three and a half-year Tribulation, he definitely taught that the Rapture occurred *before* the Tribulation. What is even more interesting is that he claimed he had written the same thing as early as 1742. He may have been influenced by John Gill before him or even others whose writings or teachings were available at that time but have not been preserved.

Historically, the Protestant Reformation resulted in a proliferation of Bibles being translated, printed, and made available to the common people for the first time in 1700 years. As they began reading it, they were impressed with the many prophetic teachings it contained. I have a copy of a commentary on the Book of Revelation written by Sir Isaac Newton in the mid-seventeenth century. He was an avid Bible scholar (as well as one of the greatest scientists in all of history) and was obviously influenced by other writers before him. Thus historically, the development of prophecy is understandable; it progressed parallel with the availability of the Bible and the study of it.

By the nineteenth century, the Bible was being read by millions in the English-speaking world. It is said that "prophecy was in the air," particularly at Trinity College in Dublin, Ireland, which John Darby and other prophecy scholars attended between 1800 and 1830. Doubtless some of the Bible teachers on the faculty had a strong influence on his thinking, including perhaps S. R. Maitland, who developed the case for futurism, which is the position that most of the book of Revelation and other Bible prophecies are yet in the future. He wrote the first book on that subject in 1826.

John Darby claimed he got the inspiration for the pre-Tribulation rapture of Christ in 1828 after he saw the distinction between Israel and the Church in his study of the book of Ephesians. Few scholars who do not make that distinction see a pre-Tribulation rapture of the Church. In fact, separating Israel and the Church is one of the major keys to rightly understanding Bible prophecy. The second key is taking the prophetic Scriptures literally whenever possible.

Grant Jeffery, a current prophecy scholar and speaker, has done extensive research in the writings of many eighteenth-century prophecy scholars. In his book *Apocalypse,* he quotes many who had a definite understanding of the difference between the two phases of our Lord's coming, particularly His coming for His own people prior to the Tribulation and the revealing of the Man of Sin.

Jeffery's most important find was the electrifying discovery of a statement in an apocalyptic sermon from the fourth century. The author is designated "Pseudo-Ephrem" ("Pseudo" [meaning "false"] because there is some question whether or not it was really written by Ephrem of Nisibis [c. 306–373], a prolific Syrian church father). Some prefer a later date for this sermon, called "Sermon on the End of the World," suggesting it may have been written sometime between 565 and 627. For our purpose the date is immaterial, for even allowing it as late as the seventh century proves that Christians eleven hundred years before the time of John Darby saw the Rapture happening *before* the Tribulation. Note the statement in English, translated from its Greek and Latin versions that date to the period. Challenging Christians to holy living (always the purpose of Rapture teaching), Pseudo-Ephrem wrote:

> Why therefore do we not reject every care of earthly actions and prepare ourselves for the meeting of the Lord Christ, so that he may draw us from the confusion, which overwhelms all the world? . . . *All the saints and elect of God are gathered together before the tribulation, which is to come, and are taken to the Lord,* in order that they may not see at any time the confusion which overwhelms the world because of our sins.[8] (emphasis mine)

There can be no doubt this fourth- (or at the latest seventh-) century Bible scholar saw the saints gathered together before the Tribulation by the coming of the Lord. His statement has all the marks of a pre-Tribulation rapture of the saints as distinct from the Glorious Appearing, which our Lord promised would occur "immediately after the distress of those days ..." (Matt. 24:29). Admittedly, Ephrem saw the Tribulation lasting only forty-two months or three and a half years (as taught later in the sermon); the fact remains, however, that he saw a pre-Tribulation rapture of the Church long before it became popular during the nineteenth century. Considering that less than 10 percent of ancient Christian books ever written have been preserved to our day, we have no doubt that even though the details of the pre-Tribulation Rapture were not widely recognized back in the fourth century, there must have been other Bible students besides Ephrem who also discovered the "blessed hope" teaching.

Ephrem, the Syrian of the fourth century, was not an originator of this view, for it was seen by Victorinus, Bishop of Petau, as early as A.D. 270. Known as a biblical "literalist," he was martyred for his faith in A.D. 304 under Diocletian. Jerome, a fourth-century scholar and translator of the first New Testament text into Latin, "classified him as millenarian," earning him the distinction of having his writings suppressed by Damasus I. Froom,[9] a church historian, indicated Victorinus saw a period of three and one half years for the two witnesses to minister, followed by a similar period for the Antichrist's kingdom, totaling the seven-year period of time. In his commentary on Revelation, he compared the plagues of that period with the plagues of Leviticus and then said, "These shall be in the last time, when the church shall have gone out of the midst."[10]

Obviously Bishop Victorinus of Petau, a brilliant Bible scholar living in the third century, saw the church departing *before* the plagues during the time of God's wrath, which from his commentary on Revelation 11 he took to be seven years. "[They] shall have gone out of the midst" was his way of describing the Rapture of the Church.

The most ancient of all prophetic writers, of course, was the Apostle Paul, whose first New Testament letter gave the early church the challenge of the "blessed hope" lifestyle motivation. Not only the 1 Thessalonians 4:13–18 classic passage, but also 2 Thessalonians 2:1–8 outlines the entire subject. And these books challenging Christians to live in the light of an imminent Rapture were written before any of the Gospels or other New Testament writings—in some cases, many years before them. These proved to challenge the early Church to holiness, evangelism, and missions by the promise of the Rapture—not the threat of Tribulation followed by the Glorious Appearing, which cannot come until the man of sin has been revealed and the seven worst years of human history have run their course.

Roy Huebner, a careful pre-Tribulation scholar, has proven that many saw the Rapture before John Darby first saw it in 1827. He said, "The word 'rapture' was in use, to designate the catching up of the saints, long before 1832. For example, Joseph Mede (1586–1638) wrote, 'Therefore, it is not needful that the Resurrection of those which slept in Christ, and the Rapture of those which shall be left alive together with them in the air . . .'"[11]

This clearly indicates that Mede, the great sixteenth-century literalist, understood 1 Thessalonians 4:13–18 to teach the catching up of the saints and used the term *rapture* to designate that catching up. His statement was made 250 years before Darby taught the Rapture! Thus, we see that the term *rapture* was not unique to Darby, but had been used by others before him. Moreover, for every printed reference to Rapture teachings that have been preserved to this day, there were doubtless many other comments in print and in the messages of faithful teachers of end-time subjects that have remained undiscovered or are no longer available.

The concept of a pre-Tribulation Rapture was obviously known during the first three centuries of the church and did not lose its challenge until the Bible was effectively locked up in museums or monasteries for the 1100 years of the Dark Ages—although several who had access to the Scriptures (and who could read Greek or Latin) saw it even during those years. It was not, however, until the Bible was translated into the language of the common people that the hope of the premillennial return of Christ was reestablished in the Church. Then in the eighteenth and nineteenth centuries, the ancient truth of the Rapture before the Tribulation was rediscovered. And wherever this truth has been taught, it has had the same effect on believers that it had in the first three centuries— it produced holy living in an unholy age, a drive for evangelism, and a zeal for missions.

ELEVEN

The Throne of God

Revelation 4–5

> After this I looked, and there before me was a door standing open in heaven. And the voice I had first heard speaking to me like a trumpet said, "Come up here, and I will show you what must take place after this." At once I was in the Spirit, and there before me was a throne in heaven with someone sitting on it. (Rev. 4:1–2)

Somewhere, high in the heavens, out in the universe, a throne is set, which is the throne of God. This throne, described in the passage before us, gives us a glimpse of the heaven of God.

The Bible teaches us that there are three heavens. The first, the atmospheric heaven, where "the prince of the power of the air" holds forth, will one day be destroyed. The second heaven is the stellar heaven, known to us as the universe. The third heaven, into which John was caught up in verse 1, is the heaven of God. This could be the "empty space" referred to by Job in 26:7. Although the heavens are filled with stars wherever the telescope can reach, it seems that behind the North Star there is an empty space. For that reason it has been suggested that this could be the third heaven, the heaven of God, where His throne is.

THE THRONE OF GOD

The central object of heaven is the throne of God, referred to eight times in 4:1–6 and eighteen times altogether in chapters 4–5. It seems to be a fixed point, with everything else in heaven located in relationship to it. We find such expressions as "about the throne," "out of the throne," "before the throne," and "in the midst of the throne." The throne of God has been considered the fixed center of the universe, the immovable point of reference. Just as the North Star has been the ancient navigators' positional guide because of its fixed position among the stars, so the throne of God is the place of authority and the center of God's rulership for the activities of heaven.

This throne before which everyone in Heaven worships may well be the Judgment Seat of Christ before which all Christians will stand (Rom. 14:2; 2 Cor. 5:10) immediately after the Rapture to receive their rewards (1 Cor. 3:10–15) or to have them "burned up," depending on how faithfully we have served our Lord. Dr. Henry M. Morris, my friend and colleague in helping me found Christian Heritage College in San Diego, has an interesting insight on this.

> This judgment must have been completed prior to the millennium [described in chapter 20], because the believers will by then have been arrayed in white garments representing the "righteous acts" of the saints and given thrones of judgment reserved for "overcomers" during the millennium. The judgments described in Revelation chapters 6–19 have to do with the earth and its Christ-rejecting inhabitants, and nothing is said concerning the judgment of believers in heaven for rewards. Consequently, the latter can only have occurred immediately after the rapture and prior to the unleashing of the plagues on earth.[12]

SEVEN THINGS AROUND THE THRONE OF GOD

The remainder of chapter 4 conveys to us seven distinct characteristics of the throne of God. We will examine them individually.

1. The Triune God

"At once I was in the Spirit, and there before me was a throne in heaven with someone sitting on it." Verses 2–3, when carefully studied, reveal all three members of the triune God. When John said "At once I was in the Spirit," he was referring to the Holy Spirit. John, as a Christian, was always filled with the Holy Spirit. But as he indicated in 1:10, he was "in the Spirit" in a special revelatory sense as God was revealing to him, in the same manner he had "moved" the prophets and apostles in time past to write the Holy Scriptures (2 Pet. 1:20–21). Here the Spirit was revealing to him "the things that shall come hereafter."

Verse 2 indicates someone sitting on the throne. Greek does not denote singular or individual characteristics; instead, it refers to a presence on the throne but does not denote how many. Consequently, we know that God the Father is there. However, verse 3 suggests that God the Son is likewise present; as taught in other passages of Scripture, He is "seated at the right hand of God." Note that "the one who sat there had the appearance of jasper and carnelian. A rainbow, resembling an emerald, encircled the throne." This verse describes the Lord Jesus Christ, for we know from several passages of Scripture that God the Father cannot be seen (John 1:18; 6:46; 1 Tim. 6:16). Thus, the one John looked on is none other than the only member of the Trinity that can be seen, the Lord Jesus Christ, who is described in two ways.

First, Christ is our High Priest. John's description of the one he looked on as ". . . appearance of jasper and carnelian" is most illuminating. Dr. Harry Ironside, in his book on Revelation, says this about John's description.

> The jasper of the Revelation is not the opaque stone we know by that name. It is later described as a crystal (chapter 21:11). It is probably the diamond, the most brilliant of all the precious jewels. The other stone is blood red, and may really be the ruby. Thus the two together give the idea of glory and sacrifice. Remembering that many of the first readers of the Revelation were converted Jews, we might ask, what would these stones suggest to them? Surely every instructed Hebrew would instantly recall that they were the first and last stones in the breastplate of the High Priest (Exodus 28:17–20). As these stones bore the names of the tribes of Israel, arranged according to the births of the twelve patriarchs, the one would suggest at once the name of Reuben, "behold a son," and the other Benjamin, "son of my right hand." It is Christ enthroned; the Son about to reign in power Who was before the seer's vision.[13]

One might well ask the question: Why is it that the first thing we notice about Christ here presents Him in His priestly role? The answer to that is seen in the location of this description. Coming right after the Church Age and before the Tribulation, it represents the first time Christ has had His entire priesthood together at one time. The priesthood of believers began at the day of Pentecost. Every member of the body of Christ is a member of the priesthood of believers; actually we are called in 1 Peter 2:9 "a royal priesthood." The Church of Jesus Christ, made up of that "royal priesthood," is not now in the presence of Christ, at least in its entirety. Only after the Rapture of the Church, when the dead in Christ are raised and we are changed, will the entire priesthood of Christ be united at one time. Therefore, the sardius and jasper stones are used to depict Christ as our High Priest.

Second, Christ is the Eternal One. Another phase of the description of Christ as seen by John is that "a rainbow, resembling an emerald, encircled the throne." This is not an ordinary rainbow but a perfectly circular rainbow. We only see half of the rainbow on earth, but in heaven we will see a perfectly circular rainbow, which, like a green emerald, presents the eternal nature of Christ. Truly He is the Eternal One.

As we examine these two descriptions of Christ, the first to greet the Christian after the Rapture, they remind us that we are in heaven not because of anything we have done, but because Christ, our faithful High Priest, has given us a royal priesthood, freely, by His grace. Similarly, He has imparted of His eternal nature to us, entitling us to share His everlasting life. When we take this into consideration, certainly it should not be difficult for us to offer to God "continually ... a sacrifice of praise" (Heb. 13:15).

One of the most commonly neglected Bible subjects among Christians today is the priesthood of all believers—that is, that we today are priests of God. As His priests, we should be faithful in exercising our privileges and responsibilities. What are our responsibilities? Basically they are twofold: intercession and sacrifice.

Intercessory prayer should occupy much of the life of the believer (1 Tim. 2:1). If we really understood that unbelievers cannot pray and that Christians out of fellowship with God cannot pray, then we would be burdened to pray for our brothers and sisters in Christ and for the unsaved. The course of history could well have been changed had we Christians been more faithful in this regard.

Another work of the priest in the Old Testament was to sacrifice. The New Testament tells us of four sacrifices that Christians can make:

Romans 12:1–2—your body
Hebrews 13:15—the sacrifice of praise (worship)
Hebrews 13:16—good works
Hebrews 13:16—giving

2. The Twenty-Four Elders

"Surrounding the throne were twenty-four other thrones, and seated on them were twenty-four elders. They were dressed in white and had crowns of gold on their heads." The next thing we see "surrounding the throne" are twenty-four other thrones, with "elders," in white clothing and with crowns on their heads, sitting on the seats. One of the most controversial questions raised by this vision of the throne of God is the identity of the twenty-four elders. Some Bible scholars, good ones indeed, believe them to be men, whereas the others, equally competent, believe them to be angels. Let us examine both views.

John Darby, one of the first to write on this subject, said, "The number twenty-four represents twice twelve. One might perhaps see here the twelve patriarchs and the twelve apostles—the saints in the two dispensations." This is better than to make them "represent" the *Church;* but it leaves them symbolic rather than actual elders.[14]

Dr. Ironside explains,

> But now the fourth verse brings before us a sight never beheld in heaven on any previous occasion: twenty-four thrones (not merely "seats") surrounding the central throne, and upon them twenty-four elders seated, with victors' crowns (not diadems) upon their heads, and clothed in priestly robes of purest white. Who are these favored ones gathered around the glorious central Being? I do not think we need to be in any doubt as to their identity, if we compare scripture with scripture and distrust our own imagination, which can but lead us astray.

In 1 Chronicles, chapter 24, we read of something very similar; and again I would remind you that many of John's readers were Hebrews, thoroughly familiar with the Old Testament. Can we question for a moment that every Jewish believer would instantly remember the twenty-four elders appointed by King David to represent the entire Levitical priesthood? He divided the priests into twenty-four courses, each course to serve for two weeks at a time in the temple which Solomon was to build. The same arrangement was in force when our Lord's forerunner was announced. Zacharias was "of the course of Abiah," the eighth in order (Luke 1:5).

The priests were many thousands in number; they could not all come together at one time, but *when the twenty-four elders met* in the temple precincts in Jerusalem, *the whole priestly house* was represented. And this is the explanation. I submit, of the symbol here. The elders in heaven represent the whole heavenly priesthood—that is, all the redeemed who have died in the past, or who shall be living at the Lord's return. In vision they were seen—not as a multitudinous host of millions of saved worshipers, but just twenty-four elders, symbolizing the entire company. The church of the present age and Old Testament saints are alike included. All are priests. All worship. There were twelve patriarchs in Israel, and twelve apostles introducing the new dispensation. The two together would give the complete four and twenty.

Then, observe further: these persons are not angels. They are redeemed men who have overcome in the conflict with Satan and the world, for they wear victors' wreaths upon their brows. Angels are never said to be "crowned," nor have they known redemption.

There are two kinds of crowns mentioned in this book: the victor's crown, and the ruler's diadem. The former is the word here used.[15]

Thus two of numerous great men of God believe that the elders are men.

When I studied with Dr. David L. Cooper some years ago, he said of these twenty-four elders that nothing in the context would indicate that these elders are used representatively. Never should one resort to a figurative, symbolic, or secondary meaning of any passage of Scripture unless there is a warrant for the same in the context. One will seek in vain for such justification. There is nothing that suggests the idea of representation. The language simply states that there were twenty-four thrones and twenty-four elders seated on their thrones, with crowns of gold on their heads.

Another popular suggestion is that these elders are heavenly beings that are of an especially high order, who, under God, are assisting in the administration of the universe. Dr. William R. Newell, who held that view, explains it:

We can only assume, not prove, that the "elders" are not of our race at all. The cherubim are not; nor the seraphim nor the "chief princes" (Daniel 10:13). Because the term "elders" is so often mentioned (over 200 times) in Scripture, both in connection with Israel and the Church, many are willing to assume that the elders are human beings. But the elders do not testify of their own *salvation* at all: although they celebrate that of *others,* as in Revelation 5:8, 9 (R.V.).

Inasmuch as God had "elders" over His people *Israel,* and "elders" were also to be appointed in each *Church* (Titus 1:15); and inasmuch as twenty-four seems God's governmental order, we do not see why it may not be that there are "elders" over God's creation; that they were created so; and they are twenty-four in number ... so these "elders" were created and associated by God with His government. When Christ, with His Bride, the Church, comes to reign in power, in Revelation 19, we hear no more of these twenty-four elders: for God then subjects *all* to the *Man;* Psalm 8 is fulfilled. The elders as all other heavenly beings, have their place, but under Christ and the Church.[16]

The word "elder" means leader. Actually it is a title of rank. It has been pointed out that, militarily speaking, we have a similar expression in English. The commanding officer of any unit is often called "the old man." This has nothing to do with his age or the size unit that he heads, for he may be the commanding general of an entire army. On the other hand, he may be a twenty-four-year-old first lieutenant who is a company commander. Both are more or less affectionately referred to as "the old man." Essentially that is what the word "elder" means: "the old man." This word is used of pastors and church leader to indicate leadership.

Obviously good Bible scholars can be found on both sides of this issue of the identity of the heavenly "elders." Very honestly, I have changed my view since I originally wrote this commentary. Then I leaned toward the "twenty-four elders" being special representative angels who administered the universe of God. Three things worked to change my mind.

1. Further Bible study convinced me that these "elders" had been redeemed by the blood of the Lamb (5:9). Angels have not been redeemed, so it could not be angels. I had been misled by the study note in the *Scofield Reference Bible* that indicated the word "us" in the KJV was not found in the most ancient manuscripts. Actually, it is indeed found in twenty-three of the twenty-four oldest manuscripts of the book of Revelation!

2. The NIV translators identify the "twenty-four elders" in 5:9: "With your blood you purchased men for God from every tribe and language and people and nation." Nothing could be clearer, these are indeed redeemed men!

3. The following quote comes from my esteemed friend Dr. Henry Morris:

> The word "seats" is the Greek *thronos*, the same word as used for "throne." The elders were seen by John seated on thrones exactly as he had seen the divine presence seated on the throne (4:2). The identity of these elders, sometimes mistakenly interpreted as angels, is very important.
>
> The elders are undoubtedly redeemed and glorified men, or, at the least, representative of such men, in view of the following considerations: (1) although there are principalities and powers in the angelic hierarchy, there can be no "elders," since all angels are of the same age, created probably on the first day of creation; (2) the term "elder" is always used elsewhere in the Bible only of men; (3) elders are always chosen representatives and leaders of the people, both in Israel and in the church; (4) there are no elders in the visions of God's throne in Isaiah 6 and Ezekiel 1–10, in consequence of the fact that prior to the cross the spirits of all the redeemed were still confined to Hades; (5) the elders were wearing white raiment (as promised to overcoming believers in Revelation 3:5) and victors' crowns (Greek *stephanos*, "wreath," as also promised to overcomers in Revelation 2:10 and 3:11); angels, being "ministering spirits" (Hebrews 1:14) are never described in the Bible as wearing crowns of any kind; (6) in Revelation 5:9–10, these elders sing a song of praise to the Lamb who had redeemed them by His blood.
>
> But why twenty-four elders? The Israelites used seventy elders (Exodus 24:1), and no indication is given as to the number of elders in the early church. There were twenty-four orders of priests in Israel (I Chronicles 24:7–19), but these were not the elders and, even though believers are to be kings and priests (Revelation 1:6), there seems no reason why the office of the priest should be commingled with that of the elder in heaven. The number twenty-four has often been held to be symbolic of the twelve patriarchs plus the twelve apostles. The latter, however, are specifically assigned to the job of judging the twelve tribes of Israel on twelve thrones in the millennial kingdom (Revelation 19:28), whereas the twenty-four elders are at the throne in heaven. If twelve of these are the twelve apostles, assigned to judging the twelve tribes, then the identity and function of the other twelve are left up in the air. It is barely possible that they are the twelve sons of Jacob.[17]

To bring this subject to a conclusion—with all due respect to my friends and many I admire who hold the view that I once did, that the "twenty-four elders" are some kind of five-star generals of the angelic hosts who are always before the throne of God—I no longer believe that is accurate. Instead, as John Darby, a careful student of Bible prophecy who lived a century and a half ago, taught—these are men who represent Israel and the church, representatives of the twelve tribes of Israel and the twelve apostles to represent the Church. This view of a future event in heaven is a beautiful picture of the many things we share with the redeemed members of the nation of Israel.

This view also highlights the difference between Israel and the Church (1 Cor. 10:32). After the Church is raptured to be with Christ in His Father's house, Israel will go through the Tribulation here on earth. We will join them and the Tribulation saints after their resurrection, and we will all share the blessings of the Millennium and eternity together. Our Lord evidently has a slightly different relationship planned for Israel than He does for His Church, even in the Millennium. But we all will share its blessings and that of the eternal heaven as individuals, who can all sing the song of the redeemed because we have personally received Him who is "the Lamb of God, who takes away the sins of the world."

3. The Signs of Judgment

"From the throne came flashes of lightning, rumblings and peals of thunder." Three things are mentioned here: "lightning," "rumblings," and "peals of thunder," all proceeding from the throne of God. Lightning and thunder have long been associated with the concept of judgment; thus we conclude, since they come from the throne of God, that they are a prelude to the judgment that is about to fall upon the earth, as described in chapters 6–19. It should be remembered that the tribulation judgments come from the throne of God. They are not the result of the evil one human being does to another, but appear as the direct judgment of God.

4. The Seven Spirits of God

"Before the throne, seven lamps were blazing. These are the seven spirits of God." The seven lamps of fire, burning before the throne, are defined as "the seven spirits of God." We have already seen this description in Revelation 1:4, where John was apparently referring to the sevenfold characteristics of the Holy Spirit as revealed in Isaiah 11:2—

1. the Spirit of the Lord
2. the Spirit of wisdom
3. the Spirit of understanding
4. the Spirit of counsel
5. the Spirit of power
6. the Spirit of knowledge
7. the Spirit of the fear of the LORD.

The seven Spirits do not mean seven different Spirits, but the seven characteristics of the one Holy Spirit. It should be borne in mind, however, that these characteristics are not limited to His role in heaven, His role during the Tribulation, or His role during the Church Age, but are an eternal part of the Holy Spirit. Therefore, when we are filled with the Holy Spirit, in addition to the fruit of the Spirit found in Galatians 5:22, we should expect to manifest these characteristics—wisdom, understanding, counsel, power, knowledge, and reverence for the Lord.

5. The Sea of Glass

"Also before the throne there was what looked like a sea of glass, clear as crystal." It is impossible to be dogmatic as to the meaning of the sea of glass, though one can conclude it is meant to convey stability, for a glassy sea is a calm sea, untroubled by winds and storms. Two suggestions for the sea itself are (1) the Church at rest or (2) the Word of God, the latter taken from the sea of glass in Solomon's Temple, which symbolized the Word of God for the means of sanctification. So we are cleansed by "the washing with water through the word" (Eph. 5:26).

A sea in Scripture usually refers to people, and this is in accord with what we find in Revelation 15, where the Tribulation saints that have been martyred by the Antichrist stand on the sea of glass.

It would seem, then, that the sea of glass represents the sure foundation, the Word of God, our means of cleansing. The stability speaks of the completed sanctification and security of believers. One of the things that shakes our confidence or our feeling of security is sin. The strife that goes on in the lives of believers between the old self and the new self causes them to yearn for ultimate sanctification, when they will no longer be tossed about by the winds of life. Here we see the Tribulation believers after the Rapture, standing on a solid, untroubled foundation, the sea of glass.

6. The Four Living Creatures

"In the center, around the throne, were four living creatures, and they were covered with eyes, in front and in back." It is most unfortunate for readers of the KJV that the translators rendered the Greek word used here (*zoa*) as "beast." This word, from which we get our word "zoology," is better rendered "living creatures" or "animals." As we look at the description of these creatures, we find that they take on animal-like characteristics. These four living creatures are seraphim, described by Isaiah in his vision of the throne of God (Isa. 6:1–3). They have six wings and cry, "Holy, holy, holy is the Lord God Almighty."

There are many orders of angels of which the elders are leaders, but over the elders are seraphim, which number only four. It seems that they are engaged in the worship of God constantly, but their form suggests that they also have other duties to perform. Because of their characteristics, it may well be that they are leaders of the realm they depict. For example, note their forms:

A lion—leader of the kingdom of wild animals
A calf—leader of domestic animals
A man—leader of the angelic hosts responsible for the human race
A flying eagle—leader of the kingdom of the fowls of the air

7. The Heavenly Worship of Christ

"The living creatures give glory, honor and thanks to him who sits on the throne and who lives for ever and ever." This describes the fact that the Lord Jesus Christ is the object of worship in heaven. He is the One who sits on the throne, the object of their affections. The cause for this worship may well be linked with the fact that the Church will be raptured at this point, and for the first time believers will be gathered together before the throne in resurrected bodies, thus bringing to fulfillment the purpose of Christ's incarnation. Only the Lord Jesus Christ could have left the glories of heaven to take on the form of a man, identified himself with human beings, become their sin, and thus paid the penalty for their sin, as He did on Calvary's cross. As mighty as these celestial beings of the angelic order are, none of them could have qualified to redeem the human race from their sin. However, the blood of God's own Son could—and did!

These angelic beings seem to be responsible to God for humanity and were no doubt frustrated because Satan had perverted himself and subverted God's plan by bringing sin into the world. They stood by helplessly while generation after generation of human beings fell into sin and lost fellowship with God. This present act of worship seems to be their expression of devotion and adoration to the Lord Jesus Christ for redeeming from the earth what they could not redeem.

> "You are worthy, our Lord and God,
>   to receive glory and honor and power,
> for you created all things,
>   and by your will they were created
>   and have their being."   (Rev. 4:11)

The song these celestial beings sing is a song of glory and honor to God because He is the Creator of all things. This, of course, on the basis of John 1:3, is another evidence that the Lord Jesus Christ is the One being worshiped.

One cannot help but be moved at the loving concern and the feeling of adoration and worship in the heart of celestial beings because the Lord Jesus Christ redeemed human beings from sin. How much more should our hearts rejoice as we worship Him? We are the recipients of His redemption!

TWELVE

The Seven-Sealed Scroll

Revelation 5

"Then I saw in the right hand of him who sat on the throne a scroll with writing on both sides and sealed with seven seals" (Rev. 5:1). Whenever a chapter in the Bible opens with the Greek word *kai* (often translated "and"; NIV here, "then"), we know it should be joined to the preceding chapter. This is not only true in subject matter but also in chronology. It is as if after John has seen the throne of God, his attention focuses on an object in the hand of God, which brings us to the seven-sealed scroll.

Although the word "book" is used in the KJV, we should bear in mind that there were no hard-covered flat books during the lifetime of John. In those days and in the days of the Old Testament all books were scrolls of either papyrus or vellum.

There are three characteristics of this scroll. First, it was in the right hand of God; second, it was written on both sides; and third, it was sealed shut by seven seals. Someone has said, "The little seven-sealed book in the hand of the one on the throne mentioned in Revelation 5 contains the secret of the chapter that follows and is the key that opens the entire book of Revelation." There can be no question that this is a significant scroll, as determined by the events that follow.

THE CAUSE OF JOHN'S WEEPING

John saw "a mighty angel proclaiming in a loud voice, 'Who is worthy to break the seals and open the scroll?' But no one in heaven or on earth or under the earth could open the scroll or even look inside it" (Rev. 5:2–3).

It is evident at the outset that this is a scroll intensely related to the human race, for angelic beings are excluded from opening it. Instead the angel is looking for a human being. We therefore conclude that the book has something to do with human beings and their relationship to the earth, the home of the human race. In spite of that fact, no redeemed person in heaven, on earth, or under the earth (in Hades) is considered worthy to open the book.

The importance of the book is seen in the fact that John weeps when it is discovered that "no one was found who was worthy to open the scroll or look inside." What could cause a Spirit-filled man like John, lifted into heaven, to weep? These are not idle tears, induced because John just cannot satisfy his curiosity. No, his tears have a far deeper meaning!

The prophet Jeremiah warned Israel that if they did not repent of their sin and turn to God, they would go down into captivity for seventy years. Because they refused to heed the warning of God, their judgment was imminent. Through the same prophet of judgment, God promised that they would go down into captivity for seventy years but would one day return to the land. To prove to them that they would return, God told Jeremiah to do a strange thing. Hanamel, Jeremiah's cousin, had a piece of ground that he knew would soon be worthless. Since Nebuchadnezzar was about to capture Jerusalem, God caused Hanamel to go to Jeremiah and offer to see it. Jeremiah bought the property for

> seventeen shekels of silver. I signed and sealed the deed, had it witnessed, and weighed out the silver on the scales. I took the deed of purchase—the sealed copy containing the terms and conditions, as well as the unsealed copy—and I gave this deed to Baruch son of Neriah . . . in the presence of my cousin Hanamel and of the witnesses who had signed the deed and of all the Jews sitting in the courtyard of the guard. (Jer. 32:9–12)

The prophet then instructed his secretary, Baruch, to place the sealed scroll in an earthen jar, thus preserving it for his heirs. It was placed with the other papers, verifying the legal owners of property.

Although Jeremiah never lived to see the day when Israel went back into the land, his legal heir one day went before the proper authorities and, on the basis of his kinship to Jeremiah, proved that he was "worthy to open the book" and to own the property.

Essentially that is the scene in heaven. For all intents and purposes the seven-sealed scroll is the title deed to the earth. This title deed was given by God to Adam, who lost it through sin to Satan; for that reason Satan is in control of the world from the time of Adam until the glorious appearing of Christ. John weeps because he knows that this scroll represents the title deed to the earth and that as long as it is left sealed, Satan will remain in control of the earth.

THE LION-LAMB IS WORTHY

> Then one of the elders said to me, "Do not weep! See, the Lion of the tribe of Judah, the Root of David, has triumphed. He is able to open the scroll and its seven seals."
>
> Then I saw a Lamb, looking as if it had been slain, standing in the center of the throne, encircled by the four living creatures and the

> elders. He had seven horns and seven eyes, which are the seven spir-
> its of God sent out into all the earth. (Rev. 5:5–6)

As John looks, he sees a Lamb that appears as if it has been sacrificed already, possessing seven horns, seven eyes, and seven spirits. This gives us five characteristics of the Lord:

1. "The Lion of the tribe of Judah." The names of our Lord are never given by accident, but all convey a part of His nature. Since the lion is the king of beasts and since Judah is the ruling tribe of Israel, this indicates that Christ is to come as King to reign over human affairs.

2. "The Root of David." This, of course, refers to Jesus' incarnation or His first birth with His roots in the family of David.

3. "A Lamb, looking as if it had been slain." When Christ completed the work of redemption, He earned the title deed to the earth; as by Adam came sin, so by Christ came redemption. It is a beautiful picture that we see here! Even though the angel refers to our Lord in His glory as a Lion, indicating His power and might, John sees Him as a sacrificial Lamb, for John sees Him through eyes of faith. Those who reject Christ will see Him as a Lion when He comes to judge and to reign over them. Those who believe in Him will see Him as their sacrificial Lamb.

4. "He had seven horns." This indicates that the Lamb is not weak. A horn in Scripture indicates power (see Zech. 1:18, and the little horn of Dan. 7). The Lord Jesus said of Himself, "All authority in heaven and on earth has been given to me" (Matt. 28:18). When Christ came the first time, as a Lamb, though He displayed certain powers, He did not manifest all of His power. When He comes the next time, as a Lion, at His Glorious Appearing, it will be in the manifestation of His omnipotence, His all-consuming power.

5. "Seven eyes, which are the seven spirits of God sent out into all the earth." These eyes speak of the judgment of our Lord, including the seven characteristics of the Holy Spirit that rests on Him without measure (Isa. 11:2; John 3:34). When our Lord comes, He will know all that human beings have ever thought or done. Every deed will be brought into judgment. Note that seven is God's number of perfection; therefore when Christ, the Lion of the tribe of Judah, comes to judge the world at the end of the Tribulation, it will be as the perfect judge, who has all power and who knows all about humankind. It should also be borne in mind that He was the sacrificial Lamb, but people rejected Him. The unsaved rarely contemplate that the One who will judge them in eternity is the very One they spurn by rejecting today Christ Jesus as Savior and Lord.

The moment Christ takes the seven-sealed scroll, all the angelic beings in heaven fall down before Him, including the four living creatures and the twenty-four elders. Almost as a footnote, they are mentioned as having two things in their hands: (1) harps, indicating the music of heaven, and (2) golden bowls filled with the prayers of the saints. Although it is impossible to be dogmatic about these prayers, one is almost led to believe that they are unanswered prayers that will be answered at the Glorious Appearing of Christ. Many a Christian has gone out into eternity with the prayer of the Apostle John, "Come, Lord Jesus," still unanswered; this prayer will be answered in that day. Many a Christian has prayed as our Lord taught us to pray, "Your will be done on earth as it is in heaven." This will not be accomplished until Christ comes to set up His millennial rule. This is another indication that all prayer is answered, though we may not receive the answer in our lifetime.

A beautiful new song is sung by the heavenly singers that is self-explanatory (5:9–10):

> You are worthy to take the scroll
>   and to open its seals,
> because you were slain,
>   and with your blood you purchased men for God
>   from every tribe and language and people and nation.
> You have made them to be a kingdom and priests to serve our
>   God,
>   and they will reign on the earth.

As was pointed out in our discussion of the identity of the twenty-four elders, these elders are not singing about themselves, but about the worthy one who has redeemed the human race on the earth.

We must keep in perspective the dramatic scene in heaven. When John sees the book and discovers what it represents, the title deed to the earth, he sorrows because no one is worthy to open the book. Suddenly he finds that "the Lamb of God, who takes away the sin of the world" is worthy to open the book on the basis of what He has done for the human race. The angels' song indicates that He is worthy for three reasons:

1. "Because you were slain." This refers, of course, to Christ's mediatorial work on Calvary's cross.

2. "With your blood you purchased men for God from every tribe and language and people and nation." Since someone from every tribe and nation and tongue will be included in redemption, the 270 million people in the world today that do not have the Bible in their own mother tongue will hear about the Savior and His love. (More will be said concerning this in our study of Revelation 7.) This verse is particularly delightful for me when I think of the ministry of Mr. and Mrs. Phil Bair, Wycliffe Bible translators to the Lacondone Indians of Mexico. When I as in their home many years ago, they had been ministering to these Indians for eighteen years. One of the promises of God that spurred them

on was the assurance that one day a Lacondone Indian would be included in the redeemed. They have the promise of Almighty God as found in this verse.

3. "You have made them to be a kingdom and priests to serve our God, and they will reign on the earth." This, of course, refers to the fact that we are members of God's spiritual kingdom, into which we are born when we believe on the Lord Jesus Christ. It bears repeating that we are His priests, doing the work of priests, conveying to people the gospel in this age. When Christ comes again in His glory, we believers will be with Him to rule and reign with Him.

ANOTHER PROOF OF PRE-TRIBULATION RAPTURE

As mentioned in the preceding chapter, once I was convinced that the word "us" in 5:19 was indeed in most of the ancient manuscripts, it became apparent that the elders were all redeemed men. Once their human nature was confirmed, it became obvious that the Rapture was pictured by 4:1 as occurring before the Tribulation. For this scene, which is of the throne of God in heaven just before the seven-year Tribulation as defined in chapters 6–19, pictures twenty-four men or "elders" in the presence of God.

John, "the faithful witness," observes these events immediately *after* the Church Age has been concluded and just prior to the beginning of the Tribulation. These men, whether twelve who represent Israel and twelve who represent the church, or twenty-four outstanding Christian leaders in all church history, makes no difference—they all are redeemed men! They are redeemed saints who are in heaven just before the revelation of the Tribulation that follows. Like John, they are part of the pre-Tribulation Rapture in their glorified bodies, worshiping all three members of the Trinity. This scene in heaven does not occur in the middle of the Tribulation or at its end, but *before it begins*!

All of this points out a serious difficulty faced by our friends who hold to the post-Tribulation view that Christ will rapture his saints at the end of the Tribulation and return immediately for His Glorious Appearing. That view leaves little or no time for the Judgment Seat of Christ, the Marriage of the Lamb, and the Marriage Supper of the Lamb. Obviously the pre-Tribulation view allows ample time for these exciting events in heaven while the earth goes through the seven years of Tribulation.

Besides, verse 10 indicates that the redeemed saints will "be a kingdom and priests to serve our God, and they will reign on the earth." When will that reigning on earth occur? In the Millennium, of course. We will join the redeemed of the Tribulation to "reign with Christ a thousand years" (20:4).

Then I looked and heard the voice of many angels, numbering thousands upon thousands, and ten thousand times ten thousand. They encircled the throne and the living creatures and the elders. In a loud voice they sang:

> "Worthy is the Lamb, who was slain,
> to receive power and wealth and wisdom and strength
> and honor and glory and praise!"   (Rev. 5:11–12)

The enormity of the numbers here bedazzles the minds of most Christians. We are used to thinking about Christians in the vast minority when it comes to the billions who travel the "broad . . . road that leads to destruction . . ." in contrast to the "the [narrow] road that leads to life, and only a few find it" (Matt. 7:13–14). Personally, I think we are going to be amazed at the enormous number who will be in heaven through the sacrifice of the Son of God. This verse gives us a rare glimpse of the enormity of those in heaven, both angelic and human. My friend Dr. Morris captures that in the following explanation of the above verse:

> As John shared in the anthem of the redeemed multitudes, he next became aware of an even greater group joining in the heavenly chorus. The tremendous host of heaven was there too. The term "ten thousand" is actually "myriad," so that the number of angels is said to be "myriads of myriads, and thousands of thousands." This is not meant to be a precise count, of course, but simply to convey the thought of "innumerable." In fact, the same word ("myriad") is translated "innumerable" in Luke 12:1 and Hebrews 12:22. The latter reference, in fact, probably looks forward to this very gathering. "But ye are come unto Mount Zion, and unto the city of the living God, the heavenly Jerusalem, and to an innumerable company of angels, to the general assembly and church of the first-born, which are written in heaven, and to God the Judge of all, and to the spirits of just men made perfect, and to Jesus the mediator of the new covenant, and to the blood of sprinkling, that speaketh better things than that of Abel."
>
> Whatever the number of saved men and women there may be—quite possibly several billion at least—the number of angels must be still greater, since every believer probably has several angels assigned to his care in addition to all the angels with other ministries. The number is no doubt a finite number, but is so great it cannot be even estimated. And all this numberless host of mighty angels, assembled from the far reaches of the cosmos there at the throne in the heavenly city, suspended high above the earth, will be united with the redeemed saints in singing beautiful praises to the worthy Lamb.[18]

THE DESCRIPTION OF CHRIST BY ANGELS

Then I looked and heard the voice of many angels, numbering thousands upon thousands, and ten thousand times ten thousand. They encircled the throne and the living creatures and the elders. In a loud voice they sang:

"Worthy is the Lamb, who was slain,
to receive power and wealth and wisdom and strength
and honor and glory and praise!"   (Rev. 5:11–12)

In a day when humanistic people are unwilling to acknowledge Jesus Christ as more than a good man or a model example, we should note carefully what the angels of heaven, who know Him best, say of Him. They proclaim Him worthy to receive seven things—power, wealth, wisdom, strength, honor, glory, and blessing—which far outshadow any obeisance due to mortals. I joyfully accept the description of the angels as the only authentic portrait of Christ.

THE UNIVERSAL WORSHIP OF CHRIST

Then I heard every creature in heaven and on earth and under the earth and on the sea, and all that is in them, singing:

"To him who sits on the throne and to the Lamb
be praise and honor and glory and power,
for ever and ever!"

The four living creatures said, "Amen," and the elders fell down and worshiped.   (Rev. 5:13–14)

These verses, which almost seem like the second stanza of the song of the heavenly hosts, carry John beyond the Tribulation, beyond the Glorious Appearing, to the end of the Millennium, to the time of the Great White Throne Judgment, when every living creature will worship Christ. This passage of Scripture should be studied in connection with Philippians 2:9–11:

Therefore God exalted him to the highest place
and gave him the name that is above every name,
that at the name of Jesus every knee should bow,
in heaven and on earth and under the earth,
and every tongue confess that Jesus Christ is Lord,
to the glory of God the Father.

Both of these passages of Scripture clearly indicate that every living creature in heaven, on earth, under the earth, or in the sea, awaiting the

Day of Judgment, will one day worship Jesus Christ. That includes all those who in this life have voluntarily rejected Him. All those on earth will worship Him; all those under the earth and those in the sea, awaiting judgment, will at their resurrection be forced to worship Him just before they are cast into the lake of fire. What a tragedy!

THIRTEEN

The Tribulation Period

Daniel 9:24–27

As we come to Revelation 6, it becomes immediately apparent that we have reached the very heart of the book. As John beholds the Lord Jesus Christ, represented by a Lamb, breaking the first seal, we encounter the first of a long series of events that begin in heaven and are consummated on earth. A seal is broken in heaven and a horseman appears on earth. Each seal broken in heaven introduces a tragedy on earth.

With the breaking of the first seal and the appearance of the first of the horsemen of the apocalypse the dreaded period of time known as the Tribulation begins. This seven-year span of future world history, graphically described in 6:1–19:21, will be the darkest time the world has ever known.

The Tribulation is one of the most significant periods of God's dealing with humankind and certainly occupies a most prominent place in His prophetic plan. More space is dedicated to that little seven-year period than any other comparable time frame in the Bible. It is mentioned over fifty times in the Old Testament by such expressions as "the day of calamity," "day of wrath," "the day of the Lord's wrath," "the day of Jacob's trouble," "the day of vengeance of our God," "time of trouble," and "the day of the LORD." In every case it is talking about the nation of Israel.

There are over a dozen references to that period in the New Testament, the best known of which and the one from which it receives its official title is our Lord's designation translated in the KJV as "tribulation" in His Olivet Discourse (Matt. 24:21). Referring to the second half of that seven-year period and the most severe time the world has ever known or "ever will know" is rightly translated in the NIV as a time of "distress unequaled" in all of history.

It has been my observation that our mid-Tribulation friends tend to push the "distress" of that terrible time of persecution of saints and tribulation for the world into the latter half of the period—after they are gone. In the case of post-Tribulationists, they tend to soften the reality of the prophecies of the entire period and make them less than the trying time they will actually be. It is difficult to see how the killing of half the world's population and about a billion martyred Christians can be anything but a time of enormous tribulation or "distress," unlike anything the world has ever known. Escaping this period in a pre-Tribulation Rapture is one reason it qualifies to be called "the blessed hope."

To understand the Tribulation period as described in the book of Revelation, one should understand that it is a very special day in God's plan for His nation, Israel. To see this clearly, we must turn to the book of Daniel and examine Daniel's seventy weeks of years.

THE SEVENTY WEEKS OF DANIEL

Daniel 9 reveals that after the nation of Israel had been in captivity about sixty-eight years, Daniel was diligently studying the prophetic word of God. He saw in Jeremiah 25:11–12 that Israel would serve the king of Babylon for seventy years:

> This whole country will become a desolate wasteland, and these nations will serve the king of Babylon seventy years.
>
> "But when the seventy years are fulfilled, I will punish the king of Babylon and his nation, the land of the Babylonians, for their guilt," declares the LORD, "and will make it desolate forever."

Daniel tells us in 9:2, after the Persians had conquered the Babylonians, "I, Daniel, understood from the Scriptures, according to the word of the LORD given to Jeremiah the prophet, that the desolation of Jerusalem would last seventy years." At this point Daniel begins to pray, confessing his sins and the sins of the nation of Israel. After that the Lord sends the angel Gabriel with a special message to Daniel, which according to verses 22–23 is to "to give you insight and understanding" that he should, "therefore, consider the message and understand the vision." Here is the exact vision given to Daniel.

> "Seventy 'sevens' are decreed for your people and your holy city to finish transgression, to put an end to sin, to atone for wickedness, to bring in everlasting righteousness, to seal up vision and prophecy and to anoint the most holy.
>
> "Know and understand this: From the issuing of the decree to restore and rebuild Jerusalem until the Anointed One, the ruler, comes, there will be seven 'sevens,' and sixty-two 'sevens.' It will be rebuilt with streets and a trench, but in times of trouble. After the sixty-two 'sevens,' the Anointed One will be cut off and will have nothing. The people of the ruler who will come will destroy the city and the sanctuary. The end will come like a flood: War will continue until the end, and desolations have been decreed. He will confirm a covenant with many for one 'seven.' In the middle of the 'seven' he will put an end to sacrifice and offering. And on a wing of the temple he will set up an abomination that causes desolation, until the end that is decreed is poured out on him." (Dan. 9:24–27)

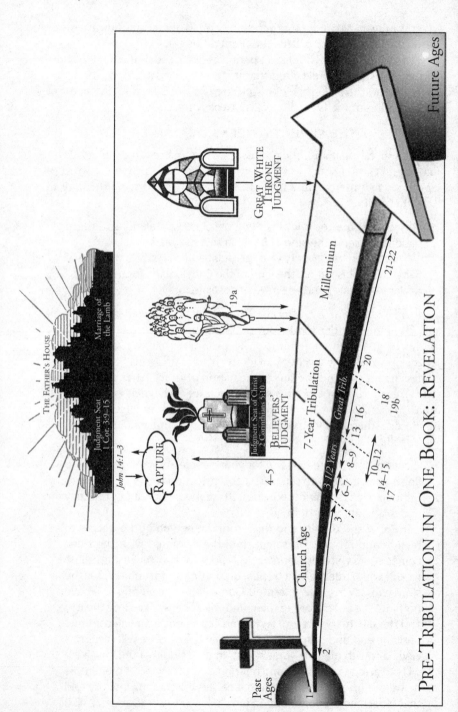

PRE-TRIBULATION IN ONE BOOK: REVELATION

Seventy Weeks Means Seventy Years

It is most important to understand the time element involved. The Hebrew word translated "seven" actually means a unit of seven rather than seven days, and only the context reveals how much time is involved. The word should literally be translated "sevens" or "heptads."

We have a similar expression in English. For example, if I say a dozen, I could mean a dozen weeks or a dozen years; or I could say a gross, which limits me to a unit of 144 but does not tell me what that 144 is. The same is true of this Hebrew word.

This is not as complicated as it may seem. For if we study the context, it is clear from both Daniel and Revelation 12 that these sevens are weeks of years or heptads of years. Thus we find that Daniel's seventy weeks are literally seventy units of seven years, or 490 years.

The Three Divisions of the Seventy Weeks of Years

Daniel 9:25 tells us that these 490 years are divided into three groupings, which we must understand in order to comprehend the time element.

1. Seven sevens of years equals forty-nine years. "Know and understand this: From the issuing of the decree to restore and rebuild Jerusalem until the Anointed One, the ruler, comes, there will be" seven heptads or forty-nine years. A study of Jewish history reveals that from the going forth of the decree of Cyrus, it took the Jews under both Ezra and Nehemiah forty-nine years to complete the building of the walls of the city of Jerusalem. Thus we have the first unit predicted.

2. Sixty-two sevens (or "weeks" in the older translations) of years equals 434 years. These next 434 years, described as 62 heptads, were predicted to be "times of trouble," and certainly that is accurate. It was a period of silence from God until John the Baptist came on the scene. It was a time of weakness in Israel, culminating in Roman domination at the time of Christ. This period was predicted to end when the "Anointed One will be cut off and will have nothing." Thus we see that this second period of time extended from the rebuilding of the Temple to the crucifixion of Christ, a total of 434 years.

Verification of the exact dates is impossible, since the Medo-Persians were notoriously poor historians. The best evidence we have is fulfilled prophecy. Since all other prophecies about Christ have been fulfilled without deviation, we can well assume the fulfillment of this one. Sir Robert Anderson's masterful book, *The Coming Prince,* shows that Christ's coming into Jerusalem the Sunday before His crucifixion occurred in exactly the right year. To my knowledge, his book has never been refuted.

3. One week equals seven years. Daniel 9:27 predicts that *he* ("the ruler who will come," or the Antichrist, who will obviously be a Roman, since he will be of the people that are to destroy Jerusalem) will make a covenant with Israel for one week. That covenant, which will cover seven years, has not been made since the crucifixion of Christ but is a covenant that will be made in the days of the Antichrist. Even though he will break the covenant in the midst of the seven years, it will still be part of the period of time that Gabriel predicted would be "decreed for your people and your holy city" (9:24).

The first two periods of these seventy units of years total 483 years. Please see the chart on "The Seventy Weeks of Daniel" and note that from the going forth of the decree of Cyrus to the crucifixion of Jesus Christ, the Messiah, was 483 years. Thus all but one "week," or heptad, of Israel's prophetically determined history has been accomplished. The final period of time will be such a time in history that the people of God are referred to as "the desolate."

The latter part of Daniel 9:26 indicates that there will be a predicted time of interruption in this prophetic calendar: "War will continue until the end, and desolations have been decreed." This corresponds with Isaiah's reference to "the year of the LORD's favor" (Isa. 61:2), which is the Christian dispensation—the year of God's grace to the Gentiles. This, however, culminates in Isaiah 61:2 with "the day of vengeance of our God," which is the resumption of God's prophetic calendar for Israel, called the seventieth week of Daniel or the Tribulation period.

Man Will Never Destroy the World

We hear a great deal of speculation as to whether or not human beings will ever destroy the world. That this could never happen is seen by the fact that God projects seven years in the future destined for His people Israel, which will be consummated in the physical coming of Christ to the earth to set up His millennial kingdom. Everything God determines and predicts in His Word will happen. Therefore we can say without reservation that human beings will not destroy the world.

THE CHRONOLOGY OF REVELATION

Turning again to Revelation 6, which introduces the Tribulation period, we must examine this book carefully for the chronology or sequence of events. To assume that the book of Revelation is intended to unfold step by step is to prepare oneself for hopeless confusion. Because of the variety of subjects dealt with, there must be some overlapping, but because the first six chapters fall into a natural sequence, some readers are inclined to assume that this is true of the entire book.

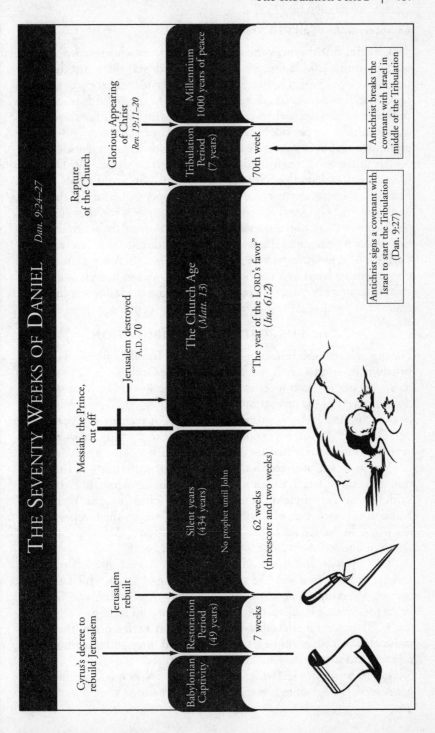

THE SEVENTY WEEKS OF DANIEL   *Dan. 9:24–27*

Cyrus's decree to rebuild Jerusalem

Jerusalem rebuilt

Messiah, the Prince, cut off

Jerusalem destroyed
A.D. 70

Rapture of the Church

Glorious Appearing of Christ
Rev. 19:11–20

Babylonian Captivity

Restoration Period
(49 years)

Silent years
(434 years)

No prophet until John

The Church Age
(*Matt. 13*)

Tribulation Period
(7 years)

Millennium
1000 years of peace

7 weeks

62 weeks
(threescore and two weeks)

"The year of the LORD's favor"
(*Isa. 61:2*)

70th week

Antichrist signs a covenant with Israel to start the Tribulation (Dan. 9:27)

Antichrist breaks the covenant with Israel in middle of the Tribulation

Chapters 6, 8–9, and 16 Are the Keys

Chapter 6 introduces the seal judgments, which make up the first quarter of the Tribulation period. The seventh seal then introduces the seven trumpets, which indicates that we are carried into the second quarter of the Tribulation (described in chs. 8–9). The seventh trumpet, in turn, introduces the seven bowl judgments, which comprise the last half of the Tribulation period. Everything else between chapters 7–8 must be placed within the consecutive events of these three judgments.

An illustration often used by the late Bible teacher, Dr. David L. Cooper, will explain this. He suggested that in a fireworks display, bright objects will scatter through the heavens in proper sequence and then suddenly one will explode into seven others. Then, just when they are almost gone, one of them bursts into several more. John saw the seven seals broken one at a time; then the seventh one introduced the seven trumpets. Each of these judgments, whether breaking a seal, blowing a trumpet, or pouring out a bowl, is a symbolic announcement in heaven of an event that actually takes place on earth. By examining the following chart, the reader can see that these judgments take place consecutively.

THE PURPOSE OF THE TRIBULATION

Having pointed out the fact of the seven-year Tribulation period that will yet come upon this earth, we should examine God's purpose in sending it. We are not left to conjecture, for it was revealed to Daniel at the same time he received the prediction of the "seventy 'sevens'" (which both the context and the Hebrew word mean "weeks" of years or 490 years; note esp. Dan. 9:24). God never does anything without a purpose, and in this verse we find that He had six things in mind.

1. "To finish transgression." This time of suffering will finish the transgression of Israel, which is the rejection of her Messiah. During the Tribulation, the people of Israel will turn to Christ in great revival and will become witnesses who will go forth and preach the Gospel around the world, as we will see in the study of Revelation 7. Actually, the Tribulation period will help cause a great revival in Israel.

2. "To put an end to sin." The words "put an end" literally mean "to seal up." This period will end with the binding of Satan, which will "seal up" sin. Humanity's cup of iniquity is filled to overflowing, and God will bring judgment on the earth for their rejection of His Son.

3. "To atone for wickedness." Again, this is a reference to the revival of Israel, when they will be reconciled to God through Him whom they rejected and whom they asked Pilate to crucify.

4. "To bring in everlasting righteousness." When Israel experiences her revival, the age of righteousness or the millennial kingdom of Christ

Seal Judgments Rev. 6

Trumpet Judgments Rev. 8, 9

Bowl Judgments Rev. 15, 16

RAPTURE

GLORIOUS APPEARING

FIRST HALF OF TRIBULATION | THE GREAT TRIBULATION

will be ushered in. Though there will be a brief insurrection at the end, it will be so short-lived as not to interrupt this final period of everlasting righteousness that will lead into the new era of the future, described in Revelation 21–22.

5. "To seal up vision and prophecy." When Israel has turned to Christ, there will no longer be a need for prophets' visions and prophecy.

6. "To anoint the most holy." This could refer to the holy place on Mount Moriah where Solomon's Temple was built over the place where Abraham had prepared to offer Isaac as a sacrifice, symbolically preparing the way for Israel to have her sins cleansed through the anticipation of the eventual death of Christ on the cross. This purpose may also refer to the millennial kingdom that will consummate the Tribulation and usher in that age of righteousness for which all Christians yearn—the only answer to the heartaches and problems of this world.

WHAT BEGINS THE TRIBULATION PERIOD

The actual event that inaugurates the Tribulation is found in Daniel 9:27 when the Antichrist, "the ruler who will come," makes a covenant with

Israel for seven years. Even though he will break that covenant, his signing will trigger the prophetic clock of God, and from that moment on only seven years will be left for the human race on the earth. One of the reasons we know Christ is coming *before* the Tribulation to rapture His Church is because the Rapture is a secret thing. The Glorious Appearing will not be secret but well known, for exactly seven years will elapse from the signing of the covenant to the Glorious Appearing of Christ on the earth.

When Christ raptures the Church, the Antichrist may make a covenant with Israel the next day, the next week, or who knows when. There are sufficient signs existing today to indicate that this event could take place soon: for example, Israel's return into the land of Palestine to become a nation, with whom the Antichrist will deal; the one-world church that will dominate the first half of the Tribulation period; and the craze for one-world government, already in existence and continuing to gather momentum until it culminates in the signing of the covenant between the Antichrist and Israel. From that point God's prophetic clock will begin to tick and humanity will have only seven years left.

WHO WILL BE IN THE TRIBULATION

Since it seems evident that the coming of Christ is close at hand, people living today are keenly interested in whether or not they will have to live under the Antichrist during the Tribulation. In all probability most of the present generation *will* go into the Tribulation.

The great exception to that is the Church of Jesus Christ. If you are a member of the body of Christ—that is, if you have personally invited Jesus Christ into your heart—you will *not* go into the Tribulation. The Bible tells us in 1 Thessalonians 1:10 that the Lord Jesus "rescues us from the coming wrath," referring to the Tribulation period. Revelation 3:10 also clarifies that the church of Philadelphia, which is the present-day church of true believers, will be delivered from the Tribulation: "Since you have kept my command to endure patiently, I will also keep you from the hour of trial that is going to come upon the whole world to test those who live on the earth."

In the final analysis, then, *you* decide whether or not you will go into the Tribulation. Your acceptance or rejection of Jesus Christ determines your relation to that time of great misery and heartache. If you accept Jesus Christ, you will be raptured out before it begins. If you have rejected Him, then according to all that the Bible teaches you will be one of those unfortunate individuals who will live at the time of the greatest misery in all the history of humankind.

FOURTEEN

The Seal Judgments

Revelation 6

This tired old planet has come under cruel times of famine, catastrophe, dictatorship, and many other causes of suffering. But Revelation 6 introduces the most awesome period of time the world has ever known. This seven-year period decreed by God is for the primary purpose of shaking human beings loose from a false sense of security. Then perhaps they may call on the name of the Lord just before the end of the age. How well God achieves this purpose will be seen in our study of chapter 7.

The first of the three chronological judgments—seals, trumpets, and bowls—is set forth in chapter 6. Some Bible teachers see enough similarity in these judgments to suggest that they run concurrently. That is, the first seal will occur at the same time as the blowing of the first trumpet and the pouring of the first bowl. Certainly all three sets of judgments tend to build up intensity as they get to numbers five, six, and seven. The problem with that idea is that it completely overlooks the fact that the opening of the seventh seal introduces the trumpet judgments of chapters 8–9, and the blowing of the seventh trumpet introduces the seven bowls of chapter 16. Therefore we may conclude that the three judgments run chronologically and represent periods of the Tribulation.

The seal judgments cover approximately the first quarter of the Tribulation or the first twenty-one months.

THE FOUR HORSEMEN OF THE APOCALYPSE

The first four seals reveal horses and riders in the form of striking imagery. An examination of the context indicates that it is clearly a dramatic presentation of literal facts. It is not God's intent to convey individual personality through these horsemen but world conditions. That they all do not refer to specific people can readily be seen by noting that the fourth horseman is called death, and death is not a person.

The four horsemen present the picture of man's inhumanity to man. They seem to be a divine prediction of the affairs of humankind that will cause much human suffering. This is not new, for those in control of the affairs of this world have a history of causing their fellow human beings much suffering, with false hopes of peace followed by wars, famines, and death.

THE FIRST SEAL — THE RIDER ON THE WHITE HORSE

I watched as the Lamb opened the first of the seven seals. Then I heard one of the four living creatures say in a voice like thunder, "Come!" I looked, and there before me was a white horse! Its rider held a bow, and he was given a crown, and he rode out as a conqueror bent on conquest.   (Rev. 6:1–2)

Immediately after the Lamb opens one of the seals, the first of the prophetically well-known "Four Horsemen of the Apocalypse" appears. Since there are three more horses and riders to follow with the successive breaking of the other seals, it is important that we identify this first rider, as a key to understanding the three that follow him.

The Antichrist

The Antichrist and his kingdom are obviously what is symbolized by the rider on the white horse. Emperors such as Napoleon, Alexander the Great, and many other would-be conquerors rode on horses. The purpose of this rider is clearly stated: "a conqueror bent on conquest." This is none other than "the little horn," that "willful king" that Bible students have been anticipating for many years. One interesting characteristic of his coming is that he has a bow in his hand, symbolic of aggressive warfare, but no arrow, indicating that he will conquer by diplomacy rather than by war. Ushering in a false peace, he will be the superman who promises to solve all the world's problems. That he will be ultimately victorious is seen by the fact that he has a crown on his head.

Interdependence among nations today is increasing at a rapid pace. In spite of the obvious and flagrant uselessness of the United Nations, it is being heralded by many world leaders as the only answer to world peace. The international hysteria of nuclear warfare has created a phobia in the minds of people who will never be satisfied until they have a one-world government. The stupidity of such a possibility is completely ignored by the idealistic aspirations of millions. The fact that socialist thinking and subversive activity dominates the United Nations does not deter the advocates of one-world government. Neither does the fact that socialism has never worked in any country of the world to improve the quality of life. These people dream of a one-world socialist world (without God).

Their enthusiasm has not abated over the years, although many small new nations are given equal vote with mature nations like our own, and two-thirds of the voting power resides in the hands of 10 percent of the world's population, which won 5 percent of the world's land area. Dr. J. Vernon McGee once told of a woman in Arkansas who named the United Nations as the beneficiary of her $700,000 estate in the fervent hope that this relatively small contribution could be of some effect in bringing about universal peace on earth and good will among humankind. Doubtless this poor woman never dreamed that her money would be used for a spying headquarters by communists and socialists against her own nation. Nor did she ever dream that her money would be used to help finance the butchery of innocent victims in Katanga in an effort to force the typical communist coalition government upon the people.

In spite of all these things, some of the wealthiest foundations in the United State are doing everything humanly possible to brainwash the population through television and other mass communication with the idea that the only solution to the world's problems is the United Nations. If this is not setting the United Nations in a perfect position to make room for the Antichrist and his one-world government, it is at least preparing the thinking of the people for Antichrist's eventual government.

Russia to Be Destroyed

The way this master diplomat, the Antichrist, *could* conquer the world through his sudden diplomacy is to offer peace and prosperity to humankind. In all likelihood, this could be accomplished if Russia and her cohorts were out of the way. Ezekiel 38–39 tells us that Russia will conceive of the idea of conquering Israel. Just at the moment when she is preparing to do so, God will supernaturally destroy Russia. In the wake of this destruction, the Antichrist could very well offer peace to the entire world in order to avoid any further wars between nations.

When will Russia be destroyed? It is impossible to be dogmatic in answering this question. At the latest, it will occur at the beginning of the Tribulation, for it will take seven years to burn the implements of war after God has wrought His destruction on Russia (Ezek. 39:9). It is unthinkable that this would go on during the Millennium; therefore it must come at the very beginning of the Tribulation or even before it.

It is *possible* that Russia will be destroyed before the Rapture of the Church. There is nothing that demands it, for the Lord can come at any time. However, there is no reason to believe that Russia will not be destroyed before the Rapture. Ezekiel 39:9–10 indicates that for seven winters the people of Israel will burn the leftover implements of war. Since the Jews will be persecuted by the Antichrist for the last three and a half years of the Tribulation, that may suggest Russia and her Arab allies will be destroyed at least three and a half years prior to the beginning of the Tribulation. It could, of course, be more. One of the mysteries of prophecy is whether Russia is destroyed before the Rapture or after it occurs.

If the Antichrist signs a covenant with Israel immediately after the Rapture of the Church, thus beginning the Tribulation, it is highly probable that Russia will be destroyed *before* the Rapture. However, if there is a period of time between the Rapture of the Church and the beginning of the Tribulation, the Church could be raptured, Russia destroyed, and then the Antichrist set up his one-world government. All the more reason Christian's should be ready at any moment to "depart and be with Christ" in the Rapture. It can come at any time.

Although all the world leaders promise peace to the masses, the human race does not have the capacity to fulfill that promise, no matter who they are or what nation they represent. The Antichrist will be no exception! For we will see that his false promises of peace, though giving him control of the world, are impossible for him to fulfill.

THE SECOND SEAL — THE RIDER ON THE RED HORSE

When the Lamb opened the second seal, I heard the second living creature say, "Come!" Then another horse came out, a fiery red one. Its rider was given power to take peace from the earth and to make men slay each other. To him was given a large sword.   (Rev. 6:3–4)

The red horse is obviously a symbol of war, for he has the ability to "take peace from the earth and to make men slay each other." This is also evidenced by the fact that a great sword is given to him. Obviously, in the Antichrist's takeover of the world, some dissatisfied nations will have waited too long to make their play to avoid his domination. Yet, rather than remain slaves, they will revolt, thus inaugurating a world war. Although their attempt to throw off the shackles of the Antichrist will be unsuccessful, it is evident from the opening of the next seals that this will be a widespread and bloody war.

THE THIRD SEAL — THE RIDER ON THE BLACK HORSE

When the Lamb opened the third seal, I heard the third living creature say, "Come!" I looked, and there before me was a black horse! Its rider was holding a pair of scales in his hand. Then I heard what sounded like a voice among the four living creatures, saying, "A quart of wheat for a day's wages, and three quarts of barley for a day's wages, and do not damage the oil and the wine!"   (Rev. 6:5–6)

The black horse is an evident symbol of famine. Black is used to depict famine in other portions of Scripture (Jer. 4:28; Lam. 4:8–9), and famine often follows war (as it did after World War I).

Inflation also tends to grip the world right after a world war. Such will be the case during the Tribulation. The balances in the hand of the rider on the black horse indicate the scarcity of food. In fact, a penny is the biblical reference to the equivalent of a person's wage for one day (Matt. 20:2, 9). Three measures of barley are about a pint, a minimum daily sustenance diet. This, then, indicates that a person will have to work for a whole day just to earn enough money to live, which will leave nothing for the family or the elderly. On this basis we can predict that all Social Security and other means of "preparing for our old age" will come to an untimely and unsuccessful end.

The rich, however, are not so injured, as indicated by the fact that the rider on the black horse is instructed not to "damage the oil and the wine," which are traditionally foods of the rich. As in the case of all war and resulting famine, this famine will take a heavy toll on the common people.

THE FOURTH SEAL — THE RIDER ON THE PALE HORSE

When the Lamb opened the fourth seal, I heard the voice of the fourth living creature say, "Come!" I looked, and there before me was a pale horse! Its rider was named Death, and Hades was following close behind him. They were given power over a fourth of the earth to kill by sword, famine and plague, and by the wild beasts of the earth. (Rev. 6:7–8)

The pale horse is literally livid or corpse-like, signifying death. The death rate of the first twenty-one months of the Tribulation period will be tremendously high as a result of war, famine, and inflation. In fact, one-fourth of all the world's population will die. According to the present world census, that would total about a billion and a half people—some killed by the edge of the sword, some by hunger, and some by "wild beasts of the earth." This latter phrase may mean a revolt against humanity on the part of the animal kingdom, or it may be a symbolic use of the words "beasts," relating to human governments. In the book of Daniel, human kingdoms are pictured by God as beasts. Also in Revelation 13, the beast that comes out of the sea symbolizes the Antichrist and his government. In any event, one-fourth of the world's population will be wiped out as a result of the Antichrist's greedy confiscation of world power.

The fact that Hades follows the pale horse of death indicates that these are unsaved dead. A believer who receives Christ during the Tribulation will not go to Hades, which is a place reserved for unbelievers as they await the Great White Throne Judgment (Rev. 20). Without being dogmatic, I suggest for your consideration that individuals who receive the mark of the beast (Rev. 13) will be those who die during this period. My reason for stating so will be given more clearly when we get to chapter 13.

THE FIFTH SEAL — THE MARTYRED TRIBULATION SAINTS

When he opened the fifth seal, I saw under the altar the souls of those who had been slain because of the word of God and the testimony they had maintained. They called out in a loud voice, "How long, Sovereign Lord, holy and true, until you judge the inhabitants of the earth and avenge our blood?" Then each of them was given a white robe, and they were told to wait a little longer, until the number of

their fellow servants and brothers who were to be killed as they had
been was completed.   (Rev. 6:9–11)

Chapter 7 will introduce the fact that at the beginning of the Tribulation there will be a great soul harvest throughout the world. The opening of this fifth seal clearly teaches that after this has begun, there will be
a time of great personal persecution for the children of God. These are
Tribulation saints, individuals who had not received Christ at the time of
the Rapture, before the Tribulation began, but did receive Him as a result
of the faithful witnesses depicted in chapter 7. They will be martyred
"because of the word of God and the testimony they had maintained."

The world despises a clear-cut testimony based on God's Word, and
that hatred will be given free reign during the Tribulation period, resulting in an agonizing time of persecution for God's people. Even though
these saints inquire of the Lord, "How long, Sovereign Lord," others will
be killed for their testimony. Their prayer will not deter persecution,
because it is a time that must be "completed." We know that these people
are believers, for verse 11 indicates that each one is clothed in "a white
robe." It is comforting to know that although this time must be "completed," it is also only "a little season" (KJV). This will probably be the
greatest period of cruelty to Christians the world has ever known. Many
of the believers referred to in Revelation 7:9 as "a great multitude that
no one could count," will probably be slain.

THE SIXTH SEAL — CATASTROPHE ON EARTH

"I watched as he opened the sixth seal. There was a great earthquake. The
sun turned black like sackcloth made of goat hair, the whole moon
turned blood red" (Rev. 6:12). When the sixth seal is opened, the earth
is violently shaken by a giant earthquake, indicating that it is the great day
of God's wrath. Following the persecution of His saints, He will show
His displeasure on the earth for this persecution.

Although there is some conjecture to the contrary, this seems to be a
description of a physical shaking of the earth caused by earthquakes and
volcanic eruptions. Such things have happened before. Earthquakes in
Northern Peru in 1970 took almost 67,000 lives. A professor once stated
that in the last four thousand years earthquakes have caused a loss of
thirteen million lives, and he claimed the most awful earthquake is yet to
come. Dr. Robert Thieme tells of the eruption on August 27, 1883, of
Krakatau on an island in the Dutch East Indies. The explosion was heard
in Rodriguez, South America, three thousand miles away. As a result of
the volcano, the sun was blotted out. Volcanic ash makes the moon look
red and blots out the sun, for after the eruption of Krakatau, it is said
that the sun was blotted from view at Batavia, a hundred miles away. At
Bondune, 150 miles away, the sun was blotted out and the moon

appeared red. Tidal waves traveled as far as Cape Horn, seven thousand miles away, and in all 36,000 people were killed.

"And the stars in the sky fell to earth, as late figs drop from a fig tree when shaken by a strong wind" (Rev. 6:13). This verse indicates that meteors will fall to the ground and hit as hard, unripe things.

"The sky receded like a scroll, rolling up, and every mountain and island was removed from its place" (Rev. 6:14). This catastrophe will apparently bring about fantastic changes on the physical earth.

"Then the kings of the earth, the princes, the generals, the rich, the mighty, and every slave and every free man hid in caves and among the rocks of the mountains" (Rev. 6:15). Great fear will grip human hearts, but because of their stubborn, willful, rebellious ways, instead of turning to God in the hour of peril they will hide in the rocks and the dens of the earth. The cataclysm will be so gigantic in proportions that even the great people of the earth will have no place to hide. Who knows what will happen to the poor?

"They called to the mountains and the rocks, 'Fall on us and hide us from the face of him who sits on the throne and from the wrath of the Lamb! For the great day of their wrath has come, and who can stand?'" (Rev. 6:16–17). It seems evident from these verses that the world will know that this is a judgment from the Lord Jesus Christ, for they refer to Him as "the Lamb."

These people will also be fully aware that they are in the Tribulation period. The fact that the fifth seal delineates the large scale persecution of Christians during the Tribulation prepares us for the opening of the sixth seal. That is followed suddenly by this great catastrophe, which in turn leads the world to recognize that this is the judgment of God because they have persecuted the followers of the Lamb of God. Suddenly they will recognize that they are being judged and will be conscious that there is no place to hide. Oh, that people in that day will have enough sense to recognize that the Lord is their defense, as did the people in Nahum's day (Nah. 1:5–7) in a similar experience. These sixth-seal catastrophes are only an introduction to the great cataclysms that will come on the earth during the remainder of the Tribulation.

The first twenty-one months of the Tribulation period consist of horrifying events. After the Antichrist assumes worldwide control, world war, famine, inflation, and the death of 25 percent of the world's population will follow. Then will occur a great persecution of God's people, followed by the catastrophic judgment of God. If this passage of Scripture teaches anything, it instructs us that the Tribulation is a period no one should enter. The wonderful thing is, you don't have to! If you have received the Lord Jesus Christ as your Savior, you will never go into this period of the Tribulation.

FIFTEEN

The 144,000 Servants of God

Revelation 7

Every spiritually minded Christian is interested in revival! One of the most frequent questions I am asked when holding prophetic conferences is, "Do you think there will ever be a great worldwide revival?" My answer to this is always an unqualified "Yes, but not as you think." I then go on to explain the biblical teaching that until the time of the Rapture of the Church, there will be a falling away, apostasy, a decline in the moving of the Spirit of God, so much so that the Lord Jesus said of those days, "However, when the Son of Man comes, will he find faith on the earth?" (Luke 18:8).

However, the greatest revival the world has ever known is yet to come. It will not occur within the Church Age but during the Tribulation period. This coming worldwide revival is prophetically described in Revelation 7, appearing right after the seal judgments to indicate that it will take place during the first twenty-one months of the Tribulation. Evidently, while the Antichrist is making his political advance, the Holy Spirit will move in the hearts of millions of people, leading them to a saving knowledge of Christ.

THE WORK OF ANGELS

A detailed study of the work of angels in the book of Revelation reveals that they are the special ministers of God, administering His plans for the earth. In chapters 2–3 they are seen as messengers assigned to individual churches. In chapter 8 they present the trumpet judgments. Here we find that they control the forces of nature. Actually, in chapter 7 the angels supervise the administration of two things:

1. They control the wind from the four corners of the earth. "After this I saw four angels standing at the four corners of the earth, holding back the four winds of the earth to prevent any wind from blowing on the land or on the sea or on any tree" (Rev. 7:1).

2. They seal the servants of God, the 144,000 Tribulation witnesses. Since the sixth seal takes place toward the end of the first quarter of the Tribulation, we find that the destroying angel is ordered to wait until the work of sealing is finished. This indicates that at the beginning of the Tribulation, the 144,000 servants of God will be sealed and begin their

ministry of preaching the gospel, attended by a mighty worldwide soul harvest that will culminate in a time of severe persecution for believers, inspired by the Antichrist. This accords with the breaking of the fifth seal; at this time the sealing angel will have finished his work and the destroying angel will be permitted to hurt the earth and the sea, ushering in the sixth seal.

THE 144,000 SERVANTS OF GOD

Few passages of Bible prophecy have been so misunderstood and distorted as to their proper meaning as verse 4. Dr. Harry A. Ironside gives this explanation.

> I am sure that many of my hearers have often been perplexed by conflicting theories regarding the 144,000. The way in which so many unscriptural and often positively heretical sects arrogate to themselves this title would be amusing, if it were not so sad. You are perhaps aware that the Seventh-Day Adventists apply it to the faithful of their communion, who will be found observing the Jewish Sabbath at the Lord's return. They suppose that these will be raptured when the Lord descends, and judgment poured out upon the rest of the church. Then we have the followers of the late Pastor Russell (Jehovah's Witnesses) who teach that the 144,000 include only the "overcomers" of their persuasion who continue faithful to the end, following the teaching of the system commonly called "Millennial Dawnism." That very absurd and weird cult known as "The Flying Roll" makes claim to the same thing; only with them, the 144,000 are those who will have their blood so cleansed that they cannot die, but will have immortal life on this earth! Besides these, there are many other sects, whose leaders consider their own peculiar followers will be the 144,000 sealed ones at the end time. All of these, however, overlook a very simple fact, which if observed, would save them from their folly. That is, *the 144,000 are composed of 12,000 from each tribe of the children of Israel. There is not a Gentile among them....* Whenever I meet people who tell me they belong to the 144,000, I always ask them, "Which tribe, please?" and they are invariably put to confusion for want of an answer.[19]

Who Are the 144,000?

Because of widespread confusion in regard to these 144,000, we must take time to examine the subject. If we let the "plain sense of Scripture make common sense," it becomes clear that the 144,000 are Jews. For John specifically states, "Then I heard the number of those who were sealed: 144,000 from all the tribes of Israel" (Rev. 7:4).

Twelve thousand from each of the twelve tribes means exactly 12,000! First Kings 19 tells us that in Elijah's day God had kept for Himself seven thousand prophets who had not bowed their knees to Baal. No one seems to question the fact that He had "seven thousand prophets." Why should there be any difference regarding the 144,000? It simplifies the Bible interpretation greatly if we accept God's Word at face value and do not try to force upon it any other meaning than that which it naturally conveys. There will be twelve thousand Jews from each of the twelve tribes of Israel, making a total of 144,000.

The word "servants," from the Greek word *doulos,* is the same word used by the Apostle Paul and by James when referring to themselves as the "servants" or bond-slaves of Jesus Christ. The chief function of a servant of Jesus Christ, no matter what his or her occupation or dispensation, is to communicate the gospel of the grace of God. That these "servants of God" will be faithful in communicating His message is seen from the fact that they experience such fantastic results, as will be described from verse 9 of our text.

These servants will be inspired by the fact that they will understand the book of Revelation, which is given of God "to show his servants what must soon take place" (Rev. 1:1). Although they will go through a great time of persecution, they will have the comfort of knowing the duration of the Tribulation and can actually anticipate the astounding events that will take place through a study of this last book in God's revealed plan.

God's Seal on Their Foreheads

In some manner, these servants will have the seal of God on their foreheads (Rev. 7:3). We do not know of what this seal will consist, but the text suggests it will be visible. It is interesting to note that during this same period of time, people will be forced to receive the "mark of the beast" on their foreheads (Rev. 13:14–18). It may be that believers will have the mark of God on their foreheads, whereas unbelievers will feature the mark of the Antichrist. I am inclined to believe that both marks are final. Once a person receives the Antichrist as his or her master, he or she will have made a decision for eternity. The same will be true when one believes on the Lord Jesus Christ.

The evangelization of the 144,000 will proceed among those who have not yet had the opportunity to succumb to the "counterfeit miracles, signs and wonders" of the Antichrist (2 Thess. 2:9). This suggests that there may well be vigorous campaigning on the part of the followers of the Antichrist and the 144,000 to get people to voluntarily submit to the mark of their master during the early days of the Tribulation. After the Antichrist instigates a wave of persecution against all Christians (the fifth seal), and after he sets himself up as God in the midst of the Tribulation, there will be few on the earth who are uncommitted, one way or the other. That there will be some is seen in the teaching of our Lord from Matthew 25:31–46. Those individuals referred to as "sheep" will have befriended the Jews during the Tribulation at the risk of their own lives, thus earning the right to enter the millennial kingdom in the flesh. They will be the ones who populate the millennial earth.

The Holy Spirit and the 144,000

A good deal of confusion exists among many splendid Christian people relative to the ministry of the Holy Spirit during the Tribulation period. Much of the confusion is caused by the footnote in the *Scofield Reference Bible* on 2 Thessalonians 2:1–12. This footnote indicates that the Holy Spirit, the restraining influence on the devil today, will be taken out of the world when the Church is raptured just before the Tribulation begins. Most prophecy scholars today hold that here Paul means that the Holy Spirit in the church (today's morally restraining influence) will be raptured, but the Holy Spirit as a member of the Trinity will still be on earth as a convicting agency, much as He was during the Old Testament.

The Holy Spirit will most assuredly be here to empower the ministry of the 144,000. The prophet Joel foresaw this ministry of the Spirit of God in Joel 2:28–32a:

> And afterward,
>   I will pour out my Spirit on all people.
> Your sons and daughters will prophesy,
>   your old men will dream dreams,
>   your young men will see visions.
> Even on my servants, both men and women,
>   I will pour out my Spirit in those days.
> I will show wonders in the heavens
>   and on the earth,
>   blood and fire and billows of smoke.
> The sun will be turned to darkness
>   and the moon to blood
>   before the coming of the great and dreadful day of the LORD.
> And everyone who calls
>   on the name of the LORD will be saved.

This passage makes it clear that the outpouring of the Holy Spirit experienced on the day of Pentecost (referred to by Peter in Acts 2:17–21) will be the type of outpouring experienced by the 144,000 witnesses of the Tribulation. Although it did occur on the day of Pentecost, as Peter said, the primary teaching of Joel 2:28–32a concerns the work of God on the earth during the Tribulation period. "And it shall come to pass afterward" (KJV) is a direct reference to the Tribulation.

Jews Everywhere

One can scarcely imagine a country in the world where Jews are not scattered throughout the leading cities and, in many cases, hold prominent positions of leadership. The 144,000 witnesses will not have to learn the language of the people to whom they communicate the gospel message, for they will already be citizens of those countries and will suddenly leave all to follow Jesus Christ. No mission boards or deputation programs will be needed, for these Jews will immediately put everything else aside in their spontaneous desire to preach. It will be like having 144,000 Apostle Pauls proclaiming the gospel of Christ at the time of the outpouring of the Holy Spirit, just like the day of Pentecost.

What Message Will the 144,000 Preach?

For some strange reason, good and able Bible scholars have been confused about the kind of message the 144,000 will preach. Some have suggested that they will preach "the gospel of the kingdom," meaning they will revert to the same message that John the Baptist preached. This cannot be so, for since Jesus Christ died on Calvary's cross and rose again, there has only been one way and one person of salvation!

Some have tried to stipulate that several gospels are referred to in the Scriptures. Let us look at some of them:

1. "the gospel of God's grace" (Acts 20:24)
2. "my gospel" (Rom. 2:16)
3. "the gospel of God" (Rom. 15:16)
4. "the gospel of Christ" (Rom. 15:19)
5. "the gospel of peace" (Eph. 6:15)
6. "the eternal gospel" (Rev. 14:6)

A careful examination of these passages will indicate that these terms are interchangeable and refer consistently to *one* gospel. In fact, at the close of the book of Acts (28:30–31) we read: "For two whole years Paul stayed there in his own rented house and welcomed all who came to see him. Boldly and without hindrance he preached the kingdom of God and taught about the Lord Jesus Christ." The text does not say that Paul was preaching the gospel but "the kingdom of God," which *is* the gospel of Jesus Christ! "There is no other name under heaven given to men by which we must be saved" (Acts 4:12).

If the terms for the gospel as listed above are not interchangeable, then the Apostle Paul would be guilty of his own indictment, for he insisted in his letter to the Galatians (1:8–9) that there is just one gospel.

> But even if we or an angel from heaven should preach a gospel other than the one we preached to you, let him be eternally condemned! As we have already said, so now I say again: If anybody is preaching to you a gospel other than what you accepted, let him be eternally condemned!

It is apparent from this that the 144,000 witnesses will be preaching the same message that the Apostle Paul or the Apostle Peter preached, the same message that we preach. This so-called sophisticated society in which we live must bear in mind that the Church of Jesus Christ dare not alter its gospel message one iota or try to adapt it to human traditions. Like the 144,000 witnesses, we will one day stand before God to give an account of how we have *preached* the gospel. The great need of the ministry and the laity today is to say with Paul, "Woe to me if I do not preach the gospel!" (1 Cor. 9:16).

THE GREAT SOUL HARVEST OF THE TRIBULATION

> After this I looked and there before me was a great multitude that no one could count, from every nation, tribe, people and language, standing before the throne and in front of the Lamb. They were wearing white robes and were holding palm branches in their hands.
>
> (Rev. 7:9)

Uppermost in the mind of God is the salvation of souls. Second Peter 3:9 makes it clear that it is not God's will that any should perish. The same principle is found in other Bible passages (note esp. Matt. 18:14). As a special climax to God's ministry of salvation, Revelation 7:9 indicates that during the first part of Tribulation the greatest soul harvest in all history will take place. In fact, it is this writer's belief that more people will accept Christ during the early months of the Tribulation, before the Antichrist really has a chance to consolidate his one-world government and set up his one-world religion of self-worship (Rev. 13:5–7), than have been converted in the nearly two thousand years of the Church Age.

To assert that a soul harvest of such gigantic proportions is scheduled to take place in the future is admittedly to controvert the thinking of most prophecy students. It is nevertheless exciting to think that more people will be saved during that time than responded under the preaching of the apostles, the early church fathers, the Reformation preachers, modern missions, fragmented denominationalism, radio and television preaching, and even the present day, when Bible-teaching local churches seem to be gathering in such a large number of souls. This concept is more than an optimistic dream, for it is a reasonable conclusion of a number of prophetic realities, all climaxing with the text of Revelation

7:9: "a great multitude that no one could count, from every nation, tribe, people and language."

Only infrequently can a prophetic concept be reduced to an equation, but the accompanying chart indicates that the soul harvest during the tribulation will exceed in number all the conversions of the almost two millennia of church history. I challenge you to study it and the succeeding explanation to see if you agree. One of the features that has been such a thrill to the millions of readers of our *Left Behind* prophetic novels is the enormous *Soul Harvest* described in volume 4 of that same name.

THE EFFECTS OF THE RAPTURE ON THE WORLD

Although the Antichrist and his followers will be delighted that the Church has been taken out of this world, many thoughtful individuals will be seriously impressed by the mysterious evacuation of millions of people. Some have suggested, and I think rightly, that the Rapture will leave its mark on humankind. Consider for a moment what would happen if the Rapture took place while Christian airline pilots were flying their 747s or DC 10s loaded with people. Or think of the impact on humanity when hundreds of Christian train engineers and bus and automobile drivers are suddenly snatched from the controls of their moving vehicles.

Because Christians have invaded almost every legitimate profession, the Rapture will leave an unprecedented vacancy and cause the most chaotic and disruptive consequences that have ever been created by a single event. Yes, the world will be fully aware of the supernatural aspect of the Rapture of millions from all over the world, particularly when they discover that the only common denominator of those raptured is their personal faith in Christ.

The impact of these strange events will soon be forgotten by the majority of those living in the Tribulation because of the lies and deceit of the Antichrist, who will sign a covenant with Israel and start his diplomatic conquest of world government. But many reflective, perceptive individuals will not forget the effects created by this strange Rapture, which will doubtless stir a revival of interest in prophetic studies among them. Such a mental climate will provide fertile ground for the 144,000 Jewish evangelists.

The 144,000 Apostle Pauls

We have already examined the identity of the 144,000 Jewish witnesses of the Lord God who go out to serve Him during the first few months of the Tribulation. Their zeal to serve God can only be compared to that of the Apostle Paul, who was such a successful harvester of souls.

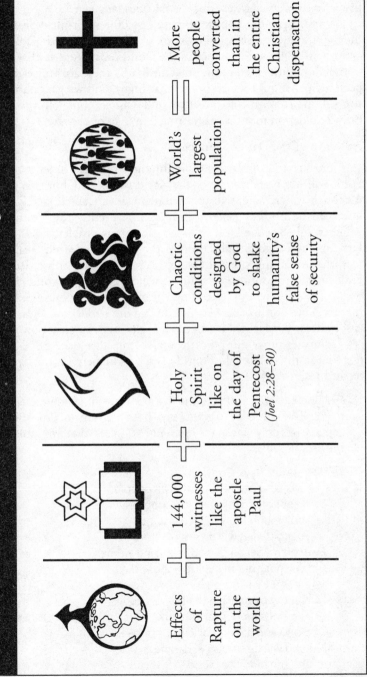

TRIBULATION SOUL HARVEST EQUATION

Effects of Rapture on the world

+ 144,000 witnesses like the apostle Paul

+ Holy Spirit like on the day of Pentecost (Joel 2:28–30)

+ Chaotic conditions designed by God to shake humanity's false sense of security

+ World's largest population

= More people converted than in the entire Christian dispensation

As a result of their preaching, an innumerable multitude will respond from "from every nation, tribe, people and language."

To appreciate the impact of these 144,000 Spirit-filled preachers on the earth, one need only compare them with the approximately 25,000 or so Spirit-filled missionaries in the world today. Add to that an equal number of Spirit-filled ministers (admittedly these are only estimates—personally, I think they are somewhat high), and we gain almost three times as many Spirit-filled, zealous soul winners going out during those early Tribulation months, harvesting a myriad of converts.

A Return of the Day of Pentecost

Contrary to popular opinion among prophecy students, the Holy Spirit will not be taken out of the world when the Church is raptured. Although widely accepted, this erroneous idea (caused largely by footnotes in the *Scofield Reference Bible*'s interpreting the "restrainer" of 2 Thess. 2:3–8 as the Holy Spirit) creates more problems than it solves. First, it is not a good translation of the Greek text, which really has in view the restraining kings of Daniel 11, not the Holy Spirit. Second, the Holy Spirit is omnipresent and thus will not leave the world. Third, no one can be saved without the Holy Spirit, and since our text clearly states there will be countless conversions during the Tribulation (Rev. 7:9, 14), it is evident that He will be on earth at that time in great power.

To further prove our point, we must consider Joel 2:28–32 in context and in the light of the Apostle Peter's statement on the day of Pentecost in Acts 2:14–21:

> "Fellow Jews and all of you who live in Jerusalem, let me explain this to you; listen carefully to what I say. These men are not drunk, as you suppose. It's only nine in the morning! No, this is what was spoken by the prophet Joel:
>
> > "'In the last days, God says,
> >   I will pour out my Spirit on all people.
> > Your sons and daughters will prophesy,
> >   your young men will see visions,
> >   your old men will dream dreams.
> > Even on my servants, both men and women,
> >   I will pour out my Spirit in those days,
> >   and they will prophesy.
> > I will show wonders in the heaven above
> >   and signs on the earth below,
> >   blood and fire and billows of smoke.
> > The sun will be turned to darkness
> >   and the moon to blood

> before the coming of the great and glorious day of the Lord.
> And everyone who calls
> on the name of the Lord will be saved.'"

Although the Apostle Peter's text here is the passage from Joel, the prophecy will be more completely fulfilled during the Tribulation period. The great soul harvest on the day of Pentecost was *like* that which is yet to come, but it was not the complete fulfillment. For there was no evidence of "wonders in the heaven above and signs on the earth below, blood and fire and billows of smoke." Joel prophesied, "The sun will be turned to darkness and the moon to blood *before* the coming of the great and glorious day of the Lord." Pentecost did not experience these phenomena—but the Tribulation period *will* culminate with these events (Matt. 24:29). We see, then, that the soul harvest of the day of Pentecost is only a type or first installment of what God has scheduled for the tribulation.

Chaotic World Conditions

The main purpose of the Tribulation is to compress into seven years of trauma, conditions that will be conducive to bringing every person to a decision about Jesus Christ or the Antichrist. We will see in subsequent studies that the majority of people will accept the mark of the beast as followers of Antichrist. But in the early days of the Tribulation many other millions will decide for Christ.

The sixth seal judgment, which we studied in the previous chapter, contains the description of the conditions designed by God to shake human beings from their false sense of security that the earth is a permanent structure, so they will be more prone to look to God for help. As long as people can stand on *terra firma*, they maintain a self-sufficient attitude toward God. But when a great earthquake occurs, stars fall from heaven, the sky rolls back like a scroll, and every mountain and island are moved out of their places (Rev. 6:12–14), many terrified people will look to God for help.

A miniature illustration of this occurred in San Diego some years ago. I had been invited by the Lions Club president, who had recently become a Christian, to address their December luncheon meeting. As I stood up, I sensed the usual "ho hum" attitude that often greets preachers at such events. About five minutes later we felt an earthquake! The ground shook, lights went out for a moment, and the chandeliers swung to and fro. When I commenced my message a moment later, I was impressed with the fact that I now had their undivided attention. Never have I addressed a more attentive secular audience. If such a change can be created by a minor earth tremor, can you imagine the transformation after all the chaotic conditions of the sixth seal judgment occur? But keep in mind that they will come after war, pestilence, famine, and death—certainly no time to foster independence from God!

When all of these momentous occurrences are added together, we find that the ideal mental climate created in the minds of millions by the Rapture, plus 144,000 Apostle Paul types, plus an outpouring of the Holy Spirit as in the day of Pentecost, plus chaotic conditions designed by God to shake human beings from their false sense of security will certainly produce conversions double or possibly triple the percentage of those who have accepted Christ throughout the history of the church. By multiplying all this by the unprecedented population that will exist at that time, we can easily conceive of a greater ingathering of souls than those who have been won to Christ during the entire Church Age.

Unprecedented Population

Most people are acquainted with the effects of today's population explosion, but few have applied it to the spread of the gospel in the end time. The accompanying chart has been based on accepted population statistics, past, present, and future. By studying it, you discover that there are probably more people living in the world today than have lived from the time of Christ to the generation before this present generation. If the population continues to grow as expected, and if, as suggested above, the spiritual conditions during the first half of the Tribulation more than double the percentage of people won to Christ during that period, because of the enormous population, this will result in more souls harvested to Christ than have been saved during the entire history of the Church. From all this we can realize the full significance of 7:9–10, 14 when it says:

> After this I looked and there before me was a great multitude that no one could count, from every nation, tribe, people and language, standing before the throne and in front of the Lamb. They were wearing white robes and were holding palm branches in their hands. And they cried out in a loud voice:
>
> > "Salvation belongs to our God,
> > who sits on the throne,
> > and to the Lamb."
>
> ..."These are they who have come out of the great tribulation; they have washed their robes and made them white in the blood of the Lamb."

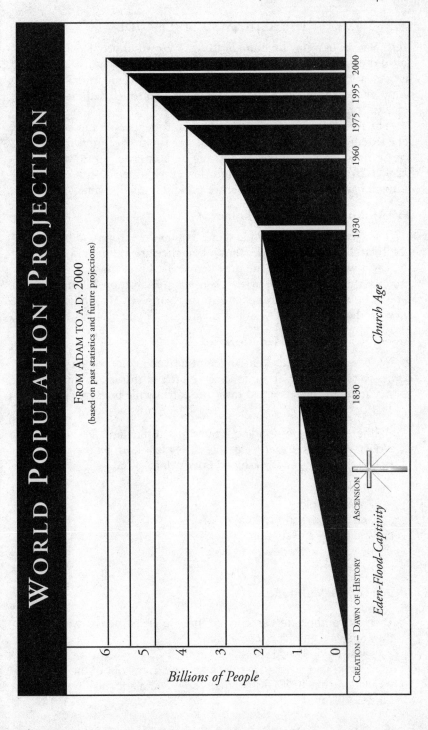

WORLD POPULATION PROJECTION

FROM ADAM TO A.D. 2000
(based on past statistics and future projections)

Billions of People

6
5
4
3
2
1
0

CREATION – DAWN OF HISTORY

ASCENSION

1830 1930 1960 1975 1995 2000

Eden–Flood–Captivity

Church Age

THE REDEEMED MULTITUDE

Verse 9 gives us a small picture of this vast crowd of people who will be saved during the Tribulation period, a crowd so vast that it is described as "a great multitude that no one could count." This mighty soul harvest shows the power of God's Holy Spirit working through dedicated vessels who are already scattered around the world.

The people will be from "every nation, tribe, people and language." The extent of the revival will approximate the first-century moving of the Spirit of God, when "every creature under heaven" heard the gospel (Col. 1:23). However, here we find that every tribe will not only hear, but will have some of its members respond. Praise His name!

The Multitude Before the Throne

The fact that this multitude stands before the throne and before the Lamb clothed in white robes shows that they are redeemed ones from the earth who now are in the presence of the Lord; the palm branches indicate their victory in Christ. Their song, "Salvation belongs to our God, who sits on the throne, and to the Lamb" (v. 10), indicates that they are the recipients of personal salvation.

Angels Rejoice When Men Are Saved

We often hear it said, "The angels of heaven rejoice when one sinner comes to repentance" (cf. Luke 15:7). Note the attitude of these angels as they look on the redeemed from the earth while praising God (Rev. 7:11–12):

All the angels were standing around the throne and around the elders and the four living creatures. They fell down on their faces before the throne and worshiped God, saying:

"Amen!
Praise and glory
and wisdom and thanks and honor
and power and strength
be to our God for ever and ever.
Amen!"

Identity of the Multitude

Then one of the elders asked me, "These in white robes—who are they, and where did they come from?"

I answered, "Sir, you know."

And he said, "These are they who have come out of the great tribulation; they have washed their robes and made them white in the blood of the Lamb." (Rev. 7:13–14)

The exact identity of this multitude is carefully spelled out. The elder asks the question as to the identity of the multitude. John does not recognize them, indicating that if they had been members of the Church or of the Old Testament, he could have identified them. Since they are the redeemed from the Tribulation, however, he does not know them. These Tribulation saints constitute a distinctive category, just as the Church and Israel or Old Testament saints form a special company. Each group has its own relationship to Christ, depending on the period of time in which these individuals are converted. That these are believers is unquestionable in view of the fact that they have "washed their robes and made them white in the blood of the Lamb."

Eternal Rewards for This Multitude

Eternal rewards are to be given to this multitude. "Therefore, they are before the throne of God and serve him day and night in his temple; and he who sits on the throne will spread his tent over them" (Rev. 7:15).

1. "They are before the throne of God and serve him day and night in his temple." These people, like the Apostle Paul, are "absent from you in body, [yet] present with you in spirit." They are not on the earth but in heaven; in order to be there, they must have died. Their position before the throne makes it clear that they have just as much eternal blessing as the believers of the other periods.

2. "... and he who sits on the throne will spread his tent over them." This is the same promise given to us in 1 Thessalonians 4:17: "And so we will be with the Lord forever." One of the promises imparted to all those who put their faith in Christ is that in the next life they will forever be with the Lord.

3. Their every need will be supplied: "Never again will they hunger; never again will they thirst. The sun will not beat upon them, nor any scorching heat. For the Lamb at the center of the throne will be their shepherd; he will lead them to springs of living water" (Rev. 7:16–17). These verses suggest that the Tribulation saints will sustain much personal suffering and human deprivation. They will evidently hunger and thirst during the Tribulation and will undergo excruciating exposure to the elements, but they will endure to the end and thus be delivered by the Savior.

4. "And God will wipe away every tear from their eyes" (Rev. 7:17b). This promise to "wipe away every tear from their eyes," offered to His children in the life to come, is similarly extended to the Church after the Great White Throne Judgment in 21:4. Although it is impossible to say exactly what is meant by wiping away every tear, I am inclined to believe it relates to removing our capacity to recall unpleasant things, including those eternally lost. If we could remember our loved ones suffering the

torments of the damned in hell, the joy of heaven would be extinguished unless God in His marvelous grace removed the capacity for such suffering. This fact further points out the seriousness of our need of salvation and the blessings God has prepared for those who love Him.

The Great Multitude Individually Saved

One consistent principle throughout the Scriptures is graphically illustrated in regard to this multitude that no one can number: Human beings must choose individually to accept or reject Jesus Christ. Regardless of the period of time in which a person lives, each one must make his or her own decision.

When the Lord Jesus was on this earth, "he was in the world, and though the world was made through him, the world did not recognize him. He came to that which was his own, but his own did not receive him. Yet to all who received him, to those who believed in his name, he gave the right to become children of God" (John 1:10–12).

The same is true during the present period of God's working with human beings, and it will continue in the Tribulation. The multitude is not merely composed of people from every language, tribe, and nation, but those, as stated in verse 14, who have been cleansed by the Lamb. That they stand before God appears in the words of verse 15. They are permitted to stand before the throne of God because they voluntarily "washed their robes and made them white in the blood of the Lamb."

This expression offers a beautiful picture of our personal acceptance of salvation. When someone is willing to come to God by the blood of His Son, acknowledging personal sin, then his or her filthy rags are cleansed by the blood of the Lamb, Jesus Christ, and that person is made white as snow.

SIXTEEN

The Seven Trumpet Judgments

Revelation 8–9

"When he opened the seventh seal, there was silence in heaven for about half an hour" (Rev. 8:1). "Silence is golden," people tell us. But there will be a silence in heaven so ominous that its very nature foreshadows the enormous difficulties that are about to come on the earth. The significance of this silence is twofold: (1) It is entirely opposite the usual sound pattern of heaven, and (2) it is the result of the revelation by Jesus Christ to the angelic hosts concerning what is about to fall on the earth.

The usual sound pattern of heaven, as we have seen in chapters 4–5, is one of great joy and worship. John heard "the voice . . . speaking to me like a trumpet"; thunder; celestial beings crying out continually, "Holy, holy, holy is the Lord God Almighty"; and the twenty-four elders crying out, "You are worthy, our Lord and God." He heard over a billion angels join in songs of praise to the "Lamb of God" and the Lord Jesus Christ saying, "Worthy is the Lamb, who was slain, to receive power and wealth and wisdom and strength and honor and glory and praise!" (Rev. 5:12). Suddenly, amid all this crescendo of sound, there comes universal silence. This may aptly be described as "the lull before the storm."

OPENING THE SEVENTH SEAL

We have already seen that the seven-sealed scroll represents the title deed to the earth. But it also contains the awful future that awaits those who reject the Lamb of God who came to take away the sin of the world. The opening of the first five seals reveals the activities of humankind, bringing about great misery on the earth. The opening of the sixth seal seems to be God's reaction against the people for their cruel persecution of His saints. The opening of the seventh seal introduces the seven trumpet judgments, which are all judgments of God sent on the earth. In these judgments, God is exclusively the sender and people are exclusively receivers.

These judgments are so terrible that the angels stand breathless in wonder. Would to God that those today who so easily reject Jesus Christ would stand still and heed the voice of God. They, too, would be "silent" if they knew the horrible doom of judgment that is coming upon this earth because people are rejecting God's Redeemer, the Lord Jesus Christ.

THE SEVEN ANGELS

As the seventh seal is broken, the seven angels receive trumpets. Since the covenant between the Antichrist and Israel will start the Tribulation and the first seal is the Antichrist, the first six seals cover the first twenty-one months of the Tribulation. The breaking of the seventh seal may very well occur at the close of the twenty-first month; it introduces the second quarter, or the seven trumpets.

"And I saw the seven angels who stand before God, and to them were given seven trumpets" (Rev. 8:2). The opening of the seventh seal does not cause the seven angels to stand before God. Apparently they are always there, awaiting a special assignment from their Creator. The opening of the seal results in each one being given a trumpet that will be blown in proper sequence, introducing a future form of judgment.

One of these seven angels is the angel Gabriel. We learn this from Luke 1:19, for when he appeared to Zechariah, the father of John the Baptist, he said, "I am Gabriel. I stand in the presence of God." We find this same angel sent by God to bring a message to the prophet Daniel (Dan. 9:21). Since Gabriel has been named as one of the seven angels who stand before God, carrying out His bidding to humankind, it may be that the other six serve the same purpose, though we have no Scripture to identify them.

WORSHIP IN HEAVEN

Another angel, who had a golden censer, came and stood at the altar. He was given much incense to offer, with the prayers of all the saints, on the golden altar before the throne. The smoke of the incense, together with the prayers of the saints, went up before God from the angel's hand. Then the angel took the censer, filled it with fire from the altar, and hurled it on the earth; and there came peals of thunder, rumblings, flashes of lightning and an earthquake. (Rev. 8:3–5)

This description of another angel taking the golden censer with "incense to offer, with the prayers of all the saints, on the golden altar" presents us with a beautiful picture that the prayers of God's people continually go up before Him. These prayers, like the prayers of the saints under the altar in 6:9, are probably the prayers that have been kept in heaven awaiting this very day. For two thousand years, God's people have been praying to God to avenge Himself on those who blaspheme against Him, revile His Son, and abuse His people. The fact that this censer is filled with fire from the altar (which stands before the throne) and is cast into the earth indicates that these prayer of vengeance are about to be answered. The action takes place in heaven but causes a response on earth of "thunder, rumblings, flashes of lightning and an earthquake." All of this signifies that the human race is about to feel the hot blast of God's wrath.

WHO IS THIS ANGEL?

There is some disagreement among Bible scholars concerning the identity of this angel. Some say that the other angel of verse 3 is the Lord Jesus Christ, for only He is worthy to receive the prayers of saints. Since He is the only "mediator between God and men" (1 Tim. 2:5), no one else is qualified to receive the prayers of the saints. Actually, all agree that Christ is the only mediator with God and that prayer should be made directly to Him through Jesus Christ the Son. However, Revelation 5:8 indicates that the four living creatures and the twenty-four elders have "golden bowls full of incense, which are the prayers of the saints." All of this means that prayers are directed to God, but when unanswerable, may be stored by these administrative angels until the time for their answer, at which time they are used in the worship of heaven.

Although it is impossible to be dogmatic, it is doubtful that this "other angel" is the Lord Jesus Christ, even though He is our great High Priest. This is not an act of redemption or propitiation, and nothing is said here about blood being sprinkled on the atonement cover. I suggest two reasons why this is not a reference to the Lord Jesus Christ.

1. The Lord Jesus, when appearing in the Old Testament to the children of God, is never referred to as "an angel." Instead, he is always introduced as "the angel of the LORD" or "the angel of God."

2. We have no record of the Lord Jesus appearing on earth as an angel after His incarnation and ascension to heaven. Here we view Him in heaven, where He is seen as a member of the triune God. Though He appears as "the Son of man" and the "Lamb who was slain," He is also uniquely, with the other two members of the Trinity, "in the midst of the throne of God." It is more likely that this "other angel" is one more angel besides the seven (Rev. 8:2) who leads in the worship of God before His throne and helps administer His universe.

"The smoke of the incense, together with the prayers of the saints" (Rev. 8:4), is a beautiful symbol that expresses the fact that our prayers are always heard by God. From our point of view, sometimes we think the heavens are as brass and that we are not getting through; but from God's viewpoint, our prayers always come before "him who sits on the throne" (5:13).

"Then the angel took the censer, filled it with fire from the altar, and hurled it on the earth; and there came peals of thunder, rumblings, flashes of lightning and an earthquake" (Rev. 8:5). The thunderclaps, lightnings, and earthquake are the result of the fire from the altar, indicating that the action of heaven initiates a responsive action on earth. As the prayers of the saints for vengeance are taken from the altar, there are frightening sounds, flashes of light, and an earthquake on the earth, introducing the fact that the seven angels are about to sound their trumpets: "Then the seven angels who had the seven trumpets prepared to sound them" (8:6).

ARE THE TRUMPET JUDGMENTS LITERAL JUDGMENTS?

The best way to decide whether the trumpet judgments are literal or symbolic is to study them in connection with the plagues of Egypt, as found in Exodus 7–11. There we see Moses performing the symbolic act of waving his rod over the waters of Egypt, which physically turn to blood. Here we see an angel performing the symbolic act of blowing a trumpet. Why should the result on earth be less physical than the event in Moses' day? Likewise, Aaron put out his rod and smote the dust of the ground; as a result of that symbolic act, physical lice appeared. Why should it be different when these angels perform their symbolic act of blowing the trumpet?

Note also that five of the plagues of Egypt are repeated in the book of Revelation. No one suggests that what happened in Egypt was not literal in its form of judgment on the rebellious Egyptians; thus, we can conclude that the same thing applies during the Tribulation period and that the trumpet judgments introduce physical judgment on the earth. The only exceptions are those trumpets that introduce events beyond human understanding, and even they affect human beings physically.

> The first angel sounded his trumpet, and there came hail and fire mixed with blood, and it was hurled down upon the earth. A third of the earth was burned up, a third of the trees were burned up, and all the green grass was burned up. (Rev. 8:7)

The hail and fire are literal judgments that fall on one-third of the earth's surface, burning up all the vegetation they light on. It should not strike us as strange that this is a literal cataclysm, for such things have happened before. God rained down burning sulfur on Sodom and Gomorrah (Gen. 19), and, as we have already seen, Egypt's water turned to blood. In fact, just such a disaster was predicted for the earth immediately prior to the "day of the Lord": "I will show wonders in the heavens and on the earth, blood and fire and billows of smoke. The sun will be turned to darkness and the moon to blood before the coming of the great and dreadful day of the LORD" (Joel 2:30–31).

THE SECOND TRUMPET

> The second angel sounded his trumpet, and something like a huge mountain, all ablaze, was thrown into the sea. A third of the sea

> turned into blood, a third of the living creatures in the sea died, and
> a third of the ships were destroyed. (Rev. 8:8–9)

A biblical allusion to "the sea" usually refers to the sea that was prominent to the land of Palestine, the Mediterranean Sea. What appeared to John as "a huge mountain" is probably a giant burning meteorite that falls into the Mediterranean Sea, killing one-third of the living creatures and destroying one-third of the ships. The result of that death and the chemical composition of the meteorite turn the water to blood.

There certainly would be an ample supply of ships in the Mediterranean Sea, since that is the permanent home of the U.S. Sixth Fleet, plus representative fleets from many other countries of the world. Since Revelation 18 indicates that Babylon will be rebuilt and become the commercial center of the world, there will no doubt be several hundred ships on the "sea" when that meteorite falls, adding further devastating details to the time of Tribulation.

THE THIRD TRUMPET

> The third angel sounded his trumpet, and a great star, blazing like a
> torch, fell from the sky on a third of the rivers and on the springs of
> water—the name of the star is Wormwood. A third of the waters
> turned bitter, and many people died from the waters that had
> become bitter. (Rev. 8:10–11)

The third trumpet judgment introduces us to a burning "torch" (ASV) that visibly falls from heaven, indicating it is another meteorite; it must bury itself so deep at just the right spot that it pollutes the water supply of a third of the world's rivers. Evidently there is a place in the earth where the headwaters of three great rivers come together. When this "Wormwood" meteorite strikes that place, it will embitter great rivers, and those who are dependent on them will die.

THE FOURTH TRUMPET

> The fourth angel sounded his trumpet, and a third of the sun was
> struck, a third of the moon, and a third of the stars, so that a third of
> them turned dark. A third of the day was without light, and also a
> third of the night. (Rev. 8:12)

The fourth trumpet deals with the luminous bodies as they affect this earth. On the first day of creation God said, "'Let there be light,' and there was light" (Gen. 1:3), and on the fourth day he created the sun, moon, and stars. The same God who created light in the first place is able to diminish it to one-third. Actually, day and night will seem to be reversed, for there will be sixteen hours of darkness and eight hours of daylight. This corresponds to the ninth plague of Egypt (cf. Ex. 10) and the prediction of our Lord in Luke 21:25–26: "There will be signs in the sun, moon and stars. On the earth, nations will be in anguish and perplexity at the roaring and tossing of the sea. Men will faint from terror, apprehensive of what is coming on the world, for the heavenly bodies will be shaken." Our finite minds can hardly fathom the tremendous forces that will be unleashed on this earth as a result of the blowing of this fourth trumpet.

THE WARNING ANGEL

As I watched, I heard an eagle that was flying in midair call out in a loud voice: "Woe! Woe! Woe to the inhabitants of the earth, because of the trumpet blasts about to be sounded by the other three angels!"   (Rev. 8:13)

This verse introduces the three woes of the book of Revelation, which in turn inform us that as horrible as the first four trumpets have been, they will be surpassed in misery by that which is to follow. The rebellion of human beings against God strangely gets progressively worse. Aware that they have sinned against God and are in the midst of judgments placed on them by the Lamb, they know they cannot stand in the "great day of their wrath" (Rev. 6:17); yet they persist in their stubborn self-will against God. This clearly answers the question often asked by people, "Will there be a second chance after death?" My answer is always the same, "What good would that do? People would make the same decision a second time."

The warning of Revelation 8:13, sounded by a special angel, threatens that worse things are yet to come. The three woes of the Tribulation period are actually the fifth, sixth, and seventh trumpet judgments. The seventh trumpet introduces the last half of the Tribulation, or the bowl judgments. The seventh trumpet and the third woe, then, are synonymous. The first woe or fifth trumpet (for they are the same) covers five months. The second woe or sixth trumpet may cover a similar period.

Even a casual reading of the fifth, sixth, and seventh trumpet judgments will acquaint the reader with the fact that they are distinguished from the previous judgments since they predict such an increase in the destructive powers to be unleashed on humanity. Someone has aptly described this period as "hell let loose on earth."

THE FIFTH TRUMPET

"The fifth angel sounded his trumpet, and I saw a star that had fallen from the sky to the earth. The star [lit., to him; cf. KJV] was given the key to the shaft of the Abyss" (Rev. 9:1). Whenever possible, we seek to interpret words in the book of Revelation literally. However, the use of the word "star" in this verse is obviously intended figuratively rather than literally, for the "star" is referred to as "him," thus clearly possessing personality. A "key to the shaft of the Abyss" cannot be given to a thing or object, but to a person. The word "star" parallels our customary reference to a "baseball star" or some other celebrity. It indicates an angel to whom is given, at this point in the Tribulation, "the key to the shaft of the Abyss."

This usage coincides with that in Revelation 20:1, where we find that at the end of the Tribulation an angel comes down from heaven "having the key to the Abyss and holding in his hand a great chain." In other words, the angel retains the key during the Tribulation period, and the awful spiritual forces about to be unleashed from "the shaft of the Abyss" are controlled by that angel. This must be a good angel to whom God can entrust such grave responsibility. His location in heaven further indicates he is a good angel, for fallen angels do not reside in heaven.

The Abyss

The Abyss ("bottomless pit," KJV) is not hell or Hades. It has been suggested that it may be at the bottom of the great gulf, fixed in Hades, that separates the place of torment and the place of comfort, described as the abode of the dead by the Lord Jesus in Luke 16:19–31.

A study of Scripture indicates two kinds of demons: those that are free, living in a spiritual realm and seeking to indwell the bodies of people, and those confined in "gloomy dungeons to be held for judgment" (2 Pet. 2:4)—evidently for some great sin.

Free Evil Spirits

The free spirits were described by the Lord Jesus in Matthew 12:43–45. He indicated that some evil spirits seek rest in human bodies. If a person who has such spirits gets rid of them, he or she must exercise great caution that they do not return at a later time and even bring their friends with them. Evidently such spirits travel in groups, and more than one evil spirit can abide in a person at a time. Apparently over a thousand evil spirits possessed the wild man of Gerasa, for they gave themselves the name "Legion" (Luke 8:30). This may indicate that one evil spirit is not sufficient to *dominate* a person's behavior. A number of spirits, however, can affect behavior, giving rise to irritable or irrational behavior. It would seem that the more numerous the evil spirits in an individual, the more control they can exercise over one's body for evil.

Where did these evil spirits come from? The best suggestion is that they are the angels who fell with Satan in his original rebellion against God, described in Ezekiel 28:11-19 and Isaiah 14. More will be said about these when we get to Revelation 12. These fallen angels, sometimes referred to as "disembodied spirits," make up the kingdom of Satan and under his leadership go about seeking to lead human beings in the defiance of God's will, just as Satan tempted Adam and Eve in the Garden. The success or failure of their objective is dependent on the number of spirits in a person's body and whether or not he or she flees for deliverance to Jesus Christ, our only defense against the attacks of Satan.

Christians need not fear these evil spirits, although they should be warned about them. The Apostle John said of those who possess the Lord Jesus, "The one who is in you is greater than the one who is in the world" (1 John 4:4). If Jesus Christ is resident within us, we do not have to fear anything that human beings or Satan can hurl against us. He is our adequate defense!

Many Christians seem to have a phobia about demon possession and a great fear of being controlled by evil spirits. This should not be our main concern, for if we remain in an abiding relationship with Jesus Christ, according to John 15:1–11 we never need fear being indwelt or oppressed by evil spirits. If we are to be marked by an obsession, let it be to abide in Christ as a branch abides in the vine. Satan's kingdom of evil spirits, who reside in "the air" or "the heavenly realms" (Eph. 2:2; 6:10–12), seeking constantly to indwell the human race, seem to be somewhat limited in their possession of human beings in Christian lands. Those who have traveled in pagan countries can tell of supernatural phenomena taking place that can only be accounted for by an evil spiritual force.

Much of the superstitious fear generated in the many religions of the world can be traced back to the work of demons. According to 2 Thessalonians 2:9–12 we can expect a great increase in the expression of this evil spiritual effect on human affairs as we get closer to the Tribulation. As the Antichrist comes on the world scene, he will be able to work "counterfeit miracles, signs and wonders, and in every sort of evil that deceives those who are perishing" (2:9–10). This power is given him by the free evil spirits. Undoubtedly some of the increasing tendencies toward spirit phenomena these days may indicate that we are getting closer to the end time.

Imprisoned Evil Spirits

Jude 6 tells us, "And the angels who did not keep their positions of authority but abandoned their own home—these he has kept in darkness, bound with everlasting chains for judgment on the great Day." It seems evident from this verse that there are imprisoned angels now kept in darkness, which may well be the "the Abyss," until the Day of the Lord. These angels are probably those who violated the laws of God in that they came to the "daughters of men "and cohabited with them, producing a strange mixtured race that had to be destroyed by the flood (Gen. 6:2–7).

This is further confirmed by 2 Peter 2:1–10, which refers to the fact that God "did not spare angels when they sinned, but sent them to hell [*tartaros*], putting them into gloomy dungeons to be held for judgment" (2:4). *Tartaros* may be "the Abyss" or the bottomless pit referred to here. Evil-spirit angels, already having manifested their evil tendencies and capabilities by almost destroying the human race, are chained there. They will be unleashed on the earth for a time of spirit persecution, the likes of which the world has never known. The description of this event is seen in the fifth and sixth trumpet judgments or, as they are also called, the first two woes.

The First Woe

> When he opened the Abyss, smoke rose from it like the smoke from a gigantic furnace. The sun and sky were darkened by the smoke from the Abyss. And out of the smoke locusts came down upon the earth and were given power like that of scorpions of the earth.
>
> (Rev. 9:2–3)

When the Abyss was opened, smoke rose from it until the air became saturated with a smoglike condition worse than anything Los Angeles or any other city has ever experienced. Out of this smog will come locust-like scorpion creatures, which have no counterpart in all history. They have been aptly called "infernal cherubim." Shaped like locusts, and like unto horses, they have faces like men, hair like women, and teeth as lions; they have breastplates of iron, their wings are as "the thundering of many horses and chariots rushing into battle" (Rev. 9:9), and they possess stings in their tails as scorpions.

Years ago someone suggested that these are B-29s because they were well-protected but had the capacity to sting from the tail. This is a fanciful suggestion, for in reality these are spirit beings that probably will not be seen by human beings but whose effects will be strongly felt. These evidently fulfill the locust-type judgment the Lord predicted would come on the earth during the Tribulation (Joel 1–2). They are not to be interpreted literally, not symbolically, but spiritually, for they depict a spirit creature able to effect a physical response on humanity. These awful creatures that come on the earth for the purpose of persecuting people are beyond our comprehension. If human beings could see these creatures, their hearts would no doubt fail them for fear.

Apollyon—"Destroyer"

"They had as king over them the angel of the Abyss, whose name in Hebrew is Abaddon, and in Greek, Apollyon" (Rev. 9:11). The leading angel of these evil spirits from out of the pit of the Abyss is, in the

Hebrew, Abaddon, and in the Greek, Apollyon (meaning "destroyer"). It is interesting to note that different generations have tried to identify this being with some particular world personage. A number of years ago I read in the *Pulpit Commentary* on the book of Revelation that this was no doubt Napoleon because of the similarity of names. Actually this is a special angelic being of a fallen state who assists Satan in his evil spirit kingdom. It is probably not Satan himself, since he is not today confined in chains of darkness in the Abyss. He is probably comparable in Satan's kingdom to the archangel Michael of the heavenly hosts. His actual name is destroyer, typical of the followers of Satan: They do not build or construct, but ever work to destroy.

Torment Five Months

Unlike any kind of locusts that have existed before them, these are not going to harm vegetation but human beings. They will not be able to kill them, but they will torment them five months. This torment is described as "the sting of a scorpion when it strikes a man" (Rev. 9:5). It has been said that the sting of a scorpion, though seldom fatal, is one of the most painful stings known. The venom seems to set the veins and nervous system on fire, and the effects last for several days. By contrast, the effects of this particular sting will extend five months.

Verse 6 speaks of a pain so intense that "men will seek death, but will not find it; they will long to die, but death will elude them." Although these infernal creatures will not be observed by the human eye, they will cause such physical pain that people will seek death, but death will be removed from them. This is a description of almost unimaginable suffering.

Believers Exempt from This Judgment

The power of God over the spirit world will protect believers from these evil-spirit creatures. Verse 4 tells us that they have power to hurt "only those people who did *not* have the seal of God on their foreheads." Just as God protected the children of Israel in the land of Goshen from the plagues of Egypt, so He will protect His children during the Tribulation period. As the Lord Jesus said, "But he who stands firm to the end will be saved [or delivered]" (Matt. 24:13). God will preserve believers from the Tribulation judgments inflicting the earth. So far the only means by which Christians will die in this period is martyrdom. "I saw under the altar the souls of those who had been slain because of the . . . testimony they had maintained" (Rev. 6:9). This further confirms the faithfulness of our God, who will give dying grace to His children in that hour and grant them the crown of life (Rev. 2:10; cf. James 1:12), which will give them great position in the Millennium.

The fact that these terrible spirit beings have power to hurt "only those people who did not have the seal of God on their foreheads" (Rev. 9:4) may serve as a clue to part of God's purpose in this fifth trumpet judgment. It may serve in the hand of God to help some uncommitted individuals during the Tribulation period realize the power of God and turn in faith to receive the Messiah.

If this seems like a terrible way for God to bring people to repentance, one should remember the seriousness of being eternally lost. The Lord Jesus Himself said, "Do not be afraid of those who kill the body but cannot kill the soul. Rather, be afraid of the One who can destroy both soul and body in hell" (Matt. 10:28). It would be an act of mercy on God's part to permit a person to be tormented five months in an effort to bring him or her to Christ in order to avoid the torments of the damned for eternity.

Verse 12 indicates that although one woe is past, "two other woes are yet to come." As terrible as is this judgment that will come on the earth, lasting five months, it will be eclipsed by the terror of the sixth trumpet judgment, which introduces the second woe. The sixth trumpet judgment reveals another army of evil-spirit beings to be unleashed on the human race from "the Abyss." This time the judgment is far more severe to the inhabitants of the earth because the spirits are not only able to inflict pain on people but also physical death.

THE SIXTH TRUMPET

The Second Woe

> The sixth angel sounded his trumpet, and I heard a voice coming from the horns of the golden altar that is before God. It said to the sixth angel who had the trumpet, "Release the four angels who are bound at the great river Euphrates." And the four angels who had been kept ready for this very hour and day and month and year were released to kill a third of mankind.   (Rev. 9:13–15)

At the blowing of the sixth trumpet, John hears a voice from the horns of the golden altar before God, which says, "Release the four angels who are bound at the great river Euphrates." This is our first introduction to these four bound angels. That they are evil angels seems obvious because they are bound. Evidently they are anxious to bring havoc on humankind but have been bound by God, prohibiting the fulfillment of their intent. Why they hate human beings we are not told; perhaps it is because they are the special object of God's love (John 3:16).

There is a day coming, however, when God will permit these awful creatures to come forth, indicating that He has a yet unfulfilled purpose and plan that will be unveiled according to His good pleasure. For it states that they had been "kept ready for this very hour and day and month and year [and] were released to kill a third of mankind." Those slain are no doubt incorrigibles who would never accept Christ and would only serve as a hindrance to "undecided" people (those who have neither the mark of the Father nor the mark of the beast).

The Euphrates River in Scripture

There is no need to spiritualize "the great river Euphrates," considered by Bible scholars to be the greatest river of boundaries in the Bible. No doubt the most prominent river referred to in the Scriptures, it formed one of the boundaries of the Garden of Eden. It was also a boundary for Israel (Gen. 15:18), the easternmost boundary of Egypt, and the boundary of the Persian Empire. It is used in Scripture as a symbol of Israel's enemies.

That these four evil angels are today bound in that area of the world is no accident, for it seems that some of the world's greatest events took place near the Euphrates River. Since it was a boundary for the Garden of Eden, near this river the first sin of humankind was committed, the first war fought, and the tower of Babel erected in defiance against God. It was near the river Euphrates that Nimrod built the city of Babylon, where idolatry received its origin and surged through the world. It was to Babylon that the children of Israel were taken captive, and it will be in this area of the world that the final sin of man will culminate. Here, according to Revelation 18, the city of Babylon will be rebuilt and become the headquarters of the commercial, religious, and military activities of the world under the Antichrist's rule. (More of this in Rev. 17–18.)

An Evil Army of 200 Million

"The number of the mounted troops was two hundred million. I heard their number" (Rev. 9:16). An army of two hundred million men would be an awesome host to confront humankind. This will be an evil army of two hundred million horselike creatures with riders on their backs called "horsemen." The four angels bound at the Euphrates River seem to be leaders of these evil spirits, riding on horselike creatures, having heads of lions and emitting fire, smoke, and sulfur. They have tails like serpents, from which their power is sent forth (9:17–19).

It is obvious that these are not to be taken as humans, for horsemen do not wear breastplates that are "fiery red, dark blue, and yellow as sulfur," nor do horses have mouths that emit "fire and smoke and sulfur." Instead, this is a literal description of unnatural, demonlike evil spirits that come out of the Abyss, advancing under the leadership of the four bound angels.

One-Third of the Human Race Killed

By the power of their tail and the "fire, smoke and sulfur" that proceeds out of their mouths, the horsemen will kill one-third of the world's population. We have already seen that 25 percent of the population will be killed by the fourth horseman of the Apocalypse (Rev. 6:8) as a result of the pestilence following the world war at the beginning of the Tribulation period. According to today's population figures, that would be one and a half billion people, depending on when the Tribulation takes place. This one-third will again involve a similar number of people—approximately another billion and a half people.

As incredible as it may seem, that indicates that one-half of the world's population (three billion people by today's standards) will be killed during the first half of the Tribulation. This is why I find it so difficult to understand why our mid- or post-Tribulation friends do not realize even the first half of this period is "tribulation."

Only the Unrepentant Killed by This Judgment

"The rest of mankind that were not killed by these plagues still did not repent of the work of their hands" (Rev. 9:20). We can assume from this verse that those killed by the evil spirits will be people who have received the mark of the beast during the Tribulation period, having rejected Christ and accepted the Antichrist to rule over them. This is not clearly stated; therefore, we say it is assumed. However, we know that unrepentant people are so killed. Once again we find that believers are exempt from the awful judgment that awaits the earth.

It seems as if the purpose of this judgment, like the preceding one, is to rid the world of the incorrigibles in the Tribulation who reject the Lord Jesus Christ and salvation through Him. Since this trumpet judgment brings us close to the middle of the Tribulation period, we find that about 50 percent of the world's unregenerate population will have died. It seems, then, that God is ridding the earth of those who will never receive Him. These people cannot possibly populate the millennial kingdom and therefore must be purged from the earth. God's judgment here is unchanged from His acts of judgment in the Old Testament. His love is expressed in the gift of His Son as the means of redemption, but if people reject this love gift, they fall under that judgment. This points out once again the need for everyone to receive Jesus Christ.

The Unregeneracy of the Human Heart

The Bible tells us that "the heart is deceitful above all things and beyond cure. Who can understand it?" (Jer. 17:9). The book of Revelation certainly answers the oft-stated suggestion of individuals that "what man needs is a second chance after death." During the Tribulation people will have unprecedented opportunity to see the omnipotent hand of God working in human affairs, yet they will stubbornly persist in their rebellion against God and their rejection of Jesus Christ. In spite of the destruction of half of the world's population and one-third of the world's vegetation, light, and water supply, people will not repent of their stubborn hearts and sinful practices. They will refuse to make the decision of Moses, who chose not to "enjoy the pleasures of sin for a short time" (Heb. 11:25) but rather chose to believe in the Lord and suffer with His people. Instead, the Tribulation population will embrace the pleasures of sin for a season and damn their immortal souls in the process.

Sins That Keep Men from Repentance

Instead of turning to God during the Tribulation period, human beings will turn in rebellion away from God. What are the sins that keep them from coming in repentance to a saving knowledge of the Lord Jesus Christ? The same sins that keep people from coming to him today!

1. Idolatry. Verse 20 states that they "did not repent of the work of their hands; they did not stop worshiping demons, and idols of gold, silver, bronze, stone and wood—idols that cannot see or hear or walk." Human beings have a built-in desire for God. They will never be happy unless they have communion with God. Because of this, the devil, the master of deceit, has used idolatry to deceive them ever since the days of Nimrod.

Not that human beings actually worship that which they have made with their hands, but they use their images to worship the spirits that they think indwell the images. Sometimes people have worshiped trees, but in reality it is the spirit in the tree that they worship. This leads to demon oppression and activity producing mystical phenomena, which in turn causes people to be superstitious and fraught with fear. If they would only turn to God, believing they can enjoy peace; instead, they turn to idolatry and reap its consequent fear.

2. "Murders." Someone has said, "Wherever the influence of the gospel is unknown, human life is cheap." This is certainly the case in Buddhist and Hindu countries of the world, not to mention unreached tribes in remote jungle areas. That is one of the reasons it is hard for the Western mind to understand the attitude of pagans toward human life if it serves their purpose. Thus violent murders will be a common practice during the Tribulation period.

3. "Magic arts." As already mentioned, superstition is a by-product of idolatry. "Magic arts" or "sorceries" (the Greek word used is *pharmekeia*) indicate that there will be a widespread use of drugs for evil purposes— drunkenness and drug addiction will be widespread. No doubt those bit-

ten by the scorpions of the fifth trumpet will seek relief in any conceivable medication, whether from a good or evil source. In the process, drug addiction will abound.

4. "Sexual immorality." Even during the Tribulation period, when life is cheap and the world is in a state of chaos, sexual promiscuity will still be a rampant disease of the human race. Who can question the fact that we are observing a wave of lust that is sweeping across the world, preparing humankind for the day of complete moral breakdown that will reach its culmination during the time of the Tribulation?

5. "Thefts." The thievery mentioned here substantiates the lawlessness that will abound in this hour of great Tribulation on the earth, for people will get money or things by any means possible. The book of Revelation teaches that this period will be a time when everyone will give in to the fulfillment of the desires and lusts of the flesh. In their mad quest for peace or contentment, people will turn further and further from God. Not only will they damn their immortal souls, but they will bring on themselves all the heartaches of their misspent lives; it will be just as true in the days of the Tribulation as in our own day, "A man reaps what he sows" (Gal. 6:7).

SEVENTEEN

The Mighty Angel and the Little Scroll

Revelation 10

The first nine chapters of the book of Revelation have brought us almost to the middle of the Tribulation. The seven seal judgments covered the first quarter, the seventh seal introduced the next quarter (the trumpet judgments), and now chapters 10:1–11:14 comprise a parenthetical section given to John just before the prophecy concerning the last half of the Tribulation. This section is to the trumpet judgments what chapter 7 was to the seal judgments: a description of conditions that existed during the particular period of time covered by the preceding judgments.

THE MIGHTY ANGEL

The identity of this "mighty angel" is debated by Bible teachers. Some contend that this is Christ. Since Christ appeared as the angel of God in the Old Testament, this would be another occasion in which He appears to the nation of Israel. Others say it is not Christ but an unidentified angel.

The Lord Jesus Christ does not appear in the book of Revelation as an angel. In fact, we look in vain for a presentation of Him as an angel after His incarnation. Ever since Jesus took on flesh, died for the sins of the human race, was crucified, rose from the dead, and ascended into heaven, He has always appeared as the Son of God in His essential deity. Although this angel possesses some Godlike characteristics, he is not God. Part of the problem may well be a failure to understand the nature of angels. Although far beneath the character of God, they are created beings of an unusually high order.

It is interesting to see how prominent a role angels play in the book of Revelation. They are mentioned more than sixty-six times throughout the book, always in a position of service. They do not create things, but fulfill the administration of God in human affairs. This is not the first time we have been introduced to a mighty angel, for in 5:2 we find the same word used.

Don't be deceived by the glorious description of this angel—"robed in a cloud, with a rainbow above his head; his face was like the sun, and his legs were like fiery pillars" (10:1). Actually, in 18:1 we find another angel, pronouncing doom on Babylon, having great power and so much glory that "the earth was illuminated by his splendor." No one seems pressed to identify this other angel as the Lord Jesus Christ; consequently we should not think it strange that God could have other mighty angels that could easily fit the description of the one in our text.

This mighty angel has in his hand a little scroll, which we will describe in connection with verse 8. He stands with his right foot in the sea and his left foot on the earth, indicating that he has authority over all land and sea surfaces. He then cries with a "loud voice," the signal for seven thunderlike voices.

SEVEN THUNDERLIKE VOICES

The voices that sound like seven thunders are a unique feature in the book of Revelation. John is prepared to write down what these thunderlike voices say when he hears another voice: "Seal up what the seven thunders have said and do not write it down" (10:4). This is the only proclamation in the entire book of Revelation that is sealed up. These voices could be the voices of other angels that sounded in such mighty volume as to resemble thunder, but since we are not told in Scripture the exact identity of the voices, it is dangerous to speculate further.

Even more important to our curiosity is what these voices say. Dr. J. Vernon McGee, in his book, *Reveling Through Revelation,* points out that many ridiculous guesses and wild speculations have been proposed. For example, "Vitringa interpreted them as the seven crusades; Danbuz made them the seven nations that received the Reformation; Elliott makes them the pope's bull against Luther; and Seventh-Day Adventism has presumed to reveal the things which were uttered."[20] Since the Apostle John is commanded by the voice to "seal up" their utterances, it is foolish to conjecture any further.

THE MIGHTY ANGEL PROVES HE IS NOT THE LORD JESUS CHRIST

The unusual action of the angel's lifting his hand toward heaven and swearing "by him who lives for ever and ever, who created the heavens and all that is in them, the earth and all that is in it, and the sea and all that is in it" (10:6) certainly indicates that this mighty angel is not the Lord Jesus Christ. The angel is making an oath by the only sure guarantee, that is, God Himself. Hebrews 6:13 tells us of an Old Testament promise made by God to Abraham in which "since there was no one greater for him to swear by, he swore by himself." This angel in Revelation 10 swore by someone greater than himself, for he lifted up his hand toward heaven and cried and swore by the Creator, the Lord Jesus Christ (John 1:3), who obviously he was not.

This angel, then, is swearing or giving oath on the authority of the Lord Jesus Christ: "There will be no more delay!" The Greek word *chronos*, used here, has two meanings, "time" and "delay." It is obvious that time is not the appropriate meaning, for there *is* time after this event. In fact, three-and-a-half years of Tribulation follow the utterance made here, plus the one thousand years of the millennial kingdom.

The New International Version has correctly translated this word "delay": There will be delay no longer. Humanity has been living in the time of God's delay for centuries, but this angel warns the human race that God is about to conclude His patience in the face of their rebellion against His will, and that soon the final consummation will take place. This consummation occurs three-and-a-half years after the utterance is made, for it is given at approximately the middle of the Tribulation period.

THE MYSTERY OF GOD

"The mystery of God will be accomplished, just as he announced to his servants the prophets" (10:7). The word "mystery" (*mysterion*) appears several times in the Bible, meaning that God is going to disclose a truth that is only possible to know in his Word. Human wisdom never has comprehended nor ever will be able to deduce these truths apart from that Word.

"The mystery of God" here referred to can only mean salvation. One of the characteristics of salvation involves the mystery of how a holy God could love sinful human beings sufficiently to send His only Son into the world to die for their sins. This was made known to the prophets, God's servants in both the Old Testament and the New Testament. For all these thousands of years people have been living under the mystery of God, where it is possible for the sinful, fallen human race to be reinstated into fellowship with God by being born into His family without works but by faith. That this mystery is soon coming to a close is apparent by the act that forty-two months of the Tribulation period have expired when this statement is given, and, as we will see in 12:6, at this point there are only 1,260 days of humanity's known history left, apart from the kingdom age.

Revelation 10:2 tells us that the mighty angel holds a little scroll open in his hand. John is to take this scroll from the mighty angel (10:8).

WHAT IS THE LITTLE SCROLL

Several suggestions have been made as to the identity of the little scroll. Some say it is the seven-sealed scroll taken from the hand of God by the nail-scarred hand of Christ, given to the mighty angel, who in turn gives it to John. If this is true, the little scroll is the title deed to the earth, with the title description on one side and the seven seal judgments on the other. Since the seven seals have been broken and it has been revealed what the seven seals are, perhaps there is no longer need for this book. Thus, John is told to eat it.

Another suggestion is that the little scroll is the new revelation to John of events from this point on to chapter 19. In either case it is the prophecy of God concerning future events. Since the mighty angel is pictured as standing with one foot in the sea and one foot on the land, John must no longer be in heaven. He has apparently returned to the earth to take the little scroll. It is a scroll, therefore, that has to do with events that are to happen on the earth.

After John asks the angel for the little scroll, he is told to take it and eat it, though warned that it will be sweet to the taste and bitter to the belly. Eating a scroll is a symbolic reference in the Scriptures to digesting a scroll. Note Jeremiah 15:16: "When your words came, I ate them; they were my joy and my heart's delight, for I bear your name, O LORD God Almighty." Ezekiel 3:1–3 contains the admonition of the Lord to the Old Testament prophet to "eat this scroll," and it "tasted as sweet as honey in my mouth." After he had eaten the book, he was told to go speak to the house of Israel.

The obvious meaning of these symbolic references to "eating the word of God" is that before someone can be a spokesman for God, he must digest the Word of God. He obviously does not eat mechanically, but mentally feeds on the Word of God. One of the reasons for so much sterility and stagnation in the Church of Jesus Christ today is that in spite of all the translations and vernacular writings available, God's people are not "digesting the Word of God." If they read, they have a tendency to read more about what other people have said concerning the Word of God than to read the Word of God itself.

After John has eaten the scroll, the mighty angel says to him, "You must prophesy again about many peoples, nations, languages and kings" (10:11). Through the written book of Revelation, this command to the Apostle John has been fulfilled, for the book of Revelation has been studied by "peoples, nations, languages and kings."

The picture of sweetness in the mouth and bitterness in the belly indicates the typical quality of God's Word, which is sharper than a two-edged sword. The sweetness comes to John in the predictions concerning our blessed Lord's return; the bitterness comes to John in being confronted by the fact that judgment is pronounced on the earth.

The gospel is much like this. It is sweet to those who hear and respond, thus being guaranteed eternal salvation as the free gift of God. It is bitter to those who reject it, however, for the same gospel that guarantees salvation to those who receive it, guarantees judgment and damnation to those who do not.

EIGHTEEN

Two Super Witnesses

Revelation 11:1–14

Revelation 11 is an integral part of the small parenthesis that began in 10:1 and continues to 11:14. This chapter has to do with the spiritual life of Israel; chapter 12 concerns the coming persecution of Israel. In chapter 11 we find that Israel will revert to the Old Testament form of worship. They will rebuild the temple apart from the Messiah since they believe He has not come. Thus they will construct the temple of rejection. In addition, this chapter unfolds the revelation that two supernatural witnesses will be recalled from Old Testament days to convey God's message to the Jerusalem area. These two witnesses are another illustration in this book that God is so keenly interested in the souls of people that He will even send two supernatural witnesses to convince lost humanity. In spite of these witnesses and the 144,000 of chapter 7, the majority will reject God's offer of salvation. Israel will basically remain in unbelief until the time of her great persecution. Before proceeding any further, you should read all of chapter 11.

We have already seen that preterists try desperately to find some internal biblical evidence to establish the date of Revelation during the reign of Nero (A.D. 64) in an attempt to prove the book was written before the fall of Jerusalem. This helps them to avoid facing the fact that the prophecies of Revelation are yet future. For instance, they like to use this command to John to measure the Temple as proof it is still in existence when he receives this vision. As we have seen, this would solve the post- and amillennial theory's most difficult problem: how to interpret the "thousand-year" time limit of the millennial kingdom mentioned six times in Revelation 20. Understandably, they would love to spiritualize it away by having it buried in the A.D. 70 destruction of the temple.

One problem with their reasoning is that we have Biblical precedent for God's commanding His servant Ezekiel (Ezek. 40–44) to measure the Temple long after it had been destroyed by the armies of Nebuchadnezzar six hundred years before Christ. Daniel also prophesied a desecration of the temple when it was still nonexistent. Obviously, if the temple referred to by these Old Testament prophets was of a future temple, then it follows that John in vision (in A.D. 95) saw a future Temple, one that is yet to be desecrated by the Antichrist (a Temple yet to be rebuilt during the Tribulation period). The fact that many Jewish groups are preparing materials today for just such an occasion to rebuild the Temple leads many to think we are coming close to the time of these prophesied events.

HISTORY OF THE JEWISH TEMPLE

After Israel was established in the land of Palestine, David, the "man after [God's] own heart" (1 Sam. 13:14; Acts 13:22), desired to build a great temple for the Lord God, but David had bloodied his hands in wars to the degree that it was impossible for God to use him for that purpose. He was permitted instead to raise much of the money and material that later went into the building of what came to be known as Solomon's Temple.

The Temple was built in Jerusalem at God's command, for Jerusalem was to be the city where He would place His name and where His people would come to worship (Pss. 71:65–72; 87:1–3; 132:13–15). The Shekinah Glory of God appeared in the Temple and became a symbol of the protecting hand of God on the nation Israel. In their apostate days, toward the end of the kingdom era, the nation thought itself impregnable as long as the Temple stood. They were deaf to the cries of Jeremiah and Ezekiel, even after some had been taken away into Babylonian captivity. Finally, the Temple and the city of Jerusalem were destroyed by Nebuchadnezzar.

Seventy years later a decree was given for the rebuilding of the city and eventually the Temple. This Temple, under the direction of Zerubbabel and Joshua the high priest was much inferior to the Temple of Solomon—so much so that some of the elders who recalled the earlier Temple wept when they saw the foundation of the new Temple. This Temple served Israel until it was desecrated by Antiochus Epiphanes, one of the Greco-Syrian rulers. This desecration was a type of the desecration of the Temple by the Antichrist at the end time or Tribulation Period. About forty years before Christ, Herod the Great had this whole temple destroyed piecemeal and rebuilt. That temple was known during New Testament days as Herod's Temple (John 2:20).

Matthew 24:2 contains the prediction of the Lord that the Temple would be destroyed: "Not one stone here will be left on another; every one will be thrown down." This prophecy was fulfilled during the time of Titus, the Roman general who laid siege to the city of Jerusalem. Although he gave orders that the Temple should not be destroyed, the Jews burned it rather than allow it to fall into pagan hands. Jesus' prophecy was fulfilled exactly, for today the site of the old Jewish Temple is occupied by the Muslims, who built a mosque called the "Dome of the Rock." One will look in vain for a single stone of the Temple of Herod resting upon another that has not been thrown down, for the

Dome of the Rock that now occupies that space is made entirely of different material. Because of Islam's present-day hatred for Israel, it is very likely that not one stone has been left upon another.

The Temple to Be Rebuilt

Several passages of Scripture refer to the Temple of the end time. In Matthew 24:15 the Lord Jesus referred to the "abomination that causes desolation, spoken of through the prophet Daniel," indicating that at the end time, in the middle of the Tribulation period as Daniel predicted, a temple will be desecrated by the Antichrist. In order for this to be fulfilled it must first be rebuilt. Likewise, in 2 Thessalonians 2:1–13 the Apostle Paul predicted that the Antichrist, in the middle of the Tribulation, would defy God by sitting in the Temple of God and presenting himself to the world as God. In order for him to do this that temple has to be rebuilt.

Ever since Jews have been returning to the land of Palestine, rumors have circulated concerning the accumulation of materials for the eventual rebuilding of the Temple. The one piece of ground that the Jews want most is the site now occupied by the Dome of the Rock, the second most holy shrine in the Moslem world—second only to Mecca, the birthplace of Mohammed. Jewish interest has been aroused, because the Dome of the Rock is built right over Mount Moriah, the place considered to be the site of Abraham's willingness to offer Isaac as a sacrifice in obedience to God.

It is difficult to substantiate any of the rumors about the planned Temple rebuilding. Some years ago a friend gave me a clipping from the *San Francisco Chronicle* entitled "Jerusalem Is Talking About Rebuilding the Temple," but it gave no specific details. In addition to this it stated, "Sometime ago the wife of a Chicago lawyer, Anna Ravens, left a legacy of $50,000 to be used toward the rebuilding of the Jewish temple in Jerusalem." No doubt her case has been repeated hundreds of times, and when the day comes that Israel can send a call to the Jews all over the world for this rebuilding, be assured that there will be millions of dollars pouring into Jerusalem immediately.

News of a mobile model of the future Temple has appeared as being transported throughout America for fundraising purposes. This fact indicates two things. One, the plans have already been drawn and millions of dollars have already been raised for that purpose. Also the collection of building materials and fabrics are already being prepared. It is estimated that with unlimited money, modern technology, and the signing of the covenant with the Antichrist for seven years (Dan. 9:27), which will give the Jews access to the Temple Mount and permission to rebuild, it could be accomplished in as little as nine to eighteen months.

Rebuilding the Temple Is a Rejection of Christ

Believers in the Lord Jesus Christ are not taught to build a temple; on the contrary, we are taught that God does not live in temples made with hands, but that the Holy Spirit uses the believer's body as a tabernacle or dwelling place (1 Cor. 6:19–20). The fact that Israel will rebuild the Temple indicates that she has not received the Messiah. Therefore we suggest the following chronology of events:

The act that will start the Tribulation period is the signing of the covenant with the Antichrist (Dan. 9:27), which will become an ungodly league with an evil power, indicating that Israel at the beginning of the Tribulation will not be predominately Christian. Then 144,000 servants of the Lord will go forth witnessing, reaching a multitude of Gentiles that no one can number; but they represent the remnant, not a major portion of the Jewish nation. Instead, the Jews will make this ungodly league with the Antichrist, permitting them to take the city of Jerusalem from the hands of the Arabs. They will build the Temple and once again institute the sacrificial system, rejecting Christ.

The fact that John is told to measure the Temple indicates that he will find it woefully inadequate as compared with the Temple of Solomon, which was inspired by God. The word "measure" may well refer to the fact that Israel will be severely judged for her rejection of the Messiah in view of the astounding light she has and will have. This Temple, then, will be built at the beginning of the Tribulation, for in the middle of it, as we will see in chapter 13:2, the Antichrist will break his league with the Jews and set up his idol in the midst of the Temple, indicating that the outer court is to be unmeasured, for it is in the hands of the nations (Gentiles). Two periods of time are measured here: 42 months and 1,260 days. Since they are identical, they may well refer to the equal division of the Tribulation period. These two measurements of time could refer to the first half of the Tribulation period; those mentioned in Revelation 12:16 and 13:5 probably refer to the last half, since here again both types of description are used.

THE TWO WITNESSES

"And I will give power to my two witnesses, and they will prophesy for 1,260 days, clothed in sackcloth" (Rev. 11:3). At this point, colorful and dynamic individuals come on the scene as the special witnesses of God. God will give *power* to them. These two witnesses will have the power to send fire out of their mouths and to kill those that try to persecute them. They also will have the power to shut up the heavens "so that it will not rain" (11:6), that the earth might be covered with a great drought. They also will have power over waters to turn them to blood and to smite the earth with all manner of plagues. This power is for the purpose of witnessing God's power in distinction to that of the Antichrist.

Who Are These Two Witnesses?

A variety of fanciful suggestions have been offered as to the identity of these two witnesses. Because God has not chosen to tell us exactly who they are, we can only offer a suggestion. Some of the most reliable suggestions are Elijah and Enoch, Elijah and John the Baptist, or Elijah and Moses.

Malachi 4:5–6 predicted that Elijah would come before "that great and dreadful day of the LORD comes." Moreover, we find that the use of fire in the Old Testament was limited to Elijah, who called down fire to consume the altar in the days of Ahab (2 Kings 18:20–40). He also withheld rain from the earth for three years. Therefore, it seems more than likely that Elijah is one of the two witnesses.

We do not find that John the Baptist demonstrated the power of Elijah, and he freely admitted he was not Elijah. Both he and the angel Gabriel made that clear. In Luke 1:17 Gabriel told Zechariah, the father of John the Baptist, that John would come "in the spirit and power of Elijah"; but that does not mean he would be Elijah. John was asked by the priests and Levites from Jerusalem, "Are you Elijah?" He said, "I am not" (John 1:21). John wore sackcloth and was a type of Elijah, but he did not minister to the Jewish nation as Elijah did.

There are only two good reasons for suggesting Enoch. First, he did not die, whereas Hebrews 9:27 tells us that "man is destined to die once, and after that to face judgment." Second, Jude 14–15 states that Enoch prophesied that "the Lord is coming with thousands upon thousands of his holy ones to judge everyone." Although these are good reasons, there are others to the contrary, sufficient to eliminate Enoch from consideration.

Enoch was a Gentile who lived hundreds of years before Abraham; therefore he is not identified in any way with Israel. The fact that Enoch and Elijah never died is not sufficient evidence to suggest they will be the two witnesses, for all believers living at the time of the Rapture of the Church will be exceptions to Hebrews 9:27. When the Lord comes, we "will be raised imperishable" (1 Cor. 15:52–58). At the Rapture, believers will be snatched out of the world and taken to be with the Lord without ever tasting of death (1 Thess. 4:13–18). According to Hebrews 11:5 the purpose of Enoch's translation was "that he did not experience death." The two witnesses in Revelation 11:3–14 do taste death; therefore, it would seem that Enoch cannot be one of these witnesses.

There are, however, three good reasons why Moses is the second witness during the first part of the Tribulation period.

1. In Matthew 17:1–5, when the Lord Jesus was transfigured before His Jewish witnesses—Peter, James, and John—two representatives of

the Old Testament were brought before their view: Moses and Elijah. Their purpose was to discuss with Christ His impending death.

2. Moses manifested power to bring plagues on the earth and to turn water into blood during the days of Pharaoh. Elijah did not do these things, but had power to call down fire from heaven and to stop rain. Therefore it reasonably follows that these two men will be given the miraculous powers they already demonstrated while on the earth.

3. Moses is an integral part of Jewish family tradition. It seems logical, therefore, that he will become one of the witnesses, for Moses and Elijah combined represent the entire Old Testament to the Jewish nation. When the rich man asked Abraham to send Lazarus back to his father's house to warn his five brethren to repent, "so that they will not also come to this place of torment," Abraham embraced the Jewish concept of the entire Old Testament by saying, "They have Moses and the Prophets; let them listen to them" (Luke 16:27–29). Moses represents the first five books; Elijah, the outstanding prophet of Israel, represents the prophetic books. "Moses and the Prophets" includes almost all those who had a hand in writing the Old Testament. Thus the two men in Jewish history who most speak of God's dealing with the nation Israel are Moses and Elijah.

The Work of the Two Witnesses

The work of the two witnesses is outlined in our text. They will primarily be witnesses of God. This is seen by virtue of the fact that they are likened to the two lampstands and the two olive trees of the book of Zechariah. Since this Old Testament symbol is used to convey the message of two men proclaiming God's faithfulness, we assume Elijah and Moses will do the same. They will be on the scene during the first half of the Tribulation period to counteract the lying wonders of the Antichrist. They will also "prophesy" (Rev. 11:3), which means they will preach concerning the things to come. No doubt they will be warning people on the basis of the book of Revelation concerning events and interpreting them as they relate to the people. Malachi 4:6 tells us that Elijah's ministry will be to "turn the hearts of the fathers to their children, and the hearts of the children to their fathers."

This seems like normal living to us, but we should remember that the Antichrist will be deceiving the people, turning the fathers against the children and the children against the fathers. Therefore the witness of these two men will be helping those who receive the Lord to return to normal thinking. It is probable that they will be the special witnesses of God to the Holy Land, whereas the 144,000 are witnesses throughout the entire earth (Rev. 7:9). We find further that they will testify, for 11:7 tells us that "they have finished their testimony." Evidently this indicates the preaching of the gospel. True testifying is preaching the gospel, whether it be in the Church Age, the Tribulation, or the Millennium.

The Witnesses Killed

"Now when they have finished their testimony, the beast that comes up from the Abyss will attack them, and overpower and kill them" (Rev. 11:7). "The beast that comes up from the Abyss" refers to the beast described in Revelation 13:1–7. "The beast" is an expression used here for the first time; the fact that he will come up out of the Abyss is a reference to the death and resurrection of the Antichrist, as we will see in more detail in chapter 13. The beast or Antichrist, the man of sin, will hate the two witnesses, make war against them, and kill them. However, note that he will have no power over them until "they have finished their testimony." In other words, they will be "immortal until their work is done"—which can be said of all God's servants who walk in obedience to His will.

The completely degenerate and inhuman characteristics of people living during the Tribulation period is seen in Revelation 11:8, which informs us that the bodies of the two witnesses will be left open in the streets of Jerusalem. The Holy City will be so degenerate spiritually that she will be called Sodom and Egypt—Sodom being a symbol of immorality and Egypt a symbol of materialism. The lives of the people going back to occupy the Holy Land today are anything but holy. They seldom even attend synagogues on the Sabbath.

"For three and a half days men from every people, tribe, language and nation will gaze on their bodies and refuse them burial" (Rev. 11:9). Someone has suggested that the modern medium of television makes possible the fulfillment of this verse. The only way in which people all over the world can see two bodies lying in the streets of a city over a three-day period of time is through the medium of television; in fact, in recent years it has been possible by the launching of television satellites for many parts of the world to view the same sight at the same time. CNN International newscasts are already beamed into more than two hundred countries of the world. In fact, ours is the first generation that can literally see the fulfillment of 11:9 in allowing the people of the entire world to see such an awesome spectacle.

This is one more indication that we are coming closer to the end of the age, because it would have been humanly impossible just a few years ago for the entire world to see these two witnesses in the streets at a given moment of time. Not content to look on them, verse 10 tells us that people throughout the world will enjoy a Christmas-like celebration, giving and receiving gifts because these preachers of righteousness and holiness are now dead.

The Witnesses Resurrected

> But after the three and a half days a breath of life from God entered them, and they stood on their feet, and terror struck those who saw them. Then they heard a loud voice from heaven saying to them, "Come up here." And they went up to heaven in a cloud....
>
> (Rev. 11:11–12)

Then suddenly "a breath of life from God entered them, and they stood on their feet." As our Lord was crucified, buried, and in three days rose from the dead, these men, after being slain and exposed to the eyes of the world, will hear the voice of God resurrecting them. A cloud will receive them out of sight in the face of their enemies. It is no wonder that "terror struck those who saw them." The resurrection of these men will be the final confirmation that they were men of God, another illustration that God does not forget His own.

This will provide a frightening scene for the peoples of the earth when they see on their favorite TV newscast these two despised witnesses caught up into heaven. But the universal hatred of the world's population for these two prophets of God gives us unusual insight of what the moral conditions of the majority of the world will be at that time. They will love Antichrist and his immoral standards for society and rebel against God and hate morality. Then, as now, there will be three kinds of people on earth: the followers of Antichrist, the Tribulation saints (who have received the Savior by faith), and the still undecided. Fifty percent of the world's population will have been killed in the seal and trumpet judgments, and "a great multitude that no one could count" (Rev. 7:9) will be saved by this midpoint in the Tribulation period. Only God knows how many believers will have already been martyred.

Since those unbelievers slain by God were the wearers of the mark of the beast (meaning they have already chosen Antichrist over Christ as their Savior), the antagonism of the people of the earth towards the two prophets suggests that even the undecided majority of the remaining population hates God and His moral values and vent that hatred at these prophets. That may suggest that even though some evangelizing will continue during the last half of the Tribulation period—what Jesus called the "great tribulation"—will continue while the 144,000 witnesses remain. But it will not be like the great soul harvest of the first three and one-half years.

DOES REVELATION 11:11–12 TEACH A MID-TRIBULATION RAPTURE?

One of the principal texts that mid-Tribulationists use to indicate that the Rapture of the Church will occur during the middle of that period is this scene of the two witnesses being supernaturally resurrected and a loud voice from heaven saying to them, "'Come up here.'" And they went up to heaven in a cloud, while their enemies looked on." There are several problems with this idea . . .

1. The two witnesses are not New Testament Christians; they are Jews who prophesy and minister to Israel. In no way can they be representative of the Church. They are special cases and are resurrected and raptured up to heaven as special cases.
2. There are no saints included with this Rapture. In Paul's narration in 1 Thessalonians 4:16–17 it is clear that "the dead in Christ will rise first. After that, we who are still alive and are left will be caught up together with them in the clouds to meet the Lord in the air." The resurrection and rapture of the two witnesses as servants of God when their work is completed is a special resurrection for them only.
3. There has been no mention of the church for three and one-half years (in Rev. 4:2–11:12). Yet the church was mentioned in chapters 1–3 seventeen times! Now mid-Tribulationists would have us believe these two Israelites being raptured in the middle of the Tribulation is proof the Church will be raptured. There is no mention of the Church or Christians here to support such a mid-Tribulation position.

Mid-Tribulationists do not recognize John's rapture in 4:1–2 as a picture of the Rapture, yet John was a far better representative of the body of Christ than these two Old Testament prophets. I am inclined to believe the only reason they see this as a proof text of their position is its occurrence in the middle of the Tribulation. They do point out that the seventh trumpet judgment sounds at this point and claim that is synonymous with "the last trumpet" of 1 Corinthians 15:52, which they locate here. The problem is that many trumpets are used in Scripture. Every day had a first and last trumpet just as armies do today. Paul's "last trumpet" reference is the last trumpet for the Church to be raptured from the earth. The seventh trumpet is one of an entirely different set of trumpets for Israel during the Tribulation. And again, there is no evidence that the Church is on earth during the first half of the Tribulation.

God's Judgment on Jerusalem

At that very hour there was a severe earthquake and a tenth of the city collapsed. Seven thousand people were killed in the earthquake, and the survivors were terrified and gave glory to the God of heaven.

(Rev. 11:13)

As a result of the shocking treatment of these two faithful witnesses of God by the inhabitants of the city of Jerusalem, the Lord will send a great earthquake, destroying a tenth part of the city and slaying seven thousand people. This cataclysmic judgment of God on the city of Jerusalem may be the event that triggers a revival that will sweep across Israel during the latter half of the Tribulation, for the passage reads, "and the survivors were terrified and gave glory to the God of heaven." This remnant may refer to the Jewish inhabitants of the city who, after seeing the judging hand of God slay seven thousand of their residents and destroy a tenth part of their city, will turn in faith to embrace the message of the two witnesses so recently resurrected. All of these events take place before the third woe is sounded in verse 14, which identifies these two witnesses who live, preach, die, and are resurrected during the first half of the Tribulation period. In addition to closing this second parenthetical passage, it also sets the stage for the events of the latter half of the Tribulation period.

NINETEEN

The Seventh Trumpet Judgment

Revelation 11:15–19

The blowing of the seventh trumpet (which is the third woe) does not initiate anything on the earth. Instead, it is much like the breaking of the seventh seal of Revelation 8:1. It merely introduces the next series of judgments, the seven bowls. Occurring exclusively in heaven, the scene introduces activities that project a meaning to the earth to be disclosed in subsequent chapters.

In order to comprehend the chronological events of this passage of Scripture, one should understand that immediately after this heavenly introduction to the seven bowls, there is another lengthy parenthetical passage that conveys details of events that will take place during the entire Tribulation period. These events include the persecution of God's children (ch. 12), the Antichrist, or the "beast coming out of the sea," and the "false prophet" (ch. 13), a heavenly vision (ch. 14), and the introduction to the last half of the Tribulation (ch. 15). This is a heavenly setting, announcing the great events that will come on the earth. Awesome beyond description, it is called the "Great Tribulation" because it reveals the most fantastic events the world has ever known.

THE FIRST ANGELIC CHORUS

The seventh angel sounded his trumpet, and there were loud voices in heaven, which said:

> "The kingdom of the world has become the kingdom of our
>   Lord and of his Christ,
>   and he will reign for ever and ever."   (Rev. 11:15)

John hears "great voices" singing in heaven, evidently angelic voices in chorus. They announced two things:

1. "The kingdom of the world has become the kingdom of our Lord and of his Christ." John has in view the kingdom of the Antichrist at the time of the Glorious Appearing (Rev. 19:11). Thus the angels will announce in heaven at the beginning of the last half of the Tribulation period that the one-world kingdom of the Antichrist will be conquered by the kingdom of Christ when He returns to this earth.

2. "And he will reign for ever and ever." In the Greek language this is the strongest term possible for "ages of ages," indicating that once Christ comes to earth, there will be no interruption of His government. Rebellion will break out at the end of the Millennium when "Satan will be released from his prison" (Rev. 20:7), but our glorified Lord will quell it so quickly that it will not interfere with His kingdom.

THE SONG OF THE TWENTY-FOUR ELDERS

And the twenty-four elders, who were seated on their thrones before God, fell on their faces and worshiped God, saying:

"We give thanks to you, Lord God Almighty,
     the One who is and who was,
because you have taken your great power
     and have begun to reign.
The nations were angry;
     and your wrath has come.
The time has come for judging the dead,
     and for rewarding your servants the prophets
and your saints and those who reverence your name,
     both small and great—
and for destroying those who destroy the earth."   (Rev. 11:16–18)

The twenty-four elders fall on their faces before God and worship Him, announcing His eternity with the words, "the One who is and who was."

This is a song of thanksgiving ("We give thanks to you, Lord God Almighty"). The elders use the prophetic perfect tense, indicating that they anticipate in heaven the final stage of God's activity on the earth before the coming of Christ, and they rejoice over the eventual consummation of His kingdom ("because you have taken your great power and have begun to reign"). Christ will not reign until the end of the Tribulation, but He certainly reigns then! The twenty-four elders proceed to make three predictions on the basis of the coming Christ:

1. "The nations were angry; and your wrath has come" indicates that at the time of His coming the nations will resent His coming and rebel against Him. Psalm 2 should be studied in this connection.

2. "The time has come for judging the dead" refers to the Old Testament saints and Tribulation saints who have been slain. This does not refer to unbelievers, who will be judged a thousand years later at the end of the Millennium (Rev. 20:11–15). The resurrection of Old Testament saints and the Rapture of Tribulation saints will take place at the end of the Tribulation, at the glorious appearing of our Lord. That subject is described in Psalm 50:1–6:

> The Mighty One, God, the LORD,
> speaks and summons the earth
> from the rising of the sun to the place where it sets.
> From Zion, perfect in beauty,
> God shines forth.
> Our God comes and will not be silent;
> a fire devours before him,
> and around him a tempest rages.
> He summons the heavens above,
> and the earth, that he may judge his people:
> "Gather to me my consecrated ones,
> who made a covenant with me by sacrifice."
> And the heavens proclaim his righteousness,
> for God himself is judge.

Here the Lord is seen, not in heaven but in the air, calling to His Old Testament saints who are still in heaven. The Church will not be in heaven at this point, since they will have been "caught up . . . to meet the Lord in the air" (1 Thess. 4:17) before the Tribulation. This will be a call, then, for the Old Testament saints who are still in heaven to be joined with the Tribulation saints in rapture and resurrection. Just as our Lord Himself has a "shout" for the Church at the beginning of the Tribulation, He has a "cry" for the Old Testament saints who will be resurrected and the Tribulation saints who will be raptured: "Gather to me my consecrated ones."

3. "And for destroying those who destroy the earth" (Rev. 11:18) indicates that Christ will take the Antichrist (the beast) and the False Prophet alive and throw them into the lake of fire. Their followers also will be killed (19:20). This text teaches that the followers of Antichrist, like all human beings who die without Christ, will go in soul and spirit to the "place of torment" (as did the rich man in Luke 16) until the Great White Throne Judgment, when they will appear for the final judgment and be cast into the lake of fire. This fact again indicates the eternal seriousness of a rebellious attitude against Almighty God and His divine offer of salvation.

THE TEMPLE OF GOD IN HEAVEN

Then God's temple in heaven was opened, and within his temple was seen the ark of his covenant. And there came flashes of lightning, rumblings, peals of thunder, an earthquake and a great hailstorm.

(Rev. 11:19)

We should keep in mind that the subject of this passage is the Rapture of Israel and Tribulation saints, who are redeemed because they have entered into a covenant with Him by sacrifice (Ps. 50:5). The Church does not have a temple or tabernacle, but Israel did. The vision of the Ark of the Covenant could be a reminder to Israel that they are dealing with a covenant-keeping God, and on the basis of His past faithfulness their redemption is guaranteed.

Israel, Christians, and Tribulation saints share in common this essential: They enter into a covenant with God by sacrifice, the covenant of a blood sacrifice—Israel temporarily by animal sacrifices; Christians and the Tribulation saints through the Lord Jesus Christ, who sacrificed Himself "once for all."

The "lightning, rumblings and peals of thunder" indicate that the scene in heaven is over and events are about to be disclosed that have to do with the affairs of human beings. These catastrophes bespeak the mounting confusion and terror that will come upon the earth in the latter half of the Tribulation period. In view of the destruction that awaits the earth, any intelligent being is left with only one decision, and that is to avoid that awful period in the world's future through receiving Jesus Christ as Savior and Lord by personal invitation.

TWENTY

Satan Versus Israel

Revelation 12

It should not come as a surprise that so much space is given in the book of Revelation to the nation of Israel. She dominates the pages of the Old Testament because she is God's nation of destiny. That He is not through with her is seen in the prophetic "time of Jacob's trouble" outlined in chapter 13 and described in Daniel 9:24–27. The "seventieth week of Daniel" or Tribulation period is covered in Revelation 6–18. It would naturally include an extensive prediction of Israel's part in that time that will try the whole earth.

So far in our study we have discovered that Israel will make a league or covenant with the Antichrist for seven years (Dan. 9:27). Revelation 7 indicates that 144,000 servants of God will go forth to preach the gospel of Christ. Because of (1) the effects of the Rapture of the Church, (2) the outpouring of the Spirit of God as on the day of Pentecost (Joel 2:28–31), making them like 144,000 Apostle Pauls, (3) world conditions of chaos designed by God to lead people to Christ, and (4) the population explosion, placing more people on the earth than ever before in the history of the world, these 144,000 servants may well reach more people for Christ than have been won during the entire Christian dispensation.

Such a host is described in Revelation 7:9: "a great multitude that no one could count, from every nation, tribe, people and language, standing before the throne." It should be kept in mind that the 144,000 Jewish witnesses represent a remnant of Israel, for according to Revelation 11 the Jews will rebuild the temple in Jerusalem, indicating that they return to the land in unbelief. We also have found that God will send two special witnesses with supernatural powers like those of Elijah and Moses to counteract in Palestine the supernatural powers of Antichrist (2 Thess. 2:9–12).

THE MIDDLE OF THE TRIBULATION

Chapter 12 introduces the second half of the Tribulation period by giving a heavenly recap of the great conflict of the ages, bringing us up to date. Before the human race was ever created in the Garden of Eden, there was a conflict between God and His most powerful angel, Satan. For some reason Satan thought he was equal with God. Even today he evidently thinks he can wrest control of this universe from God himself. The Bible shows that from the creation of humankind to the present there has been an endless conflict for the will and soul of people to see if they would use that free will to obey God or Satan.

As we will see, the principal forms Satan has used to deceive human beings about God is religion and government. Humanity has had a running romance with government since just after the Flood; but instead of doing them good, government has been the principal cause of much suffering to the present day. Take the twentieth century, for example: More people have been murdered, starved, or imprisoned by government in these past one hundred years (between 160–180 million people killed) than in all the rest of human history put together. And Satan has been behind almost all of these rapacious governments that had no regard for humanity.

FOUR KEY PERSONAGES

Chapter 12 introduces the fact that in the middle of the Tribulation period Israel will be confronted with the worst wave of anti-Semitism the world has ever seen. Yet "God is faithful" as usual! Four key personages appear in this chapter. We will examine them carefully.

1. The Sun-Clothed Woman

> A great and wondrous sign appeared in heaven: a woman clothed with the sun, with the moon under her feet and a crown of twelve stars on her head. She was pregnant and cried out in pain as she was about to give birth. (Rev. 12:1–2)

Many suggestions have been offered as to the identity of this "woman clothed with the sun." The church of Rome has maintained that she represents the Virgin Mary. In 1678 the Spanish artist Murillo created his famous painting "Mystery of the Immaculate Conception," a painting of the "woman clothed with the sun." For some reason he did not show her standing on the moon with a crown of twelve stars on her head. Thus the passage has been used to teach Mary's bodily assumption into heaven.

Others have proposed that the sun-clad woman is the Church, and still others have tried to use it to define themselves. In his *Book of Revelation,* Dr. Lehman Strauss writes,

> Then there is the blasphemous teaching of Mary Baker Glover Patterson Eddy, who was conceited enough to claim that this woman of Revelation 12 represented herself. She added that the "man child" that she brought forth is Christian Science; that the "dragon is mortal mind" (whatever that is) attempting to destroy her new religion.

I shall not go beyond Dr. Ironside's answer to Mrs. Eddy's interpretation: ". . . I need not take up the time of sane people."[21]

Dr. J. Vernon McGee further notes, "A female preacher in California, who became famous or infamous—however you care to express it—toyed with the idea that she might be the woman mentioned in this chapter."[22]

The importance of the identity of this woman is stressed in Dr. H. A. Ironside's commentary on Revelation.

I think I may say without exaggeration that I have read or carefully examined several hundred books purporting to expound the Revelation. I have learned to look upon this twelfth chapter as the crucial test in regard to the correct prophetic outline. If the interpreters are wrong as to the woman and the man-child, it necessarily follows that they will be wrong as to many things connected with them.[23]

The woman is referred to as "a great and wondrous sign [that] appeared in heaven" (Rev. 12:1). The word "sign" appears here for the first time in the book of Revelation, indicating that the woman is not to be taken literally as a woman but represents something else. Furthermore, it is impossible to conceive of Mary giving birth to her child "in heaven," and this woman is pictured in heaven.

Joseph, the son of Israel (Jacob), related a dream to his father and brothers:

Then he had another dream, and he told it to his brothers. "Listen," he said, "I had another dream, and this time the sun and moon and eleven stars were bowing down to me." When he told his father as well as his brothers, his father rebuked him and said, "What is this dream you had? Will your mother and I and your brothers actually come and bow down to the ground before you?" His brothers were jealous of him, but his father kept the matter in mind.

(Gen. 37:9–11)

As will be shown shortly, the man child (Rev. 12:5–6) is none other than Jesus Christ the Lord. Religions such as Christian Science, or even the Church, will not qualify as the mother of Christ. Instead, this is a reference to the nation of Israel, which gave birth to the Messiah. From Abraham to the days of Mary, the nation of Israel was preparing to bring forth a man child that would bless the entire world.

The fact that this woman is seen "clothed with the sun, with the moon under her feet" is most illuminating. These objects are light-conveying objects: The moon is a reflector, the sun, a source of light. They are symbolic of Israel as God's light-bearer to humankind. This Israel was in Old Testament days, for God intended her to propagate His message from the Holy Land to the entire world. Unfaithful in the dissemination of this message, the nation of Israel fell under the judgment of God. However, she will be God's light-bearer in the form of the 144,000 witnesses during the Tribulation. It should be noted from Revelation 2–3 that today the Church, God's "lampstand," is His torchbearer to get His message out to this generation.

2. The Devil

"Then another sign appeared in heaven: an enormous red dragon with seven heads and ten horns and seven crowns on his heads" (Rev. 12:3). The world today does not believe in a literal devil, accepting merely "an evil principle from without." But the Bible teaches an evil *personality* from without called the devil. This passage alone details several things about him.

Names Used for the Devil

"an enormous red dragon" (v. 3). He is red because he is the motivating force behind much of the bloodshed in human history, from Cain and to the present.

"that ancient serpent" (v. 9). This refers to the first time the devil is seen in the Bible, in the Garden of Eden.

"the devil" (v. 9). This is the name used in the Gospels for this enemy of God. It means "slanderer" or "accuser."

"Satan" (v. 9). This name means "adversary." The devil is the adversary of all God's children.

"the accuser of our brothers" (v. 10). This indicates his work before the throne of God today, seeking to discredit the saints before God.

Satan's Governmental Operation

Satan is revealed as "an enormous red dragon with seven heads and ten horns and seven crowns on his heads." More details related to Satan's governmental operations will be revealed as we study the Antichrist in chapter 13, but the seven-crowned heads probably refer to the seven stages of the Roman Empire, the embodiment of evil government. Just because Rome has sunk beneath the sands of time does not mean that Roman government is not in force today. In fact, Roman government or Caesarean imperialism is in its sixth stage (head) and today covers a vast amount of the earth's population. Any dictatorial government belongs to this category.

The ten horns refer to the ten kings who will be dominant during the Tribulation, from whom the Antichrist (the seventh head) will receive his power and authority. Antichrist is the human pawn or tool of Satan himself, for Satan uses human governments. Many modern governments and governmental leaders are his pawns today, which is the main reason for so much chaos in the world! Nothing has caused more havoc and evil to humanity than government. Power in the hands of evil men in the form of government has given license to murders, wars, famine, heartache, and suffering beyond human comprehension. This can be attributed to Satan, who, by using world dictators and key leaders, has manipulated the affairs of human beings, all to their harm. The combination of such practices will reach a climax during the Tribulation.

The Fall of Satan

Verse 4 tells us regarding that great dragon that "his tail swept a third of the stars out of the sky and flung them to the earth." This probably refers to the original fall of Satan described in Isaiah 14. Some have suggested that the glacial age was a period of judgment on the earth long before humankind ever came into being because of Satan's pride, which induced rebellion, and the casting from heaven of one-third of the angels, those who chose to follow him. The original casting of Satan out of heaven was not his final overthrow, for although his forces have been limited to the atmospheric heaven around the earth, Satan himself still has access to the throne of God to accuse believers (v. 10).

Satan's Conflict With the Seed of the Woman

The vision of Satan standing before the woman "who was about to give birth, so that he might devour her child the moment it was born" refers to the attitude of Satan ever since Genesis 3:15. This promise was given to humanity, predicting eventual deliverance from the domination of Satan. God guaranteed deliverance through the "seed of the woman." In response, Satan initiated what Bible scholars call "the conflict of the ages," attempting to stamp out the seed of the woman from the time of Adam and Eve to the Tribulation period, from Genesis to Revelation.

Satan tried to stop the seed by the murder of Abel by Cain (Gen. 4), by his effort to pollute the human race (Gen. 6), by his attempt to cut off the Hebrew nation in Egypt (Ex. 1–2), and by the decree of Haman (Esth. 3:8–15). Several times during the life of Christ he tried to destroy the "seed of the woman"—Herod's decree to kill babies, the storm on the Sea of Galilee, and the attempts to throw Christ over a cliff.

During the Christian dispensation the conflict is seen in Satan's persecution of the Church; his propagation of Islam; the Dark Ages, when the Word of God was kept from ordinary people; and false religions that spring up everywhere but offer no remedy for sin. This conflict will reach its climax during the Tribulation, when Satan through the Antichrist will seek to get people to worship him.

3. The Man Child—Christ

The identity of the man child should not be difficult for anyone familiar with the Word of God, for only Jesus Christ fits this description. The man child "who will rule all the nations with an iron scepter" (12:5) refers to Christ's rule during the millennial kingdom, when he will be the absolute ruler of the world. The man child's identity is further clarified in the statement, "her child was snatched up to God and to his throne," which is exactly what happened to Jesus Christ after his resurrection. He was caught up to heaven, where He is now seated at the right hand of God; John reveals Him in chapters 4–5 as at the throne of God. It should be noted that He is the only one who has "ascended into heaven."

The entire picture of the sun-clad woman is best understood when one keeps in mind that the Christian dispensation of almost two thousand years is entirely omitted here. This parallels the seventy weeks of Daniel, which predicts 483 years until "Messiah the Prince shall be cut off" and then, making no reference to the Gentile Church Age, goes right on to the Jewish seven-year Tribulation period, completing the seventy weeks of years. Between Revelation 12:5 and 12:6 have occurred thus far nearly two thousand years of Church history. Just like Daniel 9, they are Gentile in scope, whereas this passage concerns Israel. Verse 6 refers to the Tribulation period, when it says "the woman fled into the desert" where God had prepared a place for her. As He provided for the nation Israel for forty years in the desert, so He will feed Israel during the Tribulation's 1,260 days.

Daniel 11:40–45 speaks of a world war during the middle of the Tribulation, which will affect all the countries of the world except Edom, Moab, and Ammon. These ancient countries, which now constitute Jordan, may well be the place God has prepared for the nation of Israel to hide. In any case, they will flee during the last half of the Tribulation Period, persecuted by the greatest anti-Semitic campaign that Satan has ever unleashed against them. God, however, will be faithful to His children during that period and will provide for them. Isaiah 33:15–16 indicates that during that time He will so supply them that of Israel it will be said, "His bread will be supplied, and water will not fail him" (Isa. 33:16). No matter what the generation, to them that look for Him, God is faithful.

4. The Archangel Michael

"And there was war in heaven. Michael and his angels fought against the dragon, and the dragon and his angels fought back" (Rev. 12:7). That

Satan will make one final attempt to wrest control of the universe from Almighty God is suggested by the coming war in heaven between the holy angels, led by the archangel Michael, and the fallen angels, led by Satan. Before we review that coming war in heaven, let us examine the fourth key personage of this passage. The two angels whose names are given in Scripture are Gabriel and Michael. Gabriel is the "announcing angel"; Michael seems to be the "commanding general" of the heavenly hosts.

It is suggested on the basis of Isaiah 14 and Ezekiel 28 that Michael is superior to the majority of the angels, but somewhat lower in created order than Satan himself. He has had previous confrontations with Satan, as noted in Jude 9, where he contended with the devil and disputed about the body of Moses. Satan wanted the body of Moses, no doubt to use as a sacred shrine, relic, or object of worship to further mislead the Israelites. Michael preserved the body of Moses against that eventuality, but even he "did not dare to bring a slanderous accusation against him, but said, 'The Lord rebuke you!'" Michael does not seem able to cope with Satan himself but must rely on God's power for his defense. This is an excellent object lesson to Christians! If the archangel Michael, commander of God's heavenly host, is not adequate to take on Satan in conflict, neither are we! Our only defense against the devil is to flee to God: "Submit yourselves, then, to God" (James 4:7).

Daniel 10:13 reveals that Michael was hindered by "the prince of the Persian kingdom," either a reference to Satan himself or someone on Michael's own level who was in charge of the demonic forces. Daniel 12:1 predicts that "at that time Michael, the great prince who protects your people, will arise. There will be a time of distress such as has not happened from the beginning of nations until then." We see from this that Michael was the angel specially assigned by God to work for the protection of Israel as a nation.

THE WAR IN HEAVEN

It has been suggested by Bible scholars that the war in heaven is not a single battle but a series of battles that culminate in the middle of the Tribulation period with the expulsion of Satan from the court of God. Satan and his hosts will battle vigorously with Michael and his heavenly hosts immediately after the Rapture of the Church, for when Christ comes for His Church "with a loud command," He will come with "the voice of the archangel" (1 Thess. 4:16). The Tribulation, then, will not only be a time of war on the earth, in which human beings are the participants, but, unseen by them, battles will be fought between the hosts of God and the hosts of Satan.

In a sense, this will parallel what must have occurred during the days of Christ, for when Satan did his best to slay Christ or to tempt Him,

Christ was "ministered" to by the angels. One cannot help but surmise that the atmosphere around the cross was "charged" with conflicting spiritual forces, the holy angels on behalf of Christ conflicting with the demons who exulted in triumph over Him. The resurrection of Jesus Christ on the third day after His crucifixion was a devastating blow to the aspirations of Satan and his host of demons!

In the middle of the Tribulation period the conflicts between Michael and his hosts and Satan and his hosts will reach a climax. When God gives the order, Michael will cast the great dragon down to the earth, and "his angels with him." We can scarcely imagine the effect this will have on Satan, who for all these years has maintained access to the throne of God "day and night" to accuse believers. Suddenly, halfway through the Tribulation period, he will be banished to the earth and confined there. His fury will know no limitations, except the power of God. Three and one-half years later, at the glorious appearing of Christ (Rev. 19:1–20:3), he will be cast into the Abyss for one thousand years.

The fact that Satan is once and for all cast from the throne of God along with his evil hosts, who will no longer be the principalities and powers of the air (cf. Eph. 2:2) but beings limited to the earth, will be cause for great rejoicing in heaven. "Then I heard a loud voice in heaven say: 'Now have come the salvation and the power and the kingdom of our God, and the authority of his Christ'" (Rev. 12:10). The first giant step toward the eventual establishment of the kingdom of Christ will be the banishment of Satan from heaven. The fact that Satan no longer can accuse believers will be cause for great rejoicing. "Therefore rejoice, you heavens and you who dwell in them!" (12:12).

Verse 10 states that Satan's particular ministry in this age is to appear before the throne of God "day and night" to accuse the saints of sin or weakness, much the same function as a prosecutor before a judge. The saints have overcome these accusations by the three sources of victory over the devil (v. 11).

1. "They overcame him by the blood of the Lamb." Whether in casting out demons or victory over sin, the blood of the Lamb of God, which takes away the sins of the world, is the only true means of victory. This certainly emphasizes the power of the blood of Jesus Christ. No wonder the hymn writer was inspired to write,

> Would you be free from your burden of sin?
>   There's power in the blood, power in the blood,
> Would you o'er evil a victory win?
>   There's wonderful power in the blood.

2. "They overcame him . . . by the word of their testimony." Another way to overcome Satan is a decisive testimony for Jesus Christ. The fact

that these people who overcame Satan loved not their lives unto death emphasizes that their supreme desire was to serve Jesus Christ (Matt. 6:33). The Lord Jesus Christ promised, "Whoever finds his life will lose it, and whoever loses his life for my sake will find it" (Matt. 10:39). Satan would have us reverse the procedure and think more highly of our lives than they are truly worth in comparison to our eternal soul.

3. "They did not love their lives so much as to shrink from death." Those who try to save their lives end up losing them. Only a Christian who can assert with Paul that he or she has "a desire to depart and be with Christ, which is better by far" (Phil 1:23) is ready to "resist the devil" (James 4:7). Overcomers are more concerned with pleasing their Lord than with saving their lives.

SATAN'S FINAL ANTI-SEMITIC CRUSADE

"But woe to the earth and the sea,
   because the devil has gone down to you!
He is filled with fury,
   because he knows that his time is short."

When the dragon saw that he had been hurled to the earth, he pursued the woman who had given birth to the male child.
(Rev. 12:12–13)

Although heaven will rejoice because Satan is out, earth will not share this rejoicing, for Satan will personally take command of the earth and its operations against his greatest enemy, the nation Israel. Knowing he has but a short time (three and one-half years), he will be filled with wrath and hatred. The extent of his activities is sketched for us in 12:14–17.

The woman was given the two wings of a great eagle, so that she might fly to the place prepared for her in the desert, where she would be taken care of for a time, times and half a time, out of the serpent's reach.
(Rev. 12:14)

The faithfulness of God to the woman is seen in the fact that she is given two wings of a great eagle so that she might fly into the desert to a place prepared for her where for three and one-half years God will supernaturally protect her.

"Then from his mouth the serpent spewed water like a river, to overtake the woman and sweep her away with the torrent" (Rev. 12:15). It is hard to establish the identity of this "torrent." The best three suggestions are as follows:

1. Satan will divert actual rivers and bodies of water into the desert, where Israel is being kept by God, and will try to drown her.

2. He will attempt to flood her with false teachings.

3. Since this passage has already referred to symbols of "the woman" and the "enormous red dragon," the word "torrent" may be a symbol similar to the one used in Isaiah 59:19, which speaks of an army as it invades a country. It seems likely that the latter is the best definition. The Antichrist will marshal a great horde of men, arm them, and send them into the desert to kill the children of Israel.

"But the earth helped the woman by opening its mouth and swallowing the river that the dragon had spewed out of his mouth" (Rev. 12:16). God will protect Israel supernaturally. As in the days of the rebellion of Korah (Num. 16) in the desert, when the earth opened and swallowed those who were serving Satan and rebelling against the known will of God, so in the Tribulation the earth will swallow up the anti-Semitic armies of the Antichrist.

Dr. Seiss, in his classic commentary on the book of Revelation, suggests:

> It is the region and time of miracle when this drinking up of the river which the Dragon sends against the woman occurs. It is the region and time when there is to be a renewal of wonders, "like as it was to Israel in the day that he came up out of the land of Egypt," (Isaiah 11:15, 16). It is the region and time of great earthquakes and disturbances in the economy of nature. (Zechariah 14:4; Luke 21:25, 26; Revelation 11:13, 19.) And there is reason to think that it is by some great and sudden rending of the earth that these pursuing hosts are arrested in their course, if not en masse buried up in the convulsion. At least, the object of their bloody expedition is thwarted. They fail to reach the Woman in her place of refuge. The very ground yawns to stop them in their hellish madness.[24]

Whatever the enemy, it is apparent that God will use the earth to preserve Israel supernaturally.

"Then the dragon was enraged at the woman and went off to make war against the rest of her offspring—those who obey God's commandments and hold to the testimony of Jesus" (Rev. 12:17). Even though Satan will be thwarted in his attempt to exterminate the Jews, not until the end of the Tribulation, when he is cast into the Abyss, will he stop trying. A glance at history reveals a fore-glimpse of his consistent hatred and diabolical wrath against God's chosen people. It would almost seem that all the animosity and hatred he directs toward God in the last days of his freedom will be hurled against the nation Israel.

That Israel will be saved during the latter half of the Tribulation period is clarified by this reference to the "remnant of her seed," denoting the last generation of the "seed of the woman" living during this period. Their faith is seen in that they (1) "obey God's commandments" and (2) "hold to the testimony of Jesus." They will turn to God in

206 | REVELATION UNVEILED

complete obedience (something Israel has not done since the days of David), accepting their Messiah, Jesus Christ.

The final act of anti-Semitism on the part of Satan will be used of God to cause a worldwide revival to spread throughout Israel. Would to God that Israel two thousand years ago had accepted the offer of her Messiah and started then to "hold to the testimony of Jesus." How this would have altered the course of human history!

TWENTY-ONE

The Antichrist

Revelation 13

Revelation 13 introduces a personage well known to students of Bible prophecy. Called by at least twenty names, he is most commonly referred to as the Antichrist. In an effort to thoroughly understand the detailed description of his activities during the Tribulation Period given in Revelation 13, we will devote this chapter to a compilation of other Bible passages relative to his person, his work, and his ultimate end. Then, by comparing this introductory study with chapter 13, we will gain a comprehensive picture of the work of the Antichrist.

THE FACT OF THE ANTICHRIST

Just as Jesus Christ is the promised "offspring" of the woman (Gen. 3:15), the Antichrist is the promised "offspring" of the serpent. Counterfeiting the work of God has ever been the work of Satan, the master enemy of the human soul. For six thousand years he has tried to counterfeit everything God has done for the human race. The crowning piece of counterfeit will appear when Satan raises up a man to be a substitute for the Lord Jesus Christ—a man referred to as the Antichrist.

It should be pointed out that the term *the Antichrist*, which has been universally accepted by fundamental Bible teachers and prophetic students, is nowhere in the Bible used in connection with a specific person. The title is employed by the Apostle John in 1 John but repeatedly refers to one who opposes Christ, particularly someone teaching anything contrary to the deity of Christ. The Bible repeatedly predicts, however, that one person will arise as the embodiment of all anti-Christian attitudes, purposes, and motives that Satan has implanted in his emissaries throughout past centuries. We call him the Antichrist because he is opposed to everything which Christ represents.

TITLES OF ANTICHRIST

Many titles are given to Antichrist in the Scriptures—at least twenty in number. Some are given below as examples.

Isaiah 14:4: "king of Babylon"
Isaiah 14:12: "Lucifer" (KJV)

Daniel 7:8; 8:9: "little horn"

Daniel 8:23: "a stern-faced king"

Daniel 9:26: "the ruler who will come"

Daniel 11:36: "mighty king"

2 Thessalonians 2:3–8: "man of lawlessness," "the man doomed to destruction"

1 John 2:18: "the antichrist"

Revelation 13:1: "a beast coming out of the sea"

Of all the titles given to him, the one used by the Apostle Paul in 2 Thessalonians 2:3, "the man of lawlessness," is the most descriptive. As "the man of lawlessness" he will come on the scene in the last days as the embodiment of all the sinful people who have ever lived. Second Thessalonians 2:4 offers an appropriate description of his conduct: "He will oppose and will exalt himself over everything that is called God or is worshiped, so that he sets himself up in God's temple, proclaiming himself to be God."

A CONTRAST TO JESUS CHRIST

In his masterful book *Dispensational Truth*, Dr. Clarence Larkin has listed the following fourteen contrasts between the Antichrist and the Lord Jesus Christ.[25]

1. Christ came from above —John 6:38	Antichrist will ascend from the pit —Rev. 11:7
2. Christ came in His Father's name—John 5:43	Antichrist will come in his own name—John 5:43
3. Christ humbled Himself —Phil. 2:8	Antichrist will exalt himself —2 Thess. 2:4
4. Christ was despised —Isa. 53:3; Luke 23:18	Antichrist will be admired —Rev. 13:3–4
5. Christ will be exalted —Phil. 2:9	Antichrist will be cast down to hell —Isa. 14:14–15; Rev. 19:20
6. Christ came to do His Father's will—John 6:38	Antichrist will come to do his own will—Dan. 11:36
7. Christ came to save —Luke 19:10	Antichrist will come to destroy —Dan. 8:24
8. Christ is the good shepherd —John 10:1–15	Antichrist is the "idol [evil] shepherd"—Zech. 11:16–17
9. Christ is the "true vine" —John 15:1	Antichrist is the "vine of the earth" —Rev. 14:18

10. Christ is the "truth" —John 14:6	Antichrist is the "lie" —2 Thess. 2:11 (ASV)
11. Christ is the "holy one" —Mark 1:24	Antichrist is the "lawless one" —2 Thess. 2:8 (ASV)
12. Christ is the "man of sorrows" —Isa. 53:3	Antichrist is the "man of sin" —2 Thess. 2:3
13. Christ is the "Son of God" —Luke 1:35	Antichrist is the "son of perdition" —2 Thess. 2:3
14. Christ is "the mystery of godliness: God . . . manifest in the flesh"—1 Tim. 3:16	Antichrist will be "the mystery of iniquity," Satan manifest in the flesh—2 Thess. 2:7

NATIONALITY OF THE ANTICHRIST

One of the most frequently asked questions about the Antichrist concerns his nationality. Revelation 13:1 indicates that he "saw a beast coming out of the sea," meaning the sea of peoples around the Mediterranean. From this we gather that he will be a Gentile. Daniel 8:8–9 suggests that he is the "small [horn]" that came out of the four Grecian horns, signaling that he will be part Greek. Daniel 9:26 refers to him as the ruler of the people that will come, meaning that he will be of the royal lineage of the race that destroyed Jerusalem. Historically this was the Roman Empire; therefore he will be predominantly Roman. Daniel 11:36–37 tells us that he regards not "the God of his fathers" (KJV). Taken in context, this suggests he will be a Jew. In all probability the Antichrist will appear to be a Gentile and, like Adolph Hitler and others who feared to reveal Jewish blood, will keep his Jewish ancestry a secret. It may be known only to God, but the Bible teaches that he will be a Roman-Grecian Jew, a composite man representing the peoples of the earth. This technically qualifies him to be the embodiment of all evil men.

FUTURE ACTIVITIES OF ANTICHRIST

There is ample description of the work of Antichrist in Revelation 13 to warn the entire world of this awful personage who will come on the earth to assume control. With characteristic biblical inspiration, these principles harmonize with other teachings in the Word concerning this person. We will consider these teachings particularly in the light of the following seven events.

1. His Rise to Power

As already seen in Revelation 6:2, the Antichrist will come on the scene in the "latter times" and assume power by the stealth of diplomacy.

He will not gain control by war but by tricking the leaders of the world into the idea that he can offer peace and by gaining enough support from each of the ten kings of the earth. Eventually he will end up controlling all of them. This subtle method of diplomacy is confirmed by an examination of Daniel 8:25. "He will cause deceit to prosper, and he will consider himself superior. When they feel secure, he will destroy many and take his stand against the Prince of princes. Yet he will be destroyed, but not by human power."

2. His One-World Government

This one-world government is predicted in the image of Nebuchadnezzar (Dan. 2). The ten toes of the image represent an amalgamation of the ten kings under the dominance of the Antichrist. Revelation 17:12–15 reveals that the kings of the earth will finally come to the conclusion that they are not capable of governing themselves in peace with other nations of the world; thus they "will give their power and authority to the beast." Verse 13 suggests that for the sake of world peace they will establish a world government that they will consider the solution to the world's problems. That we have already entered into a day when humanity's political concept of government is one world in scope can scarcely be doubted. The monstrosity on Manhattan Island known as the United Nations, which has already deceived the American people and robbed the U.S. Treasury, is a classic example.

3. The Antichrist Will Dominate World Economy

When Revelation 17:13 states that the kings of the earth "will give their power . . . to the beast," this means not only their armies but also their economic power. It is inconceivable that a one-world government be established without an interrelated one-world economy. Such an economy has been suggested in the European Common Market, which is scheduled to go into effect on the eve of the next millenium. Although it is still in its infancy, because of economic necessity it could spread throughout the entire world and eventually become the type of instrument used by the Antichrist to control the monetary and financial affairs of the world.

4. The Antichrist's Atheistic Religion

The religion of the Antichrist appears in several places in Scripture, primarily Daniel 11:36–39 and 2 Thessalonians 2:1–12. These passages teach that the Antichrist will exalt himself "over everything that is called God or is worshiped, so that he sets himself up in God's temple, proclaiming himself to be God" (2 Thess. 2:4). This evil personage will be a master of deceit even in the religious realm.

According to Revelation 17 the Antichrist will give tacit approval to the ecumenical world church, which after the Rapture merges all the religions of the world, not because he believes in it, but because of its tremendous political overtones and his aspiration to control the world. He apparently will be dominated by the ecumenical church, as we will see in Revelation 17, since the prostitute (the ecumenical church) rides the beast, indicating that she will actually limit or dominate many of his governmental activities. But this will all be subterfuge on his part until he can gather sufficient control to throw her off and kill this idolatrous ecumenical religion that is even today gathering momentum in our own generation.

The Antichrist's true religion will be atheism, which has been increasing in prominence since the early days of German rationalism and today is given the respectability of intellectualism. People today demand religious tolerance for all, which is why Christians and the Tribulation saints cannot go along with it. Antichrist's religion of atheism is rapidly increasing already, particularly in key positions of influence. It is well known that the headwaters of the educational system in America rise from Columbia University, which, thanks to John Dewey and others, is predominantly atheistic in philosophy. The atheists have propagated and enforced a purely secular education for our young people, contrary to all American principles. The current amoral attitude toward moral values can be traced to secular humanism in education.

All of these things fitted together are merely pieces of a puzzle that will spread the philosophies of atheism. This does not even include the fact that the foundation stone of communism and socialism is atheism. Wherever these "isms" are propagated (and they cover a third of the world today), we find the seeds of atheism that will in the last days spring up in the worship of the Antichrist. Socialism will be the basic philosophy of Antichrist's government, economic systems, and religion, for polytheism that makes everything good is little different from atheism.

5. His Covenant With Israel

Daniel 9:27 indicates that the Antichrist will make a covenant with Israel for seven years, which, as we have already seen, will be broken in the middle of the Tribulation when it suits his purposes. This covenant will only serve to keep the children of Israel from seeking God; just as they looked to Egypt in the Old Testament, they will look for help and alliance to the Antichrist for the first three and one-half years of the Tribulation.

6. His Death and Resurrection

As already seen, Antichrist will die and be resurrected. Revelation 17:8 states that "the beast, which you saw, once was, now is not, and will come up out of the Abyss and go to his destruction. The inhabitants of the earth whose names have not been written in the book of life from the creation of the world will be astonished when they see the beast, because *he once was*, now *is not*, and *yet will come.*" In other words, the Antichrist will die in the middle of the Tribulation. Since we have already seen that Satan will be cast out of heaven, aware that his time is short, he will indwell the Antichrist and duplicate the resurrection. Thus he will come up out of perdition and again contrast the supernatural work of Christ.

From that point, on, indwelt by Satan himself, Antichrist will have power to perform "counterfeit miracles, signs and wonders" (2 Thess. 2:9–12) and can potentially deceive "those who are perishing." He will have absolute authority by virtue of his supernatural powers and the submission of the kings of the earth to his control and dominance. It is then that he will unleash his attack on the nation of Israel. It will be the greatest anti-Semitic movement the world has ever known. He will seek to put to death all those who do not bear his mark or bow down and worship him as God.

7. The Ultimate Destruction of the Antichrist

Second Thessalonians 2:8 declares, "And then the lawless one will be revealed, whom the Lord Jesus will overthrow with the breath of his mouth and destroy by the splendor of his coming." This destruction of Satan by our Lord at His coming is graphically described in Revelation 19:11–20. Christ will destroy Satan and his armies all at one time and will cast him alive into the lake of burning sulfur. We have no record of his judgment. Only the Antichrist and the false prophet will not be judged, but because of their activities they will be cast alive into the lake of sulfur before the Great White Throne Judgment.

Thus we have prophesied the bitter end of the man of lawlessness, the Antichrist. But consider the millions deceived by him who will share his fate—the lake of fire.

We will see how these basic practices of the Antichrist are further confirmed in chapter 13, and later we will encounter his own private religious leader, the False Prophet. Of all the names used for Antichrist, the most significant is that in 2 Thessalonians 2:8, where he is called "the lawless one" (ASV). The present generation is preparing for the rule of Antichrist by its insistent, contagious desire for lawlessness. One of the plaguing problems of the younger generation is that of rebellion against law and order and a desire to reject restraint. Instead of morality, honesty, and decency based on the fixed standard of God's Word, we find immorality and self-expression. Self-indulgence is the watchword of life today!

The Bible defines the spirit of lawlessness as sin in 1 John 3:4. The root word is identical: "Everyone who sins breaks the law; in fact, sin is lawlessness." The spirit of rebellion in the heart of any person signifies that he or she is a subject of the Antichrist even before he arrives. The spirit of submission to the law of God is a supernatural result of having invited Jesus Christ into one's life.

TWENTY-TWO

The Beast Out of the Sea

Revelation 13:1–10

Just as God uses human beings to accomplish His objective for humankind, so Satan uses human beings. Revelation 13 is a good example of that fact, for in it we meet two men, referred to as beasts, who will be used by Satan during the Tribulation period.

> And I saw a beast coming out of the sea. He had ten horns and seven heads, with ten crowns on his horns, and on each head a blasphemous name. The beast I saw resembled a leopard, but had feet like those of a bear and a mouth like that of a lion. The dragon gave the beast his power and his throne and great authority.　(Rev. 13:1–2)

As we begin to examine one of the most awesome chapters in the Bible, we see Satan, having been cast out of heaven, angry and standing on "the shore of the sea." He observes this "beast" (or world government system), as we are about to study, and contemplates how he will control it. This scene takes place at the midpoint of the Tribulation period.

A DESCRIPTION OF THE BEAST

This beast is obviously unlike any animal we have ever seen. Therefore we apply the Golden Rule of Interpretation: "When the plain sense of the Scripture makes common sense, seek no other sense." Because the plain sense of this passage does not make common sense, we naturally seek another sense. Since there are no seven-headed animals, this composite picture of a leopard, lion, and bear must be a symbol.

There is much controversy as to the identity of this beast. Some would have us believe that it is a religious organization, because in chapter 17 we find the scarlet woman astride a similar beast. Others would have us believe that this beast is a kingdom, not a king. This is not the first time that the Holy Spirit has used the symbol of a beast to describe either a king or a kingdom. In Daniel 7 we find that several beasts are employed to convey the meaning of coming world governments, with the lion referring not only to the Babylonian Empire, but to Nebuchadnezzar himself (Dan. 2:38). This is significant because Daniel said to Nebuchadnezzar, "You are that head of gold."

The late Dr. David L. Cooper noted that the symbol of the beast can refer either to a king or his kingdom, depending on the Holy Spirit's point of view. He used the illustration of a floodlight and a spotlight: When the spotlight is on, the king was in focus; but when the floodlight is on, the Holy Spirit would have us look at the entire kingdom. Such is the case in Revelation 13. Some details about this beast can apply only to an individual, whereas others apply to his kingdom.[26] We find that the beast opens his mouth and speaks blasphemy, indicating a reference not only to a kingdom but to a specific personage. We have already examined in detail the other Scripture passages about the Antichrist. Now we find in Revelation 13 the description of the end-time king and his kingdom.

THE SEVEN HEADS

The characteristics of this beast, as observed by John, are strange indeed. He has seven heads, ten horns, and crowns on each horn. Each head has on it a "blasphemous name." The beast has a body like a leopard, feet like a bear, and a mouth like a lion. The source of his power and authority is the devil himself. The seven heads are probably the most difficult part of this beast to describe. The ten horns obviously correspond to the ten toes of the vision of Daniel 2 and the ten horns of the nondescript beast that represents the Roman Empire in Daniel 7. They are the ten kings who give the Antichrist their power during the Tribulation period. The features of a leopard, a bear, and a lion characterizing the animal are most informative. In fact, they afford a model indication of the absolute accuracy of Scripture.

Daniel's four beasts in chapter 7 represented future kingdoms, beginning with the lion, which represented the Babylonian Empire. Then he saw a bear, which represented the Medo-Persian Empire, followed by a leopard, representing the Grecian Empire, and a nondescript beast, portraying the Roman Empire. These four animals, representing the four world kingdoms, are most interesting, for no world powers have existed other than the four described by Daniel, who wrote at the beginning of this chain of conquests.

John pens his description when the last governmental beast is in control; therefore his description is in reverse order. Whereas Daniel began with the lion, John ends with the lion. Because these two prophets lived some six hundred years apart, Daniel was looking forward to what would come to pass in relationship to these world kingdoms, but John is looking backward, for the Babylonian, Medo-Persian, Grecian, and Roman Empires have already appeared on the world scene.

The seven heads of this beast are mentioned in Revelation 17:10 as kings of the Roman Empire. The best definition I have heard is that they represent five kings up to the time of John; the sixth, Domitian, was the

Roman king at the time of John, who then skips forward to the end time for the seventh head, the Antichrist. Others suggest that these are the seven phases of Roman type of government through which the nondescript beast, which represents Caesarean imperialism, passed. In any case, the whole animal represents a bestial kingdom that will be in dominant control of the earth during the Tribulation.

A rather interesting side note regarding the Holy Spirit's description of the beast to represent kingdoms appears in the contrasts in the book of Daniel. When one thinks of world governments, they take on a beautiful shape, as did Nebuchadnezzar's image in Daniel 2. Each section of that image represented one of the four coming world kingdoms. However, when God describes the coming world kingdoms, He uses beasts to symbolize them. Human beings look favorably on government as a great help to them, whereas God looks on government as a great hindrance to them, as does anyone who has studied history and observed government's bestial treatment of humanity.

The time of the setting of this beast, as described in Revelation 13, should be noted on the accompanying chart of this period. Chapter 13 describes the work of Antichrist during the entire seven years of Tribulation. It is a parenthetical insertion coming between the trumpet and bowl judgments, not to indicate that he will begin his reign in the middle of the Tribulation period but that his governmental reign will run through the entire period and reach its climax at the middle of the Tribulation. The first three and one-half years will be spent in trying to gain control of the world (see Rev. 17). The Antichrist will lead the governmental organization that will be dominated by the religious system of the day, which we will cover in our discussion of that chapter, but in the middle of the Tribulation he will throw off the scarlet woman and assume absolute control of the world. He then will begin His covenant with the Jews and persecute them three and one-half years.

Verse 1 indicates that the beast rose "out of the sea." Whenever the Bible refers to the "sea," it means the Mediterranean Sea, unless the sea is used symbolically, as it is here. Sometimes "sea" describes people—a sea of people. The meaning, then, is that the Antichrist arises from among the people around the Mediterranean Sea, which is in accord with the nationality description we saw in the previous chapter. It is no wonder the late Dr. Wilbur Smith described this period of time rapidly coming on the world as "the darkest hour of human history."

THE DEATH AND RESURRECTION OF THE BEAST

"One of the heads of the beast seemed to have had a fatal wound, but the fatal wound had been healed. The whole world was astonished and followed the beast" (Rev. 13:3). Verse 3 indicates that the beast, or

Seal
Judgments
Rev. 6

Trumpet
Judgments
Rev. 8, 9

Bowl
Judgments
Rev. 15, 16

RAPTURE

GLORIOUS APPEARING

FIRST HALF OF TRIBULATION | THE GREAT TRIBULATION

Antichrist, will be given a deadly wound. It is possible that at the midway point of the Tribulation period, in the great war referred to as the second war of the Tribulation, the Antichrist will be killed. (Apparently of the ten kings the three not in unanimity with the Antichrist will try to wrest control from him, probably at the same time the scarlet woman of chapter 17 is thrown out of control.)

Revelation 17:8 indicates that his spirit will go down into the pit of the Abyss where it belongs, but he will be resurrected. One must keep in mind that this beast is the Antichrist. In other words, he will try to duplicate everything Jesus Christ has done. This is significant in view of the fact that the sign of our Lord's deity appears in His resurrection. He said that no sign would be given unto people except "the sign of the prophet Jonah. For as Jonah was three days and three nights in the belly of a huge fish, so the Son of Man will be three days and three nights in the heart of the earth" (Matt. 12:39–40). Christianity is unique in that we worship a resurrected, living Lord. The power of this testimony is beyond refutation to those who are real seekers after truth. When studied in the light of 2 Thessalonians 2, it may well be the tool he will use to deceive humankind.

"Men worshiped the dragon because he had given authority to the beast, and they also worshiped the beast and asked, 'Who is like the beast? Who can make war against him?'" (Rev. 13:4). Presumably after his resurrection thousands of individuals across the world, previously undecided about the Antichrist, will make him an object of worship and fall down before him.

THE BLASPHEMIES OF THE BEAST

The beast was given a mouth to utter proud words and blasphemies and to exercise his authority for forty-two months. He opened his mouth to blaspheme God, and to slander his name and his dwelling place and those who live in heaven. (Rev. 13:5–6)

Satan has long been the author of blasphemy against God. That blasphemy will reach its climax when, not content just to damn or curse in the name of God, he will set up a form of worship that leads people to fall down before him as though he were a god. This accords with Isaiah 14, which describes Satan's secret desire to have other creatures worship him. The Jews accused Jesus of blasphemy because He said He was God, and He was crucified for blasphemy. But declaring that one is God is blasphemous only when untrue. In the case of Antichrist during the Tribulation period, it will be untrue, but such supernatural powers will be given him by the devil himself that he will appear to have Godlike characteristics and thus deceive many human beings. Thus during the first three and one-half years of the Tribulation the Antichrist will be merely a man endowed with demonic power, but during the last three and one-half years, he will actually be Satan himself, clothed with the Antichrist's body.

Satan, it must be remembered, is not divine. He does not have the power to create—that is, to make something out of nothing. He can only take what God creates and manipulate it or manufacture it into something else. He can, however, indwell individuals. Even his demonic imps have that power. Jesus, of course, demonstrated His power over demon spirits by casting them out every time they confronted Him. In one celebrated case He cast out "a Legion," or a thousand demons from a man.

Since Satan has had access to the throne of God, he has served as "the accuser of our brothers" (12:10). Consequently, he has not actually indwelt many human beings personally, although some kings and dictators acted as if he did (e.g., Belshazzar, Nero, Domitian, Hitler, and, more recently, Saddam Hussein, to name just a few). In the case of most evil rulers, it has been demon-possession that accounts for their inhumane actions. But in the middle of the Tribulation, when Antichrist is fatally wounded, Satan has just been kicked out of heaven and is free to take on the dead body of Antichrist and simulate the resurrection. If other rulers were demon-possessed, can you imagine what social conditions will be like when Satan himself indwells the Antichrist and uses his body to rule the world for three and one-half years?

We are given many insights of life during that awesomely troubled time, one of which is massive worldwide deception. One of those deceptions that will fool millions who may be about to receive the resurrected Christ as their personal Lord and Savior, according to 2 Thessalonians 2, is through imitating the resurrection of Jesus. Satan will actually enter the body of the Antichrist and bring him back to life, deceiving many into thinking he has Godlike powers.

From then on Antichrist will seem to manifest even greater supernatural powers. People will worship the dragon, as Paul predicted, "He will oppose and will exalt himself over everything that is called God or is worshiped, so that he sets himself up in God's temple, proclaiming himself to be God" (2 Thess. 2:4).

THE POWER OF THE BEAST

"He was given power to make war against the saints and to conquer them. And he was given authority over every tribe, people, language and nation" (Rev. 13:7). Today the world is prepared for a one-world governmental philosophy. That philosophy, propagated by Satan and advocated by the intellectual, godless, atheistic leaders of world governments today, is rapidly spreading across the earth. As already seen, humankind has just about come to the conclusion that the only solution to the problem of continuous war is a one-world government. That government will be the devil's government, established during the Tribulation. In the midst of that time he will assume control himself and, as verse 7 tells us, will exercise power over "every tribe, people, language and nation."

During that period he will do two things: exert power over all peoples and nations and persecute the saints. In accord with the fifth-seal judgment, the latter half of the Tribulation will be a time of increased persecution of saints; and as we have already seen from chapter 12, the devil will also persecute Israel. Therefore, we may conclude that Satan will try to control all the people of the world and will launch a gigantic anti-Christian, anti-Semitic crusade.

One comforting truth gleaned from Revelation is that although Antichrist will have power over all peoples and languages, he will not deceive every individual; Revelation 7:9 makes it clear that the preaching of the gospel by the 144,000 Jewish witnesses will reach a multitude that no one can number, from every language, tribe, and people. Therefore, even Satan's control will not keep people from receiving Christ individually. This is in accord with the way it has been all during the Christian dispensation. Nations and peoples have rejected Christ, but individuals have received Him. According to John 1:10–11, "He was in the world, and though the world was made through him, the world did not recognize him. He came to that which was his own, but his own did not receive him." But the text continues: "Yet to all who received him, to those who believed in his name, he gave the right to become children of God" (v. 12).

THE WORSHIP OF THE BEAST

All inhabitants of the earth will worship the beast—all whose names have not been written in the book of life belonging to the Lamb that was slain from the creation of the world.
He who has an ear, let him hear.

If anyone is to go into captivity,
    into captivity he will go.
If anyone is to be killed with the sword,
    with the sword he will be killed.

This calls for patient endurance and faithfulness on the part of the saints.   (Rev. 13:8–10)

It is evident even today that human beings seek to worship what they can see. This is reflected in the widespread use of idols and holy relics in conjunction with the worship of the religions of the world. During the Tribulation period, Satan will provide a visible god with seemingly divine powers. Those who prefer a comfortable religion that does not demand righteous behavior will find just what they are looking for. On the basis of verse 8 alone it seems that the majority of the people on the earth, even during the Tribulation, will worship the Antichrist rather than Christ Jesus the Lord.

Some, however, will refuse to bow down and worship Antichrist. We will see shortly that he will set up an image of himself to be worshiped by everyone. Just as the three Hebrews refused to worship Nebuchadnezzar's image, which foreshadowed the day when during the Tribulation all will be commanded to worship the beast, so there will be some faithful who refuse. In this text it is those whose names are "written in the book of life belonging to the Lamb."

The significance of this expression cannot be bypassed. The Book of Life is introduced in several passages of Scripture, particularly in Revelation 20:15: "If anyone's name was not found written in the book of life, he was thrown into the lake of fire." The Book of Life contains the names of the living. It is God's book of anticipation. That is, whenever a human being is born, God writes that person's name in his book; if he or she dies without receiving Christ (Rev. 3:5), that name is blotted out of the book so that in eternity the only people whose names remain in the Book of Life are those who have received Christ by faith while they lived.

The Lamb's Book of Life is quite a different matter! There is no doubt as to the identity of the Lamb, for John the Baptist pointed to Jesus Christ as "the Lamb of God, who takes away the sin of the world!" (John 1:29). The Lamb's Book of Life includes only those who have come to the Lamb for life. Jesus said that He came to give unto people "eternal life," and many times He stated that His believers would have life everlasting. In fact, He proclaimed that those who believe on Him will "never die." He was not, of course, referring to the flesh, but to the real inner self, the eternal soul. We conclude, then, that the Lamb's Book of Life contains the names of those who have by faith received the Lamb of God and thus had their names "written in the book of life belonging to the Lamb."

Not everyone has his or her name written in the Lamb's Book of Life! One's name is not written in at birth, nor does he or she have it written in by the sovereign choice of God. A person's name is written in the Lamb's Book of Life only because he or she chooses to ask God to place it there. Jesus Christ offers us eternal life if we receive Him, if we invite Him into our hearts. If we heed His call and ask Him to come in as Lord and Savior, He enters our lives (Rev. 3:20), and the recording angel writes our names into the Lamb's Book of Life, from which it can never be blotted. Is your name written in the Lamb's Book of Life? If not, may I urge you to invite Jesus Christ into your life right now and let Him write it there.

TWENTY-THREE

The False Prophet

Revelation 13:11–18

The Lord Jesus Christ predicted that in the last days "false Christs and false prophets will appear and perform great signs and miracles to deceive even the elect—if that were possible" (Matt. 24:24). Although many false prophets have arisen, seeking to deceive human beings, and though many exist in this present day, there has never been an adequate fulfillment to our Lord's prediction quite like that which will culminate during the Tribulation.

Since humanity is incurably religious, a world dictator must provide people with an outlet for their religious inclinations. We have already seen that Antichrist will come on the scene during the Tribulation period to take control of world government. We will soon observe that the ecumenical church, described in Revelation 17, will exert such power that it will dominate him during the first three and one-half years while he is solidifying the power of his empire. That he will resent the church and attempt to throw off these shackles is clear from the fact that he will destroy her in the middle of the Tribulation period and set up his own form of worship. To propagate that worship, the devil will provide a special man on the scene, the other awesome personage described in Revelation 13 as the "beast coming out of the earth."

That these two beasts (the first beast that comes up out of the sea, the Antichrist, and this beast that comes up out of the earth) are men is clear from what will happen to them when our Lord returns at the end of the Tribulation.

> But the beast was captured, and with him the false prophet who had performed the miraculous signs on his behalf. With these signs he had deluded those who had received the mark of the beast and worshiped his image. The two of them were thrown alive into the fiery lake of burning sulfur. (Rev. 19:20)

This verse can apply only to the two beasts described in Revelation 13. The first is the governmental leader, called the Antichrist, who will set himself up as God; the second is his religious leader, who will incite men to worship Antichrist.

CHARACTERISTICS OF THE FALSE PROPHET

Then I saw another beast, coming out of the earth. He had two horns like a lamb, but he spoke like a dragon. He exercised all the authority of the first beast on his behalf, and made the earth and its inhabitants worship the first beast, whose fatal wound had been healed.

(Rev. 13:11–12)

In these two verses five characteristics chart the role of the False Prophet.

1. "Then I saw another beast, coming out of the earth." Many Bible teachers suggest that his coming up out of the earth indicates that he will not come up out of the sea of peoples, as the first beast does. That is, he will not be of mixed nationality; that he comes out of the earth (around Palestine) may indicate that he will be a Jew. This points to an apostate Jew who, during the first three and one-half years, will lead Israel to make a covenant with Antichrist and deceive them by hiding his apostasy until the middle of the Tribulation period, at which time he will serve his purpose by revealing his apostate beliefs and practices.

2. "He had two horns like a lamb." The Lord Jesus Christ is often referred to in the Gospels and in the book of Revelation as "the Lamb of God." As such He has taken away the sin of the world. The False Prophet coming on the earth will look like a lamb with two horns. Lambs do not have horns, which are symbols of authority; instead, they are meek and mild animals. The Lord Jesus said in the Sermon on the Mount, "Watch out for false prophets. They come to you in sheep's clothing, but inwardly they are ferocious wolves" (Matt. 7:15). The False Prophet will come to Israel in sheep's clothing, but God terms him "a beast."

3. "He spoke like a dragon" suggests that he will derive power of speech from the devil who, as we found in chapter 12, is the dragon. This False Prophet, then, will deceive human beings by acting like a lamb; but really he will speak the words of Satan. Let it be understood that Satan is not against religion. He is, however, against personal faith in Jesus Christ. Therefore, the beast will be one of the chief spokesmen in the Holy Land for the ecumenical power described in Revelation 17.

4. "He exercised all the authority of the first beast on his behalf." The close relationship between these two world leaders is seen in the fact that the False Prophet will be given power by the Antichrist himself. His whole purpose will be to work toward the complete dominance of the earth by the Antichrist, including a form of religion satisfactory to the Antichrist.

5. "[He] made the earth and its inhabitants worship the first beast." The False Prophet's basic purpose and operation with all of this power from the Antichrist and speech from the devil will be to drive people to

worship the Antichrist. When indwelt by Satan in the midst of the Tribulation, the Antichrist will be so deceived about himself that he will deem himself God and seek the worship of human beings (2 Thess. 2:3–8). This form of worship will be propagated by the second beast or False Prophet. He may well be described as the high priest of the Antichrist's religious system during the Tribulation period.

THE SATANIC TRINITY

Revelation 13:11–12 couples the three evil personages of the Tribulation that counterpart the person of God. Just as the dragon has already been anti-God and the first beast is anti-Christ, so the second beast will be anti-Spirit. His capacity in working for the worship of the Antichrist will correspond with the present ministry of the Holy Spirit. He will not seek to cause people to worship himself. He will not court his own personal prestige but will work purely for the purpose of getting others to worship the Antichrist. This evil scheme will be used by the devil and his two cohorts to deceive people during the Tribulation. They will victimize many individuals because they will traffic in amorality.

SUPERNATURAL POWERS OF THE FALSE PROPHET

Every tribal witch doctor, false religious teacher, and false prophet has tried by magic, voodoo, trickery, or demonic power to deceive people by a display of supernaturalism. Religions of the world are bound by superstition. Only Jesus Christ is able to give us peace and confidence before God, and this is not dependent on supernatural displays or signs.

None of the false teachers to the present time has ever possessed the supernatural powers that will be exhibited by the False Prophet on behalf of the Antichrist during the Tribulation period. Notice their description in this text.

"And he performed great and miraculous signs" (Rev. 13:13). The word translated "miraculous signs" is the same word used by the Apostle John in his Gospel, describing the ministry of Jesus. This leads us to believe that the False Prophet will be equipped by Satan and the Antichrist with authority and power to do such supernatural miraculous signs as to "deceive the inhabitants of the earth" (13:14). This should come as no surprise to Bible students, for the devil has great power. When Moses threw down his rod before Pharaoh, it turned into a serpent. The false magicians of Pharaoh, however, were also empowered to make their rods turn into serpents, thus duplicating the miracle of the man of God. However, God caused Moses' serpent to eat up their serpents. Missionaries have told us of phenomena so fantastic that they can only be explained on the basis of supernatural power.

During the Tribulation period the Antichrist will have the power to perform "counterfeit miracles, signs and wonders" (2 Thess. 2:9). It does not seem surprising that the False Prophet will be able to reproduce everything that the special witnesses of God, described in Revelation 11, will be able to do, even to the point of reproducing the miracles of Jesus. This predicted demonstration of supernatural, miraculous power should warn us of the significant truth that the mere display of supernatural power does not suffice as evidence that a matter or practice originates with God. All supernatural power is for the purpose of giving credentials to a person or a teaching. We have something far more important to stand as a test of all teaching, regardless of its accompanied signs—the Word of God. If a teaching is not in accord with that Word, it is false!

"And . . . even causing fire to come down from heaven to earth in full view of men" (Rev. 13:13). The fire test of Elijah the prophet, which proved to the children of Israel that the prophets of Baal were powerless to communicate with God, will probably be repeated during the Tribulation period. That may be one of the reasons for the coming of Elijah at the time. The difference between this confrontation and the previous one is that the false prophet will be able to call down fire from heaven. Lest this take us by surprise, we should be reminded that Satan, the real force behind the False Prophet, brought fire down from heaven and burned up Job's sheep and servants in Job 1:16.

We may well ask ourselves, Why will God permit such power to be in Satan's hands? It is because even during the Tribulation period people will be forced to worship God by faith. If all the supernatural power were on one side, it would not take faith but merely common sense to recognize the source of power. But the principle of salvation as a gift of God will still rest on the basis of faith: "And without faith it is impossible to please God" (Heb. 11:6).

The False Prophet will cause an image of the Antichrist to be built and will have power to "give breath to the image of the first beast" (Rev. 13:14–15). In the midst of the Tribulation, after the Antichrist has been slain and resurrected, the False Prophet will cause people to build an image like Nebuchadnezzar's image and will demand that it be worshiped. By some mysterious means unknown in the previous history of the world, he will give life to that image. How long it will manifest life we are not told. What characteristics it will have we are not told. Possibly the only characteristic it will manifest is that it can "speak" (v. 15). This speech will be caused by the False Prophet, who in turn will get his authority from the Antichrist and the dragon, Satan himself. He will issue an order that all who do not worship him will be killed. Revelation 20:4 tells us that many will be slain by the guillotine.

This scene is so similar to what happened to the Israelites as a result of Nebuchadnezzar's image that we begin to realize Satan's tactics do not vary significantly. Once again, an order will be given that those who do not bow down and worship him will be killed; instead of confronting a fiery furnace, they will be beheaded (Rev. 20:4). This certainly establishes the high cost of knowing Christ as personal Savior during the Tribulation. I have heard unthinking people make such statements as, "I am going to wait until the Tribulation to receive Christ." What they do not understand is the personal suffering and persecution that believers will endure during the Tribulation period because of the animosity of Satan against God and those who worship Him. Both the fifth seal and Revelation 20:4 indicate that a martyrdom of true believers will exceed even that of the Dark Ages, when the Roman Catholic Church persecuted those who held to a personal faith in Jesus Christ.

Many things coincide with the middle of the Tribulation period, one of which is Satan's persecution of the nation Israel. It may be persecution that will awaken Israel to the fact that the Antichrist is its enemy. It may, however, be the disclosure of the False Prophet's true theological persuasion that will awaken Israel. The Holy Spirit through the pen of Moses in Deuteronomy 13 determined the test of all prophets. As stated above, it is not sufficient merely to regard the manifestation of supernatural power, but one must hear what a prophet says. If a prophet declares, "'Let us follow other gods' (gods you have not known) 'and let us worship them,' you must not listen to the words of that prophet or dreamer. The LORD your God is testing you" (Deut. 13:2–3). When the False Prophet erects his idol worship, it may be that Israel, who does not seem to embrace Jesus as the Messiah in the first half of the Tribulation, will embrace Him in the second half, thus rejecting the deceiving, idolatrous religion of the Antichrist.

As we approach the end of the age and these signs in their initial stages begin to occur, we should not let miraculous power deceive us, but judge everything according to God's Word.

THE FALSE PROPHET'S USE OF THE MARK OF THE BEAST

> He also forced everyone, small and great, rich and poor, free and slave, to receive a mark on his right hand or on his forehead, so that no one could buy or sell unless he had the mark, which is the name of the beast or the number of his name. This calls for wisdom. If anyone has insight, let him calculate the number of the beast, for it is man's number. His number is 666.
> (Rev. 13:16–18)

What is the mark of the beast? It is much easier to state what the mark of the beast is than what it means. The plain sense of Scripture tells us that it comprises the numbers: six, six, six. Perhaps some of the most fanciful suggestions for prophetic interpretation revolve around the meaning of this number. Some have by mathematical computations come to the conclusion that the name of Adolph Hitler, Mussolini, and many others equaled 666. It is dangerous to make such suggestions. We only know that six is the number of a human being. It is one short of the perfect number seven, and humankind was created on the sixth day; therefore in Bible numerology it is used to refer to humankind.

Why three digits are used we do not know. Someone has suggested that it is the concentration of all that is human. The text does indicate that it somehow will mathematically speak the name of Antichrist. Since so many mistakes have been made in this regard, we ought not offer any further suggestions. Since the number will not be revealed until the middle of the Tribulation period and the Church will be raptured before the Tribulation, it seems more than likely that we will not be given a hint as to the full meaning or even the name of the Antichrist.

More important than the meaning is the use of these three numbers, 666. The False Prophet will use them as a means of forcing people to worship Antichrist. He will demand that everyone have his mark on their foreheads or on their hands in order to buy or sell. This economic pressure will be instrumental in causing many weak, worldly individuals to succumb to the establishment of this monarch, which will be tantamount to the personal rejection of Christ and acceptance of Antichrist. One can scarcely imagine the pressures of having to possess such a mark in order to secure the necessary food for his family. The U.S. government in World War II furnished a device of this kind in the form of food rationing. It was not enough to have money sufficient to pay for an item, for one had to have food stamps. The same will be true during the second half of the Tribulation, for the Antichrist will so control the economy that no one can live if he or she does not worship him.

Physically speaking, it will be necessary for every human being to have the mark of the beast. Spiritually speaking, it will be fatal. For we have repeatedly seen that those who are redeemed by the Lamb, those who have the seal of God, do not have the mark of the beast. But those who receive the Antichrist's mark will have made the final decisions for eternity to reject Christ and worship his archenemy. This fact alone should cause us to fall down before the Lord Jesus Christ and worship Him today. For He has promised to save us from the hour of Tribulation, "to test those who live on the earth" (Rev. 3:10), if we put our faith in Him.

TWENTY-FOUR

Another 144,000 Servants

Revelation 14

Anyone who would accurately interpret the book of Revelation must locate the scene of the activity before he or she begins interpretation. Chapter 14 is a good illustration of that fact. Many Bible scholars consider this to be a scene in heaven, while others regard it as a scene taking place on earth. The difference in viewpoint will seriously affect one's interpretation.

Another rule to be kept in mind is that the time should be pinpointed. This passage, which falls within the "great parenthesis" that covers Revelation 11:16–15:4, takes place in heaven at the middle of the Tribulation period. An examination of the chart in chapter 10 shows that the seventh seal judgment at the end of the first quarter of the Tribulation opens up into the seven trumpet judgments (chs. 8–9). Chapters 12–13 describe events that culminate in the middle of the Tribulation. Now, before we begin the bowl judgments that come out of the seventh trumpet, covering the last half of the Tribulation, we are about to look on the upheaval that will take place at the end of the three-and-a-half-year period, or the middle of the Tribulation.

Actually, several things occur at that time. The Global Unity Church or the prostitute of Revelation 17 will be thrown off by the Antichrist and the ten kings of the earth. He will break his covenant with Israel and drive her out of the Holy Land. The revival under the witnessing of the 144,000 servants of God (ch. 7) will come to a close. The great persecution of Tribulation saints, referred to in the fifth seal of chapter 6, prior to the middle of the Tribulation, will evidently come under the auspices of the ecumenical church; this church will function much like the National Council of Churches today in that it will not oppose evil such as communism, secularism, or immorality, but will persecute those who believe in the supernatural resurrected Christ and salvation in His name. It will be violently overthrown by Antichrist, as we will see in chapter 17. This chapter introduces a scene in heaven in the middle of the Tribulation.

CHRIST AND 144,000 OUTSTANDING CHRISTIANS

Then I looked, and there before me was the Lamb, standing on Mount Zion, and with him 144,000 who had his name and his Father's name written on their foreheads. And I heard a sound from heaven like the roar of rushing waters and like a loud peal of thunder. The sound I heard was like that of harpists playing their harps. And they sang a new song before the throne and before the four living creatures and the elders. No one could learn the song except the 144,000 who had been redeemed from the earth. These are those who did not defile themselves with women, for they kept themselves pure. They follow the Lamb wherever he goes. They were purchased from among men and offered as firstfruits to God and the Lamb. No lie was found in their mouths; they are blameless. (Rev. 14:1–5)

The contrast between chapters 13 and 14 is remarkable. From the fleshly, debased scene of earth, we are lifted to the lofty heights of heaven, where Jesus Christ's name is honored rather than profaned and where He is the central figure before whom all bow and to whom all voices are raised in adoration.

Each time we are given a new glimpse of heaven, we gain additional knowledge of the details surrounding the throne. Such is the case on this occasion, for we are introduced to the 144,000 outstanding Christians from all ages standing before the throne. We know that this is a scene in heaven because John sees "the Lamb standing on Mount Zion." There are only two possible meanings for Mount Zion in the Scripture. One is the Mount Zion at the earthly site of Jerusalem; the other is the Mount Zion of the heavenly Jerusalem. That the Lamb of God will not be on the earth in the midst of the Tribulation period is apparent from chapter 13. This must be a scene in the heavenly Jerusalem, described by the Holy Spirit in Hebrews 12:22–24:

But you have come to Mount Zion, to the heavenly Jerusalem, the city of the living God. You have come to thousands upon thousands of angels in joyful assembly, to the church of the firstborn, whose names are written in heaven. You have come to God, the judge of all men, to the spirits of righteous men made perfect, to Jesus the mediator of a new covenant, and to the sprinkled blood that speaks a better word than the blood of Abel.

The identity of this group of 144,000 subjects has for some reason eluded many outstanding Bible scholars. Most commentators have a tendency to assume that they are identical with the 144,000 described in chapter 7. Therefore we must examine them in detail.

A COMPARISON OF THE 144,000 IN CHAPTER 7
AND THE 144,000 IN CHAPTER 14

144,000 of Revelation 7:1–9	144,000 of Revelation 14:1–5
vv. 1–3: a scene on earth	v. 1: a scene in heaven; the Lamb is with them on Mount Zion
v. 3: servants of our God, sealed on their foreheads	v. 1: "who had his name and his Father's name written on their foreheads"
v. 4: 144,000 of all the tribes of Israel	v. 3: "sang a new song before the throne and before the four living creatures and the elders"
vv. 5–8: 12,000 from each tribe	v. 3: "who had been redeemed from the earth"
	v. 4: "These are those who did not defile themselves with women, for they kept themselves pure."
	v. 4: "They follow the Lamb wherever he goes."
	v. 4b: "They were purchased from among men."
	v. 4c: "firstfruits to God and the Lamb"
	v. 5: "No lie was found in their mouths."
	v. 5b: "They are blameless."

The Similarities of the Two Groups

Two basic reasons are usually advanced for considering the two groups similar: (1) Both groups total 144,000, and (2) both groups have something written on their foreheads.

The Differences of the Two Groups

Far more important, however, are the differences between the two groups.

1. The Revelation 7 group is specifically Jewish—12,000 from each of the twelve tribes. The Revelation 14 group comes "from the earth" or "from among men."
2. The Revelation 7 group is sealed with the Father's seal. The Revelation 14 group has the name of both the Father and the Son.
3. The scene of chapter 7 occurs on the earth. Chapter 14 takes place in heaven, but only halfway through the Tribulation. This can be explained in that the 144,000 witnesses of Revelation 7, like their converts of verse 9, are slain and under the altar by the middle of the Tribulation. Thus they are described in chapter 14 as before the throne, in their spirit or "soulish" state—"away from the body and at home with the Lord" (2 Cor. 5:8).
4. The additional qualifications for being a member of this group (see vv. 4–5) are not recorded in chapter 7. The 144,000 of chapter 7 are "servants of our God"; the 144,000 of chapter 14 are people "purchased from among men and offered as firstfruits to God and the Lamb." This indicates that their selection was not for the propagation of the gospel on the earth during the Tribulation, but for a special position at the throne of God before Him and the Lord Jesus Christ.
5. Verse 4 tells us that "they follow the Lamb wherever he goes," which may well indicate that as a select group, they have been faithful in completely abandoning their will to the will of Christ during their lifetimes.

Not Jews—Christians

Since only two similarities and several differences exist between these two groups, we can safely conclude that they are not the same. The fact that the numbers are the same—144,000—is not so overpowering when one bears in mind a statement by Dr. William R. Newell in his book on Revelation: "The repetition of the number 144,000, one of governmental completeness and fullness, is not necessarily conclusive proof that the two companies are one and the same."[27] This suggests that for God's perfect governmental operation He has selected multiples of twelve to be His special servants in the Tribulation and another group to enjoy a relationship with Him in heaven, the difference between them being that those in chapter 14 have earned their position because of their faithfulness in doing whatever the Lord commissioned them to do.

That both have understanding on their foreheads is certainly not conclusive evidence one way or the other. The chapter 7 group is "sealed unto God"; the chapter 14 group have the name of Christ and the Father written on their foreheads. This could be a spiritual thing, exemplified by people of the stripe of the Apostle Paul, whose mind (behind the forehead) was filled with a desire to serve Jesus Christ and God the Father all the days of his life. If anyone is permitted into that group, certainly the Apostle Paul would be qualified.

The differences between the two groups limit any assuming that they are the same, particularly when one bears in mind that the scene in chapter 14 is in heaven and that these are taken "from among men" (v. 4), indicating they come from all nations rather than just from among the Jews. Dr. Newell identifies the two as Israel, but he also makes the following statement:

> For, although we have thus spoken of them, we cannot but leave the question open for further light. Because in all other Scripture we can recall Israel's victors are always named as belonging to that elect nation, and the favor of God is seen as arising from that national election. Whereas, these of Revelation 14 do not have that mark, but rather seem to be from a larger circle than Israel—even "from among men"; and their peculiar distinction appears to be a reward for their utter self-abnegation. As Dean Alford says, "We are perhaps more like that which the Lord intended us to be; but they are more like the Lord Himself."[28]

Considering the above statements carefully, I present the following possibility, not dogmatically, but with a sincere conviction that this is a more accurate interpretation than those I have come upon so far. The 144,000 found in chapter 14 are probably the most outstanding 144,000 saints of the Church from the early days of the spread of the gospel to the Rapture of the Church. For this consecrated and devoted service to our Master they will enjoy a special position before the throne of God from death until the Glorious Appearing of Christ, at which time all saints will come with Him. This position doubtless signifies that they will have great responsibility while reigning with Him during the millennial kingdom.

QUALIFICATIONS FOR THIS ELITE GROUP OF CHRISTIANS

1. They are redeemed from the earth by faith in Christ, "who had his name and his Father's name written on their foreheads" (14:1b); they "had been redeemed from the earth" (14:3b) and "were purchased from among men" (14:4b). Obviously these men were first born again by receiving Jesus Christ as their personal Savior and Lord.

2. They are morally pure. "These are those who did not defile themselves with women, for they kept themselves pure" (14:4). Much has been written about this qualification, suggesting that only unmarried men would qualify. There is no scriptural certainty to indicate that Paul was ever married, so he easily fits the pattern here, and to my knowledge we have no record of John's having been married, though it is possible it is

just not mentioned. In any case, there may well have been 144,000 in the last 1900 plus years of the Christian Church who have remained single for the Lord's sake; having met the other qualifications, they will share in that elite position with Paul, possibly John, and others.

I do not, however, insist on a literal interpretation of this expression because nowhere does the Bible teach that sexual intercourse in marriage is defiling. On the contrary, Hebrews 13:4 clearly announces, "Marriage should be honored by all, and the marriage bed kept pure, for God will judge the adulterer and all the sexually immoral." Even the Apostle Paul, when encouraging consecrated young men to abide "as I am," was doing so not for moral reasons, but that they might give themselves more completely to serving the Lord and not be encumbered with concerns for the desires and tastes of a wife (1 Cor. 7:7, 25–35).

Moreover, Boaz in the book of Ruth addresses Ruth as "a woman of noble character," even though she had been married to his relative who had died (Ruth 3:11). There is no indication that physical relations did not exist between Ruth and her first husband, and to assume so merely because she did not have children is taking unwarranted license in interpretation. I do not find where a faithful married woman is considered any less virtuous in the Scripture than an unmarried virgin. Anything else than this would mean that God's pre-Fall commandment to "be fruitful and increase in number [and] fill the earth" (Gen. 1:28) would connote defilement in the act of obedience, which contradicts other principles in Scripture that indicate that God does not tempt people with evil.

On the contrary, the Revelation text probably does not mean unmarried men, but men who are undefiled by women; that is, they have either kept the marriage contract or have never known a woman and thus in the eyes of God are considered "virgins" (in v. 4 the Greek word for "pure" is *parthenos*, lit., "virgin"; cf. KJV). It is interesting that this passage of Scripture is the only one in the Bible referring to men as virgins. The Bible does not teach celibacy; in fact, no hint of it is found in Scripture. The Bible everywhere advocates that Christians be holy and virtuous, undefiled by the world. Misuse of sex has always been one of humanity's greatest problems, infidelity and immorality one of their greatest temptations. Therefore the elite group of 144,000 who qualify to stand before the throne of God in heaven are those who have kept themselves undefiled. That is, they kept their marriage vows or remained unmarried.

3. They are obedient and available, for "they follow the Lamb wherever he goes" (14:4b). It is obvious that all of God's children, in fact, all of His servants, are not completely yielded to His will. Some have known years of yieldedness and faithful service, only to go back and "walk no more with him," whereas others have had on-again off-again periods of

obedience. This elite group of 144,000 is unusually marked by obedience. Their attitude is epitomized by the statement of the Apostle Paul immediately after recognizing Jesus, when he said, "What shall I do, Lord?" (Acts 22:10).

4. They tell the truth, for "no lie was found in their mouths" (14:5). These men are characterized by a contrast to Satan. They are faithful witnesses, always telling the truth. Lying is a part of a person's nature when one follows Satan, "the father of all lies." One prime characteristic of obedient Christians, by contrast, is that they tell the truth.

5. They live "blameless" lives (14:5b). This does not indicate that they are perfect, for these people too had to be redeemed "from among men"; they were lost sinners and had to be born again. Nor does it mean that they live in sinless perfection since their salvation, but reasserts what the Apostle Paul meant in 1 Thessalonians 2:10 when he said, "You are witnesses, and so is God, of how holy, righteous and blameless we were among you who believed." These are men who, in their desire to serve Jesus Christ and walk with Him, leaned on His power to live holy, consecrated lives. They are men who can say with Paul, "I have been crucified with Christ and I no longer live, but Christ lives in me. The life I live in the body, I live by faith in the Son of God, who loved me and gave himself for me" (Gal. 2:20).

THE REWARD OF THE 144,000 CHRISTIANS

1. They are "offered as firstfruits to God and the Lamb" (14:4b). This suggests that these 144,000 are the outstanding believers of the Lamb and have been given a special position, as indicated in verse 1, in standing with the Lamb on Mount Zion, before the throne, and before the four living creatures and the elders.

Among that throng of recipients in heaven of special rewards or commendations for a lifetime of faithful service or even martyrdom, there will, of course, be many familiar names. I often think of men like John Wycliffe, "the morning star of the Reformation," Jon Huss, William Tyndale, and many others who were burned at the stake for translating the Bible into the language of the people. It will also include those who gave or spent their lives in taking the Word of God to forgotten or lost tribes. Because our God is a just God, we can expect to see many heroes of the faith who were totally unknown during their lifetime. They may have missed rewards on this earth, but this and other passages of the Word indicate they will receive just reward in the next life—and that will last for eternity.

2. They will sing a new song which no one can learn save the 144,000 (14:3). These two rewards suggest that they will enjoy a special relationship with God the Son and God the Father from the time of their death

after a life of faithful, holy service until they come with Christ to the earth. Verse 4 states, "They follow the Lamb wherever he goes," perhaps indicating that in addition to being in a privileged position before the resurrection, they will always be in a special position of service for Christ after the resurrection.

Admittedly, the above interpretation places me in the minority among commentators of the book of Revelation. With due respect to faithful interpreters of God who have sought the Holy Spirit for their interpretation, the above is not presented dogmatically, but prayerfully, with the desire that it be given consideration. A comparison of this interpretation with the popular view that chapters 7 and 14 refer to the same group will reveal that my view creates fewer problems than the others.

AN ANGEL PREACHING THE EVERLASTING GOSPEL

> Then I saw another angel flying in midair, and he had the eternal gospel to proclaim to those who live on the earth—to every nation, tribe, language and people. He said in a loud voice, "Fear God and give him glory, because the hour of his judgment has come. Worship him who made the heavens, the earth, the sea and the springs of water." (Rev. 14:6–7)

Verse 6 introduces the first of five angels who convey a special message concerning the middle of the end time, that is, the middle of the Tribulation period.

It is astounding that an angel is commissioned to go forth preaching the everlasting gospel, for the preaching of the gospel has not been committed to angels but to human beings. *This astounding state of affairs can only be an indication of the severity of the circumstances.* If we keep in view the setting of this passage, we will be able to understand readily why this will be necessary. Prior to the Tribulation, the Church will have been raptured. The 144,000 Israelite witnesses from all over the world will be converted through the printed page left behind by the departing church. These witnesses will harvest a multitude that no one can number (Rev. 7:9). This indicates, as we saw in our study of chapter 7, that the early days of the Tribulation will experience the greatest revival in world history.

Accompanying this revival, however, is the opening of the fifth seal, when a great time of persecution during the Tribulation begins, instigated by Antichrist and in all probability administered by the ecumenical church. As we will see in our study of chapter 17, the ecumenical or prostitute church will be so powerful during the first three and one-half years of the Tribulation that it will actually exercise restraining power over Antichrist. Therefore any persecution of true believers during that time will obviously be pursued within the framework of her administration and approval. This should not take us by surprise, for when the Babylonian influence of the Church was greatest during the Dark Ages, millions of Christians were persecuted to death. This period of history is well named the "Inquisition."

An overwhelming majority of believers will be eliminated; thus, few will remain to propagate the gospel after the middle of the Tribulation period. We have already seen in our study of chapter 12 that Israel will not experience a revival in the first part of the Tribulation; instead, a Gentile revival will occur through the preaching of the 144,000, who are indicative of the minority of Israel, not the majority. Israel's revival, according to Habakkuk 3:2, will take place in "our time"; thus it seems that only the persecution of Israel will bring about her national repentance.

One of God's faithful practices in all generations has been to send adequate warning prior to judgment. The case of Noah was one example. Before God sent the Flood, Noah was a preacher of righteousness for 120 years. Before God destroyed Sodom and Gomorrah, He sent Lot, who, instead of being a faithful preacher, became corrupted by the immorality of the city. Thus we find in the middle of the Tribulation, just before the greatest suffering inflicted on the human race and in the absence or deficiency of adequate human gospel witnesses, God will make an omnipotent exception to His overall plan of committing the gospel to human preachers by commissioning an angel to go forth preaching the everlasting gospel.

THE EVERLASTING GOSPEL

What is the everlasting gospel? Is this a different gospel from that preached today? On the basis of the Word of God, absolutely not! This is the *same* gospel that we preach, the same message that was "once for all entrusted to the saints" (Jude 3). We have already seen in our study of Revelation 7 that there are several terms for the gospel, but only one gospel. It is evident from the text that the whole message committed to the angel is not here expressed, but that is not uncommon in Scripture. The message this angel preaches is one of warning!

Whenever the Holy Spirit through the Word informs us of individuals preaching the gospel, the whole message is not necessarily given. The prophet Jonah went into that pagan city Nineveh, and the Scripture tells us in Jonah 3:4 that he simply preached, "Forty more days and Nineveh will be overturned." As we read the text, we find this simple message caused the king and his people to repent of their sin and turn to God. The only conclusion we can come to is that in addition to preaching a message of warning, Jonah also told the people how to repent, for otherwise these pagans would not have known how to approach God in sackcloth and ashes.

The same picture appears in the New Testament when Philip went down to preach to the Ethiopian eunuch. In Acts 8:35 the Scripture tells us, "Then Philip began with that very passage of Scripture and told him the good news about Jesus." The first question we hear the Ethiopian asking is, "Look, here is water. Why shouldn't I be baptized?" (8:36). Obviously, then, in preaching Jesus, Philip explained that it was necessary to call on the name of the Lord to be saved and to give evidence of that act of faith through baptism.

In like manner, this angel will warn the people to fear God instead of Antichrist, to give glory to God instead of Antichrist, and he will instruct them how to do it. Otherwise, he would be proclaiming a message of doom instead of good news. The Greek word translated "gospel" (*euangelion*) literally means "good news," and the only way we can offer people eternal good news is to show them how to receive the Lord Jesus Christ by faith. A message concerning the judgment of God is only a partial presentation of the gospel of Christ. The complete story of the gospel not only clarifies that all human beings are sinners, but also includes God's remedy for sin through Christ, who "died for our sins according to the Scriptures . . . was buried . . . [and] was raised on the third day according to the Scriptures" (1 Cor. 15:3–4).

The extent of this gospel should be noted, for it will be preached "to those who live on the earth—to every nation, tribe, language and people" (Rev. 14:6). This seems to be God's last offer to humankind to flee the wrath to come before they accept Antichrist. We have already seen that Antichrist and the False Prophet will mount a great campaign, after having killed the prostitute—the ecumenical, Babylonian church—and will seek to get everyone to worship Antichrist. This blasphemous idolatry will forfeit anyone's claim to eternal life; thus all will be eternally lost. But as a prelude to that decision, the angel of 14:6 will make known the gospel to all the world so that no one can stand before God at the judgment and maintain that he or she accepted the Antichrist without due warning from God.

There is no evidence that this angel will be any more successful in preaching the eternal gospel than was Noah, the preacher of righteousness before the Flood. On the contrary, it seems that people will pit their will against God and succumb to the lying tongues of Satan's chief tools during that period, the Antichrist and False Prophet. We will discover in chapter 16 that the angel's announcement will introduce the darkest days of human history.

Some have suggested that the message preached to every nation, tribe, and language indicates a universal language at the middle of the Tribulation period. This, however, is certainly not conclusive and would imply that we are some time away from the beginning of the Tribulation, for three and one-half years are not adequate time to teach a common language to all peoples of the earth. It is much easier to assume that since an angel, a supernatural being, will be doing the preaching, he can easily use the language of the people to whom he is preaching.

THE FALL OF RELIGIOUS BABYLON

"A second angel followed and said, 'Fallen! Fallen is Babylon the Great, which made all the nations drink the maddening wine of her adulteries'" (Rev. 14:8). The message of the five angels we are presently studying should be considered in light of the fact that this scene takes place in heaven, not on earth, and is an anticipatory announcement of what will soon take place. As with the first angel's message, this event will take place in the middle of the Tribulation period and offers a foreglimpse of the destruction of the ecumenical, Babylonian, prostitute religion detailed in Revelation 17.

Bible students are well aware of the fact that Revelation refers to two Babylons, both termed "Babylon the Great." Destruction is predicted for both because they will cause people to drink of the wine of the wrath of their fornication. We may understand that this fore-glimpse refers to religious Babylon because it takes place in the middle of the Tribulation. The prediction of the destruction of the literal city of Babylon is found in Revelation 16:18–19. That the city of Babylon will be rebuilt and become the commercial center of the world is seen from such passages as Isaiah 13–14 and Jeremiah 50–51. As we will explain in detail in our discussion of Revelation 17–18, the city of Babylon has never been destroyed according to the Old Testament predictions; thus, we can only conclude that it will be rebuilt and become the commercial center of Antichrist's kingdom; then it will be destroyed at the end of the Tribulation. This again points to the fact that Babylon will become the center of the world.

Future studies will reveal that the two Babylons begun by Nimrod in the city of Babylon, which have brought more misery and heartache on humanity than any other concepts, will be destroyed at the end of time. More individuals have been ruined in God's plan for their lives because of the two Babylons than for any other reason. These two Babylons are (1) false religion, which emphasizes idolatry, and (2) governmental and commercial Babylon. Ever since the days of Nimrod, human beings have tried to rule the world. To do so they must control the economy. During the Tribulation Antichrist will rule the world, not only by an army but also by controlling commerce. People will not be able to buy or sell without his permission except on the blackmarket. Both Babylons will be destroyed at the end of the Tribulation.

THE DOOM OF ANTICHRIST'S WORSHIPERS

A third angel followed them and said in a loud voice: "If anyone worships the beast and his image and receives his mark on the forehead or on the hand, he, too, will drink of the wine of God's fury, which has been poured full strength into the cup of his wrath. He will be tormented with burning sulfur in the presence of the holy angels and of the Lamb. And the smoke of their torment rises for ever and ever. There is no rest day or night for those who worship the beast and his image, or for anyone who receives the mark of his name."

(Rev. 14:9–11)

The third angel will pronounce doom on the worshipers of Antichrist during the Tribulation period. It may be, since he follows them, that this angel will come to the earth and, like the angel who preached the eternal gospel, warn human beings of the consequences of worshiping the beast. His message is not called the gospel message. On the contrary, he issues a warning of the awful consequences of accepting the mark of the Antichrist and becoming his worshiper. We have already seen that during the Tribulation people will be required to worship the Antichrist image and receive his mark (666) on their foreheads or on their hands. Such people will "drink of the wine of God's fury, which has been poured full strength into the cup of his wrath." In other words, they will turn their backs on God's method of salvation and take to themselves human methods. This will incur the displeasure of Almighty God and bring on humankind judgment and destruction.

We have already seen that at the breaking of the fourth seal 25 percent of the earth's population will be destroyed (Rev. 6:8) and during the blowing of the sixth trumpet (9:18) a third part of the earth's population will be destroyed. Dr. David L. Cooper used to say that these were the "incorrigibles of the Tribulation period." That is, these are the ones who turn their backs on the Messiah and become the worshipers of Antichrist, thus forfeiting their chance for eternal life. Rather than be allowed to pollute others of like mind, they will be destroyed in these two great purges of the first half of the Tribulation.

During the latter half, as we will see in our study of the bowl judgments, great persecution will fall on all those who take the mark of the beast and become worshipers of Antichrist. "Burning sulfur" will be their lot while they live, and they will be tormented forever and ever and have no rest day or night (14:11). This, of course, refers to their eternal judgment. Not all ungodly people will receive judgment during this life, though all will receive it in the next. The followers of Antichrist, however, will be different, for all who worship the Antichrist during the latter half of the Tribulation period will receive the judgment of burning sulfur, plus the many other cataclysmic judgments sent by God on Antichrist's worshipers as outlined in the bowl judgments. In addition, they will also be in torment for eternity.

Dr. Clarence Larkin, in his commentary on Revelation, states: "If 'eternal punishment' is taught nowhere else in the Bible it is taught here, and if here, why is it not true as to other classes of sinners?" This is only one of the many passages in the Bible that clearly teaches the eternal suffering of the damned. I do not enjoy teaching eternal damnation for lost souls, but as a faithful teacher of the Word, I can do nothing else. Satan tries to discredit the Word of God and minimize the importance of turning from one's sin to the Lord Jesus Christ, and he does not lack for false teachers to assist him in deceiving many.

Far too many today teach a no-judgment concept, including the annihilationists. These heretics take many forms in the various cults or "isms" of our day. It is well to remember that even matter cannot be annihilated, as any scientist will confirm. Elements can be changed, but they cannot be annihilated! If matter cannot be annihilated, how much less the immortal soul of a human being.

The marvels and blessings of heaven are so magnificent that it is a great tragedy and loss indeed just to miss that marvelous place. However, according to the Bible, just missing heaven is not hell. I wish I could report that the Bible teaches that hell is a place where people will suffer for a little while and then be burned up, never to be remembered again, or where they will be given a second chance to get into heaven, but I cannot be honest to God's Word and make such a statement. Not the slightest suggestion of this is found in the Bible, nor does it hint of a second chance after death! The Bible presents no picture other than that the lake of fire is absolutely eternal and that the populace of that lake will be tormented day and night forever and ever.

THE BLESSED STATE OF TRIBULATION SAINTS

This calls for patient endurance on the part of the saints who obey God's commandments and remain faithful to Jesus.

Then I heard a voice from heaven say, "Write: Blessed are the dead who die in the Lord from now on."

"Yes," says the Spirit, "they will rest from their labor, for their deeds will follow them." (Rev. 14:12–13)

One of the consistent chords of the Scripture is the concept that present-day sufferings are inconsequential in view of the eternal blessings prepared for those who love the Lord. The present passage certainly teaches that fact, for it refers to the "patient endurance" of the saints who are characterized by obedience during the Tribulation. Jesus said, "If you love me, you will obey what I command" (John 14:15). Therefore, one who loves Him is obedient, as these saints will be obedient, even at the expense of great personal suffering at the hands of Antichrist. Because of their endurance, they will be eternally "blessed," that is, contented of heart, for this is the true meaning of the term *blessed*. Because these people have "died in the Lord" or died in saving faith, they "will rest from their labor [of the Tribulation], for their deeds will follow them." Here we see again that a day is coming when believers will be rewarded because of their faithfulness to the Lord. A just God will bring forth justice and equity in eternity.

The principle that "their deeds will follow them" is a blessed truth to the child of God. The Word clearly teaches that our investment of faithfulness to Jesus Christ today will earn eternal dividends. This conforms with the Savior's challenge to "store up for yourselves treasures in heaven, where moth and rust do not destroy, and where thieves do not break in and steal" (Matt. 6:20). The Tribulation saints will be given special blessing for their faithfulness to Christ during that awful time of Tribulation.

THE PREDICTION OF THE BATTLE OF THE GREAT DAY OF GOD THE ALMIGHTY

I looked, and there before me was a white cloud, and seated on the cloud was one "like a son of man" with a crown of gold on his head and a sharp sickle in his hand. Then another angel came out of the temple and called in a loud voice to him who was sitting on the cloud, "Take your sickle and reap, because the time to reap has come, for the harvest of the earth is ripe." So he who was seated on the cloud swung his sickle over the earth, and the earth was harvested.

Another angel came out of the temple in heaven, and he too had a sharp sickle. Still another angel, who had charge of the fire, came from the altar and called in a loud voice to him who had the sharp sickle, "Take your sharp sickle and gather the clusters of grapes from the earth's vine, because its grapes are ripe." The angel swung his sickle on the earth, gathered its grapes and threw them into the great winepress of God's wrath. They were trampled in the winepress outside the city, and blood flowed out of the press, rising as high as the horses' bridles for a distance of 1,600 stadia.　　(Rev. 14:14–20)

The fourth and fifth angels of Revelation 14 introduce the events following our Lord's return to destroy Antichrist and all his followers. This, like the passages before it, is a prophetic fore-glimpse of what is to come, details of which will be found in 16:12–16 and 19:11–20. We will reserve more exhaustive comment on this passage until we get to the bowl judgments, particularly the sixth vial.

242 | REVELATION UNVEILED

We will pause, however, to point out in this text that it is not difficult to identify what the Holy Spirit is revealing to us. The One sitting
on the white cloud "'like a son of man' with a crown of gold on his head
and a sharp sickle in his hand" can be none other than the Lord Jesus
Christ appearing in judgment. The timing is important, for we find that
He comes when "the time to reap has come, for the harvest of the earth
is ripe." What makes the harvest of the earth ripe? The fullness of the
cup of God's wrath is pictured by the harvest time of grapes. The "great
winepress of God's wrath" can be nothing other than the last three and
one-half years of the Tribulation period, when humanity's rejection of
God will have reached its ultimate and God will bring His almighty
wrath, culminating in the war of the day of God the Almighty and the
triumph of Christ over Antichrist.

In concluding this chapter, we must stress that the prediction that
Christ will bring judgment on the earth comes only after three angelic
warnings: (1) in the preaching of the everlasting gospel, (2) in the warning that the Babylonian religion will eventually be destroyed, and (3) in
the assurance that worshipers of Antichrist will be judged in this life and
in the life to come. We can only conclude that those who are thus harvested and pressed into the winepress of God's wrath are the incorrigibles,
who stumble over all kinds of divine warnings against following
Antichrist.

This tragic picture of the culmination of all things is another indication of the depravity of the human heart. With such supernatural warnings one would think that the ungodly would fall down and worship
Jesus Christ, but nothing could be further from the truth. This is another
reminder to us that when people reject the Lord, their problem is one of
the will.

TWENTY-FIVE

Another Glimpse of Heaven

Revelation 15

Chapter 15 is the shortest chapter in the book of Revelation. Its size should not be taken as an indication of its importance, however, for it reveals three things.

1. It concludes the events revealed in chapters 10–15 concerning visions in heaven or conditions on the earth to the middle of the Tribulation period.
2. It serves as an introduction to the Great Tribulation, the latter half of the Tribulation described in chapter 16, when the seven angels pour out the bowls of God's wrath.
3. It reveals important truths concerning the wrath of God.

John said, "I saw in heaven another great and marvelous sign" (v. 1). The word "another" relates back to the two signs revealed to John in chapter 12, the woman representing Israel and the great red dragon representing Satan. This third sign is described by John as "great and marvelous," indicating that it is the most significant of all the signs revealed to this point. When we bear in mind that it is the sign revealing the final act of God's judgment on earth, we will understand that it has great spiritual significance. God has inflicted judgment many times: on the Tower of Babel, on the entire world in sending a universal Flood, on Sodom and Gomorrah, on Jerusalem in A.D. 70, and on Israel for almost two thousand years. This will be God's final judgment, the result of His wrath's being "filled up."

The word "sign" should not confound or disturb us, for it occurs seventy-seven times in the New Testament. An examination of the use of this word will certainly put an end to the lie that the book of Revelation is clouded with "signs and symbols" impossible for the average person to understand. John uses this term and related words in reference to our Lord's prediction of his death: "'But I, when I am lifted up from the earth, will draw all men to myself.' He said this *to show* the kind of death he was going to die" (John 12:32–33). This is not mysterious or hidden, but a plain statement of fact that Christ will be lifted up on the cross. John uses this word again in John 18:32 in reference to His crucifixion and in 21:19 in reference to Christ's prophecy of the death of Peter. Christ refers to His own death, burial, and resurrection as "the sign of the prophet Jonah," a period of three days and three nights (Matt. 12:38–40).

The book of Revelation becomes much more understandable when one recognizes that the word "sign" really means a "symbol of revelation." That is, it is a symbol, picture, or prophetic event that conveys some great truth or principle of God that He wants to convey to His people. As one studies this book and begins to understand the meaning of these signs, he or she receives the fulfillment of Revelation 1:3: "Blessed is the one who reads the words of this prophecy, and blessed are those who hear it and take to heart what is written in it, because the time is near." As we will see in the next chapter, the sign of these seven angels before the throne of God results in literal events of judgment emanating from the throne of God to the earth.

> And I saw what looked like a sea of glass mixed with fire and, stand-
> ing beside the sea, those who had been victorious over the beast and
> his image and over the number of his name. They held harps given
> them by God. (Rev. 15:2)

This "sea of glass" is probably the same sea observed before the throne of God in 4:6. The "fire" may refer to the trials of fire endured by the Tribulation saints. On this sea of glass before God's throne are people described as "those who had been victorious over the beast and his image and over the number of his name," who stand "beside the sea . . . [hold-ing] harps given them by God." These are believers in Jesus Christ, for otherwise they would not be in the presence of God. They are not the saints of the Church Age who were raptured before the Tribulation period, however, but the saints of the Tribulation who are victorious over the beast.

Most Bible commentators suggest that these people have been mar-tyred by the beast during the Tribulation because of their personal faith in Christ. In Revelation 13 we saw that the beast and the False Prophet will come on the scene in the midst of the Tribulation period, seeking to make people worship Antichrist. The complete tyranny of the Tribulation is seen in the fact that during the first three and one-half years the ecu-menical church of Revelation 17 will be so powerful that it will dominate Antichrist and kill all believers who refuse to join with it. During the sec-ond half of the Tribulation it will be Antichrist and the False Prophet who will kill those who refuse to worship his image and receive his mark. Therefore, this group may be those who are saved out of the last half of the Tribulation, because Revelation 7:9 states that there will be a mighty harvest of souls during the first half of the Tribulation under the preach-ing of the 144,000 servants of God. This passage may suggest there will also be a great host of martyrs who will be victorious over Antichrist.

DEATH IS VICTORY FOR CHRISTIANS

How could these folks standing on the sea of glass in the presence of God be victorious when they will have been killed during the Tribulation by the wave of persecution inspired by Antichrist? The answer is found in 1 Corinthians 15:55–57: "'Where, O death, is your victory? Where, O death, is your sting?' The sting of death is sin, and the power of sin is the law. But thanks be to God! He gives us the victory through our Lord Jesus Christ." Death at the hands of a murderous dictator or anti-Christian persecutor is only defeat as human beings look on the situation. People living during the Tribulation will think the Antichrist is overcoming the saints, but in reality he will be sending them out into eternity to be with their Lord.

A vision of human beings unenlightened by the Holy Spirit renders them incapable of understanding the eternal blessings of God. If a person does not incur blessings in this life, the unenlightened consider that defeat, not realizing that what we gain in this life is inconsequential in comparison to what we gain in the life to come. One great blessing bestowed on these souls is the martyr's crown (James 1:12; Rev. 2:10), which will provide them with a special position of authority during the millennial kingdom and probably throughout the eternal ages to come.

Holding "harps given them by God" indicates that they are playing the heavenly instrument in a beautiful symphony of praise and worship. In addition to the heavenly harps, they will also sing "the song of Moses . . . and the song of the Lamb" (15:3).

THE SONG OF MOSES AND THE LAMB

These Tribulation saints sing "the song of Moses the servant of God and the song of the Lamb" (Rev. 15:3). This does not mean that they are Israelites; instead, it signifies that they are singing the song of victory over their enemy, which is the song of Moses in Exodus 15:1–21. They couple this with the song of praise to the Lamb of God.

To understand the song of Moses, we must remember that after Pharaoh released the children of Israel, he repented of his decision and pursued them furiously with a host of Egyptian troops. When the children of Israel saw their plight—the Red Sea in front of them and Egyptian troops behind them—Moses looked to God, who had instructed him to put his rod on the water. Thereupon the people walked over on dry land. It must have been a harrowing experience when the people barely got across the supernaturally created channel when they saw the Egyptian army in hot pursuit. But no sooner had the people safely arrived on the opposite shore when God permitted the channel to close and drown the Egyptians. The people were naturally overwhelmed, because what looked like complete disaster at the hands of a cruel, satanically inspired

246 | REVELATION UNVEILED

king (a brief likeness of Antichrist) was suddenly turned into victory, and they lifted their hearts in gratitude to God.

That exactly parallels the response of these Tribulation saints standing before the throne of God, realizing that they are out of the clutches of Antichrist and Satan. Their hearts are filled with rapturous joy at their deliverance. Since they are not Old Testament saints, they are not content to sing just the song of deliverance, as were the Israelites, who were merely delivered physically from an oppressor, but a song of eternal redemption by the blood of the Lamb.

CHRIST WORSHIPED IN HEAVEN AS GOD

In a day when many have been deceived about the true nature of Jesus Christ, we ought to remember that heaven is not one iota confused about His identity. Understood in the light of Exodus 15 and the song of Moses, this verse makes plain that the God whom Moses and the children of Israel addressed in the face of their great earthly victory was none other than Jesus Christ. For confirmation of this fact we quote selected portions of that great psalm.

> Then Moses and the Israelites sang this song to the LORD:
>
>> "I will sing to the LORD,
>>   for he is highly exalted.
>> The horse and its rider
>>   he has hurled into the sea.
>> The LORD is my strength and my song;
>>   he has become my salvation.
>> He is my God, and I will praise him,
>>   my father's God, and I will exalt him.
>> The LORD is a warrior;
>>   the LORD is his name....
>> You will bring them in and plant them
>>   on the mountain of your inheritance—
>> the place, O LORD, you made for your dwelling,
>>   the sanctuary, O Lord, your hands established.
>> The LORD will reign
>>   for ever and ever."   (Ex. 15:1–3, 17–18)

The fact that these saints combine this song and the song of the Lamb can only be explained on the basis that Jesus Christ is Almighty God. The song of Moses and the Lamb in Revelation 15:3–4 clearly identifies Jesus Christ with the attributes of God Himself. No person or created being has ever been addressed like this. Note the characteristics attributed to Him:

1. Creation: "Great and marvelous are your deeds, Lord God Almighty."
2. Justice: "Just and true are your ways."
3. Object of worship: "King of the ages. Who will not fear you, O Lord, and bring glory to your name?"
4. Holiness: "For you alone are holy."
5. Omnipotence and eternity: "All nations will come and worship before you, for your righteous acts have been revealed."

The most pitiful people in all the world are the religionists who, representing modernistic liberalism or the cults and "isms," do not understand who Jesus Christ is. The book of Revelation certainly clarifies His identity, and if for no other reason, it is worthy of our study because it does what its introduction predicted. Revelation 1:1 announces "the revelation of Jesus Christ." It is the only book in the world that truly presents Jesus Christ as He really is today.

THE TEMPLE OF THE TABERNACLE OF GOD

"After this I looked and in heaven the temple, that is, the tabernacle of the Testimony, was opened" (Rev. 15:5). The Tabernacle of the Temple of God is the Holy of Holies. Great significance should be attached to this scene. Dr. J. Vernon McGee points out in his commentary on Revelation:

> The temple is referred to 15 times in the Revelation. Its prominence cannot be ignored. Each reference is either to the temple in Heaven or to the absence of the temple in the New Jerusalem. In this instance the reference is specifically to the tabernacle, and the Holy of Holies in which the ark of the testimony was kept. In the ark were the tables of stone. Both the tabernacle and the tables of stone were duplicates of originals in Heaven.[29]

The Testimony that emanates from the Tabernacle is seen in the Ark of the Covenant. God has always kept His covenant with Israel or with any to whom He has entered into a covenant relationship, including the members of the Church of Christ, who have entered into the "new covenant" through the blood of Christ.

THE SEVEN ANGELS BEFORE THE THRONE

Out of the temple came the seven angels with the seven plagues. They were dressed in clean, shining linen and wore golden sashes around their chests. Then one of the four living creatures gave to the seven angels seven golden bowls filled with the wrath of God, who lives for ever and ever. And the temple was filled with smoke from the glory of God and from his power, and no one could enter the temple until the seven plagues of the seven angels were completed.

(Rev. 15:6–8)

This is the third time we have encountered a group of seven angels at once. There were seven angels assigned, one each, to the seven churches in chapters 2–3. Then each of the seven angels was given a trumpet to blow in revealing the second quarter of the Tribulation judgments. Now we see the seven angels to whom the judgments of the last half of the Tribulation period are given.

Since these angels come out of the Temple, it seems as if they are given access to the presence of God. Created as holy beings, angels are permitted entrance in the presence of God in the true Temple in heaven, of which the Old Testament Tabernacle and Temple were merely patterns or symbols. In those earthly dwelling places of God, no person was permitted except the high priest once a year, and then only after the most scrupulous preparation in righteousness. As these angels leave the heavenly Temple, having worshiped the Lord, one of the four living creatures gives each one a bowl that will be poured out on the earth, the significance of which is revealed in chapter 16.

As soon as the angels come out of the Temple, great smoke from the glory of the presence of God and His power fills the Temple so that neither angels nor human beings can go back into worship until "the seven plagues of the seven angels [are] completed" (v. 8). In other words, from the middle of the Tribulation period no created being will have access to the presence of God on His throne until the end of the Tribulation, for He will not be dealing with people in mercy, as is His usual custom. During the latter three and one-half years of the Tribulation, He will deal with human beings in judgment.

THE WRATH OF GOD

This brief section of eight verses in the middle of the book of Revelation opens and closes with the wrath of God. It depicts the scene in heaven of God's sending out His angels of judgment to perform His last act of bringing people to Himself. He uses mercy, love, circumstances, the Holy Spirit, and many other divine tools to bring us to Himself. Ordinarily, the unsaved are not judged on this earth, which explains why people can break the laws of God and seemingly get away with it. The judgment they receive on this earth is merely the judgment of their deeds—whatsoever they sow, they reap—but people do not receive God's judgment until the Day of Judgment, with but one exception. During the last three and one-half years of the Tribulation, God will bring great judgment and calamity on humankind.

FILLING UP GOD'S WRATH

Verse 1 says of the seven last plagues, "because with them God's wrath is completed." Verses 5–8 describe the judgment of God being fulfilled. Verse 1 makes it clear that this will be the last judgment before the millennial kingdom. A literal translation of verse 1a is: "And I saw another sign in heaven, great and marvelous, seven angels having seven plagues, the last ones." When this judgment is finished, the Tribulation will be concluded and the Millennium begun.

GOD'S PURPOSE IN THIS GREAT TRIBULATION

Not to understand that this impending period of Great Tribulation is of divine purpose and intent is to fail to understand significant truths relative to these coming events. Although we will probably not know the full extent of God's purpose for the Tribulation until we look down from heaven and see these events transpire, I would like to suggest the following four purposes as being discernible from the Scriptures:

- to introduce a worldwide revival when, under the preaching of the 144,000 servants of God, a multitude will be gathered that no one can number (Rev. 7:9)
- to destroy the wicked followers of Antichrist who are committed to his way, lest they pollute others and corrupt them from the truth of the gospel, thus damning their souls
- to break the stubborn will of the nation of Israel, who will confess her national sin of rejecting the Messiah and plead for His return
- to shake the earth and all things in it so that one's normal sense of security will be so disordered that one will be more prone to look to God. Crises usually cause people to look to God. The Tribulation will be a time when God creates a climate of crisis, a climate conducive for human beings to call on Him while He is near.

TWENTY-SIX

The Seven Bowl Judgments

Revelation 16

No introduction is needed for this chapter, since chapter 15 has already prefaced it. The time sequence of the seven bowl judgments is synonymous with the last half of the Tribulation.

The seven angels, each holding a bowl containing the judgments that are about to fall on the earth, seem reluctant to cast forth their bitter judgments. However, they are obedient to the voice of God when He speaks: "Go, pour out the seven bowls of God's wrath on the earth." These bowls constitute what the Lord Jesus referred to as the "great distress [KJV tribulation]" (Matt. 24:21), or the last forty-two months of the Tribulation period.

Wild and fanciful ideas have been offered through the years as a means of symbolizing or spiritualizing these judgments. There is no scriptural basis for such symbolism. In fact, four of these seven judgments occurred literally in Egypt among the ten plagues and have never been accepted by credible Bible teachers as anything but literal. In addition, part of the sixth judgment, that of drying up the Euphrates River and producing frogs, was also literally fulfilled during the history of Israel. Frogs were generated as one of the plagues of Egypt, and both the Red Sea and Jordan River were rolled back so that God's people could walk forth on dry ground. Therefore, nothing new will be transpiring when God dries up the Euphrates River in order that the kings of the East may march over on dry ground. If the plagues of Egypt were literal (and they certainly were), why should we not expect these awful judgments likewise to be literal? We will now examine the judgments individually.

THE FIRST BOWL JUDGMENT— SORES UPON HUMAN BEINGS

"The first angel went and poured out his bowl on the land, and ugly and painful sores broke out on the people who had the mark of the beast and worshiped his image" (Rev. 16:2). This first bowl judgment introduces grievous or painful sores upon human beings. Dr. Wilbur Smith notes that the same word used here for "sore" was used by the Old Testament translators of the Septuagint for boils in the story of the Egyptian plagues.

For this reason many have called it the plague of boils. This judgment delineates two essential points:

1. The time—when Antichrist is worshiped. Further confirmation that the three judgments—the seals, the trumpets, and the vials—are sequential, not concurrent, as some Bible teachers suggest, is clarified in the time of this judgment. Antichrist will not be set up as the object of worship until the middle of the Tribulation period. This judgment will fall on the human race because of their worship of Antichrist, which can only occur after the middle of the Tribulation (see ch. 13). The time of this judgment, then, will probably commence within the first one to three months of the second half of the Tribulation period.

2. The recipients—beast worshipers. The selection from among the peoples on the earth is clearly seen in this passage: Only those containing the mark of the beast and worshiping his image will be selected for those awful sores. This indicates that God in His marvelous grace will not bring judgment on believers during this latter half of Tribulation, but will protect them as He did the Israelites during the plagues of Egypt. This further confirms our assumption that in the previous judgments, when He slays 25 percent and one-third of the world's population, He will exempt believers.

THE SECOND BOWL JUDGMENT—
THE SEAS TURN TO BLOOD

"The second angel poured out his bowl on the sea, and it turned into blood like that of a dead man, and every living thing in the sea died" (Rev. 16:3). In this one short verse we encounter a catastrophe predicted for the earth that is almost beyond human comprehension. We have already seen that God will cause a third part of the sea to turn to blood during the second trumpet, but this second bowl includes the entire sea.

It does not take much imagination to see that when all living creatures in the seas die, they will float to the top, their decaying bodies discharging an unbearable stench and inaugurating potential disease. This judgment may well interfere with commercial shipping and send whole populations into confusion as people grope for an adequate supply of water, not to mention destroying what is left of the fish industry.

THE THIRD BOWL JUDGMENT—
RIVERS AND FOUNTAINS TURN TO BLOOD

The third angel poured out his bowl on the rivers and springs of water, and they became blood. Then I heard the angel in charge of the waters say:

"You are just in these judgments,

> you who are and who were, the Holy One,
> because you have so judged;
> for they have shed the blood of your saints and prophets,
> and you have given them blood to drink as they deserve."

And I heard the altar respond:

> "Yes, Lord God Almighty,
> true and just are your judgments."   (Rev. 16:4–7)

The third bowl, a sequel to the second, carries with it an interesting explanation as to why God will permit it. God will destroy the only remaining sources of water, the rivers and fountains or springs of the deep, by letting them turn to blood. Whether this means literal blood is inconsequential, for if Christ can turn water to wine, He certainly can turn water to blood. What is significant is that it will become corrupt blood, which will breed disease and pestilence.

One of the basic needs of humankind is water. Unless God provides water from another source or engineers by some process can turn this corrupted water into pure water, the world will be in a state of riot and confusion, seeking this necessity of life.

The book of Revelation reveals interesting things from time to time about the activity of angels in this universe. It seems that, in addition to other functions we have already noted, a special angel is assigned to the waters. This angel will speak when his waters are turned to blood, proclaiming the justification for such an awful miracle, for Antichrist will have put so many Christian martyrs to death that he will deserve exactly what he receives. His quest for the blood of Christians during the first half of the Tribulation will result in his water supply turning to blood in the last half. This is God's earthly vindication of the suffering martyrs from earliest times to the present, answering the prayers of the souls under the altar in Revelation 6.

THE FOURTH BOWL JUDGMENT —
SCORCHING HEAT OF THE SUN

The fourth angel poured out his bowl on the sun, and the sun was given power to scorch people with fire. They were seared by the intense heat and they cursed the name of God, who had control over these plagues, but they refused to repent and glorify him.

(Rev. 16:8–9)

The consistency of the sun, in that it rises every morning and sets every evening, producing light and heat for us according to the seasons of the year, affords a great sense of security to all people. During the Tribulation, when the fourth bowl is poured out on the earth, the human race will contend with a sun-induced heat wave the like of which has never been experienced. Even though a third part of the sun will be darkened, that which is left will be so powerful that it will scorch people "with fire."

We have all lived through acute heat waves at one time or other, but we endure them because night comes to cool things somewhat, and eventually the distressing season passes away. Even so, many deaths result through heart attacks or heatstrokes during such periods, and those not so afflicted are still miserably uncomfortable. Such will be the case during the Great Tribulation; but when we add the effect of this excruciating heat on the corrupt waterways and rivers, we find people almost tasting the torments of hell described by Jesus in Luke 1623–24, without water to satiate their thirst.

One would think that this experience will drive people to their knees in repentance to the God of creation. Instead, in this chapter is found the first of three occasions when people "cursed the name of God . . . but they refused to repent and glorify him." This illustrates the most severe rebellion and hostility to God's will found anywhere in the annals of human history.

The best commentary on this judgment comes from the pen of the prophet Malachi, who, when speaking of that same day, described it with these words:

> "Surely the day is coming; it will burn like a furnace. All the arrogant and every evildoer will be stubble, and that day that is coming will set them on fire," says the LORD Almighty. "Not a root or a branch will be left to them. But for you who revere my name, the sun of righteousness will rise with healing in its wings. And you will go out and leap like calves released from the stall." (Mal. 4:1–2)

God promises hope even in that dreadful time for those who "revere my name," for there is "healing in its wings." God in His marvelous grace seems in every age to provide supernaturally for those who put their trust in Him.

THE FIFTH BOWL JUDGMENT — DARKNESS

> The fifth angel poured out his bowl on the throne of the beast, and his kingdom was plunged into darkness. Men gnawed their tongues in agony and cursed the God of heaven because of their pains and their sores, but they refused to repent of what they had done. (Rev. 16:10–11)

The fact that the fifth bowl introduces darkness may be the singular expression of God's mercy to the rebellious citizens of the earth during the Tribulation period. Following the great heat wave occasioned by the fourth bowl judgment, it may significantly give relief to human flesh.

This is a special judgment that seems to center on the headquarters of Antichrist, for it is poured out on "the throne of the beast, and his kingdom was plunged into darkness." The seat of the beast will probably be the rebuilt city of Babylon during the Tribulation, the center of all commerce, religion, evil, and government.

Two things indicate that this darkness will prevail for some time on the earth: the predictions of other prophets, and the effects on human beings.

This judgment, a repetition of the ninth plague of Egypt, is to be understood literally:

> Woe to you who long
>   for the day of the LORD!
> Why do you long for the day of the LORD?
>   That day will be darkness, not light.   (Amos 5:18)

> Who can withstand his indignation?
>   Who can endure his fierce anger?
> His wrath is poured out like fire;
>   the rocks are shattered before him.
>   . . . but with an overwhelming flood
> he will make an end of Nineveh;
>   he will pursue his foes into darkness.   (Nah. 1:6, 8)

> That day will be a day of wrath,
>   a day of distress and anguish,
> a day of trouble and ruin,
>   a day of darkness and gloom,
>   a day of clouds and blackness.   (Zeph. 1:15)

Christ's own prediction was: "But in those days, following that distress, 'the sun will be darkened, and the moon will not give its light.'" (Mark 13:24).

The effects on people, described in Revelation 16:10 ("Men gnawed their tongues in agony"), indicate that the relief from the heat will soon produce an exasperating, frustrating darkness. If you have visited Carlsbad Caverns or Mammoth Cave, you know what true darkness really is when absolutely no light is available. We may forecast that human ingenuity in producing electricity may solve this problem, but we must remember that the water supply produces electricity, and with the tampering of the water supply, as seen in the second and third judgments, people may be incapable of continuing to draw electrical power and illumination from the rivers and bodies of water.

These judgments are so clearly supernatural that everyone will know that they descend from the God of heaven. But instead of falling down before Him to become the recipients of His mercy, people only "cursed the

God of heaven because of their pains and their sores, but they refused to repent of what they had done." They not only blaspheme God, but refuse to change their ways. Let it be understood that those who reject the Lord do so not because of philosophical doubts or unexplained answers to unanswered questions, but as a result of hardness of heart and love for sin.

THE SIXTH BOWL JUDGMENT — EUPHRATES DRIED UP

> The sixth angel poured out his bowl on the great river Euphrates, and its water was dried up to prepare the way for the kings from the East. Then I saw three evil spirits that looked like frogs; they came out of the mouth of the dragon, out of the mouth of the beast and out of the mouth of the false prophet. They are spirits of demons performing miraculous signs, and they go out to the kings of the whole world, to gather them for the battle on the great day of God Almighty.
>
> "Behold, I come like a thief! Blessed is he who stays awake and keeps his clothes with him, so that he may not go naked and be shamefully exposed."
>
> Then they gathered the kings together to the place that in Hebrew is called Armageddon. (Rev. 16:12–16)

The sixth bowl judgment comes in two parts: (1) the drying up of the Euphrates River, which will be a preparation for the "battle on the great day of God Almighty"; and (2) the tremendous demon forces that will bring the rebellious armies of the world to the Valley of Megiddo for the purpose of opposing the Lord.

The Euphrates River, one of the most prominent rivers in the Bible, since the dawn of human history has stood as a natural barrier between East and West. To those of the Western world, the peoples living east of the Euphrates River have been shrouded in darkness, while all the time their numerical superiority has been building up. The Euphrates River is the eastern border of the land God gave to Abraham (Gen. 15:18). It is about eighteen hundred miles long and so large that it forms a natural barrier against the armies of the world. Most people are not particularly conscious of the fact that it served as the eastern border of the Roman Empire. The sixth bowl judgment will dry up that river to make way for the "kings from the East."

The Kings From the East

The booming population explosion of the nations of the East has produced a new interest in Bible prophecies concerning "the kings from the East." Actually, there is little information on the subject. The literal rendering of the expression is "the kings from the sunrising," a reference to the kings from the Oriental nations of the world. Since it refers to them en masse, it indicates that they do not amalgamate or lose their identity (for they are "kings"), but instead form a massive Oriental confederacy. This confederacy may be preparing to oppose Antichrist, whose capital lies in Babylon, but because of the lying tongues of the demons we are about to study, they will be brought across the Euphrates River on the side of Antichrist in opposition to Christ.

One of the many signs that indicate we may be approaching the end times and the fulfillment of these prophecies in Revelation is the rise of China and her massive army. Not only does she have a population of more than 1,200,000,000, but she can field an army that some estimate at two hundred million. However, since 50 percent of the world's population will have been killed by this time, it will be much smaller. What is important is that in preparation for the movement of the armies of the world to go down into the Valley of Megiddo against Jesus Christ when He returns in His Glorious Appearing, China is already moving in the political direction that will make it possible for her to do what Revelation indicates she will during the Tribulation: march over the Euphrates River to participate in the Battle of Armageddon. Such an action would have been considered impossible just sixty years ago. Today it is not only feasible, but with her Communist-inspired obsession to take over all of Asia and perhaps even the entire world, it may be feasible. Just another suggestion that "the time is near."

Three Froglike Deceiving Spirits

The second part of the sixth bowl judgment reveals the three unclean froglike spirits that will come from the mouths of the devil, the Antichrist, and the False Prophet. These deceiving spirits, by working miracles before the "kings of the whole world," will trick them into coming together for the "battle on the great day of God Almighty." After the five preceding judgments of God, the earth will be in such a chaotic shambles economically, socially, and religiously that kings of the earth will not be prepared to do battle with anyone. Only by this supernatural spirit of deception on the part of Satan, the Antichrist, and the False Prophet will they be able to summon the kings and the armies of the world to the final conflict against God and His Christ. The timing of this event must be the very last days of the Tribulation, since the next bowl concludes the Tribulation with the destruction of Babylon.

Armageddon

"The battle of Armageddon" is an expression often used to describe the decisive battle between Antichrist and his God-hating forces of the earth and Christ, who will consume them with the power of His mouth (Rev. 19:11–16). Actually, it is more proper to call this "the battle on the great day of God Almighty" because that is the scriptural expression. It takes place in Armageddon, which means "the Valley of Megiddo."

The Megiddo Valley, located close to the center of the land of Palestine, offers one of the most breathtaking sights my wife and I encountered in our trip through the Holy Land a few years ago. Napoleon Bonaparte is said to have stated with deep emotion after his first sight of this great valley, "This is the ideal battleground for all the armies of the world." Little did he realize that this prophecy had preceded him, that it *will be* the world's great battleground. Actually, it has already served as the battleground of many major wars. There Barak defeated the Canaanites (Judg. 4:15), Gideon defeated the Midianites (Judg. 7), and Saul and Josiah both met their deaths. Dr. M. R. Vincent in his *Word Studies in the New Testament* notes:

> Megiddo was in the plain of Esdraelon, which has been a chosen place for encampment in every contest carried on in Palestine from the days of Nabuchodonozor, king of Assyria, unto the disastrous march of Napoleon Buonaparte from Egypt into Syria. Jews, Gentiles, Saracens, Christian crusaders, and anti-Christian Frenchmen; Egyptians, Persians, Druses, Turks and Arabs, warriors of every nation that is under heaven have pitched their tents on the plain of Esdraelon, and have beheld the banners of their nation wet with the dews of Tabor and Hermon.[30]

What could induce the kings of the earth to concentrate their forces on that one spot in such an enlightened generation? The only answer is the devastating power of the lying, froglike spirits that go forth from the satanic trinity of Satan, the Antichrist, and the False Prophet during the last days of Tribulation. Dr. Clarence Larkin makes a significant statement:

> The power of a delusive and enthusiastic sentiment, however engendered, to lead to destruction great hosts of men is seen in the Crusades to recover the Holy Sepulchre at Jerusalem. If a religious fanaticism could, at nine different times, cause hundreds of thousands of religious devotees to undergo unspeakable hardships for a religious purpose, what will not the miracle working wonders of the "froglike demons" of the last days of this Dispensation not be able to do in arousing whole nations, and creating vast armies to march in all directions from all countries, headed by their Kings, for the purpose of preventing an establishment of the Kingdom of the King of Kings in His own Land of Palestine?[31]

Christ's Challenge to Tribulation Saints

Verse 15 is our Lord's challenge to any saints still living during the closing days of the Tribulation. He will come as a thief to the ungodly world not prepared for Him, and as He challenges believers of all generations to be faithful, so in those closing days He will challenge His servants whom He has supernaturally preserved from the effects of the previous judgments to continue faithful to the very end. This little parenthetical thought reminds us again of the faithfulness of our God to all those who look to Him for the manifestation of His mercy and grace.

With the armies of the world gathering together in the Valley of Megiddo, the Lord will give one last challenge to His saints; then the time will be prepared for the final judgment to be poured out on the earth.

THE SEVENTH BOWL JUDGMENT — THE WRATH OF GOD

> The seventh angel poured out his bowl into the air, and out of the temple came a loud voice from the throne, saying, "It is done!" Then there came flashes of lightning, rumblings, peals of thunder and a severe earthquake. No earthquake like it has ever occurred since man has been on earth, so tremendous was the quake. The great city split into three parts, and the cities of the nations collapsed. God remembered Babylon the Great and gave her the cup filled with the wine of the fury of his wrath. Every island fled away and the mountains could not be found. From the sky huge hailstones of about a hundred pounds each fell upon men. And they cursed God on account of the plague of hail, because the plague was so terrible. (Rev. 16:17–21)

When the seventh angel pours out his bowl into the air a voice will be heard from the Temple of God before the throne, conveying a most welcome message: *"It is done!"* It is most welcome because it signifies the consummation of the Tribulation, the conclusion of the day of God's wrath on the ungodly, the end of the time of Jacob's trouble.

This final judgment of God will appear in the form of the world's greatest earthquake, one that "has [never] occurred [like it] since man has been on earth." It will destroy "the great city," meaning the city of Babylon, the capital of the world at that time, splitting it into three parts. In addition, "cities of the nations collapsed," meaning that the cities of the world will be wiped out. In addition, every island will vanish and the mountains will not be found. This will indicate a complete renovation of the earth, which may be a fulfillment of 2 Peter 3:10, which predicts that the entire earth will be destroyed and "the elements will be destroyed by fire, and the earth and everything in it will be laid bare."

If this were not enough catastrophe, great hailstones, weighing about 135 pounds each, will come down out of heaven. It is difficult for us to conceive of hailstones that large or of the devastating effect they will have on the people they will hit. Dr. David L. Cooper draws attention to "what the Lord said in Job 38:22, 23. He has filled His armory full of hail and snow 'against the time of trouble, against the day of battle and war.'" More details of this catastrophe will be seen in Revelation 18 under the detailed destruction of the city of Babylon and in chapter 19 with the coming of Christ on the white horse to conquer the earth and subdue it.

Humanity's Perennial Rebellion Against God

Already we have seen people refuse to repent on two different occasions in the face of these judgments. The last thing to be noted in the present passage is the hardness of the unsaved, unregenerate heart: "And they cursed God on account of the plague of hail." It is hard to conceive of human beings so rebellious that they will lift their faces in final defiance to God even in the face of such disaster. All hopes and dreams will be ended with the ultimate consummation because people will have chosen to worship Antichrist.

In conclusion, it is important for us to understand the purpose for all this judgment. The citizens of the Tribulation who take the mark of the beast and worship his image will break the first four of the Ten Commandments. Jesus said that we are to love the Lord our God with all our heart, with all our soul, and with all our mind; "this is the first . . . commandment." Exodus 20 lists the commandments: (1) Have no other gods before me; (2) you shall not make for yourselves an idol; (3) you shall not misuse the name of the LORD your God; (4) remember the Sabbath day by keeping it holy.

None of these commandments will be kept by the inhabitants of the Tribulation. The judgments of God on humankind will appear primarily because instead of worshiping Him, they worship Antichrist. Instead of worshiping God in spirit and truth through His Son Jesus Christ, they will fashion an image and fall down and worship it. Instead of worshiping in speech and word, they will "curse God." God has said, "I will not hold anyone guiltless who misuses his name." The fact that they do not remember the Sabbath day or any day is further confirmation of their unregenerate, atheistic, godless hearts. Every individual who refuses to acknowledge the coming judgment of God on the unregenerate should study this chapter of Scripture. It not only clearly depicts God's intended plan for the coming Tribulation people, but also reveals His plan to judge people for eternity.

TWENTY-SEVEN

Religious Babylon Destroyed

Revelation 17

Archaeologists tell us that Babylon is the cradle of civilization. Located on the shores of the Euphrates River, the ruins of this city have revealed some of the most ancient documents of past generations. This city begun by Nimrod, who was a rebel before the Lord, authored some of the greatest evils ever to fall on humankind. Two of these evils will be destroyed during the Tribulation period, according to Revelation 17–18.

In ancient days Satan seemed to make Babylon the capital of his evil operation. From this headquarters was started false religion, humanity's attempt for self-government in defiance of God's will, and city dwellings for commercial and social purposes contrary to God's command to "be fruitful and increase in number [and] fill the earth" (Gen. 1:28). These great evils, which have damned the souls of millions by substituting counterfeit solutions to natural human problems that would ordinarily lead a person to God, will all be destroyed at the end of the Tribulation period. Chapter 17 describes the coming judgment of God on the religious system that has enslaved the human race in superstitious darkness for centuries.

MYSTERY, BABYLON THE PROSTITUTE

One of the seven angels who had the seven bowls came and said to me, "Come, I will show you the punishment of the great prostitute, who sits on many waters. With her the kings of the earth committed adultery and the inhabitants of the earth were intoxicated with the wine of her adulteries." Then the angel carried me away in the Spirit into a desert. There I saw a woman sitting on a scarlet beast that was covered with blasphemous names and had seven heads and ten horns. The woman was dressed in purple and scarlet, and was glittering with gold, precious stones and pearls. She held a golden cup in her hand, filled with abominable things and the filth of her adulteries. This title was written on her forehead:

MYSTERY
BABYLON THE GREAT
THE MOTHER OF PROSTITUTES
AND OF THE ABOMINATIONS OF THE EARTH.

I saw that the woman was drunk with the blood of the saints, the blood of those who bore testimony to Jesus.

When I saw her, I was greatly astonished.   (Rev. 17:1–6)

The first six verses of our text reveal to us a most astounding and awful scene, portraying through symbols two great forces, one religious, the other governmental. This vision comes from "one of the seven angels who had the seven bowls." Though it is not stated by John, the context locates this judgment scene as taking place in the middle of the Tribulation period. It is a description of the global ecumenical religious system powerful enough to gain a controlling influence in the Antichrist's government.

The Vision of the Woman

Ten details delineate this woman:

1. "the great prostitute"
2. "who sits on many waters"
3. "with her the kings of the earth committed adultery"
4. "the inhabitants of the earth were intoxicated with the wine of her adulteries"
5. "a woman [in the desert] sitting on a scarlet beast"
6. "dressed in purple and scarlet"
7. "glittering with gold, precious stones and pearls"
8. "she held a golden cup in her hand, filled with abominable things and the filth of her adulteries"
9. "on her forehead: MYSTERY, BABYLON THE GREAT, THE MOTHER OF PROSTITUTES AND OF THE ABOMINATIONS OF THE EARTH"
10. "drunk with the blood of the saints, the blood of those who bore testimony to Jesus."

Even before we come to the angel's interpretation of this vision, it is clear that we are not dealing with a mere human being, for no one woman can commit fornication with the kings of the earth, nor can a woman be "drunk with the blood of the saints, the blood of those who bore testimony to Jesus." Our rule for Bible interpretation is that when the plain sense of Scripture makes common sense, seek no other sense. In this case the plain sense, "a woman," does not make common sense; thus, we must seek another sense. Fortunately, the angel gave John the interpretation to this vision, which we will consult after examining the vision of the beast.

The Vision of the Beast

Five details describing the beast are given:

1. "blasphemous names" (v. 3)

2. "had seven heads" (v. 3)
3. "and ten horns" (v. 3)
4. "[the prostitute] rides [it]" (v. 7)
5. "the beast ... was, now is not, and will come up out of the Abyss and go to his destruction" (v. 8)

THE INTERPRETATION OF THE BEAST AND THE PROSTITUTE

The careful Bible student will immediately recognize this beast even before examining the angel's interpretation. In the first place, it is similar to the beast of Revelation 13 and doubtless represents what all beasts used symbolically represent: either a king or a kingdom that opposes God's will. We will consider these in reverse order, just as the angel has interpreted them to John.

When John sees the great prostitute, he is "greatly astonished." The angel says to him, "Why are you astonished?" Actually, some parts of this vision should have been familiar to John, for it is obviously the same beast as that described in chapter 13. The angel introduces his explanation with the words, "This calls for a mind with wisdom" (v. 9), which indicate that only someone with the wisdom of God (found in the Word of God) can understand this vision.

The Beast Explained

1. "The seven heads are seven hills on which the woman sits" (Rev. 17:9). The seven hills of this passage of Scripture have caused some to suggest that since the city of Rome is built on seven hills, she is the one designated here as the beast with seven heads. But there are good reasons for not accepting this interpretation. Geographically, it would be difficult to establish the seven hills of Rome. In addition, the context seems more to indicate that these are seven kings. It is not uncommon for mountains to designate kings or kingdoms (cf. Isa. 2).

As pointed out in the commentary on chapter 13, these seven hills are kings: "Five have fallen, one is, the other has not yet come." As stated there, I am inclined to believe that the first five represent five kings of the Roman Empire through John's lifetime; the existing king, Domitian, was the sixth; thus we have the five that were, the sixth that is, and the seventh who is to come, referring to Antichrist at the end of time.

2. "The beast who once was, and now is not, is an eighth king. He belongs to the seven and is going to his destruction" (Rev. 17:11). This strongly suggests that the Antichrist is the seventh head. He will die in the middle of the Tribulation period, duplicate the resurrection of Jesus Christ by coming back to life, but at the end of the Tribulation will be destroyed (19:20).

3. "The ten horns you saw are ten kings who have not yet received a kingdom, but who for one hour will receive authority as kings along with the beast" (Rev. 17:12). The ten horns coincide with the ten toes of Nebuchadnezzar's vision of Daniel 7 and Revelation 13. These are the ten kings who will make up the Antichrist's world confederacy of nations. Since they get their power from Antichrist, perhaps he will appoint them kings of certain countries after he has taken over world governments. Their oneness of mind is seen in Revelation 17:13 in that they "will give their power and authority to the beast"; that is, during the last three and one-half years of the Tribulation period they will promise complete allegiance and cooperation to the beast.

4. The end of the beast. Looking forward to the end of the Tribulation, the angel explains to John that these ten kings will continue to function until they bring their armies to the Valley of Megiddo in the last great rebellious act of humankind against Christ, who will "overcome them" at the battle of the great day of God Almighty. He will overthrow them because He is "Lord of lords and King of kings" (Rev. 17:14).

5. Full of names of blasphemy. Of the five characteristics in John's vision of the beast, the first is not interpreted here by the angel. He has already interpreted this clearly in chapter 13 when telling about this same beast, for he said, "on each head [was] a blasphemous name" (13:1), "the beast was given a mouth to utter proud words and blasphemies" (v. 5), and "he opened his mouth to blaspheme God, and to slander his name and his dwelling place and those who live in heaven" (v. 6). The blasphemous nature of world government is not limited to Nimrod's time but has been characteristic of all world governments that continue in opposition to God's will. The one-world organization that contains the dreams and aspirations of the one-worlders of today affords a good example of this. About the only person to whom they have not granted some kind of recognition is Jesus Christ. He was excluded in the founding of the United Nations and is also excluded from the conduct of its business. That is one reason for its futility and a major reason why we can be so confident that it will continue to be futile and detrimental to humanity.

The Prostitute Explained

1. The peoples the prostitute sits on: "Then the angel said to me, 'The waters you saw, where the prostitute sits, are peoples, multitudes, nations and languages'" (Rev. 17:15).

The angel first explains to John the meaning of the water on which the woman is sitting: It is the peoples of the earth. Peoples, multitudes, nations, and languages designate all humanity in the book of Revelation. We note this in 7:9, where the 144,000 are used by the Spirit of God to harvest in "a great multitude that no one could count, from every nation, tribe, people and language. ..." This, then, establishes a fundamental principle in interpreting Babylon the Great, the prostitute who sits on the bestial world kingdom: She is a worldwide system that has dominance over all peoples; this is why she is sitting on them.

2. The woman is a great city: "The woman you saw is the great city that rules over the kings of the earth" (Rev. 17:18).

Many have taken this to mean that the woman represents the capital city of Antichrist's kingdom, but this cannot be, for Antichrist himself rules over the kings of the earth. If, then, the woman is not the Antichrist, what other possible explanation can we have for such unanimous world dominance? The only answer is the one system before which all kings, dictators, and nations have been forced to bow down throughout history, that is, the Babylonian religion of idolatry. One cannot go anywhere in the world without being confronted with some semblance of the idolatry. No system in the world's history has enslaved more people than this awful religion. It has not only brought them into the decadence of superstitious ignorance, but it has darkened their understanding, making it difficult for them to grasp the simple plan of salvation as revealed in the person of God's Son, Jesus Christ.

It should not take us by surprise that this prostitute woman, the religious system, is referred to as a city. The Bride, who is Christ's raptured and resurrected Church, is described in Revelation 21:2 as "the Holy City, the new Jerusalem, coming down out of heaven from God, prepared as a bride beautifully dressed for her husband" (see also 21:9–10). In other words, a city can be symbolized by a woman. When used symbolically, a woman is always intended throughout the Scripture to signify a spiritual or religious movement. If a good woman, it is "Jehovah's wife" or "the bride of Christ." If an evil woman, such as "a prostitute," it represents the evil religious system of idolatry.

Returning to the parts of the vision not explained in detail by the angel because they are referred to so frequently throughout Scripture, we find that such is exactly the picture here. This prostitute who sits on many waters is the religious prostitute of Babylonian idolatry. Taking many forms, she will have encircled the globe during the first half of the Tribulation, causing kings of the earth to commit fornication and making the inhabitants of the earth "intoxicated with the wine of her adulteries" (17:2). The religions of the world are synonymous with depravity, debauchery, and a contemptibly low standard of morality.

In viewing the Hindus, Buddhists, Confucianists, Taoists, Muslims, and primitive religionists, I have found that none of them teaches the moral standards of God. Instead, their practices are based on a loose form of behavior that permits sensual activities, producing guilt complexes that the religion in turn uses to enslave its people in forms of personal sacrifice and self-abuse to atone for their own sin. The Babylonian religions of the world, whether they be Greek, Indian, African, Roman, or Chinese, are arrayed in gold, precious stones, and costly array. They use mystery and idolatry.

Being the "mother of prostitutes and of the abominations of the earth" (17:5) means idolatry. The Babylon religion that Nimrod founded centuries before Christ has always been an idolatrous religion, which is why God called it "abomination." Abomination in the Old Testament refers to the worship of idols, and that is exactly the form of religion Satan has used to deceive men and women and lead them away from God. Such religions have unanimously been opposed to the saints and martyrs of Jesus.

3. Religion dominates politics: ". . . that rules over the kings of the earth" (Rev. 17:18).

The fact that the prostitute is seated on the beast and defined as the one who "rules over the kings of the earth" indicates the tremendous power she will exercise over the world government during the first half of the Tribulation. This is nothing new. The leaders of the Babylonian religions of the world have always vied with the political leaders for dominance over their country or the world, in distinction from the true Christian Church, which has never sought political power. Jesus said, "My kingdom is not of this world" (John 18:36). He came the first time to establish a spiritual kingdom, to which one gains entrance by being born again (3:3). When He comes the second time in His Glorious Appearing, He will establish His earthly kingdom, but He will not need any help from those who come with Him. Instead, He will be the sole warrior, generating all the power to combat Antichrist and his cohorts.

The Church, Christ's Bride, will merely be accompanying Him on her honeymoon, prepared to rule and reign with Him for a thousand years. Whenever the church as an organization has involved herself in politics, she has forsaken the will of God. That does not rule out individual Christians being good citizens and participating in offices of government, but nowhere in Scripture is the Church taught to usurp authority from the kings of the earth. Such, however, has been the practice of Babylonian idolatry.

The People of That Period

Almost obscured by the two great personages, the beast and the prostitute who rides the beast, are the millions of individuals living on the earth during the time of these events. They are referred to as the "waters," or the "peoples, multitudes, nations and languages."

All people in any age fall into one of two classifications throughout Scripture—believers or unbelievers. Such is the case in this passage.

Revelation 17:8 records for us the people living during the time of the death of Antichrist, who will "be astonished when they see the beast, because he once was, now is not, and yet will come." These folks are the unbelievers during the Tribulation, described as those "whose names have not been written in the book of life from the creation of the world." They have never by faith called on the Lord Jesus Christ to have their names written in the Lamb's Book of Life.

The other group cited here is referred to as "the saints... those who bore testimony to Jesus" (17:6), who, because of their personal faith in Jesus Christ, will have been killed by the Babylonian religious system. In verse 14 we find that when Christ comes as "Lord of lords and King of kings," then He will overcome the beast. He will bring with Him those who are "called, chosen and faithful followers." These are the individuals who demonstrated their sincere faith by calling on the name of the Lord for salvation. No matter what the age—Old Testament, New Testament, Church Age, Tribulation, and eventually the Millennium—only those who call on the name of the Lord will be saved.

THE CURRENT IDENTITY OF BABYLON THE PROSTITUTE

A careful examination of this passage of Scripture should make it easy for us to identify the current prostitute of Babylon and predict with some degree of accuracy what we can expect on the religious horizon. To do so, however, we must develop a basic understanding of the biblical meaning of "Babylon." This word occurs 290 times in the Bible. The greatest book ever written on this subject is the masterpiece *The Two Babylons,* by Rev. Alexander Hislop, published in 1858. This book, containing quotations from 275 authors and to my knowledge never refuted, best describes the origin of religion in Babylon and its present-day function. Two more recent authors who quote heavily from this book are likewise presented at length because they have so clearly and simply summarized the heart of Hislop's work and provided, in few words, the best description of these ancient events that I have found. Dr. Harry Ironside, in his commentary on Revelation, has written:

> The woman is a religious system, who dominates the civil power, at least for a time. The name upon her forehead should easily enable us to identify her. But in order to do that we will do well to go back to our Old Testament, and see what is there revealed concerning literal Babylon, for the one will surely throw light upon the other....
>
> ... we learn that the founder of Bab-el, or Babylon, was Nimrod, of whose unholy achievements we read in the 10th chapter of Genesis. He was the arch-apostate of the patriarchal age ... he persuaded his associates and followers to join together in "building a city and a

tower which should reach unto heaven." Not ... a tower by which they might climb up into the skies ... but a tower of renown ... to be recognized as a temple or rallying center for those who did not walk in obedience to the word of the Lord ... they called their city and tower Bab-El, gate of God; but it was soon changed by divine judgment into Babel, Confusion. It bore the stamp of unreality from the first, for we are told "they had brick for stone, and slime had they for mortar." An imitation of that which is real and true has ever since characterized Babylon, in all ages.

Nimrod, or Nimroud-bar-Cush ... was a grandson of Ham, the unworthy son of Noah.... Noah had brought through the flood, the revelation of the true God.... Ham on the other hand seems to have been all too readily affected by the apostasy that brought the flood, for he shows no evidence of self-judgment.... His name ... means "swarthy," "darkened," or, more literally, "the sunburnt." And the name indicates the state of the man's soul ... darkened by light from heaven....

Ham begat a son named Cush, "the black one," and he became the father of Nimrod, the apostate leader of his generation.

Ancient lore now comes to our assistance, and tells us that the wife of Nimrod-bar-Cush was the infamous Semiramis the First. She is reputed to have been the foundress of the Babylonian mysteries and the first high-priestess of idolatry. Thus Babylon became the fountain-head of idolatry, and the mother of every heathen and pagan system in the world. The mystery-religion that was there orig- inated spread in various forms throughout the whole earth ... and is with us today ... and shall have its fullest development when the Holy Spirit has departed and the Babylon of the Apocalypse holds sway.

Building on the primeval promise of the woman's Seed who was to come, Semiramis bore as one whom she declared was miraculously conceived! And when she presented him to the people, he was hailed as the promised deliverer. This was Tammuz, whose worship Ezekiel protested against in the days of the captivity. Thus was introduced the mystery of the mother and the child, a form of idolatry that is older than any other known to man. The rites of this worship were secret. Only the initiated were permitted to know its mysteries. It was Satan's effort to delude mankind with an imitation so like the truth of God that they would not know the true Seed of the woman when He came in the fullness of time....[32]

Dr. Clarence Larkin, in his book *Dispensational Truth,* includes these interesting details:

Babel, or Babylon, was built by Nimrod. Gen. 10:8–10. It was the seat of the first great Apostasy. Here the "Babylonian Cult" was invented, a system claiming to possess the highest wisdom and to reveal the divinest secrets. Before a member could be initiated he had to "confess" to the Priest. The Priest then had him in his power. This is the secret of the power of the Priests of the Roman Catholic Church today.

Once admitted into this order men were no longer Babylonians, Assyrians, or Egyptians, but members of a Mystical Brotherhood over whom was placed a Pontiff or "High Priest," whose word was law. The city of Babylon continued to be the seat of Satan until the fall of the Babylonian and Medo-Persian Empires, when he shifted his Capital to Pergamos in Asia Minor, where it was in John's day. Rev. 2:12, 13.

When Attalus, the Pontiff and King of Pergamos, died in B.C. 133, he bequeathed the Headship of the "Babylonian Priesthood" to Rome. When the Etruscans came to Italy from Lydia (the region of Pergamos), they brought with them the Babylonian religion and rites. They set up a Pontiff who was head of the Priesthood. Later the Romans accepted this Pontiff as their civil ruler. Julius Caesar was made Pontiff of the Etruscan Order in B.C. 74. In B.C. 63 he was made "Supreme Pontiff" of the "Babylonian Order," thus becoming heir to the rights and titles of Attalus, Pontiff of Pergamos, who had made Rome his heir by will. Thus the first Roman Emperor became the Head of the "Babylonian Priesthood," and Rome the successor of Babylon. The Emperors of Rome continued to exercise the office of "Supreme Pontiff" until A.D. 366, through the influence of the monks of Mt. Carmel, a college of Babylonian religion originally founded by the priests of Jezebel. So in A.D. 378 the Head of the "Babylonian Order" became the Ruler of the "Roman Church." Thus Satan united Rome and Babylon in one religious system.

Soon after Damascus was made "Supreme Pontiff" the "rites" of Babylon began to come to the front. The worship of the Virgin Mary was set up in A.D. 381. All the outstanding festivals of the Roman Catholic Church are of Babylonian origin. Easter is not a Christian name. It means "Ishtar," one of the titles of the Babylonian Queen of Heaven, whose worship by the Children of Israel was such an abomination in the sight of God. The decree for the observance of Easter and Lent was given in A.D. 519. The "Rosary" is of Pagan origin. There is no warrant in the Word of God for the use of the "Sign of the Cross." It had its origin in the mystic "Tau" of the Chaldeans and Egyptians. It came from the letter "T," the initial name of "Tammuz," and was used in the "Babylonian Mysteries" for the same magic purposes as the Romish Church now employs it. Celibacy, the Tonsure, and the Order of Monks and Nuns, have no warrant or authority from Scripture. The Nuns are nothing more than an imitation of the "Vestal Virgins" of Pagan Rome.[33]

After reading the above quotations, you may be inclined to think me anti-Catholic, but that isn't exactly true; I am anti-false religion. For example, I am opposed to any religious system that has enough of the truth to deceive the faithful and enough of the false to damn its followers. A false religion is worse than no religion at all.

In some respects the religion of Rome is more dangerous than no religion because she substitutes religion for truth. Human beings would be better off with their God-given desire for truth unfulfilled that they might seek after Him. Rome's false religion too often gives a false security that keeps people from seeking salvation freely by faith. Rome is also dangerous because some of her doctrines are pseudo-Christian. For example, she believes properly about the personal deity of Christ but errs in adding Babylonian mysticism in many forms and salvation by works.

With respect to sincere Roman Catholics who have personally received Christ as their Savior and Lord and to those who are evaluating the claims of Christ on their lives, I must point out that the Church of Rome today does not teach "the faith that was once for all entrusted to the saints" (Jude 6). Instead, they have added the baggage of fifteen hundred years of tradition to the original doctrines of Christianity. Most or all of that added teaching originated in pagan or "mystery Babylon." Today the Church of Rome is doctrinally a mixture of Babylonian paganism and Christianity. That is why it is a far cry from "the faith . . . once for all entrusted to the saints."

One of their leading theologians was recently on a radio talk show and was asked, "Do you believe *sola scriptura*?"—meaning, "Do you test all doctrine by the Word of God?" He replied, "No, we have the Scripture in one hand and fifteen hundred years of tradition in the other. Together they formulate our beliefs." What he does not seem to understand is that it is from that tradition of "Mystery Babylon . . . the Mother of Prostitutes" (mother of idolatry a là Nimrod) that he gets all the false doctrines listed in chapter 5 of this book, from worshiping images and relics to purgatory to prayers to Mary and even declaring the infallibility of very fallible popes. The seriousness of the situation is seen in the fact that even though our Lord Himself commanded that it was essential to be "born again" spiritually by faith in Him alone, many rarely or never hear that challenge in the Church of Rome today.

My own father was a Roman Catholic for the first twenty-six years of his life. He considered himself "a good Catholic," for he was baptized and confirmed in the church, went to Catholic schools, sang in the boys' choir, was an altar boy, and even had me baptized as an infant lest I die prematurely and go to hell or purgatory. When he heard the gospel at twenty-six and was personally "born again" by faith in Jesus Christ, it totally changed his life. Often I heard him complain, "No one in the church had ever told me I needed to be born again, by faith, not of works, but by God's grace. The sisters never told me; neither did the priest, the bishops, the cardinal, or even the pope." Yet according to John 3, Jesus our Lord made that a requirement for entering the kingdom of God. Even the Apostle Peter taught that salvation was the result of being born again (1 Pet. 1:23–25). Failing to bring him to God, my father's church had clouded the way of truth with all their Babylonian pagan innovations brought up through the centuries.

It grieves me to have to say this, but according to their own writings it is obvious that the Apostles Peter, Paul, and John, James, and the first-century Church would not approve of the mixed message the Church of Rome teaches today, consisting of some Christianity and some "mystic" Babylonism. Fortunately, with the increase in Bible study within the Catholic Church since Pope John XXIII endorsed the reading of Scripture and the publication of the Catholic Confraternity Edition of the Bible, many have been born again personally by faith. The Gallup Poll on religion indicates that at least thirteen million Catholics in the U.S. profess a "born-again" experience with Jesus Christ. I pray that millions more will join them in that life-changing experience.

THE PRE-CHRISTIAN PRACTICES
OF THE ROMAN CATHOLIC CHURCH

Many of the changes in the Church of Jesus Christ began to surface after the bishop of Rome became dominant over other church bishops. Gradually "Maryolatry" and other Babylonian practices were brought into the church. These practices had one thing in common: They existed before Christ and were not taught by Him. For example, prayers for the dead, not instituted until A.D. 300, are nowhere taught in the Scripture but are a regular part of the ancestor worship of the Chinese, who practiced it *hundreds of years before Christ.* In addition, the worship of Mary and Christ as a baby was conceived in the same form with other names by most of the major religions of the world hundreds of years before Christ.

Easter and Lent observances with forty days' fasting were practiced for the benefit of Tammuz five hundred years before Christ. To prove that Tammuz was worshiped before Christ, just turn to Ezekiel 8:7–14. The worship of Tammuz was so extensive by that time that even the women of Israel were seen "mourning for Tammuz." The title "Queen of Heaven," given to Mary, is certainly not Christian. In fact, good

Roman Catholics should be horrified to find that this expression is found in the Old Testament. Jeremiah 44:17 points out that it was used to describe the mother of Tammuz, the mother goddess of Babylon, over *five hundred years before Christ.*

The practice of establishing a celibate priesthood and having nuns is not of Christian origin; nothing in the Bible teaches this. Indeed, 1 Timothy 3:1–3 forbids it. Hundreds of years before Christ it was incorporated by the Buddhists and Hindus, who practice it to this day. Where did they get it? From Babylonian mysticism, the "mother of prostitutes." The sign of the cross used on the end of a pole is likewise not of Christian derivation. It was used in the worship of Tammuz five hundred years before Christ. We have already seen that making confession, not taught in the Scripture, was practiced in Babylon, and we can go on to include prayer beads, purgatory, and many other pre-Christian practices of the Church of Rome. Thinking people can scarcely deny the fact that Rome today is a form of Babylonian mysticism.

ROME IS NOT THE ONLY FORM OF BABYLONIAN RELIGION

It was my privilege many years ago to make a trip around the world. My wife and I visited some fifty temples and religious shrines of the major religions of the world. We were appalled to find the strange chords of similarity in all these forms of religion. Mystery, darkness, incense burning, superstition, ignorance, immorality, priesthood, nuns, sprinkling, idolatry, and many other Babylonian customs appeared repeatedly. I can only conclude that Rome is not the only form of Babylonian mysticism, but merely the one that has infiltrated Christianity. And after the Rapture, their leaders that remain will bring all the Babylonian-based religions together with one global idolatrous religion. She may be the one leading all forms of religions at the end time.

ECUMENICAL CHURCH UNITY — A PLAN OF THE DEVIL

We are living in a day of ecumenical propaganda calling on the churches of the world to amalgamate. Church unity is moving at a breathtaking pace. Many years ago I preached a sermon in our church entitled "The Ecumenical Church—A Sign of Our Lord's Return." During that message I stated that the day would come when Roman Catholicism and liberal Protestantism would begin moving together and make overtures to unite. That statement struck many in the church like a bombshell. I was accused of being radical and extreme. When I make that statement now, I find overwhelming agreement. The newspapers are filled with accounts of such strange things as Catholic and Protestant churches working together with the Jews on a common translation of the Scriptures, a

Baptist minister participating with a Catholic priest in a marriage ceremony, and a Catholic priest participating in the ordination of a Baptist
minister, after which he was quoted as saying, "It was a rich and meaningful experience." As we approach the end of the Church Age, we can
expect to see liberal Protestantism, in the form of the National Council
of Churches and the World Council of Churches, being swallowed up
by the Church of Rome.

This unity movement should not, however, be limited to apostate
Christianity. We can expect to see it move toward amalgamating all the
religions of the world under Rome's headship because our text states that
the religious system at the end time will be a one-world religion: "Where
the prostitute sits, are peoples, multitudes, nations and languages" (Rev.
17:15). This can only mean a one-world religious system.

ROME'S PERSECUTION OF CHRISTIANS

Today it is not just liberals who are trying to beat a path back to Rome,
thus nullifying the Protestant Reformation. There are leading evangeli-
cals who have held meetings to bring the faiths back together. Using the
drastic social chaos created by liberal humanism (or socialistic ideology)
in education, media, and the entertainment industry as a pretext to "get
together" on the moral issues we agree upon, some are willing to nego-
tiate away the right to evangelize Jews, Catholics, or those of other religions.

Three of the major leaders are personal friends of long standing. But
I have refused to participate in this dangerous—and what I consider
heretical—effort to do Antichrist's work for him even before he comes.
Not only are their efforts a violation of the Great Commission, it ignores
the long history of Rome's intolerance and persecution of Christians. In
Revelation 17:6 we are told that this prostitute, or idolatrous woman,
"was drunk with the blood of the saints, the blood of those who bore testimony to Jesus." Whenever in control of a country, Rome has not hes-
itated to put to death all who opposed her. Rome's frantic opposition to
the Reformation (caused by her pagan indulgences and corruption of the
true faith) is a good example. Some passages from *Halley's Bible Handbook*
will illustrate her historic brutality.

The Inquisition

The Inquisition, called the "HOLY OFFICE," was instituted by
Innocent III, and perfected under the second following Pope, Gre-
gory IX. It was the Church Court for the detection and punishment
of heretics. Under it every one was required to inform against
heretics. Anyone suspected was liable to Torture, without knowing
the name of his accuser. The proceedings were secret. The Inquisitor

pronounced sentence, and the victim was turned over to the civil authorities to be imprisoned for life or to be burned. The victim's property was confiscated and divided between the Church and the State. In the period immediately following Innocent III the Inquisition did its most deadly work in Southern France (see under Albigenses), but claimed vast multitudes of victims in Spain, Italy, Germany, and the Netherlands. Later on the Inquisition was the main agency in the Papacy's effort to crush the Reformation. It is stated that in the 30 years between 1540 and 1570 no fewer than 900,000 Protestants were put to death, in the Pope's war for the extermination of the Waldenses. Think of monks and priests directing, with heartless cruelty and inhuman brutality, the work of torturing and burning alive innocent men and women; and doing it in the Name of Christ, by the direct order of the "Vicar or Christ." The INQUISITION is the MOST INFAMOUS THING in history. It was devised by the Popes, and used by them for 500 years to maintain their power. For its record none of the subsequent line of "Holy" and "Infallible" Popes have ever apologized.

Rome's Opposition to the Reformation

In the Netherlands the Reformation was received early; Lutheranism, and then Calvinism; and Anabaptists were already numerous. Between 1513 and 1531 there were issued 25 different translations of the Bible in Dutch, Flemish and French. The Netherlands were a part of the dominion of Charles V. In 1522 he established the Inquisition, and ordered all Lutheran writings to be burned. In 1525 prohibited religious meetings in which the Bible would be read. 1546 prohibited the printing or possession of the Bible, either Vulgate or translation. 1535 decreed "death by fire" for Anabaptists. Phillip II (1566–98), successor to Charles V, reissued the edicts of his father, and with Jesuit help carried on the persecution with still greater fury. By one sentence of the Inquisition the whole population was condemned to death, and under Charles V and Phillip II more than 100,000 were massacred with unbelievable brutality. Some were chained to a stake near the fire and slowly roasted to death; some were thrown into dungeons, scourged, tortured on the rack, before being burned. Women were buried alive, pressed into coffins too small, trampled down with the feet of the executioner. Those that tried to flee to other countries were intercepted by soldiers and massacred. After years of nonresistance, under unheard of cruelty, the Protestants of Netherlands united under the leadership of William of Orange, and in 1572 began the great revolt;

and after incredible suffering in 1609, won their independence; Holland, on the North, became Protestant; Belgium, on the South, Roman Catholic. Holland was the first country to adopt public schools supported by taxation, and to legalize principles of religious toleration and freedom of the press.

In France. By 1520 Luther's teachings had penetrated France. Calvin's soon followed. By 1559 there were about 400,000 Protestants. They were called "Hugenots." Their earnest piety and pure lives were in striking contrast to the scandalous lives of the Roman clergy. In 1557 Pope Pius urged their extermination. The king issued a decree for their massacre, and ordered all loyal subjects to help in hunting them out. The Jesuits went through France persuading the faithful to bear arms for their destruction. Thus hunted by Papal agents, as in the days of Diocletian, they met secretly, often in cellars, at midnight.

St. Bartholomew's Massacre. Catherine de Medici, mother of the King, an ardent Romanist and willing tool of the Pope, gave the order, and on the night of August 24, 1572, 70,000 Hugenots, including most of their leaders, were massacred. There was great rejoicing in Rome. The Pope and his College of Cardinals went, in solemn procession, to the Church of San Marco, and ordered the Te Deum to be sung in thanksgiving. The Pope struck a medal in commemoration of the Massacre; and sent a Cardinal to Paris to bear the King and Queen-Mother the Congratulations of Pope and Cardinals. "France was within a hair-breadth of actually becoming Protestant; but France massacred Protestantism on the night of St. Bartholomew, 1572. 1792 there came to France a 'Protest' of another kind." (Thomas Carlyle)

The Hugenot Wars. Following St. Bartholomew's Massacre the Hugenots united and armed for resistance; till finally, in 1598, by the Edict of Nantes, they were granted the right of freedom of conscience and worship. But in the meantime some 200,000 had perished as martyrs. Pope Clement VIII called the Toleration Edict of Nantes a "cursed thing"; and, after years of underground work by the Jesuits, the Edict was Revoked, 1685; and 500,000 Hugenots fled to Protestant Countries.

In Bohemia, by 1600, in a population of 4,000,000, 80 percent were Protestant. When the Hapsburgs and Jesuits had done their work, 800,000 were left, all Catholics.

In Spain. The Reformation never made much headway, because the Inquisition was already there. Every effort for freedom or independent thinking was crushed with a ruthless hand. Torquemada (1420–98), a Dominican monk, arch-inquisitor, in 18 years burned

10,200 and condemned to perpetual imprisonment 97,000. Victims were usually burned alive in the public square; made the occasion of religious festivities. From 1481 to 1808 there were at least 100,000 martyrs and 1,500,000 banished. "In the 16th and 17th centuries the Inquisition extinguished the literary life of Spain, and put the nation almost outside the circle of European civilization." When the Reformation began Spain was the most powerful country in the world. Its present negligible standing among the nations shows what the Papacy can do for a country.[34]

The above quotations indicate that Rome has never been noted for her toleration. To my knowledge, she has never publicly acknowledged her sin of putting these Protestants to death. Calling us "separated brethren" is just an accommodation used today to gain acceptance by Protestants. When she is established in power, you can expect additional outbreaks of the Inquisition. Look at Catholic-dominated countries today, such as Colombia and Spain, where Protestants are treated as heretics, their churches burned, and their religious freedom denied.

In India we find that Hinduism is so parallel to the practices of Romanism that many of the Hindus can become Roman Catholics and need not give up Hinduism. Since the religions of the world all have idolatry in common, it would be a simple thing for them to amalgamate on a common basis. What do they care whether they are worshiping Semiramis and Tammuz or Mary and Jesus, just so they have an idol before which to bow down?

The color scheme of this one-world religion as defined in Revelation 17:4 is most revealing: "The woman was dressed in purple and scarlet." If you are familiar with pictures of the Vatican Council as published in national magazines, you will have observed that the bishops and cardinals wore purple and scarlet robes. You will also see that the pope and other church leaders are "glittering with gold, precious stones and pearls." They hold "a golden cup in [their] hand, filled with abominable things and the filthiness of [their] adulteries." These abominable things and adulteries are the idolatry and worship of gods other than Jesus Christ. In Rome we saw all manner of idols in the very headquarters of the Roman Church. More costly surroundings can scarcely be found than in the Vatican.

THE COMING DESTRUCTION
OF THE BABYLONIAN PROSTITUTE

Revelation 17:16–17 tell us: "The beast and the ten horns you saw will hate the prostitute. They will bring her to ruin and leave her naked; they will eat her flesh and burn her with fire. For God has put it into their hearts to accomplish his purpose by agreeing to give the beast their power to rule, until God's words are fulfilled." The Antichrist will permit the one-world Church to govern his actions during the first three and one-half years of the Tribulation while he is gathering more and more power; but in the middle of the Tribulation, when he feels he can become an autocratic ruler, he and the ten kings will throw off the prostitute because, in reality, while being dominated by her, they "hate the prostitute."

None of the world's political leaders have enjoyed subjugation to religious leaders, but have continued in a servile role only for expediency. When it is no longer necessary, the ten kings will "bring her to ruin and leave her naked," meaning they will confiscate her temples, her gold, and her costly apparel. In so doing, they will unwittingly be the instruments of God in destroying this awful Babylonian system once and for all: "For God has put it into their hearts to accomplish his purpose."

What is the will of God in regard to the Babylonian system? That she be annihilated. I am not suggesting that Christians attack her and seek to exterminate her. Instead, our responsibility is to "'come out from them and be separate,' says the Lord. 'Touch no unclean thing'" (2 Cor. 6:17), leaving her destruction to God, who will use the ten kings of the Tribulation period as His agents. The true Church of Jesus Christ must not sink into the pitfall of the religious phobia of our day, which is "religious unity." I am reminded of a statement I once heard attributed to Charles Haddon Spurgeon, that "you cannot have unity without forsaking truth, and to forsake truth for the sake of unity is to betray Jesus Christ." May God help us to be faithful to Him in these last days.

WHEN WILL THE PROSTITUTE RELIGION BE DESTROYED?

The destruction of the prostitute religion by the ten kings, as described in Revelation 17:16–17, is best understood as a parenthetical prophecy. It is one of the few things in the book of Revelation that is not chronological. The reason is because at the end of the Tribulation, when the seventh angel pours out his bowl on the earth and says "It is done!" there is a great earthquake that destroys the cities of the world, including all Babylons—religious Babylon and governmental/commercial Babylon. We have already seen that the "conflict of the ages," the battle between God and Satan for the souls of human beings, has gone on almost since the beginning of time. Now that battle is coming to an end.

The difficulty is the religious Babylon of Revelation 17, which is destroyed, comes in two parts. One occurs during the first part of the Tribulation when the governmental system of Babylon (pictured as this ugly "beast") is gaining world control but has to permit the "prostitute" to sit on and ride the beast. We see this as meaning she exercises a degree of control over the Babylonian system by bringing the nations of the world under her idolatrous religious power. During the first half of the Tribulation she incurs the wrath of the ten kings who see her use the authority of the Antichrist to advance her religious causes. So they plot to kill her.

The reason we know this killing of the prostitute of "mystery Babylon" is done in the middle of the Tribulation is twofold: (1) "The deadly wound" of Antichrist is healed by the indwelling of Satan himself, simulating the resurrection of Christ, in the middle of the Tribulation. (2) From then on the world does not worship mystery Babylon but the image of the beast. The False Prophet will do away with all religion except the worship of Antichrist Satan, which he will enforce. That begins in the middle of the Tribulation, as we saw described in Revelation 13.

Since the woman who rides the beast gets her authority from the beast, the Holy Spirit uses this description to show how religious Babylon and governmental Babylon are so intertwined they are presented together. However, they are destroyed at different times. The prostitute (religious Babylon) is destroyed by "beast and the kings of the earth," who "hate the prostitute" and kill her. This clears the way for Antichrist to fulfill the lifetime dream of Satan to get people to worship him. She is destroyed in the middle of the Tribulation; Babylon the governmental system will be destroyed at the end, when commercial Babylon is destroyed (ch. 18). With "Mystery Babylon . . . the Mother of Prostitutes" out of the way, "all inhabitants of the earth will worship the beast—all whose names have not been written in the book of life belonging to the Lamb that was slain from the creation of the world" (Rev. 13:8). Even in the dreadful last half of the Tribulation period, the worship of Antichrist will not be universal. Those who have received the Lamb of God will oppose him, even at the cost of martyrdom.

TWENTY-EIGHT

Commercial Babylon Destroyed

Revelation 18

The destruction of Babylon described in Revelation 17 and 18 will decisively rid the world of the major evils that have plagued the human race for about five thousand years. We have already seen the destruction to be unleashed on ecclesiastical or religious Babylon in the middle of the Tribulation period. The destruction of the commercial and governmental systems will not take place, however, until the end of the Tribulation. Some Bible scholars do not distinguish between the destruction of chapter 17 and that of chapter 18, but mold them altogether. The following six reasons establish that they are not the same.

1. "After this . . ." (18:1). This expression indicates that the events described in chapter 18 will not take place until after the events of chapter 17 have been fulfilled.
2. " I saw another angel coming down from heaven" (18:1). Events of chapter 17 were introduced by "one of the seven angels who had the seven bowls" (17:1). The angel referred to in chapter 18 is obviously not the same as the one who introduced the events of chapter 17. Therefore, we can expect the same sequence of events that have happened throughout the book of Revelation: When an angel fulfills his responsibility, another distinct judgment takes place on the earth.
3. The names in the two chapters are different. The name in chapter 18 is simply "Babylon the Great" (18:2). True, the Babylon destroyed in chapter 17 has the name, "MYSTERY, BABYLON THE GREAT, THE MOTHER OF PROSTITUTES AND OF THE ABOMINATIONS OF THE EARTH" (17:5), but the only similarity is the location, Babylon. When both titles are used fully, the contrast of these two Babylons is clearly seen.
4. Babylon the prostitute of chapter 17 will be destroyed by the kings of the earth (17:16). The Babylon of chapter 18 will be destroyed by the cataclysmic judgments of God.
5. The kings who destroy the Babylon of chapter 17 rejoice. In the Babylon of chapter 18, the kings and merchants lament and weep for her (18:9–15).

6. If chapters 17 and 18 take place during the last days of the Tribulation, there will be no place for the Antichrist and the False
   Prophet to do away with all religions and substitute the worship
   of the Antichrist's image as described in chapter 13.

We conclude, then, that chapter 17 describes the destruction of the
religious system, whereas chapter 18 denotes the destruction of "Satan's
seat," the commercial and governmental city of Babylon, marking the
prelude to the consummation of the Tribulation.

BABYLON THE GREAT IS FALLEN

After this I saw another angel coming down from heaven. He had
great authority, and the earth was illuminated by his splendor. With
a mighty voice he shouted: "Fallen! Fallen is Babylon the Great!" She
has become a home for demons and a haunt for every evil spirit, a
haunt for every unclean and detestable bird.   (Rev. 18:1–2)

Whether "another angel" is one of the seven angels who had the seven
bowls we are not told. But it seems doubtful, for this angel is distinctive,
with such "great authority" that he lights the earth with his glory.

The message of this angel who cries with a "mighty voice" is this:
"Fallen! Fallen is Babylon the Great!" Since chapter 18 describes the
destruction of a literal commercial city, the governmental capital of the
world during the Tribulation, we naturally ask ourselves the question,
"Where is that city?" Again, Bible prophecy students are not in agreement. I have heard some suggest the city of Rome, and some years ago
one interpreter suggested New York City because he felt it was the commercial center of the world. Those of us who believe we should take the
Scriptures literally whenever possible are inclined to believe that the city
of Babylon will be rebuilt. Admittedly, there are good Bible teachers who
do not hold that position, but I am inclined to believe that the weight of
Bible prophecy requires the literal rebuilding of Babylon.

BABYLON TO BE REBUILT

The main reason for believing that Babylon must be rebuilt relates to
some prophecies concerning her destruction that are yet unfulfilled.

1. Isaiah 13–14 and Jeremiah 50–51 describe the destruction of
Babylon as being at the time of "the day of the LORD." A careful reading
of these four chapters will reveal that the prophecies concerning the
destruction of Babylon in the Old Testament use the law of double reference; that is, they refer to the overthrow of Babylon the enemy of Israel
in the seventieth year of their captivity. But since Babylon is the headwaters of the world's governmental, commercial, and religious systems

in opposition to God's will, the second reference in these prophecies has to do with the day of the Lord, that is, the Tribulation period.

2. The ruins of Babylon have been used to build other cities, contrary to Jeremiah 51:26: "'No rock will be taken from you for a cornerstone, nor any stone for a foundation, for you will be desolate forever,' declares the LORD."

It is reliably reported that at least six cities bear the marks of having used parts of ancient Babylon in their building, including Seleucia, built by the Greeks; Ctesiphon, by the Parthians; Almaiden, by the Persians; and Kufa, by the Caliphs. Hillah, just a twenty-minute walk from the Babylonian ruins, was built almost entirely from the ruins of Babylon. The builders of Baghdad, fifty miles north of the site of ancient Babylon, also used materials from the ancient city. *The Encyclopedia of Lands and People* states in reference to Babylon:

> They found great treasure and the materials of its wonderful build-ings were used for the construction of Bagdad in 762. . . . And so, during the centuries, the greatness of Babylon and Assyria passed away. Their magnificent cities were used to supply the bricks for suc-ceeding towns and villages, and such ruins as the barbarians left fell into decay until they became shapeless mounds whose very names were forgotten.[35]

This fact alone demands the rebuilding of Babylon, because when God destroys it in chapter 18, no part of it will ever be used to build another city.

3. The prophecies of Jeremiah and Isaiah indicate that "Babylon will suddenly fall and be broken" (Jer. 51:8); and, "Babylon, the jewel of king-doms, the glory of the Babylonians' pride, will be overthrown by God like Sodom and Gomorrah" (Isa. 13:19). History reveals that ancient Babylon was never destroyed like that.

4. According to Isaiah 13:20, the ruins of Babylon were never to be inhabited: "She will never be inhabited or lived in through all genera-tions; no Arab will pitch his tent there, no shepherd will rest his flocks there." Again, a look at history reveals that such has not been the case with ancient Babylon. The best description of the history of Babylon, showing that this prophecy has never been fulfilled, is found in Dr. Clarence Larkin's book, *Dispensational Truth:*

> For a description of Babylon and her destruction we must turn to Isaiah, chapters 13 and 14, and Jeremiah, chapters 50 and 51. In these two prophecies we find much that has not as yet been fulfilled in regard to the city of Babylon.
>
> The city of Babylon was captured in B.C. 541 by Cyrus, who was mentioned "by name" in prophecy 125 years before he was born. Isa-

iah 44:28–45: 4, B.C. 712. So quietly and quickly was the city taken on the night of Belshazzar's Feast by draining the river that flowed through the city, and entering by the river bed, and the gates that surmounted its banks, that the Babylonian guards had forgotten to lock that night, that some of the inhabitants did not know until the "third" day that the king had been slain and the city taken. There was no destruction of the city at that time.

Some years after it revolted against Darius Hystaspis, and after a fruitless siege of nearly 20 months was taken by strategy. This was in B.C. 516. About B.C. 478 Xerxes, on his return from Greece plundered and injured, if he did not destroy, the great "Temple of Bel."

In B.C. 331 Alexander the Great approached the city which was then so powerful and flourishing that he made preparation for bringing all his forces into action in case it should offer resistance, but the citizens threw open the gates and received him with acclamations. After sacrificing to "Bel," he gave out that he would rebuild the vast Temple of that god, and for weeks he kept 10,000 men employed in clearing away the ruins from the foundations, doubtless intending to revive the glory of Babylon and make it his capital, when his purpose was defeated by his sudden death of marsh-fever and intemperance in his thirty-third year.

During the subsequent wars of his generals Babylon suffered much and finally came under the power of Seleucus, who, prompted by ambition to build a Capital for himself, founded Seleucia in its neighborhood about B.C. 293. This rival city gradually drew off the inhabitants of Babylon, so that Strabo, who died in A.D. 25, speaks of the latter as being to a great extent deserted. Nevertheless the Jews left from the Captivity still resided there in large numbers, and in A.D. 60 we find the Apostle Peter working among them, for it was from Babylon that Peter wrote his Epistle (1 Peter 5:13), addressed "to the strangers scattered throughout Pontus, Galatia, Cappadocia, Asia, and Bithynia."

About the middle of the 5th century Theodoret speaks of Babylon as being inhabited only by Jews, who had still three Jewish Universities, and in the last year of the same century the "Babylonian Talmud" was issued, and recognized as authoritative by the Jews of the whole world.

In A.D. 917 Ibu Hankel mentions Babylon as an insignificant village, but still in existence. About A.D. 1100 it seems to have again grown into a town of some importance, for it was then known as the "Two Mosques." Shortly afterwards it was enlarged and fortified and received the name of Hillah, or "Rest." In A.D. 1898 Hillah contained about 10,000 inhabitants, and was surrounded by fertile lands, and

282 | REVELATION UNVEILED

abundant date groves stretched along the banks of the Euphrates. Certainly it has never been true that "neither shall the Arabian pitch tent there, neither shall the shepherds make their fold there," Isaiah 13:20. Nor can it be said of Babylon—"Her cities are a desolation, a dry land, and a wilderness, a land wherein no man dwelleth, neither doth any son of man pass thereby," Jeremiah 51:43.[36]

The latest information I can glean concerning the city of Hillah, in the suburbs of ancient Babylon though perhaps not within the walls of the literal city itself, is that it is growing rapidly and is considered a wealthy city. Urban and suburban Hillah have a population of about 250,000; in fact, its population is on a par with that of any prosperous city of the modern world. It seems that the Iraqi government has awakened to the fact that the ruins of Babylon make exciting attractions for the tourists of the world. In addition, the suburbs of modern Hillah are spreading out around the ancient ruins. One writer has even gone so far as to suggest that people now live in the village of Babylon. Its population has increased remarkably since 1958 because the Iraqi government is building homes and moving in workers to bring old Babylon out of her dusty grave. The ancient city of Babylon is being "resurrected."

What all of this means is not too difficult to grasp. The one-world government, the one-world religion, and the one-world banking system that make possible the commerce of the world are already gathering momentum. It is just a matter of time before they decide to locate in a single spot. That spot will be Babylon. Recently, one of the delegates at the United Nations made a strong appeal to that body that it move its facilities out of Manhattan Island because of crowded conditions, the high cost of living, and discrimination against some of the delegates. His suggestion was that the United Nations move to Geneva, which is the headquarters for the international banking institutions of the world. Having been in Switzerland on three occasions, even I can see, as lovely as it is, that it is just too small to become the headquarters of Satan during the Tribulation. Besides, the Bible teaches us that Babylon will have that dubious honor. Instead, this suggestion to the United Nations will gather momentum in view of the difficulties of life in New York—economic, racial, and moral—until eventually such a suggestion will be favorably received.

By that time the Babylonian religion under the leadership of Rome will have consumed the World Council of Churches and its ecumenical movement and will be rapidly moving toward amalgamating the major religions of the world under the headship of the one who bears the title "Pontifex Maximus." The world bankers will be more than happy to finance the rebuilding of Babylon as the greatest city of the world to accommodate the headquarters of this one-world government and one-world religion. The fact that Iraq is one of the most oil-rich countries in the world will guarantee their investment, which, as usual, will return them a handsome profit. Railroads, river bottoms dredged to provide harbor facilities, and transatlantic air routes will make Babylon the strategic center of the world. And, like ancient Babylon in its day, it will be "the jewel of kingdoms, the glory of the Babylonians' pride" (Isa. 13:19). Unless the Lord raptures His Church soon, we can expect to see the foundation laid for the greatest city in all the world's history.

BABYLON REBUILDING UPDATED

Since writing the above material in the first edition, much has happened in both Iraq and Babylon. Saddam Hussein, the megalomaniac dictator of the country, has spent over one billion dollars on the rebuilding of that ancient city, which I believe will be taken over some day by Antichrist, titled New Babylon, and made the governmental, commercial, and religious center of the world.

During the last few years I have become a friend of two teachers of Bible prophecy, both of whom have been to Babylon. Dr. Charles Pak from Tulsa and Dr. Joseph Chambers from Charlotte are eyewitnesses of the fact that Saddam is trying to restore the ancient majesty to the city. Even amid all his self-induced problems with America and the United Nations, his rebuilding program is progressing. It is interesting to note that the first rebuilt structure in the old city was a temple to the sun. That should not be difficult to understand, as Hussein is a committed Satanist! He is a Muslim for political reasons, but at heart he is a sun-god worshiper.

THE COMING DESTRUCTION OF BABYLON

Once rebuilt, the great city of Babylon will serve as the seat of Satan, the governmental, religious, and commercial headquarters of the world during the Tribulation. In spite of her splendor and magnitude, this will be the most short-lived of the capitals of the world, for she will be earmarked for destruction by Almighty God. "In one hour she has been brought to ruin!" (Rev. 18:19).

The kings of the earth, merchants, and sailors will stand off as the city is destroyed, weeping because their great concern for making money and living to the gratification of the flesh has been cut off. No more will they be able to make merchandise; no more will people buy from them; their riches are gone, and thus they weep in despair (Rev. 18:9–17).

By contrast, the angel cries to heaven and instructs the holy apostles and prophets to "come out of her ... for ... God has remembered her crimes" (Rev. 18:5–6). For centuries, spiritually dead in their quest for material gain, the merchants, religionists, and governmental leaders of the world have tried to destroy the true prophets and apostles of God. In one hour they will receive double judgment for their iniquities and works.

This predicted judgment should certainly caution all who put their trust in stocks and bonds, houses and lands, or the making of money, that they are trusting in the wrong things. Their trust should be wholly and completely in the Lord.

BABYLON IS MILLSTONED

The mighty angel that casts down the great millstone (Rev. 18:21–22) symbolizes the permanence and suddenness of the destruction of Babylon, which we have already seen will be by earthquake, thunder, lightning, plagues, death, mourning, and famine, and "she will be consumed by fire" (18:8). My friend Dr. Charles Pak was told by his guide in the new Babylon city area that only ten feet underground is thick black tar, which may help provide the fires for the destruction of the entire area. The expression in verse 21 that she is "never to be found again" coincides with the prophecies of Isaiah 13 and Jeremiah 50–51, depicting the permanence of her destruction; the lifting of the curse during the millennial kingdom will not include her. Revelation 18:22 indicates that in addition to commerce, religion, and government, Babylon will also be the music capital of the world. If her product is similar to present-day popular music, and it no doubt will be, its noise and confusion will cease after her fall.

THE LIGHT OF LIFE DESTROYED

The darkness with which Babylon will be perpetually enshrouded is a testimony to her lifelessness for eternity. She will be solemnly and finally judged because of her slaughter of the saints and those who would communicate God's truth to people (Rev. 18:23–24). This marks the formal destruction of the most harmful religious and governmental system in the history of humankind and the destruction of the most detrimentally influential city ever built. From the ancient beginnings of this city it has been a capital of Satan's attack on the human race. Just as God chose Jerusalem as His headquarters to win the souls of people, Satan chose Babylon as his capital to destroy them. He moved his headquarters to Pergamum and then to Rome, where it is today; during the second half of the Tribulation period, he will move it again to Babylon, where God will finally destroy it forever.

As we will see, this climaxes the conflict of the ages, for Christ will come to set up His kingdom; Satan will be bound and unable to tempt the human race for one thousand years, after which he will be released one last time to deceive the last generation of human beings and then forever be thrown into the lake of fire. This will effectively end the conflict of the ages between God and Satan for human souls with a triumphal victory of Christ over Satan. The tragedy of the ages is the millions of souls Satan has deceived about God. There is nothing in Scripture to even suggest they will not suffer forever for allowing themselves to be deceived.

GOD'S MERCIFUL CALL TO HIS PEOPLE

Then I heard another voice from heaven say:

"Come out of her, *my people*,
   so that you will not share in her sins,
   so that you will not receive any of her plagues;
for her sins are piled up to heaven,
   and God has remembered her crimes."   (Rev. 18:4–5)

One thing that we purposely omitted was the voice from heaven calling God's people out of the city of Babylon *before her destruction*. Who are these people referred to by the voice from heaven as "my people"? They could be Tribulation saints, people who were not Christians at the time of the Rapture of the Church but who, during the Tribulation, received Christ as Savior and Lord. What they are doing in the capital city without the mark of the beast is difficult to comprehend, but the passage indicates that some will refuse to bow their knee to Antichrist. Another suggestion is that they may be Israelites who have not yet recognized Christ and repented of their national and personal sin by turning to Him. If Babylon is to be the headwaters of commercialism, one can be sure that many Jews will be present. God's call to these people at the end of the Tribulation period is another example of His consistent administration of mercy, as in His call to Lot and his family prior to the destruction of Sodom and Gomorrah.

One of the interesting parts of God's call to His people living in Babylon is to "come out of her, my people, so that you will not share in her sins, so that you will not receive any of her plagues." Because God works on the principle of "a man reaps what he sows" (Gal. 6:7), these people are warned that if they partake of the sins of Babylon, they will be judged accordingly. His invitation to come out of her is typical of God in His call to sinners of all ages that they turn to Him (which is repentance). The mercy of God is forever available. In every age He receives those who are willing to repent of their sin and look to Him for mercy through His Son, the Lord Jesus Christ. Only those who have done so will avoid the judgment of God that comes on all sinners.

PART THREE

Christ and the Future

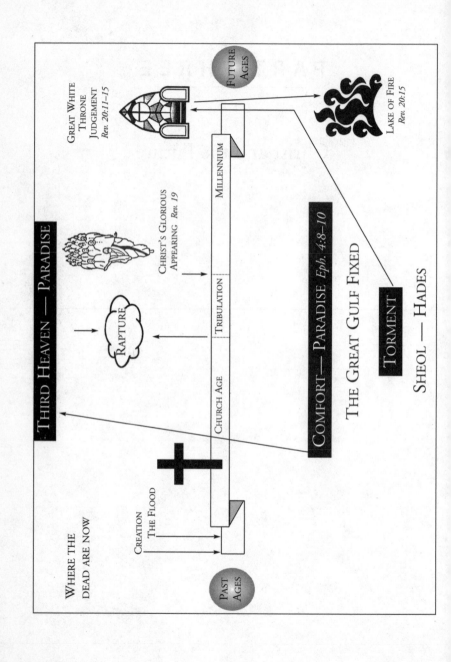

THIRD HEAVEN — PARADISE

WHERE THE
DEAD ARE NOW

CREATION
THE FLOOD

RAPTURE

CHRIST'S GLORIOUS
APPEARING *Rev. 19*

GREAT WHITE
THRONE
JUDGEMENT
Rev. 20:11–15

FUTURE
AGES

CHURCH AGE

TRIBULATION

MILLENNIUM

PAST
AGES

LAKE OF FIRE
Rev. 20:15

COMFORT—PARADISE *Eph. 4:8–10*

THE GREAT GULF FIXED

TORMENT

SHEOL — HADES

TWENTY-NINE

The Heavenly Hallelujah Chorus

Revelation 19:1–6

After this I heard what sounded like the roar of a great multitude in heaven shouting:

"Hallelujah!
Salvation and glory and power belong to our God,
for true and just are his judgments.
He has condemned the great prostitute
who corrupted the earth by her adulteries.
He has avenged on her the blood of his servants."

And again they shouted:

"Hallelujah!
The smoke from her goes up for ever and ever."   (Rev. 19:1–3)

The "Hallelujah Chorus" from Handel's *Messiah* is usually considered the most sublime expression of praise in the field of music. This paean of praise will be totally eclipsed by the magnificent heavenly "Hallelujah Chorus" of the future, described here in Revelation 19, which was the source of Handel's inspiration.

We have already seen that in order to understand the book of Revelation, one must always keep in view whether the scene is depicted in heaven or on earth. The contrast between the destruction of Babylon described in chapters 17–18 and the rapturous songs of praise in chapter 19 can be explained in terms of the specific relationship to time and location. Chapters 17–18 depict the impending doom on earth of the human race at the end of the Tribulation. Chapter 19 gives us a view of rejoicing in heaven that God's judgment is finally settled upon the earth; no longer will anyone be permitted to rebel against Him.

In a vital sense the rejoicing in heaven in chapter 19 results from the final triumph of good over evil, Christ over Antichrist, God over Satan, and the Holy Spirit over the spirit of evil. Ever since the fall of Adam the angelic creatures around the throne of God have anticipated that ultimate day when the cup of human iniquity would be filled with abominations and God would finally judge the human race. This contrasts with the attitude of people in the world, who will be weeping for the doom of the prostitute, Babylon. The scene in Revelation 19 offers a brief glimpse of what God intends to be the experience of humankind in their relationship with God, from which they fell. Human beings are seriously frustrated today because they are incapable, without Jesus Christ, of worshiping God as described here. Their spirit of self-sufficiency and pride prohibits their abandoning themselves to God. Only Christians who have voluntarily bent their knees to Jesus Christ (Phil. 2:8–9) are really able to enjoy the blessings of true worship, which is such an integral part of one's emotional desires.

Dr. Walvoord has stated that the reference to "a great multitude" in verse 1 is to the same group as in Revelation 7:9 (also translated "a great multitude"). "Though the general reference may be to all people in heaven, the allusion seems to be to the martyred dead of the great tribulation."[37] Actually, the people of verse 1 are distinct from the other beings in heaven, as we will see, for they are singing a song that includes salvation. This incorporates all believers—the Old Testament saints, the Church Age saints, and the Tribulation saints. Together they join in this great chorus, proclaiming, "Hallelujah!"

Revelation 19 is the only chapter in the New Testament where this word "Hallelujah" is found; it appears four times. Actually, it is an Old Testament word, taken from the Psalms, and means "praise the LORD." There are many things for which we should praise the Lord, as outlined in Psalms 146–150, including praise for His judgment.

Three additional words are used in the original to express this praise to the Lord our God: "salvation," "glory," and "power." Walter Scott, in his exposition of the Revelation of Jesus Christ, states, "The first of the three terms signifies deliverance, the second God's moral glory in judgment, and the third His might displayed in the execution of the judgment upon the harlot."[38]

Verse 2 establishes the cause for the judgment effected upon Babylon, here called "the great prostitute" and thus referring primarily to religious Babylon of chapter 17. But the human race has also made a religion of commercialism and government, whose destruction is described in chapter 18; thus, in this sense Babylon probably refers to all three forces that prostitute a person's basic quest for God into false religion, a lust for money and material possessions, or a lust for power through government.

These three evils have characterized the unregenerate since before the Flood. The destruction referred to here is significant because it involves more than just the city of Babylon and the commercial government and religious headquarters. It includes all that Babylon has typified since the days of Nimrod, who succeeded in carrying on the nefarious work of Cain and Lamech in the pre-Flood days, when they inaugurated systems that led away from God. In both cases these men were Satan's tools because they were unwilling to be "servants" of God.

All the iniquities of past ages will be justified in this ultimate destruction when God, in righteous judgment, "has avenged on her the blood of his servants" (Rev. 19:1). The extent of her judgment is seen in verse 3 in that "the smoke from her goes up for ever and ever," indicating that this judgment on Babylonian religion, politics, and commerce will last forever. No wonder there is rejoicing in heaven at the realization that Satan's religious, commercial, or political systems will never again be permitted to lead us astray.

THE TWENTY-FOUR ELDERS

"The twenty-four elders and the four living creatures fell down and worshiped God, who was seated on the throne. And they cried: 'Amen, Hallelujah!'" (Rev. 19:4). The twenty-four elders mentioned in verse 4 are not strangers to us. We have seen in our exposition of chapter 4 that they are probably a special group of men, twelve probably the sons of Jacob or their representatives and the twelve apostles. However, they could be twenty-four representatives of Christianity taken from all ages. These, plus the four living creatures also described in chapter 4, will join the redeemed in heaven to sing praises to God.

Five times in the book of Revelation the twenty-four elders express themselves, each time in praise and rejoicing. They frequently break out in a chorus of praise for the Lamb and His conquests. In Revelation 4:10–11 we see them honoring God for His creative power; in 5:8–9 they worship the Lamb who is found worthy to take the scroll from the Father and open its seals; in 7:11–12 they celebrate the arrival of the multitude of Gentiles in heaven; in 11:16–18 they worship God when He announces that the world has become the kingdom of Christ and He will reign forever; now in our present text we find them adding their "Amen, Hallelujah!" to God's judgment and destruction of Babylon.

Then a voice came from the throne, saying:

"Praise our God,
all you his servants,
you who fear him,
both small and great!"

Then I heard what sounded like a great multitude, like the roar of rushing waters and like loud peals of thunder, shouting:

"Hallelujah!
For our Lord God Almighty reigns." (Rev. 19:5–6)

The "voice ... from the throne" is evidently that of an angel commanding all God's servants to praise Him. All those in heaven are willing servants of God. The angels had a chance to make their choice when Satan rebelled against God. Some chose to leave; other passages suggest that additional angels have left since then. Human beings choose whether or not they will serve Him during this life. Thus, in that great heavenly chorus there will be a mixture of human and celestial voices as they sing, "Hallelujah!" They all share this in common: They have voluntarily become His servants.

The whole purpose of humankind is to glorify God. God created the human race for His good pleasure (Rev. 4:11). When people refuse to be His servants, they do not function according to His pleasure, thus living in disobedience. One gains entrance into heaven only by faith in Jesus Christ, involving the sublime act of yielding oneself to Him, not only as a Savior, but as Lord and Savior. Having once invited Jesus Christ into your life to be your Lord and Master, you have volunteered to become His servant.

THE LORD GOD ALMIGHTY REIGNS

The united song of all those in heaven anticipates the rulership of the Lord God by His Son, Jesus Christ. This song in a sense is an announcement of what will soon occur in the prophetic sequence. For shortly after this paean of praise in heaven, Jesus Christ will come to set up His glorious kingdom. For nineteen hundred years Christians have prayed in obedience to our Lord, "Your kingdom come, your will be done on earth as it is in heaven" (Matt. 6:10). That prayer will one day be answered when Christ comes physically to this earth to rule and to reign forever. This prophetic fact should be a cause of great rejoicing to all believers who understand and anticipate the event.

It was my privilege some years ago to preach part of the funeral service of Dr. David L. Cooper, a great Bible scholar under whom I studied for several years. At the conclusion of the service of rejoicing that this aged saint had gone on to join his dear wife and the many whom he had faithfully led to the Savior, the organist began to play the recessional as friends came by the casket to look into the face of their departed friend. It is difficult to describe the thrill that went through me when, instead of the traditional mournful tunes I am accustomed to hearing at funerals, I heard the dynamic chords of the organ pealing out the triumphant "Hallelujah Chorus." And the best part of all is that for the child of God, it is true. That was no time for sadness, but for rejoicing and for worship of our God. His old servant was not dead but with his Lord, awaiting that great Resurrection Day, when he will come to this earth with his Lord and all his loved ones in Christ.

THIRTY

The Marriage Supper of the Lamb

Revelation 19:7–10

"Let us rejoice and be glad
  and give him glory!
For the wedding of the Lamb has come,
  and his bride has made herself ready.
Fine linen, bright and clean,
  was given her to wear."

(Fine linen stands for the righteous acts of the saints.)
Then the angel said to me, "Write: 'Blessed are those who are invited to the wedding supper of the Lamb!'" And he added, "These are the true words of God."
At this I fell at his feet to worship him. But he said to me, "Do not do it! I am a fellow servant with you and with your brothers who hold to the testimony of Jesus. Worship God! For the testimony of Jesus is the spirit of prophecy."   (Rev. 19:7–10)

The marriage supper of the Lamb is a subject greatly misunderstood, not because of erroneous teaching, but because it is almost neglected in our preaching today. The main source of information concerning this coming event is found in Revelation 19:7–10, which falls into two main divisions: (1) the marriage of the Lamb, and (2) the marriage supper of the Lamb.

THE MARRIAGE OF THE LAMB

The marriage supper of the Lamb was one of the themes on which the Lord Jesus loved to dwell. In many of His stories or parables, He spoke of marriage suppers. For instance, in the parable of the ten virgins, He told about the preparation for the coming of the bridegroom. In Matthew 22:1–14 He spoke the parable of the marriage of the king's son. At this festive occasion the king sent out servants to invite people to come to this blessed event.

Who Is the Bridegroom?

The question "Who is the Bridegroom?" has but one answer. The Bridegroom can only be "the king's son" of Matthew 22:1–14, the Lord

Jesus Himself. In John 3:29, long after John the Baptist had introduced Jesus as "the Lamb of God, who takes away the sin of the world!" (John 1:29), John was asked to identify himself. He made it clear that he was not the Christ; in John 3:29 he referred to Christ as "the bridegroom," to himself as "the friend who attends the bridegroom [and who] waits and listens for him, and is full of joy when he hears the bridegroom's voice." Clearly Christ is here referred to as the Bridegroom as well as the Lamb. Thus, Christ is the Bridegroom at the marriage of the Lamb.

Who Is the Bride?

The answer to the question "Who is the Bride?" presents a difference of opinion. Some say that the Bride is Israel, because in Revelation 19:7 she is called "wife," as in Isaiah 54:5 Israel is called the wife of God. But the Bride cannot be Israel because a bride is not called a wife until after the marriage has taken place. Besides, there are two wives in Scripture. The Old Testament wife was "cast off" because of the spiritual adultery committed in the worship of other gods (Jer. 3:1–20; Ezek. 16; Hos. 2; 3:1–5). It is this very difference that Paul had in mind in 2 Corinthians 11:2: "I am jealous for you with a godly jealousy. I promised you to one husband, to Christ, so that I might present you as a pure virgin to him." The Church has been guilty of many sins in her nearly two thousand years of existence, but spiritual adultery is not one of them. Spiritual adultery is defined in Scripture as the worship of other gods. One cannot be a Christian, with the Holy Spirit as the witness in one's heart, and worship anyone but the Lord Jesus Christ. This fact, of course, automatically becomes the test as to the genuineness of salvation.

One other verse of importance to consider here regarding the identity of the Bride is found in Ephesians 5:32. The Apostle Paul, speaking to husbands and wives of their relationship together, likens the husband to Christ and the wife to the Church. He sums it up in verse 32 by saying, "This is a profound mystery—but I am talking about Christ and the church," clearly indicating that the perfect picture of the relationship between the Lord Jesus and His Church is that of a bride and a bridegroom. Therefore when a person accepts Jesus Christ, he or she becomes a member of the Church, the true invisible Church, and is automatically espoused or engaged to Christ. This engagement will be finalized at the marriage of the Lamb.

When and Where Will This Marriage Take Place?

The marriage of the Lamb must take place in heaven, for in Revelation 19:11, after the marriage of the Lamb and the marriage supper of the Lamb, we find the Lord Jesus coming in what we call "the Glorious Appearing" to set up His kingdom. For this reason we must conclude that the marriage and the supper have occurred in heaven. Their location in Revelation 19 shows these events to have taken place at the end of the Tribulation, just before the millennial reign of Christ on the earth.

Ephesians 5:27 indicates the manner in which the Bride will be presented to Christ: "a radiant church, without stain or wrinkle or any other blemish, but holy and blameless." This condition will exist only after the judgment of Christ when believers have been completely cleansed and the Church is made whole. For that reason we believe that the Judgment Seat of Christ, which will take place during the Tribulation, will precede the marriage supper of the Lamb, and immediately after the judgment of reward has been presented to the last believer, the marriage of the Lamb will take place. All Christians who have trusted in Christ during the age of grace, from the day of Pentecost to the Rapture of the Church, will make up His Bride.

How Does the Bride Make Herself Ready?

Years ago a bride usually made her own wedding dress; in fact, it is not uncommon for brides to make them today. The wedding dress of this Bride, made of fine linen (Rev. 19:8), is defined as "the righteous acts of the saints." That is, the Bride makes herself ready through her righteous acts. Inasmuch as this marriage comes after the Judgment Seat of Christ, most likely the position of the individual as a member of the Bride of Christ is determined by the outcome of the judgment by fire, when his works will be judged. Therefore Christians in this age must be careful to do good works (Titus 3:8). The Lord Jesus challenges Christians, "Store up for yourselves treasures in heaven" (Matt. 6:20). Although Christians are reluctant to consider working for rewards, we should remember that our relationship to Christ as members of the Bride of Christ will be determined by faithful service today.

The devil is a master liar. He tells the unsaved, "Work for salvation." If his lies fail and the individual accepts Christ, the devil immediately whispers, "Now that you're saved freely by grace, you don't have to do anything." That perspective does not agree with Ephesians 2:8–10; most Christians forget verse 10, "For we are God's workmanship, created in Christ Jesus to do good works, which God prepared in advance for us to do." The purpose of the Christian is to be available to the Lord for "good works."

We ought properly to take periodic inventories to see if we are truly serving Christ. In that Day all unfaithful Christians will rue their unfaithfulness, for it will not only keep them from the position with Christ they might desire, but will limit the extent to which they rule and reign with Christ during the millennial kingdom. The attitude of the Apostle Paul should characterize every Christian: "What shall I do, Lord?" (Acts

22:10). That kind of attitude will provide such motivation in believers that they will not only receive a "full reward" but hear the Savior say, "Well done, good and faithful servant! . . . Come and share your master's happiness!" (Matt. 25:21).

THE MARRIAGE SUPPER OF THE LAMB

The marriage supper, of course, is not the marriage, but the marriage feast of the Lamb. It seems a particular honor to be invited to this feast, for John was instructed to write, "Blessed are those who are invited to the wedding supper of the Lamb!" (Rev. 19:9). "Blessed" means "happy" or "honored." In other words, "Happy (or honored) are those who are invited to the wedding supper of the Lamb."

The Identity of the Guests

That guests will appear at this marriage supper can be deduced from the fact that some people are invited to attend the marriage ceremony. Obviously, a bride is never invited to a wedding supper, nor is a bridegroom. Those who are invited are the friends of the bride and groom. Now who are these friends or guests? There are some differences of opinion here. It cannot be the Church, for the Church is the Bride. Some try to identify the parables of the ten virgins and of the marriage supper of the king's son as illustrations of the guests at this wedding supper. But these two parables only serve to illustrate the prominence of a marriage supper in the thinking of the Lord Jesus. Note that both the foolish virgins and the guest who did not possess a wedding garment are left outside the wedding feast, whereas there is no place for anyone to be left outside at the marriage supper of the Lamb. These two parables are "kingdom of heaven" parables, teaching that one should be prepared for the coming of the Bridegroom.

John the Baptist, one of the last Old Testament saints, indicated that he was a friend of the Bridegroom (John 3:29). These Old Testament saints will be in heaven and will have their rewards, but they are not the Church, not the Bride of Christ. They are the friends of the Bride and Bridegroom, who at this point can be seen as the ones invited as guests to the feast. So then all the believing dead from Adam until the resurrection of Christ will be guests at this feast. In addition to them will appear those who have received the Savior during the Tribulation, both Jew and Gentile, many of whom will have been martyred for the testimony of Christ.

These will comprise the guests at the feast. Some would suggest that perhaps angels will be among the guests. However, I do not feel this is probable. Angels may be spectators at the marriage supper of the Lamb, but it should be noticed that the supper is distinguished by the use of the sacrificial name of the Lord—Lamb. Angels have never been the recipients of the blessings of the redeemed. Only those who have lived a human existence, have sinned, and have been redeemed by the blood of the Lamb will be in that number, either as the Bride of Christ or as the invited guests of Christ. I do not wish to imply that the Old Testament saints are inferior to the Church, or the body of Christ, but merely to point out that this is a special blessing for the Church. Now Israel, or the guests at the wedding supper of the Lamb, have promises and relationships to Him in which we shall not share; however, the marriage supper of the Lamb is an experience reserved for the Church.

THE HONEYMOON OF THE LAMB

After weddings on this earth, the wedding party customarily has a celebration or reception, which has replaced in the modern era of the old-fashioned marriage supper. But after the marriage supper, the bride and the bridegroom usually change into their traveling dress and slip away on a wedding trip. It is more than just coincidence that immediately after the marriage supper of the Lamb, John tells us, "I saw heaven standing open and there before me was a white horse" (Rev. 19:11a). From this point he launches into a description of the Glorious Appearing of the Lord Jesus Christ on this earth to set up His kingdom, when He will come with His Bride, the Church. The earth—the former abode of the Church, from which the Church will have been raptured, and the place where the Lamb Himself lived and died—will then become the place of the thousand-year honeymoon. Would to God that every marriage could enjoy the fulfillment of that symbol—one thousand years of peace.

THE BELIEVER AND THE MILLENNIUM

Immediately after the descent of Christ to this earth, the millennial kingdom will commence. Christ will set up His kingdom and believers will reign with Him. Second Timothy 2:11–12 clarifies this prospect. That reigning is based on the works of the believers, for Paul said, "If we endure, we will also reign with him."

REIGNING ACCORDING TO FAITHFULNESS

In Luke 19:11–27 we find the parable of the ten minas. This parable testifies to the quantitative element in our Christian service. Ten servants were given a mina each. The first one invested that mina, and at the coming of his Lord he had earned ten minas. Note the commendation and the injunction of the Savior in Luke 19:17: "'Well done, my good servant!' his master replied. 'Because you have been trustworthy in a very small matter, take charge of ten cities.'" Because this servant had magnified his substance, he was given the authority of ten cities during the

Millennium. The same is said in verse 18 of the second servant, who had taken his mina and gained five minas. To him was given authority to reign over five cities.

The unfaithful servant, who simply returned to the master the mina he had been given, received nothing; in fact, the mina he had was taken away, which may well indicate that the unfaithful servants of Christ, though saved ("but only as one escaping through the flames," 1 Cor. 3:15), do not have any reward, but will live a rather barren existence during the Millennium. Faithful servants, however, will be given a place of true leadership in Christ's kingdom, a position of leadership directly in proportion to the degree of faithfulness in Christian service. What a challenge to believers to be faithful in whatever way they can in this life, for in their service for Christ they are laying up for themselves treasures in heaven that will one day determine their station and position for a thousand years.

A hymn writer challenges us to "work for the night is coming, when man's work is done." The shades of night are falling rapidly; every Christian should be busy about the Master's business, "making the most of every opportunity" (Eph. 5:15), while light still remains.

THIRTY-ONE

The Glorious Appearing of Jesus Christ

Revelation 19:11–16

The Glorious Appearing of Jesus Christ is easily the most exciting event in all Bible prophecy. Every Christian who knows anything about the Bible looks forward to that blessed day when his Lord will truly be glorified. His coming in glory will be in marked contrast to His first coming, when He fulfilled the prophecies of a Savior. On that occasion He came humbly, born in a manger. He suffered Himself to be abused and buffeted by His enemies, even to the point of permitting His creatures to spit on Him and crucify Him. The next time our Lord will not come in humility, but in "power and great glory." His Glorious Appearing will significantly counterpoint His humble birth about two thousand years before.

Revelation 19:10 is the transition verse between the marriage supper of the Lamb and the Glorious Appearing. It can be considered in connection with either subject. After the vision John informs us that he "fell at his feet to worship him." Because the pronoun "him" has no antecedent, we can assume from the context and the divine instruction that this is the angel who revealed the vision to John. Like others who make the mistake of worshiping anyone but God, he is immediately corrected with the words, "Do not do it! I am a fellow servant with you and with your brothers." In the resurrection Christians will evidently be equal with angels, for in the book of Revelation they are considered as fellow servants with angels, and all bear the testimony of Jesus. Then John receives this specific command: "Worship God!"

This command of the angel to "worship God" in the sense that it is used here excludes worship directed toward any other creature. It is one of the many illustrations that demonstrate the consistency of Scripture. This scene, almost at the close of the book of Revelation, coincides with the first commandment of Exodus 20, "You shall have no other gods before me," teaching that God is the only object of worship. This consistency is also conveyed in establishing the personal deity of the Lord Jesus Christ. He is the only person in the Scripture who freely received worship of human beings without rebuke. Ten times in the New Testament Jesus was worshiped, and not once did He restrain those who did so.

That brings us to one of the most fascinating phrases in the Bible concerning prophecy: "The testimony of Jesus is the spirit of prophecy." Used in this connection, we find that the "fellow servant of God" is one who communicates the testimony of Jesus. Whether human or angelic, the true servants of God work indirectly or directly toward the testimony of Jesus.

The above expression gives the finest definition of the spirit of prophecy to be found in the Bible, "the testimony of Jesus." Prophecy is not solely the prediction of the future, as some say, nor is it only the declaration of ethical principles, as others claim. Prophecy receives its value and meaning from its relation to Christ, whether that relation be direct or indirect. From the first prophetic utterance of God (Gen. 3:15) to the last prediction of the Revelation, the heart of prophecy has been directed to the person of Christ. Errors of interpretation of details may be inescapable, but there need be no error in understanding the direction and purpose of prophecy; as a whole, it points to Christ.

We tend to think of prophecy as a revealing of future events, but in the New Testament we find that the prophetic gift is second only to that of the apostles and is a special form of the teaching gift. In reality, it is a making known of the divine will, and the divine will is that we should humble themselves and receive His Son, Jesus Christ. Therefore, any prophecy or prophetic teaching should directly or indirectly reveal the person of Jesus Christ. The study of Bible prophecy has fallen into disrepute only when teachers have become involved in peripheral areas such as date-setting or rigid predictions of events that go beyond the clear teachings of Scripture, and all at the expense of revealing "the testimony of Jesus."

Prophetic teaching, or preaching that testifies of Jesus, invariably warms the heart. The two disciples on the road to Emmaus acknowledged after their encounter with the resurrected Christ, "Were not our hearts burning within us while he talked with us on the road and opened the Scriptures to us?" (Luke 24:32). What caused their heart to burn within them? Verse 27 gives the answer, "And beginning with Moses and all the Prophets, he explained to them what was said in all the Scriptures concerning himself." For that reason, the study of the book of Revelation should cause our hearts to "burn within us," because it is the revelation of Jesus Christ, who forms the heart of all prophecy.

One quality that makes the Bible a literary masterpiece is its unusual simplicity. The words "I saw heaven standing open and there before me was a white horse, whose rider is called Faithful and True" (Rev. 19:11), present a simple introduction to the grand climax of the ages. For thousands of years it has been central to the plan of God that His Son, Jesus Christ, should reign over the earth and all things thereon. This simple expression introduces the event that shows our Lord gloriously coming to earth, fulfilling the many prophecies concerning His appearing.

Since the Glorious Appearing of Christ is such a climactic event in the Bible, we can expect to find many references to it. In that expectation we will not be disappointed. Before we examine the text in Revelation, it would help the student to examine other Bible references to this event so that we may adequately compare Scripture with Scripture and more clearly establish the proper sequence of events.

CHRIST GOES FIRST TO EDOM

Who is this coming from Edom,
>   from Bozrah, with his garments stained crimson?
Who is this, robed in splendor,
>   striding forward in the greatness of his strength?
"It is I, speaking in righteousness,
>   mighty to save."
Why are your garments red,
>   like those of one treading the winepress?
"I have trodden the winepress alone;
>   from the nations no one was with me.
I trampled them in my anger
>   and trod them down in my wrath;
their blood spattered my garments,
>   and I stained all my clothing.
For the day of vengeance was in my heart,
>   and the year of my redemption has come.
I looked, but there was no one to help,
>   I was appalled that no one gave support;
so my own arm worked salvation for me,
>   and my own wrath sustained me.
I trampled the nations in my anger;
>   in my wrath I made them drunk
>   and poured their blood on the ground."   (Isa. 63:1–6)

For some reason we find that our Lord will go first to Edom, where many Israelites have fled for safety from the Antichrist. He thus will vindicate the promises of God as He triumphs over the enemies of Israel. This text also describes Him as arrayed in red garments and reveals that this is the "day of vengeance." Human beings, having rejected God's mercy offered through the sacrificial death of Christ on the cross, will suffer God's judgment at the hands of the One they have rejected. This, and other texts, make it clear that Christ's Glorious Appearing will not be a time of joy to the unsaved but, on the contrary, a time of great sorrow because the day of God's wrath is come.

CHRIST'S COMING ATTENDED
BY SIGNS AND NATURAL PHENOMENA

"For as lightning that comes from the east is visible even in the west, so will be the coming of the Son of Man. Wherever there is a carcass, there the vultures will gather.

"Immediately after the distress of those days

'the sun will be darkened,
and the moon will not give its light;
the stars will fall from the sky,
and the heavenly bodies will be shaken.'

"At that time the sign of the Son of Man will appear in the sky, and all the nations of the earth will mourn. They will see the Son of Man coming on the clouds of the sky, with power and great glory. And he will send his angels with a loud trumpet call, and they will gather his elect from the four winds, from one end of the heavens to the other." (Matt. 24:27–31)

This prediction of our Lord Himself concerning His Glorious Appearing is taken from the Olivet Discourse. It reveals that He will come visibly and become the object of attention. The sun, moon, and stars will not give their lights, but all attention will be focused on "the sign of the Son of Man [that] will appear in the sky," after which "all the nations of the earth will mourn" because they have not prepared themselves for that Day. Then all people will see Christ, who is the Light, "coming on the clouds of the sky, with power and great glory." At this moment the second installment of the Rapture will occur, when Christ gathers together "his elect from the four winds, from one end of the heavens to the other."

THE SECOND INSTALLMENT OF THE RAPTURE

In Psalm 50:1–6 we find the Lord above the earth but below the heaven (v. 4), looking back up to heaven and down to the earth, calling His saints to Him. This indicates that He will rapture the Tribulation saints still living and the Tribulation saints whose souls are under the altar (Rev. 6). This may include the Old Testament saints, whose resurrection may wait until the end of the Tribulation. This event may take place just before the marriage supper of the Lamb previously discussed. Now, having raptured all believers from all ages, He will come to an exclusively unsaved earth.

Christ Comes to Execute Judgment with His Saints

Enoch, the seventh from Adam, prophesied about these men: "See, the Lord is coming with thousands upon thousands of his holy ones

> to judge everyone, and to convict all the ungodly of all the ungodly
> acts they have done in the ungodly way, and of all the harsh words
> ungodly sinners have spoken against him." (Jude 14–15)

This is the only passage in the Bible telling us that Enoch was a prophet. Somehow God had revealed to him that in the unfolding of the ages Christ will come with myriads of holy ones to execute judgment on humankind. That judgment will begin with Antichrist and will eventually include the nations of the earth, as explained in Matthew 25.

Second Thessalonians 2:7–10 describes Christ's coming in judgment to destroy Antichrist, which parallels the passage we will study in the next chapter, in which Christ casts the Antichrist into the lake of fire.

Christ Will Stand on the Mount of Olives

> Then the LORD will go out and fight against those nations, as he fights
> in the day of battle. On that day his feet will stand on the Mount of
> Olives, east of Jerusalem, and the Mount of Olives will be split in two
> from east to west, forming a great valley, with half of the mountain
> moving north and half moving south. You will flee by my mountain
> valley, for it will extend to Azel. You will flee as you fled from the earth-
> quake in the days of Uzziah king of Judah. Then the LORD my God will
> come, and all the holy ones with him. (Zech. 14:3–5)

Our Lord ascended into heaven from the Mount of Olives. In Acts 1:11 the angels said, "This same Jesus, who has been taken from you into heaven, will come back in the same way you have seen him go into heaven." Our Lord will not only come in "the same way," meaning visibly and physically, but He will actually come to the same place, the Mount of Olives. When His feet strike the Mount of Olives, that hill will divide in two.

Some Bible commentators have indicated that a natural division exists between the two high points on the Mount of Olives, which will cleave in two, thus creating a new passageway from Jerusalem down to Jericho at the Jordan River. There may even be a gigantic causeway from the Jordan River out to the Mediterranean. Others speak of a geological report, indicating a fault under the Mount of Olives that needs only a slight earthquake to cleave it in two. In any case, when Christ sets His feet on the Mount of Olives, His power will be manifested in that it will divide into two parts.

All of the above events, taking place in a breathtaking moment of time, will highlight the fact that our Lord has come. These passages are only some of the many that describe the great event of our Lord's Glorious Appearing.

THE GLORIOUS APPEARING

The expression "glorious appearing" is not found in the book of Revelation, but it does occur in Titus 2:13. There it describes the physical, visible return of Christ to the earth in distinction from that "blessed hope," which is the Rapture of the Church or the secret coming of Christ for His believers prior to the Tribulation period. Of all the descriptions of the Glorious Appearing in the Bible, none is more graphic than our present text:

> I saw heaven standing open and there before me was a white horse, whose rider is called Faithful and True. With justice he judges and makes war. His eyes are like blazing fire, and on his head are many crowns. He has a name written on him that no one knows but he him-self. He is dressed in a robe dipped in blood, and his name is the Word of God. The armies of heaven were following him, riding on white horses and dressed in fine linen, white and clean. Out of his mouth comes a sharp sword with which to strike down the nations. "He will rule them with an iron scepter." He treads the winepress of the fury of the wrath of God Almighty. On his robe and on his thigh he has this name written:
>
> KING OF KINGS AND LORD OF LORDS.
>
> (Rev. 19:11–16)

Verse 11 introduces this dynamic scene by telling us that John sees "heaven standing open." This is the second time John has seen the heaven opened. The first time was in Revelation 4:1, where he was invited up into heaven and as a representative of the Church looked down on the scenes of the Tribulation Period. In chapter 19 the Tribulation has been concluded and Christ is returning to the earth, so we find the heaven opened again. This time, instead of taking a man up, heaven is opened to let the rider on the white horse out, accompanied by His armies.

This rider is to be distinguished from the rider on the white horse in 6:2, who was the Antichrist. The present rider, with eyes "like blazing fire," can be none other than the Lord Jesus Christ. The significance of the white horse is typical of the difference between this coming and Christ's first coming. While on this earth our Lord fulfilled Zechariah 9:9, entering Jerusalem on a lowly beast of burden. Now His humilia-tion is done away and He will come in glory, properly using the white horse to depict His power and glory. Lest you think it strange that there are horses in heaven, I remind you that in 2 Kings 2:11 and 6:13–17 we find references to horses and chariots of fire.

Even more significant than what our Lord will do at His coming is how He is described here, for His eternal nature is revealed. "Faithful and True" presents our Lord as a contrast to the unfaithful deceivers of humankind, Antichrist and Satan. Our Lord has faithfully fulfilled all of His prophecies. "With the Lord a day is like a thousand years" (2 Pet. 3:8) suggests that a promise of God given a thousand years ago is as though it were given yesterday. The extent of His faithfulness, however, is not fully comprehended until He fulfills these promises. Believers accept His faithfulness now by faith, but in that moment all human beings will see the tangible evidence of His faithfulness. Christ is the truth; by contrast, Satan is the big lie. Christ is the true way to God; Satan is the false way, leading not to God but to hell.

The Righteous Judge

"With justice [righteousness] he judges" (Rev. 19:11). We have already seen that our Lord comes to judge this earth on the basis of what it has done concerning Himself. He is the pivot of all history and the significant factor of the ages.

The Righteous Warrior

"With justice [righteousness] he ... makes war." This world has known nothing but wars since it rejected God and His Son, Jesus Christ. During World War I the total number of war-related deaths was forty million. It is estimated that the total number of deaths caused by World War II was sixty million. Most of the wars of the world have been unrighteous wars.

When Christ comes, however, His war will consist of only one battle. He will consume all before Him, all that stand in opposition to Him, and bring every person into subjection. This will be the first clearly righteous war in the history of humankind. The ability of Christ to wage a righteous war is not only seen in His holy nature, but in that His eyes are "like blazing fire," indicating that He will judge according to truth. The best judge on earth cannot know all the facts of a given situation because he or she is limited by human frailty. Jesus Christ is not so limited. He who knows the end from the beginning will be a righteous judge, for His all-seeing eye will reveal all truth about every individual and nation.

The Righteous King

"On his head are many crowns" (Rev. 19:12). This does not suggest that Christ is doing a balancing act with a great number of crowns on His head, but should be taken symbolically to mean that He will come in much authority. All through history a crown on a person's head has symbolized authority. Kings wore crowns, the popes wear a triple crown, the Antichrist's kingdom is symbolized with crowns, even the ten kings of the Tribulation will have crowns; but when Christ comes, all power will be given to Him as the Supreme King. In fact, verses 11–12 reveal the threefold nature of Christ in His Glorious Appearing. For when He comes, He will be a judge, a warrior, and a king.

"He has a name written on him that no one knows but he himself." Many have speculated about this name, but it seems unwise to do so. A Bible name reveals the nature of the person, and there are many names that reveal facets of the nature of God and Jesus Christ. However, since Jesus is divine, it seems only natural that some aspects of His nature are incomprehensible to our finite minds. Therefore at least this one name will be unknown to us. J. A. Seiss made the following statement:

> This warrior, judge, and king has a name ineffable and unknowable, but it is a true and rightful name, a name of reality, which is above every name. We do not yet know all the majesty and attributes of being which belong to our sublime Savior; and when He comes forth out of heaven for the war on the beast, He will come in vast unknowableness of greatness, in heights of great majesty and glory, which no one knoweth but Himself.[39]

Verse 13 indicates that "He is dressed in a robe dipped in blood." This may well be a reference to the bloodshed caused by the battle of the great Day of God Almighty as He brings forth triumphs, or it may be a symbolic reference to the fact that His garments have been sprinkled with blood on Calvary's cross so that we may wear robes of righteousness.

"And his name is the Word of God." The Apostle John is the only writer of the New Testament who uses the expression "the Word of God" to describe the Lord Jesus Christ. It is a beautiful expression, coming from the Greek word *logos* and literally meaning "the expression" of God. As we reveal thoughts from one human mind to another through the vehicle of words, so Christ, the eternal Word of God, reveals God to us. If human beings want to know God, they need only study about His Son, Jesus Christ, for He "has made him known" (John 1:18).

THE ARMIES OF CHRIST

"The armies of heaven were following him, riding on white horses and dressed in fine linen, white and clean" (Rev. 19:14). The armies of heaven consist of the angelic hosts, the Old Testament saints, the Church, and the Tribulation saints. The most significant truth, however, is the garb of this army. They are "dressed in fine linen, white and clean." Military men are issued fatigue uniforms for battle dress, not only for camouflage but also because war is so dirty that light-colored clothes would be severely soiled. Here, however, the Commander-in-Chief of the heavenly forces clothes His army in white, a practice unheard of in the history of warfare. The reason should not be overlooked by the reader: No member of the armies of Christ that come with Him in His Glorious Appearing will do battle. Not one of us will lift a finger, for the battle will be consummated by the spoken word of our Lord.

THE AUTHORITY OF THE KING OF KINGS

"Out of his mouth comes a sharp sword with which to strike down the nations. 'He will rule them with an iron scepter.'" The sharp sword here has lead some to believe that it is "the sword of the Spirit, which is the word of God" (Eph. 6:17). But Dr. John Walvoord states concerning this expression:

> The word for sword indicates a long Thracian sword, or one which is unusually large and longer than most swords. The same word is sometimes used to describe a javelin, a sword sufficiently light and long to be thrown as a spear. Here the word is used symbolically to represent a sharp instrument of war, with which Christ will smite the nations and establish His absolute rule. The expression of ruling "with a rod of iron" is also found in Psalm 2:9 and Revelation 2:27, with a similar expression, "the rod of His mouth," in Isaiah 11:4. It represents absolute, unyielding government under which men are required to conform to the righteous standards of God.[40]

The coming of Christ in His Glorious Appearing with the heavenly armies will not only bring to consummation the enmity of Satan, his Antichrist, the False Prophet, and the millions they deceive, but will usher in the millennial kingdom—the righteous reign of Christ on earth. This fact is seen clearly in the name given to Christ in verse 16.

"On his robe and on his thigh he has this name written: KING OF KINGS AND LORD OF LORDS" (Rev. 19:16). A warrior goes into battle with his sword on his thigh. Christ's sword will be His spoken word. The word that called the world into being will call human leaders and the armies of all nations into control. Instead of a sword on His thigh is His name, "KING OF KINGS AND LORD OF LORDS." Christ Jesus, the living Lord, will be established in that day for what He is in reality, *King* above all kings, *Lord* above all lords. Then truly will the prophetic words of Isaiah be fulfilled, "For to us a child is born, to us a son is given, and the government will be on his shoulders. And he will be called Wonderful Counselor, Mighty God, Everlasting Father, Prince of Peace" (Isa. 9:6).

THIRTY-TWO

The Battle of the Great Day of God Almighty

Revelation 19:17–21

In the previous chapters we saw that the Glorious Appearing of Jesus Christ portrays Him coming as the righteous Judge, the righteous Warrior, and the righteous King. The present chapter, covering Revelation 19:17–21, primarily deals with Christ as the righteous Warrior, for we see Him coming to do battle with the host of Satan's armies in what is often called "the battle of Armageddon," but which in truth is a war, or campaign, of the great Day of God Almighty. This war is necessitated by the fiendishly evil ambitions of humankind and their evil source of power, Satan. It is doubtless the most horrible experience in the annals of human history.

Our Lord Himself tells when this battle will take place:

> "Immediately after the distress of those days
>
>> 'the sun will be darkened,
>>   and the moon will not give its light;
>> the stars will fall from the sky,
>>   and the heavenly bodies will be shaken.'
>
> "At that time the sign of the Son of Man will appear in the sky, and all the nations of the earth will mourn. They will see the Son of Man coming on the clouds of the sky, with power and great glory. And he will send his angels with a loud trumpet call, and they will gather his elect from the four winds, from one end of the heavens to the other."
>
> (Matt. 24:27–31)

The Glorious Appearing will take place "immediately after the distress of those days," that is, at the end of the Tribulation and before the Millennium. Our Lord will time His coming at the most dramatic point in all history. The Antichrist, the False Prophet, and Satan will inspire the armies of the world to invade Palestine in a gigantic effort to rid the world of the Jews and to fight against Christ.

This coming battle before Christ sets up His millennial kingdom is often called "the Battle of Armageddon." This is a misleading expression because Armageddon means "Mount of Slaughter" and refers to the beautiful valley to the east of Mount Megiddo, and the word "battle" here literally means "campaign" or "war." No war has ever been won by a single battle. In fact, it is possible to lose a battle and still win a war. The war of the great Day of God Almighty takes place in a single day, and the Battle of Armageddon will be just one of the battles of that war.

Actually, this war will encompass more than just the Valley of Megiddo; as we will see, it covers practically all of the land of Palestine. This conflict, when Christ defeats the armies of Antichrist, will be a series of at least four "campaigns"; therefore it is more properly called "the battle on the great day of God Almighty" (Rev. 16:14). The carnage and the horror of the scene are described only generally from our text (19:71–21). In order to get a full picture of this horrible period, we must turn to several other passages in the Word of God.

THE BATTLE OF ARMAGEDDON

We have already seen in the previous chapter that the Lord will go first to Edom and soil His garments in a bloody battle, in which He will rescue the Israelites who have been persecuted by Antichrist and his armies. Then He probably will go to the Valley of Megiddo, where the great armies of the world will be gathered in opposition to Him. It is impossible to predict the exact sequence of the battles in this war, but since everything culminates at Jerusalem, it would seem that He will go next to the Valley of Megiddo. This conflict can literally be called the Battle of Armageddon and is described in Revelation 16:12–16.

> The sixth angel poured out his bowl on the great river Euphrates, and its water was dried up to prepare the way for the kings from the East. Then I saw three evil spirits that looked like frogs; they came out of the mouth of the dragon, out of the mouth of the beast and out of the mouth of the false prophet. They are spirits of demons performing miraculous signs, and they go out to the kings of the whole world, to gather them for the battle on the great day of God Almighty.
>
> "Behold, I come like a thief! Blessed is he who stays awake and keeps his clothes with him, so that he may not go naked and be shamefully exposed."
>
> Then they gathered the kings together to the place that in Hebrew is called Armageddon.

When we discussed Revelation 16, we noted how the Euphrates River will dry up to make possible the way of the kings of the East with their vast hordes moving like a cloud to cover the land. The satanic trinity of Antichrist, the False Prophet, and the devil himself send out "three evil spirits that looked like frogs" out of the mouth of the beast and of the

False Prophet, deceiving the kings of the earth to bring them into this great battle of Armageddon, where they will fight against Christ. The importance of the Valley of Megiddo for this conflict should not be overlooked. "Armageddon," from the transliterated "Har-Magedon" of the ASV, is a Hebrew expression that means "Mount Megiddo." This place, mentioned only in Revelation 16:16, will be the final battleground between the forces of good and evil.

> The town of Megiddo guarded the pass which formed the easiest caravan route between the Plain of Sharon and the Valley of Jezreel, and the low mountains around were silent witnesses of perhaps more bloody encounters than any other spot on earth, continuing down to recent times. Hence the appropriateness of this place for the vast conflict pictured in Revelation 16.[41]

One commentator has stated that as far back as the time of Napoleon that great valley was claimed to be the most natural battleground of the whole earth. Many great military generals have fought there:

Thothmes	1500 B.C.
Rameses	1350 B.C.
Sargon	722 B.C.
Sennacherib	710 B.C.
Nebuchadnezzar	606 B.C.
Ptolemy	197 B.C.
Antiochus Epiphanes	168 B.C.
Pompeii	63 B.C.
Titus	A.D. 70
Khosru, the Persian King	A.D. 614
Omar	A.D. 637
the Crusades under St. Louis of France	A.D. 909
Saladin, who conquered Richard the Lion-hearted	A.D. 1187
the Ottoman forces	A.D. 1616

There Satan and his hordes have met God before. Three renowned mountains overlook this valley: Carmel, Gilboa, and Tabor. It was on Mount Carmel that the contest between Elijah's God and the devil-possessed, Baal-worshiping prophets of Jezebel took place. One of the mightiest conflicts in the Old Testament, it was not a battle of one man versus a nation, but God versus Satan, for on that day "the fire of the LORD fell" (1 Kings 18:38). One day it will fall again, but on that day the fire will be accompanied by the Lord himself: "On that day his feet will stand on the Mount of Olives, east of Jerusalem" (Zech. 14:4).

This great battle of Christ versus Antichrist will conclude in a display of the omnipotent Christ, for He will utterly destroy Antichrist and his armies. The carnage of this battle is well described by Ezekiel.

> "Son of man, this is what the Sovereign LORD says: Call out to every kind of bird and all the wild animals: 'Assemble and come together from all around to the sacrifice I am preparing for you, the great sacrifice on the mountains of Israel. There you will eat flesh and drink blood. You will eat the flesh of mighty men and drink the blood of the princes of the earth as if they were rams and lambs, goats and bulls— all of them fattened animals from Bashan. At the sacrifice I am preparing for you, you will eat fat till you are glutted and drink blood till you are drunk. At my table you will eat your fill of horses and riders, mighty men and soldiers of every kind,' declares the Sovereign LORD.
>
> "I will display my glory among the nations, and all the nations will see the punishment I inflict and the hand I lay upon them. From that day forward the house of Israel will know that I am the LORD their God."
> (Ezek. 39:17–22)

Ezekiel 38–39 primarily describe the destruction of the armies of Gog and Magog, who come down against Israel, which will probably take place just prior to the Tribulation. Most Bible commentators call this the Battle of Armageddon, but I think they speak amiss, for several reasons.

1. In Ezekiel 38:1–39:16 Gog's armies come against Israel and are opposed by the Western confederation of nations. Armageddon will find all the armies of the earth united against Christ.

> Sheba and Dedan and the merchants of Tarshish and all her villages will say to you, "Have you come to plunder? Have you gathered your hordes to loot, to carry off silver and gold, to take away livestock and goods and to seize much plunder?"   (Ezek. 38:13)

2. In the battle described in Ezekiel, Israel is living in the land of unwalled villages in a time of peace, which will not be their lot in the latter half of the Tribulation period.

3. Also, it takes seven years to burn the implements of war left on the ground after this great battle.

> "Then those who live in the towns of Israel will go out and use the weapons for fuel and burn them up—the small and large shields, the bows and arrows, the war clubs and spears. For seven years they will use them for fuel."   (Ezek. 39:9)

This cannot be carried out during the Millennium; therefore, we conclude it will be accomplished before the Tribulation. Whether this is before or after the Rapture of the Church is impossible to ascertain, because the Bible does not teach conclusively that the Tribulation begins immediately after the Rapture. The Tribulation, begun by the signing of the covenant between Antichrist and Israel (Dan. 9:27), may or may not commence immediately following the Rapture. Therefore Ezekiel 39:17–22 goes beyond that immediate battle when Gog's armies come down against Israel, for in this latter section it is all the armies united together, as it will be at the end of the Tribulation.

Putting these passages together (Ezek. 39:17–22 and Rev. 16:13–26), we find that when Christ meets the armies of Antichrist in the Valley of Megiddo, they will come from east and west, and from the north and south. He then will slay them with the sword that comes out of His mouth (Rev. 19:15). All that will be left of these armies is little more than a gigantic feast for the birds of prey and other parasites.

THE BATTLE OF THE VALLEY OF JEHOSHAPHAT

"In those days and at that time,
    when I restore the fortunes of Judah and Jerusalem,
I will gather all nations
    and bring them down to the Valley of Jehoshaphat.
There I will enter into judgment against them
    concerning my inheritance, my people Israel,
for they scattered my people among the nations
and divided up my land...."
Proclaim this among the nations:
    Prepare for war!
Rouse the warriors!
    Let all the fighting men draw near and attack.
Beat your plowshares into swords
    and your pruning hooks into spears.
Let the weakling say,
    "I am strong!"
Come quickly, all you nations from every side,
    and assemble there.
Bring down your warriors, O LORD!
"Let the nations be roused;
    let them advance into the Valley of Jehoshaphat,
for there I will sit
    to judge all the nations on every side.
Swing the sickle,
    for the harvest is ripe.
Come, trample the grapes,
    for the winepress is full
    and the vats overflow—

so great is their wickedness!"
Multitudes, multitudes
   in the valley of decision!
For the day of the LORD is near
   in the valley of decision.
The sun and moon will be darkened,
   and the stars no longer shine.
The LORD will roar from Zion
   and thunder from Jerusalem;
   the earth and the sky will tremble.
But the LORD will be a refuge for his people,
   a stronghold for the people of Israel.
"Then you will know that I, the LORD your God,
   dwell in Zion, my holy hill.
Jerusalem will be holy;
   never again will foreigners invade her."   (Joel 3:1–2, 9–17)

In this great battle there are "multitudes, multitudes in the valley of decision! For the day of the LORD is near in the valley of decision." These are more of the armies of the nations who will be brought into war by the lying spirits described in Revelation 16:13. This battle is also described in 14:14–20.

> I looked, and there before me was a white cloud, and seated on the cloud was one "like a son of man" with a crown of gold on his head and a sharp sickle in his hand. Then another angel came out of the temple and called in a loud voice to him who was sitting on the cloud, "Take your sickle and reap, because the time to reap has come, for the harvest of the earth is ripe." So he who was seated on the cloud swung his sickle over the earth, and the earth was harvested.
>
> Another angel came out of the temple in heaven, and he too had a sharp sickle. Still another angel, who had charge of the fire, came from the altar and called in a loud voice to him who had the sharp sickle, "Take your sharp sickle and gather the clusters of grapes from the earth's vine, because its grapes are ripe." The angel swung his sickle on the earth, gathered its grapes and threw them into the great winepress of God's wrath. They were trampled in the winepress outside the city, and blood flowed out of the press, rising as high as the horses' bridles for a distance of 1,600 stadia.

These passages show that the battle will take place at the time of God's judgment, for He will put in His sickle and reap a judgment harvest on the nations of the earth for their persecution of the nation Israel. As a result of this conflict with Christ, "blood flowed out of the press, rising as high as the horses' bridles for a distance of 1,600 stadia."

314 | REVELATION UNVEILED

THE BATTLE OF JERUSALEM

The final battle in the war of the great day of God Almighty will be the battle of Jerusalem. The Antichrist and what is left of his armies, or more properly the advance guard of his armies, will storm Jerusalem. This last conflict between Satan and Christ until after the Millennium will find Satan making one more fiendish effort to destroy the promised seed. Satan will order his armies to destroy the entire city of Jerusalem, but Christ will come to deliver her at the last moment, as is clearly seen in Zechariah 12:1–9.

> This is the word of the LORD concerning Israel. The LORD, who stretches out the heavens, who lays the foundation of the earth, and who forms the spirit of man within him, declares: "I am going to make Jerusalem a cup that sends all the surrounding peoples reeling. Judah will be besieged as well as Jerusalem. On that day, when all the nations of the earth are gathered against her, I will make Jerusalem an immovable rock for all the nations. All who try to move it will injure themselves. On that day I will strike every horse with panic and its rider with madness," declares the LORD. "I will keep a watchful eye over the house of Judah, but I will blind all the horses of the nations. Then the leaders of Judah will say in their hearts, 'The people of Jerusalem are strong, because the LORD Almighty is their God.'
>
> "On that day I will make the leaders of Judah like a firepot in a woodpile, like a flaming torch among sheaves. They will consume right and left all the surrounding peoples, but Jerusalem will remain intact in her place.
>
> "The LORD will save the dwellings of Judah first, so that the honor of the house of David and of Jerusalem's inhabitants may not be greater than that of Judah. On that day the LORD will shield those who live in Jerusalem, so that the feeblest among them will be like David, and the house of David will be like God, like the Angel of the LORD going before them. On that day I will set out to destroy all the nations that attack Jerusalem."

For more details of the fighting examine the following Scripture, where more graphic details are given.

> The seventh angel poured out his bowl into the air, and out of the temple came a loud voice from the throne, saying, "It is done!" Then there came flashes of lightning, rumblings, peals of thunder and a severe earthquake. No earthquake like it has ever occurred since man has been on earth, so tremendous was the quake. The great city split into three parts, and the cities of the nations collapsed. God remembered Babylon the Great and gave her the cup filled with the wine of

the fury of his wrath. Every island fled away and the mountains could not be found. From the sky huge hailstones of about a hundred pounds each fell upon men. And they cursed God on account of the plague of hail, because the plague was so terrible. (Rev. 16:17–21)

THE RETURN OF CHRIST

This is the most dramatic moment in world history! After winning four successive battles, Christ will set His feet on the Mount of Olives.

A day of the LORD is coming when your plunder will be divided among you.

I will gather all the nations to Jerusalem to fight against it; the city will be captured, the houses ransacked, and the women raped. Half of the city will go into exile, but the rest of the people will not be taken from the city.

Then the LORD will go out and fight against those nations, as he fights in the day of battle. On that day his feet will stand on the Mount of Olives, east of Jerusalem, and the Mount of Olives will be split in two from east to west, forming a great valley, with half of the mountain moving north and half moving south. (Zech. 14:1–4)

When Christ consumes all before Him through the earthquakes, lightnings, and the sword that proceeds out of His mouth, not only will the Holy Land be destroyed but the entire country will be literally bathed in the blood of unregenerate, God-hating, Christ-opposing people. It is hard for us to envision the hordes of troops from all over the world that will oppose Christ. Who can conceive of a time when the blood of slain men will flow as high as the horses' bridles by the space of a thousand and six hundred furlongs? That is just about the length of the entire land of Palestine! Naturally many skeptics and those who do not take the book of Revelation literally find it difficult to believe that so much blood could be shed.

A point to be kept in mind is that part of the destruction of the troops around Jerusalem will include a hailstorm. "From the sky huge hailstones of about a hundred pounds each fell upon men. And they cursed God on account of the plague of hail, because the plague was so terrible" (Rev. 16:21). Millions of pieces of ice will fall to the earth weighing a hundred plus pounds each, melting in the torrid heat of Palestine, and mingling with the blood of those slain until the land of Palestine will be literally bathed in a bloody liquid that is almost too horrible to describe. What a price human beings will pay for rejecting Christ!

HUMANKIND FEEDS BIRDS

And I saw an angel standing in the sun, who cried in a loud voice to all the birds flying in midair, "Come, gather together for the great supper of God, so that you may eat the flesh of kings, generals, and mighty men, of horses and their riders, and the flesh of all people, free and slave, small and great."

Then I saw the beast and the kings of the earth and their armies gathered together to make war against the rider on the horse and his army. (Rev. 19:17–19)

How like the futility of humankind in their pent-up wrath and antagonism against God! In one moment human beings stand in their physical might filled with hate and bitterness, attacking the very headquarters of the Christ. The next moment their flesh is food for the ravenous birds of the heavens. What a picture of the futility of humankind in pitting their will against Jesus Christ. Oh, that people might see that human wisdom is foolishness with God, who will triumph through the one He has ordained, the Lord Jesus Christ.

No one escapes the wrath of the Lord Jesus as described in Revelation 19:21: "The rest of them were killed with the sword that came out of the mouth of the rider on the horse, and all the birds gorged themselves on their flesh."

Not one person will escape the warrior Christ in this last great battle. Those who resist Him during the Tribulation will be slain by Him in His Glorious Appearing. They will then have lost whatever chance they had for eternity.

THIRTY-THREE

Satan Bound in the Abyss

Revelation 20:1–3; 19:20

The evils in this old world are caused by the devil. No living creature in the known history of the universe has brought more misery to both natural and supernatural beings. One-third of the angels in heaven and a majority of the adult population of the earth have followed him in his rebellion against God. This will earn for them eternal separation from God in what our Lord described as "the eternal fire prepared for the devil and his angels" (Matt. 25:41). The book of Revelation is not only a book of prophecy, unfolding the future, but a book of ending. The present chapter describes the doom of Antichrist, the False Prophet, and Satan.

Have you ever wondered whether or not the devil is really an individual or just a figment of the imagination? In educational circles today it is considered unrealistic to assert that there is a supernatural power conveying evil to this earth. Many would admit that the only devil is the devil within you; others would say with Goethe, when he spoke through the mouth of Mephistopheles, "I am the spirit of negation."

The popular idea of the devil, or Satan, is the caricature showing him in a red suit, long tail, horns on his head, and a pitchfork in his hand. Others present him in a similar fashion in hell, shoveling the stokers for all the workers of iniquity when they suffer the torments of the damned. These humorous presentations of Satan are, no doubt, at his instigation in an effort to minimize his importance, thus giving people a false security concerning his danger.

Like other subjects of great interest to the human mind, particularly those that delve into the spiritual realm, Satan can be understood only through the authoritative Word of God. It is obvious from the Scriptures that Satan is not just a figment of the imagination, but a living personality. Thirty-five times he is called "the devil"; fifty-two times he is called "Satan" (which means "enemy" or "adversary").

Matthew 13:19 tells us that after a person has heard the Word of God, "the evil one comes and snatches away what was sown in his heart." In the same chapter the Lord Jesus tells of a farmer who sowed the good seed of the gospel, only to have an enemy come at night and sow false seeds. The Lord Jesus said, "The enemy who sows them is the devil. The harvest is the end of the age, and the harvesters are angels" (13:39). (It is interesting to note that these two statements are not taken from the para-ble, but from Jesus' own interpretation of the parable.)

Peter believed in a personal devil, for in Acts 5:3 he asked Ananias, "How is it that Satan has so filled your heart that you have lied to the Holy Spirit?" Peter also wrote later: "Be self-controlled and alert. Your enemy the devil prowls around like a roaring lion looking for someone to devour" (1 Pet. 5:8). Obviously Peter not only believed that the devil was a living being, but that he was an adversary on the march.

John believed in a personal devil, for in John 13:2 he wrote, "The evening meal was being served, and the devil had already prompted Judas Iscariot, son of Simon, to betray Jesus." The Apostle Paul also taught the personal existence of the devil when cautioning Christians to "put on the full armor of God so that you can take your stand against the devil's schemes" (Eph. 6:11).

It is obvious from these and many other passages in the Bible that Satan is a living personality. If you disagree, you must step over Jesus Christ, the Creator of all things (John 1:3), as well as Peter, John, and Paul, who were used of God to write twenty of the twenty-seven books in the New Testament. The big question is: Where did he come from?

THE ORIGIN OF SATAN

Since Satan is a living being, he must have been created. God created all things, but how could a holy God create a wicked creature like Satan? That is one of the philosophical questions of the ages. If we turn to the philosophers, we will die in confusion, for like their conclusions on other subjects, the only thing in which they are consistent is their disagreement. We are thus obliged to turn to the source of wisdom, the Word of God.

Ezekiel 28:1–19 furnishes a picture of the background of Satan. The first ten verses comprise an oracle directed against the king of Tyre. The next oracle, however, beginning in verse 12b, obviously goes beyond the king of Tyre to a supernatural being, for it attributes to him things that are beyond the capability of a mortal human being. Note, for example, verse 13: "You were in Eden, the garden of God." The subsequent state-ments in this verse obviously refer to and describe an Eden that was for-eign even to Adam and Eve. It describes not a vegetable garden, with which they would have been familiar, but a rock garden.

It is not uncommon for world rulers to be indwelt by Satan himself. History records scores of rulers who sought to make up a government contrary to the will of God. This is the embodiment of the devil's plan, pitting his will against God's will. Ezekiel 28:3 indicates that the king of Tyre was indwelt by a supernatural power, for it tells us: "Are you wiser than Daniel? Is no secret hidden from you?" It is a known fact that Daniel was one of the wisest living men in the Babylonian Empire, for to him was given the gift of determining hidden secrets. He was able to recall Nebuchadnezzar's dream and interpret it when none of the magicians, astrologers, or wise men of the Babylonian court could do so.

In addition to this, as a righteous man Daniel had the power of God in his life, giving him wisdom; yet the king of Tyre also had this power, and in great abundance. The reason? This king was indwelt by Satan himself, which clarifies why that kingdom was so blessed economically, for by craftiness in knowing the future, the king could guide the country in its economic plans. Thus, we see that this oracle is divided between that which speaks against the king of Tyre himself and that which censures the power or person within the king of Tyre, the devil. It is to the latter part of the oracle that we direct our attention.

Ezekiel 28 twice speaks of Satan's creation: "on the day you were created" (v. 13b), and "you were blameless in your ways from the day you were created" (v. 15). The Hebrew word translated "create" means "to bring into existence that which has had no prior form or substance." God alone has the power to create. Thus there must have been a time when Satan was not, before God brought him into being. Satan is usually considered the greatest created being. Even the archangel Michael was reluctant to bring against him any railing accusations (Jude 9).

Satan was "anointed as a guardian cherub" (Ezekiel 28:14). This implies leadership of the angelic host in the presence of the Shekinah Glory of God. It seems that Satan was not just an angel, but the leader of the cherubim, for he was "anointed as a guardian cherub." As the cherubim stand in the presence of God today, so Satan once stood in charge of them.

The abode of Satan in that day was Eden, "the holy mount of God" (Ezek. 28:13–14), where this chief of the cherubim "walked among the fiery stones." This mount of God is, no doubt, the heaven that Jesus referred to, the headquarters of God. Although God is omnipresent (i.e., everywhere at one time), He nevertheless maintains a headquarters where Jesus Christ exists today, seated at His right hand. Satan, then, was created perfect—a "model of perfection" and "blameless" (vv. 12b, 15a). Not until later was iniquity found in him; verse 16 adds, "and you sinned." Like all God's creatures to whom is given the treasure of a free will, Satan sinned because he chose to do so.

THE FALL OF SATAN

Ezekiel 28:16–17 teaches that Satan sinned and was judged for that sin, for God said, ". . . you sinned. So I drove you in disgrace from the mount of God, and I expelled you, O guardian cherub, from among the fiery stones." Verse 17 indicates that it was pride, pride of his beauty and wisdom, that caused him to sin.

A more detailed description of this sin can be found in Isaiah 14. Here we find another oracle delivered against an earthly king—on this occasion, the king of Babylon. After dealing with the king living at that time, Isaiah goes on to describe a person and experiences that transcend any mortal human being, again referring to Satan within the king. In verse 12 we find that Satan at one time was called, "O morning star, son of the dawn!" (Isa. 14:12). Then we note his pride, for he said in his heart:

> "I will ascend to heaven;
> I will raise my throne
>   above the stars of God;
> I will sit enthroned on the mount of assembly,
>   on the utmost heights of the sacred mountain.
> I will ascend above the tops of the clouds;
>   I will make myself like the Most High." (Isa. 14:13–14)

This attitude on the part of Satan constituted his sin.

THE PROBLEM OF EVIL

We now return to the problem of the origin of evil. Since God is holy and cannot create evil, who did? To ascribe the power of creation to Satan would tend to make him a god. There is no indication in Scripture that Satan can create anything (i.e., make something from nothing). But like other of God's creatures equipped with a free will, Satan can manufacture items from the things God has created. Satan evidently took the forces of God that were created perfect, combined them in an imperfect manner, and "manufactured evil." The force of evil in the world today, directed by the person of Satan and his cohorts, is a misapplication of the perfect forces and creation of God.

This can be illustrated in the chemical world, composed of over one hundred elements which, when improperly combined, can become disastrous. For example, common table salt is made up in part of sodium, one of the necessities of life; but by changing the mixture and introducing other elements, sodium can become the basis for a deadly poison. In this sense Satan did not create evil any more than the chemist creates poison. He merely manufactures poison out of those things God has already created.

Evil is a matter of the will. The basic sin in the force of evil is selfishness or pride, both stemming from the same root. Satan said, "*I* will ascend"; "*I* will make myself like the Most High" (Isa. 14:14). *I* will, *I* will. His will, in opposition to the will of God, constituted the great sin, and it is so still! Those who pit their will against God's will commit evil and bring on themselves the judgment of God. It is contrary to the will of God not only for human beings to sin, but for them to reject Jesus Christ. The Word of God tells us that "in the same way your Father in heaven is not willing that any of these little ones should be lost" (Matt. 18:14). Likewise, "the Lord is . . . not wanting anyone to perish, but everyone to come to repentance" (2 Pet. 3:9). Are you like Satan, in rebellion against God's will, or have you submitted to God's will? He sinned willingly against the light he possessed. Have you?

THE CONFLICT OF THE AGES

"Misery likes company" is a popular expression aptly describing Satan's activities against God's special creature, the human being. God created Adam and Eve perfect (in His likeness), with a free will and for His pleasure (Rev. 4:11). He placed them in an ideal garden, filled with trees containing delicious fruit and two special trees. One was called the "tree of life," the other the "tree of the knowledge of good and evil" (Gen. 2:9). God invited them to eat of every tree in the garden but forbade them to eat of the "tree of knowledge of good and evil."

Actually, this was a test whether human beings would be obedient to God. Had they eaten of the "tree of life," the test would have been over. Instead, Eve and, through her, Adam were tempted by Satan (Gen. 3:1–7) and disobeyed God, introducing sin into the human race. But God immediately promised a remedy for sin, a Redeemer through the Seed of the woman (Gen. 3:15). From that time on Satan has tried to destroy that Seed of the woman in an attempt to defy God and hinder Him in fulfilling His will. Satan has also tried to incite people to do his will by urging them to do their own will, regardless of what God has said.

Many illustrations can be given of this conflict down through the ages. He had Cain murder Abel, thus eliminating the first two sons of Eve. He so polluted the human race through sin that by the time of Noah, some sixteen hundred years or so after Adam and Eve, only eight people were truly seeking God. After the Flood we see evidence of this conflict in Pharaoh's attempt to exterminate the Israelites and Haman's anti-Semitic attempt to exterminate all Jews during the Medo-Persian Empire.

Many times before and during the life of Christ, the true Seed of the woman, Satan tried to destroy Him: Caesar Augustus's decree of taxation that carried a pregnant woman, great with child, ninety miles away for a census to be taken; Herod's edict to kill all babies two years of age and under; his three temptations of Christ, seeking to make Him stoop to his fallen level; the storm on the Sea of Galilee, when Jesus lay sleeping in the ship; and many others. Failing to stop Christ's perfect sacrifice for the redemption of the world, he has done everything he can to thwart the Church of Jesus Christ. Although he has managed to keep her from fulfilling her perfect role, he has not destroyed the Church because our Lord has kept His promise, "I will build my church, and the gates of Hades will not overcome it" (Matt. 16:18).

Church history reveals that after three centuries of incessant attempts to destroy the Church through persecution and burning all copies of the Word of God, the Church was so powerful that she supplanted paganism as the state religion of Rome in A.D. 312. At this point Satan stumbled on his most effective tool—indulgence or endorsement. During the next thirteen centuries the Church gradually lost her light and spiritual power by adopting some of the satanically inspired practices of paganism contrary to the Word of God. As these practices increased, Bible light decreased, bringing on what is called the Dark Ages. No jailer ever kept his prisoner more confined than did the church of Rome keep the Bible for hundreds of years.

Not until the Reformation were people again exposed to God's Word, but again Satan made an attack. The superstitious concepts of the Roman Catholic Church, which by this time were little more than modernized pagan thought, turned many intellectuals during the Age of Enlightenment against Christianity. History affirms that many skeptics and rationalists were educated in Jesuit colleges. Being thus exposed to a characterization of Christianity through Catholic dogma and never exposed to the living Christ, these men turned to atheism and a resultant humanism that has deified the human race as proud and arrogant. The difference between John Wycliffe, John Calvin, Martin Luther, William Tyndale, and other Christian intellectuals and such men as Voltaire, Rosseau, Weishaupt, Mirabeau, and other atheistic thinkers is the Word of God. Had the latter group been exposed to the living Christ through the pages of the Bible, history may well have been different and the world today a far better place in which to live.

For more than four hundred years Satan's attack on humanity in general and Christianity in particular has taken many forms until today the Church seems surrounded by a host of different attacking armies of evil. The French skepticism of Voltaire and Rousseau that ultimately produced the French Revolution spread through Germany and became German Rationalism. Other evil forces and concepts stemming from it were evolution, psychiatry, illuminism, Nietzscheism, socialism, communism, liberalism, and Nazism.

Modern college professors ridicule those who believe in the "conspiratorial view of history," which is to deny both the events of history and the power of Satan to accomplish his devious attempts. Who can truthfully deny that he is subverting society by destroying Christianity in order to set up his blasphemous religion headed by the Antichrist, whom men will worship instead of God? Who can question that he is trying to destroy all national governments in favor of a one-world government, which he will head through the beast or Antichrist?

ANTICHRIST AND THE FALSE PROPHET DOOMED

But the beast was captured, and with him the false prophet who had performed the miraculous signs on his behalf. With these signs he had deluded those who had received the mark of the beast and worshiped his image. The two of them were thrown alive into the fiery lake of burning sulfur. (Rev. 19:20)

According to this verse Satan's two henchmen, Antichrist and his False Prophet, will be thrown bodily into the lake of fire. This should not seem strange, for if the two witnesses can be taken up into heaven, our Lord can certainly throw two wicked tools of Satan into that fiery lake.

SATAN BOUND A THOUSAND YEARS

And I saw an angel coming down out of heaven, having the key to the Abyss and holding in his hand a great chain. He seized the dragon, that ancient serpent, who is the devil, or Satan, and bound him for a thousand years. He threw him into the Abyss, and locked and sealed it over him, to keep him from deceiving the nations anymore until the thousand years were ended. After that, he must be set free for a short time. (Rev. 20:1–3)

Revelation 20 introduces the marvelous reign of Christ on the earth. This period of time is the utopia the human race has yearned for and never found. That coming kingdom age is to be an age of righteousness. History proves that the only means to secure a righteous era is for Satan to be bound; as long as he is loose, we will have trouble.

Naturally there are those who ridicule the idea of a literal angel and chain and the literal binding of Satan. As one seminary professor said, "How big a chain would it take to bind Satan and how heavy should it be? We can't take this passage literally or we introduce many problems we cannot solve." Really? What does it matter how big or heavy the chain? Is anything too hard for God? Dr. Walvoord, another seminary professor and president, has noted, "The four instances in Scripture of the word for 'chain' in Revelation 20:1 give no reason for interpreting the word in other than its ordinary sense. Whatever the physical character of the chain, the obvious teaching of the passage is that the action is so designed as to render Satan inactive."[42]

The binding of Satan will restrict him from doing the thing he does best, for Revelation 20:3 says that God's goal in this binding is to "keep him from deceiving the nations anymore until the thousand years were ended." During the Millennium Satan will not deceive human beings about themselves, God, Christ, or eternity. For this reason we conclude that the majority of people living then will be believers. But Satan will be released at the end of the period for one last bit of deception, after which he, too, will be cast into the lake of fire.

SATAN'S FINAL DOOM

"And the devil, who deceived them, was thrown into the lake of burning sulfur, where the beast and the false prophet had been thrown. They will be tormented day and night for ever and ever" (Rev. 20:10). The meaning of this verse is too clear to be questioned. God, by His supernatural hand, will take Satan and cast him forever into the lake of fire. This lake is synonymous with Gehenna, which Jesus referred to as the eternal abode of the lost. A detailed description of Satan's being cast into hell is found in Isaiah 14:9–17. Satan will be ridiculed by the kings of the earth, and he will himself be cast into the lake of fire later. He who was so great and had deceived them now shares their state.

Many have jokingly presented Satan as ruling over hell. This, of course, is not true. No king of hell is "tormented day and night for ever and ever." We should understand that hell is eternal—forever and ever. Those who refuse to believe in the existence of hell must remember that Jesus Christ believed this concept, for He said, "Then he will say to those on his left, 'Depart from me, you who are cursed, into the eternal fire prepared for the devil and his angels'" (Matt. 25:41). Unquestionably the Son of God believed and preached that there was a hell to shun.

Someone will say, "Well, hell for the devil and his angels, yes, but not humankind." Ah, that is the tragedy! Humankind will suffer in hell all the torments prepared for supernatural creatures, for I call again your attention to Revelation 20:10, where, at the end of the millennial kingdom, the beast and the False Prophet are still in torment. They have not been burned up, but are still there, obviously alluding to the fact that one does not cease to exist in hell. Also, 20:11–15 makes it clear that all human beings whose names are not written in the Book of Life will be cast into this lake of fire.

The devil, as a master of deceit, does everything he can to keep people from believing in the existence of a hell; but hell is a literal state of existence that will be the plight of all those who reject the Lord Jesus Christ. Don't aid Satan in making the mistake that will damn your soul for eternity. Receive the Lord Jesus Christ while there is still time. Call on Him while He is near. The good news of the gospel of Jesus Christ offers a remedy for sin, an escape from hell. The Lord Jesus is the Savior from sin: "I tell you the truth, whoever hears my word and believes him who sent me has eternal life and will not be condemned; he has crossed over from death to life" (John 5:24).

THIRTY-FOUR

The First Resurrection

Revelation 20:4–6

> I saw thrones on which were seated those who had been given authority to judge. And I saw the souls of those who had been beheaded because of their testimony for Jesus and because of the word of God. They had not worshiped the beast or his image and had not received his mark on their foreheads or their hands. They came to life and reigned with Christ a thousand years. (The rest of the dead did not come to life until the thousand years were ended.) This is the first resurrection. Blessed and holy are those who have part in the first resurrection. The second death has no power over them, but they will be priests of God and of Christ and will reign with him for a thousand years. (Rev. 20:4–6)

One of the most treasured subjects in the whole Bible is its indisputable presentation of life after death. Practically all human beings dream of walking from death into an eternal state of bliss, but only the Bible gives authoritative details about it. In fact, it is mentioned so frequently that if there is no resurrection of the dead, the Bible becomes unreliable. Every promise to believers concerning an afterlife is predicated on a bodily resurrection. The expression "the resurrection from among the dead" is found forty-nine times in Scripture.

Revelation 20:4–6 is the only passage that labels the "believer's resurrection." It is important to understand that just as there are two phases to Christ's second coming—(1) the Rapture of the Church and (2) the Glorious Appearing—so there are three phases to the resurrection of believers: (1) the Church, (2) seven years later the Old Testament saints, and finally (3) the Tribulation saints. John merges them all together when he says, "Blessed and holy are those who have part in the first resurrection."

CHURCH AGE SAINTS — PHASE 1

The saints of the church age will be resurrected in the first phase of the first resurrection, as outlined in 1 Thessalonians 4:13–18. This passage described the Rapture of the Church, when all Christians will be resurrected. This resurrection, according to Paul, will concern only "the dead in Christ" and those "who have fallen asleep in [Jesus]"; thus it will be limited to the Church Age. Consisting solely of those who are born-again believers, the Rapture will include no Old Testament saints. "In Christ" is uniformly used in the New Testament as a theological reference to those who have been baptized by the Holy Spirit into the body of Christ and denotes the saints after the day of Pentecost.

OLD TESTAMENT SAINTS — PHASE 2

Dr. Walvoord notes that the Old Testament seems to place the resurrection of Israel after the Tribulation. In Daniel 12, immediately after the description of the Tribulation in the preceding chapter, deliverance is promised Israel at the close of the Tribulation.[43]

> "At that time Michael, the great prince who protects your people, will arise. There will be a time of distress such as has not happened from the beginning of nations until then. But at that time your people—everyone whose name is found written in the book—will be delivered. Multitudes who sleep in the dust of the earth will awake: some to everlasting life, others to shame and everlasting contempt."
>
> (Dan. 12:1–2)

The suggestion that Israel will be resurrected prior to the Tribulation saints results from a comparison of Revelation 19:7–9 with Psalm 50:1–6. At the marriage supper of the Lamb, Israel will be in attendance as friends of the Bridegroom. Since the marriage supper will occur just prior to the Glorious Appearing, we may assume that Israel will be resurrected *before* the Glorious Appearing, while Tribulation saints are raised *during* or *at* His Glorious Appearing.

TRIBULATION SAINTS — PHASE 3

Revelation 6:9–11 presents a picture of the Tribulation saints who have been martyred for the testimony of the Lamb, waiting for the resurrection, "and they were told to wait a little longer, until the number of their fellow servants and brothers . . . was completed." This obviously refers to the end of the Tribulation period, at which time, when Christ comes in His glory to set up His millennial kingdom, the Tribulation saints will be resurrected.

This accords with our text:

> I saw thrones on which were seated those who had been given authority to judge. And I saw the souls of those who had been beheaded because of their testimony for Jesus and because of the word of God. They had not worshiped the beast or his image and had not received his mark on their foreheads or their hands. They came to life and reigned with Christ a thousand years. (Rev. 20:4)

In order to live, the tribulation saints must be resurrected; this evidently will take place while the angel is binding Satan, just prior to or at the beginning of the millennial kingdom. Note the accompanying chart of these three phases.

THE HAPPY AND HOLY ONES

Revelation 20:6 describes the eternal state of those taking part in the first resurrection as "blessed and holy." "Blessed" means "happy"; caused by the blessing of God, such happiness is linked with holiness.

Human beings cannot enjoy uninterrupted blessing today because of sin. All those resurrected in the first or believers' resurrection will be resurrected holy. Thus the blessing of God, His original intent for the human race, will never be withheld, because they will live eternally holy and therefore eternally happy.

Those who partake of this first resurrection will be unusually happy because "the second death has no power over them" (Rev. 20:6). Fear of death is one of the primary causes of present unhappiness. People today can escape mentally from it or try to amuse themselves until they are unaware of it, but if they think at all, it disrupts what happiness they may have in their present state of mind. No Christian should fear death. The book of Revelation clarifies that our Lord and Savior holds the keys of death and Hades (Rev. 1:18), and thus the second death or the lake of fire (20:14–15) has no power over us. No wonder believers are happy. Their participation in the first resurrection has made them impervious to the second death.

THE UNBELIEVING DEAD

Who are these who are called "the rest of the dead"? About this there is no question. They are the unbelievers of all ages. Luke 16:19–31 demonstrates that after death they exist in Hades. We will see in our study of the last part of this chapter that they will be brought out of Hades and judged, then cast alive into the lake of fire, which is the second death. Since these unbelievers are not resurrected to life but to death, a state of separation from God, they are referred to as having part in the "second death." The second resurrection, then, is a resurrection to death.

The chart below sharply contrasts the nature of the two resurrections.

The First Resurrection	The Second Resurrection
Involves witnesses of Jesus (Rev. 20:4)	Involves those deceived by Satan (Rev. 20:8) and unbelievers (21:8)
Will occur before the Millennium (Rev. 20:4)	Will occur after the Millennium (Rev. 20:11)
"They came to life" (Rev. 20:4)	"The dead" (Rev. 20:12)
Judged (Rev. 20:4)	Judged (Rev. 20:13)
Become priests and rulers with God and Christ (Rev. 20:6)	Tormented day and night (Rev. 14:10–11)
God's sons (Rev. 21:7)	There was found no place for them (Rev. 20:11)
Over them the second death has no power (Rev. 20:6)	Cast into the lake of fire, which is the second death (Rev. 20:14–15)
Enjoy life eternal (Matt. 25:46)	Suffer everlasting punishment (Matt. 25:46)
Happy and holy (Rev. 20:6)	Weeping and gnashing of teeth (Matt. 25:30)

WHAT DETERMINES YOUR RESURRECTION?

The answer to this question signifies clearly your relationship to the One who does the resurrecting. I can never consider 1 Thessalonians 4:13–18 without pointing out the condition of verse 14, "We believe that Jesus died and rose again." The condition of being a part of the resurrection of believers rests in personal acceptance of Christ's death for our sins according to the Scriptures and His resurrection on the third day according to the Scriptures. Right here it would be good to ask yourself, "Am I ready for that resurrection? Have I met the condition? Will I be a part of it?" If your answer is negative, may I encourage you to accept Christ now? Call on Him, assured of His promise that "everyone who calls on the name of the Lord will be saved" (Rom. 10:13).

Just as John announced, "Blessed and holy are those who have part in the first resurrection," so it follows that tragic and horrible are those who have part in the second resurrection. For to have part in the second resurrection is to be eternally lost. At any cost, avoid that resurrection by calling on the Lord Jesus today so that you may partake of the first resurrection—that you may be one of Christ's at His coming. When I think of all these momentous events taking place at the end of time, I cannot think of anyone I would rather belong to than Jesus Christ!

THIRTY-FIVE

The Millennium and Church History

Revelation 20:1–6

And I saw an angel coming down out of heaven, having the key to the Abyss and holding in his hand a great chain. He seized the dragon, that ancient serpent, who is the devil, or Satan, and bound him for a thousand years. He threw him into the Abyss, and locked and sealed it over him, to keep him from deceiving the nations anymore until the thousand years were ended. After that, he must be set free for a short time. I saw thrones on which were seated those who had been given authority to judge.

And I saw the souls of those who had been beheaded because of their testimony for Jesus and because of the word of God. They had not worshiped the beast or his image and had not received his mark on their foreheads or their hands. They came to life and reigned with Christ a thousand years. (The rest of the dead did not come to life until the thousand years were ended.) This is the first resurrection. Blessed and holy are those who have part in the first resurrection. The second death has no power over them, but they will be priests of God and of Christ and will reign with him for a thousand years. (Rev. 20:1–6)

Revelation 20 is one of the most controversial chapters in the Bible, not because it contains anything essentially complex, but because it touches on a subject of preconceived bias.

THE KINGDOM OF CHRIST IN RELATION TO HIS COMING

Revelation 20:1–7 refers six times to the kingdom of Christ lasting "one thousand years." This has triggered a major controversy, not because there is any question about the accuracy of the original text, but because it conflicts with concepts held by many theologians down through the years. This is the only place in the Bible that establishes the length of time for the coming Kingdom of Christ. That there is to be a Kingdom Age during which Christ will rule on earth is really unquestioned by sincere Bible students who believe the Bible to be the Word of God, for it is one of the most frequently mentioned subjects in the entire Bible.

This Kingdom period is often labeled "the *Millennium*," a term derived from the Latin words *mille* ("one thousand") and *annum* ("year"). It is unfortunate that the term *Millennium* has replaced the more scriptural term *Kingdom*. This period of time will literally fulfill the prayer our Lord taught His followers to pray, "Your kingdom come" (Matt. 6:10). The point of controversy throughout church history regarding the Kingdom essentially concerns whether Christ will come before the Kingdom is ushered in or whether the world will get better and better and Christ will come to a righteous earth. By spiritualizing Scripture, some have even tried to explain away the Millennium.

Three concepts, known as premillennialism, postmillennialism, and amillennialism, define the area of conflict. Before examining the nature of the Kingdom itself, we must first review the content of these views, note when they were introduced into the church, and examine them in the light of Scripture.

PREMILLENNIALISM — THE OLDEST VIEW

The premillennial view is the view that holds that Christ will return to earth, literally and bodily, before the millennial age begins and that, by His presence, a kingdom will be instituted over which He will reign. In this kingdom all of Israel's covenants will be literally fulfilled. It will continue for a thousand years, after which the kingdom will be given by the Son to the Father when it will merge with His eternal kingdom. The central issue in this position is whether the Scriptures are to be fulfilled literally or symbolically. In fact, this is the essential heart of the entire question.[44]

Generally speaking, one's view of interpreting the Scriptures determines whether or not he or she is a premillennialist. For the most part, all who believe the Bible to be literal are premillennialists. Some Bible scholars, however, separate prophecy from other passages. They interpret the rest of the Bible literally, but whenever they come to prophecy, and particularly the book of Revelation, they tend to spiritualize it. Only in taking the Bible other than literally can a person be anything but a premillennialist.

The early Christians were almost unquestionably premillennialists. The New Testament itself indicates that the apostles expected the Lord to return and set up His Kingdom in their lifetime. In Acts 1:6, just before our Lord ascended into heaven, the disciples asked a question that revealed their understanding: "Lord, are you at this time going to restore the kingdom to Israel?" The Lord did not deny that He would set up a Kingdom, but He told them, "It is not for you to know the times or dates the Father has set by his own authority." So we find the disciples and

THEORIES ABOUT THE KINGDOM AGE

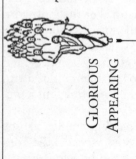

GLORIOUS APPEARING

TRIBULATION

SATAN BOUND
Revelation 20:1–3

ANTICHRIST &
FALSE PROPHET
CAST INTO HELL
Revelation 19:20

MILLENNIAL KINGDOM — 1,000 YEAR REIGN OF CHRIST

PRE-MILLENNIALISM (Chiliasm)

Peter	Ignatius	Tertullian	Brightman	Bible Institutes
John	Polycarp	Cyprian	Feming	Lightfoot
James	Justyn Martyr	Methodious	Alford	Westcott
Paul	Irenaeus	Nepos	Isaac Newton	Scofield Bible
Barnabas	Melito	Bohemian Protestants	Faussett	
		Waldensians	John Darby	
		Wycliffites	Fundamentalists	
		Joseph Bede	Brethren	

A-MILLENNIALISM

Augustine		Luther	Lutherans	World War I
			Presbyterians	Depression
Entire Church of Rome			Methodists	World War II
			Congregationalist	

POST-MILLENNIALISM

Presbyterians	Daniel Whitby
Many State & Reformed Churches	(1638–1726)
Calvin	

those whom they taught anticipating the return of Christ and the establishment of His Kingdom. Many of the detractors of the premillennial position suggest that it is a relatively new theory, having come on the scene during the days of John Darby and others. The truth of the matter is that premillennialism held sway during the first three centuries of the early church and was known as "chiliasm." Dr. Pentecost quotes from Lewis Sperry Chafer's *Systematic Theology:*

> *Chiliasm,* so named from . . . *(chilioi)*—meaning "one thousand"—refers in a general sense to the doctrine of the millennium, or kingdom age that is yet to be, and as stated in the *Encyclopedia Britannica* (14th ed., S.V.) is "the belief that Christ will return to reign for a thousand years. . . ." The distinctive feature of this doctrine is that He will return *before* the thousand years and therefore will characterize those years by His personal presence and by the exercise of His rightful authority, securing and sustaining all the blessings on the earth which are ascribed to that period. The term *chiliasm* has been superseded by the designation *premillennialism;* and . . . more is implied in the term than a mere reference to a thousand years. It is a thousand years which is said to intervene between the first and second of humanity's resurrections. . . . In this thousand years . . . every earthly covenant with Israel will be fulfilled. . . . The entire Old Testament expectation is involved, with its earthly kingdom, the glory of Israel, and the promised Messiah seated on David's throne in Jerusalem.[45]

An additional definition of premillennialism appears in the writings of John Walvoord,

> Premillennialism generally holds to a revival of the Jewish nation and their repossession of their ancient land when Christ returns. Satan will be bound (Revelation 20:2) and a theocratic kingdom of righteousness, peace, and tranquillity will ensue. The righteous are raised from the dead before the millennium and participate in its blessings. The wicked dead are not raised until after the millennium. The eternal state will follow the judgment of the wicked. Premillennialism is obviously a viewpoint quite removed from either amillennialism or postmillennialism. It attempts to find a literal fulfillment for the prophecies in the Old and New Testament concerning a righteous kingdom of God on earth. Premillennialism assumes the authority and accuracy of Scriptures and the hermeneutical principle of a literal interpretation wherever this is possible.[46]

Some in the early church taught that since there were six literal days of creation after which God rested, so there would be six thousand-year periods of time given to humanity upon the earth, after which they would rest for a thousand years of peace. This view was revived somewhat during the nineteenth century but has not been given wide acceptance, probably because modern science teaches that there are millions of years of human history, or perhaps because as we move into the twenty-first century it has become impossible for that age day theory to be proven accurate.

It is possible, of course, that drastic mistakes were made in the ancient calendar of one or two decades. That would allow several years yet before the Rapture and seven or more years yet to be fulfilled before all the prophesied events that must be fulfilled to usher in the Millennium. But that seems most unlikely! There may indeed have been one to four years added somewhere during the past six thousand years, or, as some suggest, one to seven years subtracted, which would indicate we have already been in the twenty-first century for several years. Prophecy scholars do not base their belief that the coming of the Lord is within our generation on the year 2000, but on the many legitimate signs (such as Israel's going back in the land, Daniel 12:4, people running to and fro on the earth, the move toward global government, and others) that are being fulfilled in our lifetime. My next book on prophecy, *Are We Living in the End Times?* deals with this very subject, demonstrating that our generation has more reason to expect the return of Christ than any generation before us. That does not guarantee ours is the concluding generation, but it does indicate that we have more incentive to "watch and be ready" than any other generation in almost two thousand years.

Toward the end of the third century the spiritualizing and allegorizing of Scripture began to take over theological thought, and together with the merging of ecclesiastical and governmental Rome under Constantine, premillennialism fell into disrepute. With the advent of Augustine and other Catholic theologians, theology and philosophy supplanted the study of Scriptures. The Dark Ages are well named, for the Word of God, which is the light of life, was hidden from people by the Church, which has been entrusted with the responsibility of propagating it. As the light of God's Word was extinguished, the hope of the Church, the literal return of Christ to the earth, was eclipsed.

Not until after the Reformation was there a revival of premillennialism. The first generation of reformers, such as John Calvin and Martin Luther, did not pursue the study of the Second Coming particularly but were heavily influenced by the theology of Augustine. Martin Luther had been a priest of the Augustinian order prior to his withdrawal from Rome, and thus his interpretation was affected by his previous training. The second generation of Reformation Bible scholars saw a rise in the literal interpretation of Scripture, which in turn produced a reemphasis on the ancient "chiliasm," now given the more modern title of "premillennialism."

J. Dwight Pentecost refers to some of the great post-Reformation scholars holding the premillennial view. "Among them will be found the greatest exegetes and expositors that the church has known, such as Bengel, Steir, Alford, Lange, Fausset, Keach, Bonar, Ryle, Lillie, MacIntosh, Newton, Tregeles, Ellicott, Lightfoot, Westcott, Darby, to mention only a few."[47] Even the critics of premillennialism suggest that the Brethren Movement arising in England and Ireland during the first part of the nineteenth century was largely responsible for popularizing the dispensational view of the Lord's return. It was sometimes called "Darbyism" because of the popular and practical writings of John Nelson Darby (1880–1882), one of its leaders.

After the turn of the century, Bible institutes sprang up throughout America with a heavy emphasis on a literal interpretation of the Bible. These schools have overwhelmingly advocated the premillennial view— not by premeditation, but because they are biblical literalists. No doubt the most important influence in popularizing the premillennial viewpoint has been the *Scofield Reference Bible*.[48] According to Dr. Walvoord,

> this edition of the Bible, which has had unprecedented circulation, has popularized premillennial teachings and provided ready helps of interpretation. It has probably done more to extend premillennialism in the last half century than any other volume. This accounts for the many attempts to discredit this work.... The reputation of the Scofield Bible is curious because each succeeding writer apparently believes that his predecessors have not succeeded in disposing of this work once and for all. This belief apparently is well-founded, for the Scofield Bible continues to be issued year after year in greater numbers than any of its refuters.[49]

It is probable that the premillennial view, though subject to many attacks, will remain a dominant influence upon the Church until the Lord returns.

AMILLENNIALISM

Amillennialism holds that there will be no literal Millennium on the earth following the second coming of Christ. It tends to spiritualize all the prophecies concerning the Kingdom and attributes to the Church those prophecies relating to Israel.

> Its adherents are divided on whether the millennium is being fulfilled now on the earth (Augustine) or whether it is being fulfilled by the saints in heaven (Kliefoth). It may be summed up in the idea that

there will be no more millennium than there is now, and that the eternal state immediately follows the second coming of Christ.[50]

This view believes that Satan was bound at the first coming of Christ. Those who hold the amillennial point of view concede that it was first suggested by Augustine, who more than any other Church father "molded the doctrines of the church of the Middle Ages."[51] Augustine was preceded by a dangerous philosophy introduced into the Church by Clement of Alexandria and his student, Origen, who trained Dionysius. Together these three established the Alexandrian emphasis on spiritualizing the Scriptures. Because of the Greek emphasis in Platonic philosophy and Plato's allegorical teaching methods learned by these Alexandrian scholars, the third century ended in serious controversy. Although these men did not teach amillennialism, they did condition the brilliant-minded Augustine with the spiritualization of Scripture, and he produced the doctrine. His view of amillennialism became the accepted viewpoint of the Church of Rome, which eventually took over most of the Church and thus propagated his view.

In his book *The City of God,* Augustine presented the present age as a state of continual conflict between the "City of God" and the "City of Satan." This was ultimately to climax in the victory of the Church over the world. He taught, on the basis of Luke 10:18, that Satan had been bound on the earth by Christ, and he considered the Roman government's endorsement of Christianity as a state religion evidence that the Church was winning the conflict in his day. When this Church Age was completed, Christ would return and the eternal order would be established. "In arriving at his conclusion regarding the millennium Augustine used the principle of spiritualizing Scripture freely."[52]

Augustine is widely regarded as a brilliant theologian and thinker by evangelical Christians. That his teachings have left an indelible mark on the Church cannot be doubted, but that it has been a mark for good can very well be questioned. "His view of what the City of God is led him into teachings that have given rise to unspeakable misery, the very greatness of his name accentuating the harmful effects of the error he taught. He, beyond others, formulated the doctrine of salvation by the Church only, by means of her sacraments."[53] This doctrine, plus his amillennialism and his conception of extreme predestination at the choice of God, certainly give us a right to question the true value of Agusutine's contribution to Christianity.

Naturally amillennialism during the age of Rome's dominance of the Christian scene waxed supreme. The early Reformers (such as Calvin, Luther, Melanchthon, etc.) took their cue from Augustine and similarly adopted amillennialism. Amillennialism flourished during the early

Reformation period, particularly in the formalistic churches, until today it is "without question a majority view of professing Christians." Dr. Walvoord points out that the large number of amillennialists at present come from three sources: those who have become disenchanted with postmillennialism, those who came out of the Church of Rome, and those identified with twentieth-century liberalism.[54] It is not correct to say that all amillennialists are liberal, but it is correct that all liberals are amillennialists. One cannot hold the amillennial point of view without unusual spiritualization of Scripture, which is a most dangerous interpretation to follow.

POSTMILLENNIALISM

Postmillennialism, the most recent of the three major views concerning the establishment of the Millennium, is almost extinct at the present time. Postmillennialism basically suggests that the world will get better and better until the whole world is Christianized, at which time Christ will return to a kingdom of peace. This view was originated by Daniel Whitby (1638–1726), a Unitarian controversialist in England. Although he was censored for some of his heretical views, particularly on the subject of the Trinity, "many conservative theologians rapidly embraced and propagated his viewpoint on the millennium."[55]

Although this view was popular before the turn of the century and was given some impetus during the great revival movement of the Wesleys, Finney, Moody, and others, it has been almost eliminated as a result of the two great world wars, the Great Depression, and an overwhelming rise in moral evil. It has made limited resurgence among a group of intellectuals known as Theonomists. One theological professor I heard years ago observed, "The postmillennialist does not have a post to lean on." Many of those who once held the postmillennial view have changed to the amillennial position.

REASONS FOR ACCEPTING THE PREMILLENNIAL VIEW

There are many reasons for accepting the premillennial view of our Lord's return to this earth. Dr. Clarence Larkin, in his masterful book *Dispensational Truth,* offers the following evidence:

1. When Christ comes He will raise the dead, but the Righteous dead are to be raised before the Millennium, that they may reign with Christ during the 1,000 years, hence there can be no Millennium before Christ comes. Revelation 20:5.
2. When Christ comes He will separate the "tares" from the "wheat," but as the Millennium is a period of universal righteousness the separation of the "tares" and "wheat" must take place before the

Millennium, therefore there can be no Millennium before Christ comes. Matthew 13:40–43.

3. When Christ comes Satan shall be bound, but as Satan is to be bound during the Millennium, there can be no Millennium until Christ comes. Revelation 20:1–3.

4. When Christ comes Antichrist is to be destroyed, but as Antichrist is to come before the Millennium there can be no Millennium until Christ comes. 2 Thessalonians 2:8; Revelation 19:20.

5. When Christ comes the Jews are to be restored to their own land, but as they are to be restored to their own land before the Millennium, there can be no Millennium before Christ comes. Ezekiel 36:24–28; Revelation 1:7; Zechariah 12:10.

6. When Christ comes it will be unexpectedly, and we are commanded to watch lest He take us unawares. Now if He is not coming until after the Millennium, and the Millennium is not yet here, why command us to watch for an event that is over 1,000 years off?[56]

These are only some of the reasons why we anticipate the coming of Christ before the Millennium. In addition, it is the clear teaching of the Bible. Revelation 19 pictures Christ coming literally to the earth, slaying Antichrist, and casting him alive into the lake of fire. After Satan is bound, Christ will rule with His saints. A literal interpretation of Scripture will invariably point one to the premillennial return of Christ to the earth.

THIRTY-SIX

The Coming Kingdom of Christ

Revelation 20:1–10

There can be no doubt as to the scriptural evidence for the coming Kingdom of Christ. There are literally hundreds of verses in the Bible that predict an earthly Kingdom of God, ruled by the Son of God and superseding all the kingdoms of the world. Most of the prophets treat this subject at length, often holding it out as a source of encouragement to the children of Israel in their most desperate days. In this chapter we will give an exposition of some of the longer passages. The following chapter will contain a description of the Millennium from some of the shorter passages; then the texts will be briefly compared in order to develop a composite picture of life during the Millennium.

THE KINGDOM ACCORDING TO DANIEL

In Daniel 2:31–35 we find the vision of Nebuchadnezzar recalled by Daniel, the great prophet. He sums up this description of the four world empires with these words:

> While you were watching, a rock was cut out, but not by human hands. It struck the statue on its feet of iron and clay and smashed them. Then the iron, the clay, the bronze, the silver and the gold were broken to pieces at the same time and became like chaff on a threshing floor in the summer. The wind swept them away without leaving a trace. But the rock that struck the statue became a huge mountain and filled the whole earth. (Dan. 2:34–35)

The interpretation of this vision is provided by Daniel in 2:36–45. After describing the parts of the great image as four world kingdoms— the head of gold as Babylon, the breast and arms of silver representing the Medo-Persian Empire, the belly and thighs of bronze representing the Greek Empire, and legs of iron signifying the Roman Empire—Daniel describes the ten toes and the feet of iron and clay as representing the ten kingdoms that will cooperate in establishing the Antichrist in power during the Tribulation period. In verse 44 we find the interpretation of the stone cut without hands, which grinds to powder the rest of the image.

> "In the time of those kings, the God of heaven will set up a kingdom that will never be destroyed, nor will it be left to another people. It

will crush all those kingdoms and bring them to an end, but it will itself endure forever. This is the meaning of the vision of the rock cut out of a mountain, but not by human hands—a rock that broke the iron, the bronze, the clay, the silver and the gold to pieces.

"The great God has shown the king what will take place in the future. The dream is true and the interpretation is trustworthy."

(Dan. 2:44–45)

From this prophecy and its interpretation we see that God Himself will "set up a kingdom that will never be destroyed," will pulverize all the known kingdoms of the world, and will expand His Kingdom until it will "crush all those kingdoms and bring them to an end." This can be none other than the Kingdom of God. This, then, is the Kingdom of God ruled over by Christ, who is symbolized in the Bible as a rock. His Kingdom will be firmly established, filling the whole earth.

We have already seen in Revelation 17–18 that nothing is more detrimental to humanity than religion and government. Humanity tends to look on government as a panacea to solve all of its ills. By contrast, the Bible teaches that a government without a benevolent despot of supernatural origin as its leader cannot be a happy experience, but a source of human misery. The utopian Kingdom predicted in this passage of Scripture will be the Kingdom established on earth when Christ, the only truly benevolent despot who has already demonstrated His love for humankind, will return.

THE COMING KING

Psalm 2, written by David under inspiration of the Holy Spirit, prophesies a day when the world's leaders will become so atheistic and antagonistic to God that they will pit their wills against Him in a gigantic atheistic, anti-Semitic conflict. The reaction of God, however, is laughter; He holds them in derision. This event evidently will take place in the middle of the Tribulation, when human pride is so filled with people's own importance that they think they can actually defy God. In so doing, they will incur the wrath of God, but first they will incur the laughter of God (v. 4). The next verses predict His anger in these words:

Then he rebukes them in his anger
and terrifies them in his wrath, saying,
"I have installed my King
on Zion, my holy hill."   (Ps. 2:5–6)

God will establish His King in His holy place in His due time, regardless of the atheistic antagonism of human beings. A description of that Kingdom follows in verses 7–9:

I will proclaim the decree of the LORD:
He said to me, "You are my Son;
    today I have become your Father.
Ask of me,
    and I will make the nations your inheritance,
    the ends of the earth your possession.
You will rule them with an iron scepter;
    you will dash them to pieces like pottery."   (Ps. 2:7–9)

This passage speaks of an absolute Kingdom stretching to the uttermost parts of the earth. The Lord will rid the world of all those kings who oppose Him. This great psalm concludes with God's challenge to world leaders concerning their present attitude:

Therefore, you kings, be wise;
    be warned, you rulers of the earth.
Serve the LORD with fear
    and rejoice with trembling.
Kiss the Son, lest he be angry
    and you be destroyed in your way,
for his wrath can flare up in a moment.
    Blessed are all who take refuge in him.   (Ps. 2:10–12)

If the world leaders responded that way today, this world would be an entirely different place in which to live.

EZEKIEL'S PROPHECIES OF A WORLD KINGDOM

The prophecies of Ezekiel take on logical progression when in chapters 36–37 we find the restoration of the nation of Israel to the land of Palestine. Chapters 38–39 contain the abortive attempt of Russia to come down against Israel in the latter days just prior to the Tribulation. Then in chapters 40–48 we encounter a description of the millennial Kingdom, particularly the Temple and conditions for worship during that thousand-year period.

Ezekiel goes into great detail regarding the matter of worshiping in the Temple, even pointing out that the sacrificial systems will be reestablished. These sacrifices during the millennial Kingdom will be to the nation of Israel what the Lord's Supper is to the Church today: a reminder of what they have been saved from. No meritorious or efficacious work will be accomplished through these sacrifices. Instead, they will remind Israel repeatedly of their crucified Messiah, just as the Passover Feast reminded the nation of Israel for centuries that God had delivered them by blood from the land of Pharaoh.

THE MILLENNIAL KINGDOM ACCORDING TO
ZECHARIAH THE PROPHET

Zechariah 14 contains an easily interpreted prophecy concerning the coming Kingdom.

> On that day living water will flow out from Jerusalem, half to the eastern sea and half to the western sea, in summer and in winter. . . .
>
> Then the survivors from all the nations that have attacked Jerusalem will go up year after year to worship the King, the LORD Almighty, and to celebrate the Feast of Tabernacles. If any of the peoples of the earth do not go up to Jerusalem to worship the King, the LORD Almighty, they will have no rain. If the Egyptian people do not go up and take part, they will have no rain. The LORD will bring on them the plague he inflicts on the nations that do not go up to celebrate the Feast of Tabernacles. This will be the punishment of Egypt and the punishment of all the nations that do not go up to celebrate the Feast of Tabernacles.
>
> On that day HOLY TO THE LORD will be inscribed on the bells of the horses, and the cooking pots in the LORD's house will be like the sacred bowls in front of the altar. Every pot in Jerusalem and Judah will be holy to the LORD Almighty, and all who come to sacrifice will take some of the pots and cook in them. And on that day there will no longer be a Canaanite in the house of the LORD Almighty.   (Zech. 14:8, 16–21)

These verses make it clear that Jerusalem will serve as headwaters for the religious life of the people, the source of the waterways of the world: "Living water will flow out from Jerusalem" (v. 8). This refers to the "living waters" that Jesus promised the woman at the well in Samaria, indicating that the way of redemption and new life would be supplied from Jerusalem, the headquarters of the King. It also refers to the physical waters provided during that age from Jerusalem to worship the King every year. Not to do so will be to incur the animosity of God "in the form of a plague."

Verse 20 refers to the holiness of the Kingdom. We have already seen that Satan will be bound during this millennial Kingdom (Rev. 20:1–3); when Christ rules, it will be a true Kingdom of holiness. The world has never known an era of holiness when standards were not established through human practices but by the mandate of God. During those days God's standards will be the law. Violators of that law will be severely punished.

THE MILLENNIUM ACCORDING TO THE PROPHET ISAIAH

The prophet Isaiah referred to the coming Kingdom of Christ many times. The last two chapters in Isaiah contain specific information concerning that period.

Behold, I will create
　　new heavens and a new earth.
The former things will not be remembered,
　　nor will they come to mind.
But be glad and rejoice forever
　　in what I will create,
for I will create Jerusalem to be a delight
　　and its people a joy.
I will rejoice over Jerusalem
　　and take delight in my people;
the sound of weeping and of crying
　　will be heard in it no more.
Never again will there be in it
　　an infant who lives but a few days,
　　or an old man who does not live out his years;
he who dies at a hundred
　　will be thought a mere youth;
he who fails to reach a hundred
　　will be considered accursed.
They will build houses and dwell in them;
　　they will plant vineyards and eat their fruit.
No longer will they build houses and others live in them,
　　or plant and others eat.
For as the days of a tree,
　　so will be the days of my people;
my chosen ones will long enjoy
　　the works of their hands.
They will not toil in vain
　　or bear children doomed to misfortune;
for they will be a people blessed by the LORD,
　　they and their descendants with them.
Before they call I will answer;
　　while they are still speaking I will hear.
The wolf and the lamb will feed together,
　　and the lion will eat straw like the ox,
　　but dust will be the serpent's food.
They will neither harm nor destroy
　　on all my holy mountain, says the LORD.　　　(Isa. 65:17–25)

This passage reveals some of the most descriptive details known of the Millennium. Such information is given to show that Jerusalem will be the place of rejoicing; no more weeping will be heard within the city. Jerusalem has known much heartache throughout its many centuries.

One of its walls is famous today as a place of wailing—wailing for the future restoration of the greatness of Israel. This will be fulfilled during the Millennium.

Verse 20 indicates that the life span of a human being will be increased as in the days before the Flood. Believers will evidently live until the end of the Millennium, some almost a thousand years. However, unsaved people will be given a hundred years in which to receive Christ. If they reject Him, they will die on their hundredth birthday.

Economic stability will be the standard during that period. For instance, people will not build houses and let others occupy them because of death or sickness. It will be a stable time when people can enjoy the fruits of their efforts. "They will not toil in vain or bear children doomed to misfortune" (Isa. 65:23).

The text also indicates that God will answer His people speedily during the millennial Kingdom, even while they are in the midst of praying, and sometimes "before they call." God will anticipate the needs of His people, supplying those needs in many cases before they call on Him.

The curse will be lifted from the animals, who will enjoy peace one with another, for "the wolf and the lamb will feed together." The only exception seems to be the serpent, which will continue to crawl on his belly and eat dust.

THE RENOVATION OF THE EARTH BY FIRE

Most prophetic teachers acknowledge that the earth will be renovated by fire, but for some reason they insist on locating this event at the end of the Millennium. Isaiah 65:17, however, preceding the description of the Millennium, indicates that God will "create new heavens and a new earth" *before* the Kingdom is established. That means He will create a new atmospheric heaven around the earth and reestablish the earth on a far better basis. We learn from other passages that the waste areas of the world will be recreated. Today three-quarters of the earth is wasted by water, making much of the earth unusable. At that time vast mountain ranges will be leveled, and the earth will enjoy a complete resurfacing before the Millennium.

The same period of time is referred to in 2 Peter 3:1–16. The apostle predicts that in the last days scoffers will come, "scoffing and following their own evil desires" and suggesting that since no changes have occurred in creation since the beginning, there is no reason to believe the fact of Christ's coming. They reject the change of the Flood and the destruction of Sodom and Gomorrah. The apostle points out to believers that they are not so limited by such biased concepts.

Peter further states that "with the Lord a day is like a thousand years," meaning that God's promises of two thousand years ago are only two days old. Then he predicts that the Day of the Lord will usher in a time of cataclysmic change on the earth. The earth will be dissolved, meaning the surface of the earth in the Day of the Lord. The Day of the Lord, then, will dawn with the destruction of this old earth and the refurbishing of its surface, on which God will establish His Kingdom of righteousness.

The times described by Peter are upon us. Certainly every child of God today should heed His words: "Since everything will be destroyed in this way, what kind of people ought you to be? You ought to live holy and godly lives as you look forward to the day of God" (2 Pet. 3:11–12a).

SATAN'S FINAL CONFLICT

When the thousand years are over, Satan will be released from his prison and will go out to deceive the nations in the four corners of the earth—Gog and Magog—to gather them for battle. In number they are like the sand on the seashore. They marched across the breadth of the earth and surrounded the camp of God's people, the city he loves. But fire came down from heaven and devoured them. And the devil, who deceived them, was thrown into the lake of burning sulfur, where the beast and the false prophet had been thrown. They will be tormented day and night for ever and ever.   (Rev. 20:7–10)

We have already seen that at the beginning of the millennial Kingdom Satan was bound by a great angel in the Abyss (Rev. 20:1–3). That means that people will not be tempted by Satan for a thousand years. Today there are three forces of temptation: the world, the flesh, and the devil. Because the world will be a Kingdom of righteousness administered by the Lord, the righteous Judge, no lewd, suggestive, worldly temptations can mislead them. Neither will they be tempted by Satan, for he will be chained. Therefore the only source of temptation will be the flesh. In such an environment an overwhelming number of people will no doubt be saved.

Isaiah 65:20 casts some interesting light on this future time of great world blessing:

Never again will there be in it
   an infant who lives but a few days,
   or an old man who does not live out his years;
he who dies at a hundred
   will be thought a mere youth;
he who fails to reach a hundred
   will be considered accursed.

This verse suggests that believers will live after birth to the end of the Millennium, since a person will be reckoned a child when he or she is a hundred years old. But it also indicates that if a person reaches a hundred years of age and is not a believer, he or she will be accursed, or die. In other words, those living during the Millennium are given a hundred years to make a decision to receive Jesus Christ as Savior and Lord. If they do so, they will continue living to the end of the Millennium, paralleling the age of the human race before the Flood. If they do not receive Jesus Christ, they will die at a hundred years of age. If we add to this the absence of worldly temptation and the absence of satanic temptation, plus the fact that the whole world will know the gospel of Christ in that day, we can reasonably conclude that this will be the most ideal environment in which to raise children.

Like Adam and Eve and others after them until the Flood, couples in the Millennium can have children not only the first hundred years but for hundreds of years thereafter. Since it will be a time of unprecedented blessing and food supply, a couple will conceivably have as many children as they desire. The conclusion seems justifiable, then, that the overwhelming majority of people on the earth during the last nine hundred years will be Christians.

Of course, some born during that age will reject Christ and die by their hundredth birthday. And even though they die at a hundred years of age, there will be ample time for these unsaved to propagate a generation of unbelievers to follow Satan when he is released at the end of the Kingdom age to "deceive the nations in the four corners of the earth—Gog and Magog—to gather them for battle. In number they are like the sand on the seashore" (Rev. 20:8). Their number "like the sand on the seashore" does not necessarily mean that the overwhelming majority of the world population at that time will follow Satan. Instead, it indicates that a fantastic population explosion will occur during the Millennium and that many born during the last century will follow Satan. Comparatively speaking, this will be a youth movement, since all who follow Satan in his last rebellion will be under a hundred years of age.

THE MASSIVE MILLENNIAL SOUL HARVEST

It is most encouraging to realize that many times more people will be converted during the millennial Kingdom than will be lost. Because the millennial population will undoubtedly exceed the total world population during the whole of biblical history, and since the majority living at that time will be Christian, it follows that there will be more people in heaven than in hell. Consequently, God will achieve His grand purpose for the majority of humankind—their salvation (2 Pet. 3:9).

Another truth revealed in Revelation 20:8 concerns the consistency of the work of Satan in every generation. After being incarcerated for a thousand years, he will immediately proceed to do what he has done for centuries—*deceive the nations.* Satan is the master deceiver of the human race. His conflict-of-the-ages program, as previously outlined, is just a sample of the extent of his consistent deception. He will inspire Antichrist to be a master deceiver during the Tribulation (2 Thess. 2:9–10). This deception always finds itself in opposition to God's will. Whenever a person rebels against God, whether the person be Cain, Lamech, Nimrod, Pharaoh, Judas, Voltaire, Thomas Paine, or Robert Ingersoll, one is deceived by the devil.

In a practical sense Satan tries two basic approaches with people today: He either gets them to turn against Christ because they love unrighteousness, or he gets them to rebel against God by willfulness. It is most practical here to pause and ask yourself, reader, if you have received Jesus Christ as your personal Lord and Savior. If you have not, then you are deceived by the devil. You may dress up your deception with a host of excuses and a long list of reasons, but it is nothing more than Satan's deception. It would be well for you to contemplate the final outcome of Satan's own rebellion lest you share it with him. "And the devil, who deceived them, was thrown into the lake of burning sulfur, where the beast and the false prophet had been thrown. They will be tormented day and night for ever and ever" (Rev. 20:10).

God, in his infinite wisdom, did not cast Satan into the lake of fire at the time He cast in his two chief tools, the beast and the False Prophet. They were cast in at the end of the Tribulation, before the Millennium began (Rev. 19:20). He saved Satan out of that judgment because He wanted to give the last generation who would not live to be a hundred years of age a final choice. This will make unanimous the experience of all people who have ever lived, from the time of Adam and Eve to the very end of human history. All human beings have been tempted of Satan and have had to decide whether to respond to God or Satan. All have sinned, but God through the gift of His Son, Jesus Christ, on Calvary's cross has given everyone a second chance. That second chance, available only on this earth, involves the acceptance of God's gift of salvation in the person of His Son. If you have never made that decision, you are making a contrary decision right now.

It should be pointed out here that although the beast and the False Prophet, or Antichrist and the False Prophet, were cast into the lake of fire a thousand years before the devil, they remained there, for the passage says, "where the beast and the false prophet had been thrown" (Rev. 20:10). Since these are men, suffering the torments of the damned for a thousand years, we may clearly discern the capability for people to suffer that length of time. The plight of Satan for eternity in this same verse is the same plight as that shared by all those who have been deceived by him: "They will be tormented day and night for ever and ever."

There is no reason to symbolize these simple words. The same words used to describe the eternal blessings of those who receive Christ and the eternal nature of God are used to describe the plight of the lost—"for ever and ever." If God is eternal and believers will enjoy Him eternally, why should we arbitrarily suggest that it is not possible for humankind and Satan to be tormented day and night forever and ever?

THIRTY-SEVEN

The Great White Throne

Revelation 20:11–15

Then I saw a great white throne and him who was seated on it. Earth and sky fled from his presence, and there was no place for them. And I saw the dead, great and small, standing before the throne, and books were opened. Another book was opened, which is the book of life. The dead were judged according to what they had done as recorded in the books. The sea gave up the dead that were in it, and death and Hades gave up the dead that were in them, and each person was judged according to what he had done. Then death and Hades were thrown into the lake of fire. The lake of fire is the second death. If anyone's name was not found written in the book of life, he was thrown into the lake of fire. (Rev. 20:11–15)

You have just read the most awesome passage found anywhere in the Bible. It confronts us with the sobering truth of our ultimate encounter with God. The story is told of the great statesman Daniel Webster, toward the twilight of his life, attending a luncheon meeting with some younger government leaders. The chairman of the group turned to Mr. Webster and asked, "What is the greatest thought that has ever passed through your head?" Quick as a flash Daniel Webster replied, "My accountability to God." Nowhere is one's accountability to God more clearly defined than in this passage of Scripture.

One truth must be emphasized at the outset of this study: This ultimate judgment of the Great White Throne is for unbelievers only. Who are these "dead, great and small"? They are *dead* now in trespasses and sins because of their rejection of Jesus Christ, and they will be resurrected in order to appear at this judgment. Revelation 20:5 states that "the rest of the dead did not come to life until the thousand years were ended. This is the first resurrection." It is noteworthy that in 20:12 the dead are referred to as "great and small." This would mean the "great and small" intellectually, physically, financially, positionally, and in every other way. This group will include *all* the dead without Jesus Christ.

Verse 13 adds further information: "The sea gave up the dead that were in it, and death and Hades gave up the dead that were in them, and each person was judged according to what he had done." The sea will give up all those who were drowned or buried at sea, never having accepted Jesus Christ. "Death" represents the grave, "Hades" the place of torment where their spirits have gone. What these two verses teach is that we may expect a physical resurrection uniting the dead, whether their ashes are in the grave, in a mausoleum, on the earth, or in the sea. Those ashes will be resurrected and united with the soul and spirit as they arise from the place of torment, and in this resurrected form they will stand before the Great White Throne.

THE BOOKS OF ONE'S DEEDS OPENED

At this point we find a set of books and a book being opened. Notice the wording in verse 12: ". . . and books were opened. Another book was opened, which is the book of life." For the identity of these "books" we must look beyond our immediate text to another passage in God's Word. Galatians 3:10 contains the description of the second book by which the human race will be judged. Those who have lived under the hearing of the law of God will be judged by it. Unless people accept the mercy of God in the person of His Son, there is no way they can be found righteous, "for all have sinned and fall short of the glory of God" (Rom. 3:23).

Revelation 20:12 indicates that some of the books at this Great White Throne Judgment will be the books of a person's works, for "the dead were judged according to what they had done as recorded in the books." The same thing is said in verse 13b. In some way every person must have a recording angel who in this life is tabulating everything he or she does. In connection with this thought it is well to consider Ecclesiastes 12:14: "For God will bring every deed into judgment, including every hidden thing, whether it is good or evil." In this final hour the books of one's works or deeds will be open.

If people today are able by means of photography to capture the action of people's lives and by the means of plastic recordings to record their voice, certainly Almighty God can play His divine film and recording at the judgment. Not only will the actions and words of a person be recalled at this judgment, but "every hidden thing." This indicates that God has a special X-ray camera that takes photographs of the thoughts and intents of the heart, which will be revealed in that day.

D. L. Moody, the famous evangelist, used to say that if someone ever invented a camera that could take a picture of the human heart, that person would starve to death, for people would refuse to have this revealing picture exposed. In that awesome day, however, all the secret thoughts and intents of the heart will be revealed by the projection of God's special X-ray, taken from the books of the deeds of the human race.

THE BOOK OF LIFE OPENED

Verse 12 indicates not only that the dead will be judged out of the books according to their works, but that another book is opened, which is the Book of Life. Here we discover that a recording angel maintains a book called the Book of Life. The New Testament refers to this Book of Life eight times; and although the Old Testament does not call it the Book of Life, three times it mentions a book in which names are written.

To properly understand the Book of Life, you must realize that there are really two Books of Life. One is called "the book of life"; the other, "the Lamb's book of life." These are definitely not the same! "The book of life" contains the names of the living; "the Lamb's book of life" is a book belonging to the Lord Jesus Christ, the "Lamb of God, who takes away the sin of the world!" (John 1:29). Jesus Christ came into the world to save sinners and, as He repeatedly said, "to give them eternal life." Clearly, then, the Lamb's Book of Life is the book of Jesus Christ in which are entered the names of those who have received His eternal life (Rev. 13:8). I am personally inclined to believe that in this book will appear only the names of the believers who have lived since the cross.

Revelation 13:8 indicates that during the Tribulation period the people who will worship the Antichrist are "all those whose names have *not* been written in the book of life belonging to the Lamb that was slain from the creation of the world." Revelation 21:27 tells us that the only people who will enter into the Holy City are "those whose names are written in the Lamb's book of life." It is therefore essential that one have his or her name written in this book.

There are two major differences between these two Books of Life. (1) The Book of Life seems to contain the names of all living people, whereas the Lamb's Book of Life includes only the names of those who call on the Lamb for salvation. (2) Without doubt more important, it is possible to have one's name blotted out of the Book of Life, but not out of the Lamb's Book of Life. In Revelation 3:5 we find that "he who overcomes will, like them, be dressed in white. I will never blot out his name from the book of life." An overcomer here is one clothed in the white garments of Christ, for he or she is a believer to whom is imputed the righteousness of Christ. Therefore that person's name will not be blotted out of the Book of Life. In Exodus 32:33 we read: "The LORD replied to Moses, 'Whoever has sinned against me I will blot out of my book.'" It is therefore possible to have one's name blotted out of the Book of Life because of sin. But it is impossible to have one's name removed from the Lamb's Book of Life.

> And if anyone takes words away from this book of prophecy, God will take away from him his share in the tree of life and in the holy city, which are described in this book. (Rev. 22:19)

Some try to tell us that this reference to God's taking away a person's "share" out of the Book of Life suggests that anyone who detracts from the book of Revelation and its prophecy will lose his or her rewards; but this cannot be, for the only "share" we have in the Book of Life is our name. We have no indication in Scripture that anything but our name is written in the Book of Life, for our deeds are not recorded there, but in the books of our works.

We see, then, that the Bible offers three reasons for having one's name blotted out of the Book of Life: (1) for sinning against God, (2) for not being clothed in the righteousness of Christ through the new birth, and (3) for taking away from the words of the book of this prophecy.

Revelation 20:15 establishes the importance of the Book of Life, for it tells us, "If anyone's name was not found written in the book of life, he was thrown into the lake of fire." In a sense this is God's double check at the Great White Throne Judgment, for as a person comes forward, he or she will be judged by the book of law, by the Lamb's Book of Life, and by the deeds done in the flesh taken from the books of human works. Then, just before that person is cast into the lake of fire, he or she is given a double check. The recording angel will look through the Book of Life, and "if anyone's name was not found written in the book of life, he was thrown into the lake of fire."

This double check in the Book of Life points out a consistent scriptural principle—that there are only two kinds of people. The Bible repeatedly refers to the believing or unbelieving, the saved or unsaved, the condemned or not condemned, the righteous or unrighteous, the just or unjust, the wise or unwise. This principle is maintained here: There are those whose names are written and others whose names are not written in the Book of Life. In that hour there will be no hesitation, no indecision, for either a person's name is written or it is not written in the Book of Life. It must be one way or the other.

One does not need to have one's name entered in the Book of Life, for if he or she is alive it is already there; God is "not wanting anyone to perish, but everyone to come to repentance" (2 Pet. 3:9). But to keep it there, one must also have his or her name written in the Lamb's Book of Life.

Jesus Christ said, "I am the bread of life. He who comes to me will never go hungry, and he who believes in me will never be thirsty" (John 6:35). The Lord Jesus repeatedly invited people to come to Him, for He alone is "the way and the truth and the life" (14:6). John 5:24 tells us, "I tell you the truth, whoever hears my word and believes him who sent me has eternal life and will not be condemned; he has crossed over from death to life." The steps of salvation here are clear: (1) "whoever hears my word" and (2) "believes him who sent me." That means trusting in Jesus. Trust that Christ is the way of salvation, the One who has come to seek and to save that which was lost, including you. The one who trusts has everlasting life. Those whose names are written in the Lamb's Book of Life are those who have received this everlasting life. *Have you?*

Revelation 20:11–15 includes two books of vital importance. Your name is already written in the Book of Life, but is it written in the Lamb's Book of Life? That depends entirely on what you have done with the Lord Jesus Christ. If you have accepted Him, it is; if you have not accepted Him, it is missing. The answer to that question determines your eternal destiny.

THIRTY-EIGHT

The New Heaven and New Earth

Revelation 21

Revelation 21 introduces the eternal future planned by God, the ultimate purpose of God for the human race. Not much space in Scripture is given to this eternal state, but enough is revealed to assure every believer's heart about the future. Revelation 21–22 provide more details of this state that can be found anywhere else in the Bible.

SEVEN NEW THINGS

There are seven new things revealed in these two chapters that form a fitting introduction to the eternal future God has prepared for those who love Him.

- a new heaven (21:1)
- a new earth (21:1)
- new Jerusalem (21:2)
- new things (21:5)
- a new paradise (22:1–5)
- a new place for God's throne (22:3)
- a new source of light (22:5)

THE DESTRUCTION OF THIS EARTH

Three destructions of the earth are described in the Bible, one past and two yet to come. The first destruction came when the Flood covered the earth in the days of Noah, sparing only eight righteous persons (Gen. 6–8). In one of the best-known promises in the Old Testament, however, signified by the rainbow, God promised Noah that He would never again destroy the earth by a flood.

Nevertheless, two passages in the Bible predict that God will yet destroy the earth. One destruction will come by fire, after which He will restore all things. Isaiah 65:17–20 speaks of a restored earth, and 2 Peter 3:4–14 describes the judgment of fire reserved or kept in store "for the day of judgment." The other destruction is described in our text (Rev. 21:1).

Many Bible scholars identify Isaiah 65:17–20 and 2 Peter 3:4–14 with Revelation 21:1. This presents some serious problems. A thorough examination of the two passages suggests that since death appears in the

Isaiah 65 passage, Isaiah was obviously not talking about the eternal order, but the millennial Kingdom. And since 2 Peter 3:10 refers to the Day of the Lord, I am inclined to believe that he meant the second catastrophic event that will come upon the earth, producing a refurbished earth to begin the Millennium. We have already examined Revelation 20:7–10 concerning the final insurrection of Satan, when again the heaven and the earth will be polluted by the rebellion of Satan. Therefore the words of our Lord, "Heaven and earth will pass away, but my words will never pass away" (Matt. 24:35), evidently will be fulfilled when the prophecy of Revelation 21:1 is completed: "Then I saw a new heaven and a new earth, for the first heaven and the first earth had passed away, and there was no longer any sea."

THE DESTRUCTION OF HEAVEN

Why will God destroy the heaven? Very simply, because the atmospheric heavens are filled with evil. Whenever we read about heaven in the Bible, we should keep in mind that there are three heavens: the atmospheric heaven around the earth, the stellar heaven, which contains the great galaxies that we view on a starry night, and the third heaven, or the throne of God (see 2 Cor. 12:2; Rev. 4–5). Our text in no way indicates that God will destroy the stellar heaven or the place of His headquarters, but He will destroy the atmospheric heaven, where Satan lives. Ephesians 6:12 indicates that Satan, who is the god "of this dark world," and his emissaries are performing spiritual wickedness in heavenly realms. Therefore, after the final rebellion of Satan, God will destroy this earth that is so marred and cursed by Satan's evil. He will include the atmospheric heaven to guarantee that all semblance of evil has been cleared away.

THE NEW HEAVEN AND THE NEW EARTH

Because it is God's plan for humankind to inhabit the earth forever in fulfillment of His promises, after He does away with this planet as we know it, He will create a new heaven and a new earth, better than anything this world has ever known, including the Garden of Eden. Many changes will be made, as seen in verse 1: "And there was no longer any sea." Two-thirds of the present earth's surface is covered with water; the remaining one-third includes a large area rendered worthless because of mountains and deserts. Thus only a small percentage of the earth's surface is today inhabitable.

Nothing in the text indicates a new earth limited to the twenty-five thousand miles in circumference and eight thousand miles in diameter of the present earth. It may be much larger; the Bible does not say. But one thing is certain—the new earth will be the Christian's heaven. When Christians talk about going to heaven, they mean in the soul state, provided they die before the Rapture. After the resurrection of the body, believers will come to earth to reign with Christ during the Millennium. After that thousand years we will live forever on the new earth described in our text. Although it will have a river and an abundance of water, it will not have land surface wasted by seas.

"I saw the Holy City, the new Jerusalem, coming down out of heaven from God, prepared as a bride beautifully dressed for her husband" (Rev. 21:2). The Holy City, which our Lord went to prepare for His saints (John 14:1–3), will come down from heaven to this earth. This New Jerusalem, fully described in Revelation 21, will be the city of righteousness, prepared by God for the enjoyment of His people. The expression "prepared as a bride beautifully dressed for her husband" is a symbolic reference to the preparation of a virtuous young woman for the day of her marriage. God has been preparing the city for almost two thousand years. Since Christ instantly called worlds and universes into being, one can scarcely imagine the glories of this city that has been so long in preparation.

"Now the dwelling of God is with men, and he will live with them" (Rev. 21:3). Another outstanding characteristic of this new city is that God's Tabernacle will no longer be in the third heaven, for He will move His headquarters to the new earth and will literally take up His abode in the New Jerusalem. We simply do not have the mental capacity to comprehend the significance of living in an economy where God Himself exists.

"They will be his people, and God himself will be with them and be their God" (Rev. 21:3). The people who inhabit the new eternal earth will be those who voluntarily received Christ by faith—before the Flood, before Abraham, before Christ, during the Church Age, and throughout the Tribulation and Millennium. As indicated in our study of the Millennium, far more people will inhabit heaven than hell. God has a special love for humankind. That love will have all eternity to express itself upon His obedient creatures. To true Christians heaven is not just a place where all things are new, but a place where they can enjoy unbroken fellowship with God.

"He will wipe every tear from their eyes" (Rev. 21:3). The wiping away of all tears means that the normal reaction of present life, sorrow, will be eliminated. As the book of Job tells us, "Yet man is born to trouble as surely as sparks fly upward" (Job 5:7). Trouble produces sorrow, sorrow produces tears. But these tears will be wiped away. The present passage may also indicate that we will lose the power to remember loved ones who rejected Jesus Christ. With the keenness of mind that we will possess in the Resurrection, doubtless the compassionate heart of God's people would burst with sorrow and heaven would be ruined were they to contemplate the lost plight of their loved ones condemned for eternity. God in His marvelous mercy will wipe away all tears from their eyes. That probably means He will erase all remembrance of the unsaved from the minds of believers.

"There will be no more death" (Rev. 21:4). The specter of death, the natural result of sin, will at last be removed.

"... or mourning or crying or pain, for the old order of things has passed away" (Rev. 21:4). Since sin produces death and sickness, a sinless eternity will not admit these miseries.

"He who was seated on the throne said, 'I am making everything new!'" (Rev. 21:5). This is an almost certain indication that God will create for us a dimension that we cannot yet comprehend. He plans an entirely new way of life for his people. For instance, many have wondered about the marital status of Christians during the Millennium (cf. Matt. 22:30), but I think that whatever remorse we experience when thinking of life for eternity without marriage can easily be offset by faith when we accept the fact that all things will be new. As marvelous as a good Christian marriage is today, it will be totally eclipsed by sheer delight and unquenchable joy during the eternal future in whatever experience that newness possesses.

THE LORD REITERATES HIS EARTHLY OFFER

"He said to me: 'It is done. I am the Alpha and the Omega, the Beginning and the End. To him who is thirsty I will give to drink without cost from the spring of the water of life'" (Rev. 21:6). When the Lord Jesus walked this earth, He said to the people of His day, "If anyone is thirsty, let him come to me and drink. Whoever believes in me, as the Scripture has said, streams of living water will flow from within him" (John 7:37–38). To the woman at the well, who was drinking natural water, He said, "But whoever drinks the water I give him will never thirst. Indeed, the water I give him will become in him a spring of water welling up to eternal life" (John 4:14). The Lord "Jesus Christ is the same yesterday and today and forever" (Heb. 13:8). Two thousand years after He made these promises we find Him prophetically reiterating the same thing: "I will give to drink without cost from the spring of the water of life."

HUMANITY'S THIRST FOR GOD

Anyone who has ever traveled will testify that the ancient civilizations and present cultures are extremely religious. Humanity's religious inclination is a testimony of one's thirst for God. Human beings will not thirst in the eternal state, but will be satisfied over and above all that they can ever ask or think. Their thirst will be supplied by Christ Himself. If nothing else, this speaks of the complete satisfaction of the place that lasts forever.

ONLY BELIEVERS WILL INHABIT THE ETERNAL ORDER

"He who overcomes will inherit all this, and I will be his God and he will be my son" (Rev. 21:7). One of the most wonderful concepts in the Bible is the Father-child relationship between God and a Christian. This verse indicates that it will go on forever in heaven as on earth.

THE ETERNAL STATE OF THE LOST

But the cowardly, the unbelieving, the vile, the murderers, the sexually immoral, those who practice magic arts, the idolaters and all liars—their place will be in the fiery lake of burning sulfur. This is the second death.   (Rev. 21:8)

Since God has been talking about the eternal state of the blessed, He contrasts that with the eternal state of the lost, described more fully in 20:11–15. Here He refers to them as those that have part in the second death. These are the individuals who through fear, unbelief, or a lust for sin rejected Jesus Christ.

The location of verse 8 in the eternal plan of God revealed in this book should be carefully examined. It once and for all repudiates the suggestion of many that there is a second chance for sinners after death. This unscriptural concept is made to appease the conscience of those libertines who have rejected Jesus Christ and prefer sin. But not one shred of evidence in the Bible substantiates it! And certainly the location of this verse pronounces an everlasting death sentence on the idea. Here in the eternal order human beings are pictured already in their eternal state as based on their own personal decision about God; He refers to them one last time, revealing their part in the "fiery lake of burning sulfur. This is the second death."

ONLY TWO KINDS OF PEOPLE

Verses 7 and 8 confirm the consistent presentation throughout the entire Bible that God sees only two kinds of people, believers and unbelievers. Either they are overcomers who have their part with God eternally or unbelievers who have their part in the lake of fire. You who read this chapter should examine yourselves to see which kind of person you represent. Are you one who has trusted Jesus Christ and thus through Him will inherit all things, or are you among those who have rejected Him? If so, you will have your part in the lake of fire. It is not too late to heed the Savior's call: "I will give to drink without cost from the spring of the water of life" (Rev. 21:6). He will receive you right now if you will call on Him. If there is any question in your mind as to whether you have ever invited Jesus Christ into your life, may I urge you to get down on your knees right now and ask Him to save you.

THIRTY-NINE

The New Jerusalem

Revelation 21:9–27

The dazzling glory of the new city of Jerusalem that is to come down from God out of heaven is beyond our ability to comprehend. It is pictured in Revelation as the ultimate preparation of God for human habitation. This same difficulty of comprehension may be observed in the ministry of many of our missionaries. As they live amid a primitive tribe for a period of time and try to communicate to them scenes of the outside world, the natives look at them in bewilderment. How can one describe an electric stove to a native who has never seen anything but an open wood fire? How can one describe refrigeration to a native who has known nothing but the cool of the mountain stream that runs by his thatched hut? Only by comparing the unknown with the known is the missionary able to convey facts of the outside world or, more importantly, the eternal truths of God. Thus it is with us as we try to comprehend the glories God has prepared in the Holy City for those who love Him. He has used terms and descriptions with which we are familiar to describe the things that are beyond our finite frame of reference.

THE NEW JERUSALEM — THE BRIDE OF CHRIST

One of the seven angels who had the seven bowls full of the seven last plagues came and said to me, "Come, I will show you the bride, the wife of the Lamb." And he carried me away in the Spirit to a mountain great and high, and showed me the Holy City, Jerusalem, coming down out of heaven from God. It shone with the glory of God, and its brilliance was like that of a very precious jewel, like a jasper, clear as crystal. (Rev. 21:9–11)

Inviting John to a high mountain, the angel showed him the Bride, the Lamb's wife. But the Bride is described in verse 10 as that "great [city] ... the holy City, Jerusalem." This does not suggest that the Bride of Christ is a city. Since chapter 19 described the marriage of the Lamb to the Bride, we find that the Bride is not a physical city but the Church. The Holy Spirit here is telling us about that city that the Lord promised His disciples in John 14:2 when He said, "I am going there to prepare a place for you." Now that prepared city is coming to the earth, and its inhabitants are the members of the Bride.

When this city comes to the earth, it will be a people-filled city—people in their resurrected bodies after the Millennium, prepared to dwell with Christ for eternity. That is why this city, which surpasses the splendor of anything we can comprehend, is called the Bride, the Lamb's wife. A city is more than buildings and streets, for these are merely the means of providing for the inhabitants that compose the real city. As we will see, others will be permitted into the city, but the city, which will be the capital of the eternal order of God, is "the bride, the wife of the Lamb . . . the Holy City, Jerusalem."

"It shone with the glory of God" (Rev. 21:11). This city is the crowning feature of the creation of God, the unique habitation of the redeemed for eternity. To emphasize the glory of God, the verse pictures a dazzling light "like a jasper, clear as crystal." Someone has suggested that perhaps the city will be surrounded with a ball of crystal light; just as the earth is round, this square city would have a round sphere of light. Certainly it will reflect the glory of God.

THE CITY FOURSQUARE (REV. 21:12–21)

"It had a great, high wall" (Rev. 21:12). The great wall around this city suggests that it will be an exclusive city. It will not be built for protection, of course, since no enemies will threaten in the eternal order, but it will stand as a visual reminder that all do *not* have access to God.

". . . with twelve gates, and with twelve angels at the gates. On the gates were written the names of the twelve tribes of Israel" (Rev. 21:12). Obviously the number twelve takes on great significance in this city. Since the Bible is inspired by God, we can expect, in spite of the various authors and the length of time engaged in its writing, that there will be an unusual, even supernatural continuity in the use of numbers.

Students of Bible numerology point out this thrilling thread of consistency that attests to divine authorship. For example, it is suggested that the number *one* stands for unity, *two* for union, *three* for the Trinity; *four* is the number of the earth (four directions: east, west, north, south), *five* the divisional number (five wise and five foolish virgins), *six* the number of humankind. Everything in the Bible that has to do with humanity seems to be in the realm of six. For instance, "Six days you shall labor" (Ex. 20:9). The height of the average person is about six feet. The Antichrist uses for his number three sixes, called "man's number" (Rev. 13:18).

Seven seems to be the perfect number, or God's number. He instructed Solomon to put seven steps in the throne of the temple. He established the divine calendar on the basis of seven days, and He has described seven millennia of time relating to humankind's activity on earth.

Twelve seems to be the governmental or administrative number. Thus we find multiples of twelve in the administration of God's universe—twenty-four thrones around the altar and 144,000 outstanding Christians (see Rev. 14), who will probably gain special leadership positions during the millennial Kingdom. Note the many references to "twelve" in this picture of the Holy City that will come down from heaven (21:9–21):

- *Twelve gates.* Twelve entrances will always be open for God's people to have access to the New Jerusalem. Revelation 21:13 indicates there will be three gates on each of the four sides of this gigantic city.
- *Twelve angels.* Again we see the relationship of angels in the eternal order and their work with the human race.
- *The names of the twelve tribes.* These indicate that the children of Israel will have ready access to this splendid heavenly city. Since angels are mentioned, it seems that each of the tribes has its angel, just as each of the churches has its angel (see Rev. 2–3).
- *Twelve foundations.* The foundation walls of the city will be magnificent beyond comprehension. In verses 19–21 they are described as "decorated with every kind of precious stone." Dr. Walvoord described the twelve foundations as follows:

The various foundations are represented as layers built upon each other, each layer extending around all four sides of the city.

Jasper—gold in appearance but like clear glass in substance, namely, glass with a gold cast to it;

Sapphire—a stone similar to a diamond in hardness and blue in color;

Chalcedony—an agate stone from Chalcedon (in Turkey), thought to be sky blue with other colors running through it;

Emerald—introduces a bright green color;

Sardonyx—a red and white stone;

Sardius—refers to a common jewel of reddish color, also found in honey color which is considered less valuable. The Sardius is used with Jasper in Revelation 4:3 in describing the glory of God on the throne;

Chrysolyte—a transparent stone, golden in color, according to the ancient writer Pliny, and therefore somewhat different from the modern pale green Chrysolyte stone;

Beryl—is sea green;

Tolpaz—is yellow-green and transparent;

Chrysoprasus—introduces another shade of green;

Jacinth—is a violet color;

Amethyst—is commonly purple.

Though the precise colors of these stones in some cases are not certain, the general picture here described by John is one of unmistakably beauty, designed to reflect the glory of God in a spectrum of brilliant color. The light of the city within shining through these various colors in the foundation of the wall topped by the wall itself composed of the crystal-clear Jasper forms a scene of dazzling beauty in keeping with the glory of God and the beauty of His Holiness. The city is undoubtedly far more beautiful to the eye than anything man has ever been able to create, and it reflects not only the infinite wisdom and power of God but also His grace as extended to the objects of His salvation.[57]

- *The names of the twelve apostles of the Lamb.* The foundation stones of the city contain the names of the apostles, indicating that the Holy City will contain the redeemed by the blood of Christ, who heard the Word through the faithful witnessing of the servants of God in the first century, the apostles. The gates of the city contain the names of the twelve tribes, indicating that they were the vehicles through which the oracles of God were revealed in the Old Testament days, and to whom Messiah came. Both the Old Testament saints and the Church will have access to this city, but each time they enter they will be reminded of their debt to the nation of Israel and to the apostles.

The angel who talked with me had a measuring rod of gold to measure the city, its gates and its walls. The city was laid out like a square, as long as it was wide. He measured the city with the rod and found it to be 12,000 stadia in length, and as wide and high as it is long.

(Rev. 21:15–16)

Most Bible scholars agree that the root meaning of the Greek word for "furlong" in the KJV or "stadia" in the NIV indicates that each side of this city is approximately fifteen hundred miles long. Thus the city itself would stretch from about the eastern seaboard of the United States to the Mississippi River on one side and from the Canadian border to the Gulf of Mexico on the other. In addition to the length and breadth, the city will be the same in height. Bible scholars do not agree as to whether this will be a cube-shaped or a pyramid-shaped city. Even though the pyramid concept seems more in keeping with our understanding, the literal interpretation of the text suggests it will be a cube. The great size, of course, will afford sufficient space for a habitation of the saints of all ages.

My friend and colleague, Dr. Henry M. Morris, an expert engineer and author, has done the math on this and concluded that given the estimated population of possibly twenty billion residents each person would enjoy a block of space of approximately one cubic mile, or its length, breadth, and height would be "a little over a third of a mile in each direction."[58] Can you imagine the view from your apartment house overlooking the Holy City and extending as far as the eye can see from an elevation of fifteen hundred miles?

"The twelve gates were twelve pearls" (Rev. 21:21). Every gate will be one pearl, large enough to cover the gateway to this huge city, so they will be larger than people. In addition, the streets of the city will be "pure gold, like transparent glass," indicating that we will walk on gold.

In our mind's eye, gazing at this city with its fantastically beautiful and expensive stones for foundations, its gigantic pearl gates, and its gold streets, we are impressed with the superiority of this city over anything known to us. Today we use concrete and stone for foundations, scarcely the most beautiful material on earth, but selected because of its durability, supply, and low cost. Our streets are made of concrete or blacktop for the same reasons. By comparison, the Holy City of God will be so magnificent that we will literally walk on precious metals that today are used for costly bracelets, necklaces, and rings. The city's foundation will consist of precious stones that today are used for ornaments only and, because of their expense, are small. This presentation, when taken literally, emphasizes the phenomenal omnipotent power of our God.

NO TEMPLE IN THE CITY

"I did not see a temple in the city, because the Lord God Almighty and the Lamb are its temple" (Rev. 21:22). From the very beginning of the creation of humanity, God has chosen to fellowship with us. He maintained fellowship with Adam and Eve before they sinned. After the Fall, a place of sacrifice had to be established. In Genesis 4, we find that Cain and Abel both knew about building an altar on which to place a sacrifice. The antediluvian and postdiluvian patriarchs also used this approach to God through sacrifice.

In the days of Moses God established the Tabernacle, where He would come to dwell in the midst of the people in what is known as the Holy of Holies. Under the reign of Solomon this was transferred to the Temple, but because of Israel's apostasy they lost this choice position with God. Finally the Lord Jesus Christ came to tabernacle with us and to become the complete sacrifice. When He departed, He sent His Holy Spirit to dwell in the bodies of believers.

In the millennial Kingdom a memorial Temple will provide a place for people to worship God because they will still be in the deciding process, exercising their free will to worship God or reject Him. However, in the eternal order there will no longer be a need for a "temple" (or dwelling place of God, as the Greek word implies). Instead, God Himself will be there with His Son and with the Holy Spirit. This will make not only the Holy City one grand and glorious temple or place of worship but also the eternal earth.

This perspective coincides with Hebrews 11:9–10, where Abraham specifically is described as looking for a city, meaning the heavenly Jerusalem. This will be realized by Abraham and his children who have responded to Jesus Christ their Messiah (Heb. 12:22–24). One can scarcely visualize the Holy City without the resurrected Abraham because of that passage of Scripture. This certainly indicates that though the Holy City is referred to as the Bride of the Lamb, it will be inhabited not just by the Church, but by all who have been redeemed through His blood.

GOD IS THE LIGHT OF THE CITY

The Bible teaches us that "God is light; in him there is no darkness at all" (1 John 1:5). Therefore the sun and the moon will no longer be needed in the eternal order. God Himself will provide sufficient light by His very presence. Several times Revelation 21:22–24 declares that God will be the light of this city. One of the most beautiful statements I have ever read on this subject came from the pen of Dr. Lehman Strauss:

> In that city which Christ has prepared for His own there will be no created light, simply because Christ Himself, who is the uncreated light (John 8:12), will be there.... The created lights of God and of men are as darkness when compared with our Blessed Lord. The light He defuses throughout eternity is the unclouded, undimmed glory of His own Holy presence. In consequence of the fullness of that light, there shall be no night.[57]

Think of it! No darkness forever!

EVERYONE HAS ACCESS TO THE HOLY CITY

> The nations will walk by its light, and the kings of the earth will bring their splendor into it. On no day will its gates ever be shut, for there will be no night there. The glory and honor of the nations will be brought into it. (Rev. 21:24–26)

Some have suggested that because "nations" and "kings" are referred to here, during the eternal order God will continue to separate the people by nations. This may well be His intent and meaning, fully in accord with His planned purpose for the human race since Genesis 10. However, hundreds of years transpired before the Flood, when He apparently did not interject difference of nationalities. The word "nations" comes from the root word "Gentiles" and is so translated in many places in the Bible. Thus, this reference could be to Gentiles who have received Christ. The "kings" would be saved men who were kings or world leaders, men of renown, who during the eternal order will come into the Holy City and give their glory to Christ.

If this is the interpretation, it would concern men who have come to God, not on the basis of being kings, but as poor, lost sinners who need a Savior. I am inclined to believe that this is the best interpretation, indicating that the Holy City will contain the Old Testament saints and the Church, plus the Tribulation saints who are redeemed from every language and tribe and nation (Rev. 7:9). It will also include the people of many nationalities who become believers during the millennial age. This may reach back into the days of Israel, when God had His witnesses in other nations of which we have little or no record. Many of these people no doubt responded to God but, knowing nothing of Israel, were thus not Jewish proselytes.

THOSE EXCLUDED FROM THE HOLY CITY

"Nothing impure will ever enter it, nor will anyone who does what is shameful or deceitful, but only those whose names are written in the Lamb's book of life" (Rev. 21:27). As a reminder of God's consistent pattern in dealing with people, those who reject His Son will not be admitted to His city. For we learn that "nothing impure will ... enter ... nor will anyone who does what is shameful or deceitful" be admitted. That would include everyone in human history who has not received Christ. Thus all those who have died in their defilement and lies and abominations are excluded from the city. In essence, only by acceptance of Jesus Christ does anyone have access to the ultimate blessing that God has prepared for him or her.

This closing scene of chapter 21, with its inspired presentation of the glories that God has established for people in the eternal order, should inspire every individual to receive Jesus Christ as Lord and Savior and thus have their names written in the Lamb's Book of Life.

FORTY

Heaven on Earth

Revelation 22

The last chapter of Revelation contains a final description of that heaven-like earth that God has prepared for those who love Him. It also contains a final challenge of a loving Savior who came into this world to die for the sins of the human race and has consistently sent His Spirit through His servants to convey His loving gospel message to them.

It is a fitting way to end not only this greatest of all books on prophecy, *The Revelation of Jesus Christ,* but also the library of God's Word. The Bible opens and closes with basically the same type of setting. In the first two chapters of Genesis we encounter God's description of creation and the heavenlike conditions on the earth prepared for humankind. The last two chapters of Revelation describe the eternal heaven that God will reestablish for them. All the chapters between contain the great conflict of the ages as human beings turn their backs on God and as He seeks to draw them to Himself. In all these books the human race is consistently presented with the opportunity to worship God freely by faith or reject Him by rebellion of will.

Revelation 22:1–5 contains six challenging descriptions of the heaven-like earth. As you bear in mind the heavenly city and the new earth described in chapter 21, we turn now to additional details to make this utopian state even more ideal.

1. "Then the angel showed me the river of the water of life, as clear as crystal, flowing from the throne of God and of the Lamb" (Rev. 22:1). We cannot live without water in this life or seemingly in the life to come. A study of history shows that humankind has always looked for water. The ideal fortress cities of the world have been located on high points of ground that had an adequate water supply. Many have died and nations have had to change their homeland because there was no adequate water supply. In the eternal paradise God has planned for us, an abundance of water will proceed out of the throne of God Himself, indicating that God will be the source of that life-giving substance.

2. "... the tree of life, bearing twelve crops of fruit, yielding its fruit every month" (Rev. 22:2). When Adam and Eve sinned, God forbade them to eat of the Tree of Life. Genesis 3:22–24 states:

> And the LORD God said, "The man has now become like one of us, knowing good and evil. He must not be allowed to reach out his hand and take also from the tree of life and eat, and live forever." So the LORD God banished him from the Garden of Eden to work the ground from which he had been taken. After he drove the man out, he placed on the east side of the Garden of Eden cherubim and a flaming sword flashing back and forth to guard the way to the tree of life.

This text clarifies that the eating of the Tree of Life makes a person live forever. Adam and Eve were forbidden to eat of that tree because they had first taken of the Tree of the Knowledge of Good and Evil, but in the eternal future human beings will be able to eat of it; this testifies of the eternity of our blessed future state.

The fruit of this tree will spring forth all year. In our backyard we have two avocado trees that yield fruit alternately every six months. In the paradise of God trees will continually bring forth fruit twelve months of the year, possibly with a variety of fruit. Thus, we will be able to eat and drink without fear of want in the eternal future. Whether we will eat meat or not is not mentioned, but we will be able to eat fruit.

One aspect of the Tree of Life has brought some controversy relative to the expression that "the leaves of the tree are for the healing of the nations" (Rev. 22:2). It would be better to translate the word "healing" as "health," not indicating that anyone will be sick during the eternal order, but that the Gentiles or nations that have been inhuman to each other throughout their known history will be healed in their relationships toward each other and will thus live equitably and fairly.

3. "No longer will there be any curse. The throne of God and of the Lamb will be in the city, and his servants will serve him" (Rev. 22:3). The curse that God placed on the earth as a result of the sin of Adam and Eve in the Garden of Eden will be partially lifted during the Millennium, but completely lifted during the eternal order. Therefore, the unlimited potential of the planet God gave to the human race will be realized for the first time. As proof that it will be an uncursed earth, God will place His throne here. His angelic hosts and human beings will be with Him as His servants. No rebellious servants of God will exist in the eternal order.

4. "They will see his face, and his name will be on their foreheads" (Rev. 22:4). The seal of God in the forehead of a person indicates that he or she is the blood-bought child of God through faith in Jesus Christ. The superiority of the future status of humanity in relationship to God is seen in the fact that we will actually be able to see God. Today we know that "no man has ever seen God" (John 1:18); in that order we will literally see God.

5. "There will be no more night. They will not need the light of a lamp or the light of the sun, for the Lord God will give them light" (Rev. 22:5). As expressed in Revelation 21, God Himself, who is light, will be the light of that eternal order, suggesting a consistency of heat and light. Today we are dependent on the sun for light and heat, changing our apparel or place of residence or habits of agriculture in accordance with the cycle of the sun. At that time we will not be limited to external objects, for God Himself will provide a consistent pattern of light that is ideally suited for us.

These first five characteristics bring beauty and warmth into the heavenlike condition of the new order. The description in chapter 21 of the stone city with golden streets, pearl gates, and rock foundations does not suggest the warmth that the water, vegetation, and light described in this chapter convey. These elements indicate that it will not be a cold city, like some of our concrete jungles, but a city furnishing the warmth of natural life that is so advantageous to human beings. Ecology-minded Christians will be happy to know that.

6. "And they will reign for ever and ever" (Rev. 22:5). Just as we rule with Christ for a thousand years, so we will reign with Him forever. Whether that will involve universes, galaxies, and other planets can only be guessed at. But one thing is for certain: We will reign with Him forever.

Since the Bible does not in any one passage offer a complete presentation of God's plan for our activities during the eternal order, it would be good to examine the characteristics delineated by Dr. Pentecost in his book *Things to Come*:

A. A life of fellowship with Him.

> For now we see through a glass darkly; but then face to face (1 Cor. 13:12).

> Beloved, now we are the sons of God, and it doth not yet appear what we shall be; but we know that, when he shall appear, we shall be like him; for we shall see him as he is (1 John 3:2).

> I will come again, and receive you unto myself, that where I am, there ye may be also (John 14:3).

> And they shall see his face (Rev. 22:4).

B. A life of rest.

> And I heard a voice from heaven, saying unto me, Write, Blessed are the dead which die in the Lord from henceforth. Yea, saith the Spirit, that they may rest from their labours; for their works do follow them (Rev. 14:13).

C. A life of full knowledge.

... now I know in part; but then shall I know even as also I am known (1 Cor. 13:12).

D. A life of holiness.

And there shall in no wise enter into it any thing that defileth, neither whatsoever worketh abomination, or maketh a lie; but they which are written in the Lamb's book of life (Rev. 21:27).

E. A life of joy.

And God shall wipe all tears from their eyes; and there shall be no more death, neither sorrow, nor crying, neither shall there be any more pain; for the former things are passed away (Rev. 21:4).

F. A life of service.

And there shall be no more curse; but the throne of God and of the Lamb shall be in it; and his servants shall serve him (Rev. 22:3).

G. A life of abundance.

I will give unto him that is athirst of the fountain of the water of life freely (Rev. 21:6).

H. A life of glory.

For our affliction, which is but for a moment, worketh for us a far more exceeding and eternal weight of glory (2 Cor. 4:17).

When Christ, who is our life, shall appear, then shall ye also appear with him in glory (Col. 3:4).

I. A life of worship.

And after these things I heard a great voice of much people in heaven, saying Alleluia; Salvation, and glory, and honour, and power unto the Lord our God (Rev. 19:1).

After this I beheld, and lo, a great multitude, which no man could number, of all nations, and kindreds, and people, and tongues, stood before the throne; and before the Lamb, clothed with white robes, and palms in their hands; and cried with a loud voice, saying, Salvation to our God which sitteth upon the throne, and unto the Lamb.... Blessing, and glory, and wisdom, and thanksgiving, and honour, and power, and might, be unto our God for ever and ever. Amen! (Rev. 7:9–12).[60]

CHRIST'S LAST MESSAGE TO HUMANKIND

Revelation 22:6–9 takes us back to the early part of this book, when the faithful and true witness told us that He would send His angel to convey His message concerning the things that must come to pass. For the second time John bows before the angel but is forbidden to do so (v. 9), for the consistent pattern in the Word of God is that we worship God only. Again we remind you that the Lord Jesus would have to be God or a crass imposter, for ten times during His life on this earth He accepted the worship of people without rebuking them. Since angels refuse to accept the worship of human beings, certainly the only excuse Jesus Christ would have for accepting their worship is that He is indeed the Son of God.

"Behold, I am coming soon" (Rev. 22:7). Three times we find this expression in the last verses of this book. Some have been confused about the literal meaning of the expression because it was uttered almost two thousand years ago. It is more accurately translated, "Behold, I come suddenly." This saying does not refer to an appointed time soon to come but means that His coming will take place suddenly and without warning.

Significant details are given in association with each of these three promises of our Lord.

1. Verse 7 contains the promise, "Blessed is he who keeps the words of the prophecy in this book." This may be a reference to the Rapture of the Church. "Happy are those" who are sufficiently aware of the prophecy of this book to be ready when that Day arrives.

2. "Behold, I am coming soon! My reward is with me, and I will give to everyone according to what he has done" (Rev. 22:12). Added to Christ's promise of his second coming, this verse proclaims a reward by way of judgment, a standard part of the state of believers after the Resurrection. On the basis of this reward we will reign with Christ forever.

3. "Do not seal up the words of the prophecy of this book, because the time is near" (Rev. 22:10). How different is this command of God to John from what He gave Daniel at the close of his book. There the Lord said to Daniel: "But you, Daniel, close up and seal the words of the scroll until the time of the end" (Dan. 12:4). The reason for the difference in the instructions is that one lived after the time of Christ's crucifixion, the other before. In John's day it was possible to see the unfolding of the events prophesied; in Daniel's day they were a long way off.

A SEVERE WARNING TO DETRACTORS
FROM THIS PROPHECY

I warn everyone who hears the words of the prophecy of this book: If anyone adds anything to them, God will add to him the plagues described in this book. And if anyone takes words away from this book of prophecy, God will take away from him his share in the tree of life and in the holy city, which are described in this book. (Rev. 22:18–19)

This is one of the most awesome challenges in the Word of God against tampering with Holy Writ. Far too many today glibly ridicule, detract from, and cast disparaging remarks on Holy Scripture. This is their day of opportunity, but their judgment will come upon them swiftly in God's good time. It is a fearful thing to disbelieve God, and it is unbelief that causes someone to detract from His Holy Word. Although this is not a reference to Bible-believing commentators of the Word who mistakenly translate some passage and inadvertently minimize it, it does serve as a soul-stirring challenge to those of us who have taken in hand to write and preach on this marvelous book. I can well appreciate the attitude of the late Dr. Joseph A. Seiss, who wrote in his book *The Apocalypse:*

> With an honest and ever-prayerful heart, and with these solemn and awful warnings ever before my eyes, I have endeavored to ascertain and indicate in these lectures what our gracious Lord and Master has been so particular to make known and defend. If I have read into this Book anything which he has not put there, or read out of it anything which he has put there, with the profoundest sorrow would I recant, and willingly burn up the books in which such mischievous wickedness is contained. If I have in anything gone beyond the limits of due subjection to what is written, or curtailed in any way the depth and measure of what Jesus by his angel has signified for the learning of the Churches, I need not the condemnation of men to heap upon me the burden of censure which I deserve. If feebleness, or rashness, or overweening confidence in my own understanding has distorted anything, I can only deplore the fault, and pray God to send a man more competent to unfold to us the mighty truths which here stand written. . . . If I err, God forgive me! If I am right, God bless my feeble testimony! In either case, God speed His everlasting truth![61]

THE LORD JESUS' LAST INVITATION TO HUMANKIND

The Spirit and the bride say, "Come!" And let him who hears say, "Come!" Whoever is thirsty, let him come; and whoever wishes, let him take the free gift of the water of life. (Rev. 22:17)

The Lord Jesus Christ, ever concerned for the souls of the lost, closes His great revelation to the churches with a challenge for individual people to call on His name. He indicates that there are two who invite us to come to Him: the "Spirit" and the "bride." In addition, He will even use "him who hears." God the Holy Spirit will use the printed page as well as those who are just repeating what they have heard but may not even believe what they are saying. He also uses the "bride," which indicates that the primary ministry of the Church of Christ during the entire Church Age is to tell others about the Savior. All Christians everywhere should be engaged in saying to their fellow human beings: "Whoever is thirsty, let him come; and whoever wishes, let him take the free gift of the water of life." Jesus Christ, of course, is the water of life.

These closing verses of the Bible make it perfectly clear that salvation is a matter of the will—whoever *wishes* may come. This clearly implies that whoever wills *not* to come is lost. This teaching abounds throughout the Scriptures.

In contrast to those who reject Christ, we encounter the state of the blessed described in verse 14. Those who have washed their robes in the righteousness of Christ have a right to the Tree of Life and thus are entitled to live forever. He describes their state as "blessed," meaning "happy."

Every individual wants happiness. The way to eternal happiness is to receive Christ as Lord and Savior, which entitles you to entrance into the Holy City, access to the Tree of Life, and the marvelous blessings of a loving God. If there is any question in your mind as to whether or not you have received the living Christ, I urge you, on the basis of His challenge, to change your will and receive Him as your Lord and Savior today.

NOTES

1. Phillip Schaff, *History of the Christian Church*, vol. 2, pp. 750–51.
2. H. Grattan Guinness, *History Unveiling Prophecy*, pp. 41–46, as quoted by Roy Froom in *The Prophetic Faith of Our Fathers* (Washington, D.C.: Review and Herald, 1950), p. 337.
3. Gary G. Cohen, *Understanding Revelation* (Chicago: Moody, 1978), pp. 53–54.
4. Henry H. Halley, *Halley's Bible Handbook*, 24th ed. (Grand Rapids: Zondervan, 1965), p. 758.
5. Loraine Boettner, *Roman Catholicism* (Philadelphia: Presbyterian and Reformed, 1962), p. 8.
6. Harry A. Ironside, *Lectures on the Book of Revelation*, 12th ed. (Neptune, N.J.: Loizeaux Brothers, 1942).
7. Boettner, *Roman Catholicism*, pp. 8–9.
8. Grant Jeffery, *Apocalypse* (Frontier Research Publication, 1992), pp. 85–94.
9. Froom, *The Prophetic Faith of Our Fathers* (Washington D.C.: Review and Herald, 1950), p. 337.
10. St. Victorinus, Bishop of Petau, *Commentary on the Apocalypse of the Blessed John*, vol. 3, "The Writings of Tertullianus," trans. R. E. Wallis (Edinburgh: T. & T. Clark, 1870), p. 428.
11. Quote from Ray Hubner, a Brethren defender of Darby.
12. Henry M. Morris, *The Revelation Record* (Wheaton, Ill.: Tyndale , 1983), p. 85.
13. Harry A. Ironside, *Lectures on the Book of Revelation*, 12th ed. (Neptune, N.J.: Loizeaux Brothers, 1942), pp. 80–81.
14. Quoted in William R. Newell, *The Book of the Revelation* (Chicago: Moody, 1935), p. 374.
15. Ironside, *Lectures on the Book of Revelation*, pp. 81–83.
16. Newell, *The Book of the Revelation*, p. 374.
17. Henry M. Morris, *The Revelation Record: A Scientific and Devotional Commentary on the Book of Revelation* (Wheaton, Ill.: Tyndale, 1983), p. 87.
18. Ibid., p. 104.
19. Ironside, *Lectures on the Book of Revelation*.
20. J. Vernon McGee, *Reveling Through Revelation* (Los Angeles: Thru the Bible Books Foundation, 1962), 1:82.
21. Lehman Strauss, *The Book of Revelation* (Neptune, N.J.: Loizeaux Brothers, 1964), p. 228.
22. McGee, *Reveling Through Revelation*, 2:2.
23. Ironside, *Lectures on the Book of Revelation*, pp. 203–4.
24. Joseph A. Seiss, *The Apocalypse* (Grand Rapids: Zondervan, 1957), p. 318.
25. Clarence Larkin, *Dispensational Truth* (Philadelphia: Rev. Clarence Larkin Estate, 1920), p. 120.

26. David L. Cooper, "An Exposition of the Book of Revelation: The Great Parenthesis (11:15–15:8)," *Biblical Research Monthly*, 20 (May 1954): p. 84.

27. Newell, *The Book of Revelation*, p. 209.

28. Ibid., p. 210.

29. McGee, *Reveling Through Revelation*, 2:542–43.

30. Marvin R. Vincent, *Word Studies in the New Testament* (Wilmington, Del.: A. P. & A., 1972), 2:542–43.

31. Clarence Larkin, *The Book of Revelation* (Philadelphia: Rev. Clarence Larkin Estate, 1919).

32. Ironside, *Lectures on the Book of Revelation*, pp. 287–91.

33. Larkin, *Dispensational Truth*, p. 140.

34. Halley, *Halley's Bible Handbook*, pp. 291–92.

35. "Babylon," *Encyclopedia of Lands and People* (New York: The Grolier Society, 1960), 3:221.

36. Larkin, *Dispensational Truth*, p. 142.

37. John F. Walvoord, *The Revelation of Jesus Christ* (Chicago: Moody, 1966), p. 268.

38. Walter Scott, *Exposition of the Revelation of Jesus Christ*, 4th ed. (London: Pickering & Inglis, n.d.), p. 375.

39. Seiss, *The Apocalypse*, p. 436.

40. Walvoord, *The Revelation of Jesus Christ*, p. 277.

41. Merrill C. Tenney, ed., *The Zondervan Pictorial Bible Dictionary* (Grand Rapids: Zondervan, 1963), p. 71.

42. Walvoord, *The Revelation of Jesus Christ*, p. 291.

43. Ibid., p. 298.

44. Dwight J. Pentecost, *Things to Come* (Grand Rapids: Zondervan, 1958), p. 372.

44. Ibid., p. 370.

45. John F. Walvoord, *The Millennial Kingdom* (Grand Rapids: Zondervan, 1959), pp. 5–6.

46. Pentecost, *Things to Come*, p. 390.

47. A new edition of the *Scofield Reference Bible* has recently been printed, correcting the archaic words of the KJV but retaining the beautiful style and dignity.

48. Walvoord, *The Millennial Kingdom*, p. 12.

49. Ibid., p. 6.

50. Halley, *Halley's Bible Handbook*, p. 764.

51. Walvoord, *The Millennial Kingdom*, p. 51.

52. E. H. Broadbent, *The Pilgrim Church* (London: Pickering and Inglis, 1931), p. 26.

53. Walvoord, *The Millennial Kingdom*, p. 51.

54. Ibid.

55. Larkin, *Dispensational Truth*, pp. 10–11.

56. Walvoord, *The Revelation of Jesus Christ*, p. 325.

57. Morris, *The Revelation Record*, p. 451. Talk about high ceilings! That is many times more space than most people enjoy now on earth.

58. Strauss, *The Book of Revelation*, p. 355.

59. Pentecost, *Things to Come*, p. 581.

60. Seiss, *The Apocalypse*, p. 527.

BIBLIOGRAPHY

Boettner, Loraine. *Roman Catholicism*. Philadelphia: Presbyterian and Reformed, 1962.

Bradbury, John W., ed. *Hastening the Day of God*. Wheaton, Ill.: Van Kampen, 1953.

Broadbent, E. H. *The Pilgrim Church*. London: Pickering and Inglis, 1931.

Cooper, David L. "An Exposition of the Book of Revelation: The Great Parenthesis (11:15–15:8)." *Biblical Research Monthly*, 19 (May 1954): 84–85, 89.

_____. "An Exposition of the Book of Revelation: The Pouring Out of the Bowls of God's Wrath (16:1–21)." *Biblical Research Monthly*, 19 (October 1954), 186–87.

DeHaan, M. R. *Revelation: 35 Simple Studies on the Major Themes in Revelation*. Grand Rapids: Zondervan, 1946.

Grant, F. W. *The Revelation of Christ*. New York: Loizeaux Brothers, n.d.

Halley, Henry H. *Halley's Bible Handbook*. 24th ed. Grand Rapids: Zondervan, 1965.

Ironside, Harry A. *Lectures on the Book of Revelation*. 12th ed. New Jersey: Loizeaux Brothers, 1942.

LaHaye, Tim F. *The Beginning of the End*. Wheaton, Ill.: Tyndale, 1972.

Larkin, Clarence. *The Book of Daniel*. Philadelphia: Rev. Clarence Larkin Estate, 1929.

_____. *The Book of Revelation*. Philadelphia: Rev. Clarence Larkin Estate, 1919.

_____. *Dispensational Truth*. Philadelphia: Rev. Clarence Larkin Estate, 1920.

McGee, J. Vernon. *Reveling Through Revelation*, 2 parts. Los Angeles: Thru the Bible Books Foundation, 1962.

Newell, William R. *The Book of the Revelation*. Chicago: Moody, 1935.

Ottman, Ford C. *The Unfolding of the Ages in the Revelation of St. John*. New York: "Our Hope," 1905.

Pentecost, J. Dwight. *Things to Come*. Grand Rapids: Zondervan, 1958.

Scott, Walter. *Exposition of the Revelation of Jesus Christ*. 4th ed. London: Pickering and Inglis, n.d.

Seiss, Joseph A. *The Apocalypse*. Grand Rapids: Zondervan, 1957.

Strauss, Lehman. *The Book of Revelation.* Neptune, N.J.: Loizeaux Brothers, 1964.

Talbot, Louis T. *An Exposition of the Book of Revelation.* Grand Rapids: Eerdmans, 1957.

Walvoord, John F. *The Millennial Kingdom.* Grand Rapids: Zondervan, 1959.

_____. *The Revelation of Jesus Christ.* Chicago: Moody, 1966.

We want to hear from you. Please send your comments about this book to us in care of the address below. Thank you.

ZondervanPublishingHouse
Grand Rapids, Michigan 49530
http://www.zondervan.com